THE CIVIL COURT PRACTICE 2010

PROCEDURAL TABLES

LexisNexis®

THE CIVIL COURT PRACTICE 2010
PROCEDURAL TABLES

GENERAL EDITOR

ALAN SIMONS LLB (Hons)(Lond)

Former District Judge

Members of the LexisNexis Group worldwide

United Kingdom	LexisNexis Butterworths, a Division of Reed Elsevier (UK) Ltd, Halsbury House, 35 Chancery Lane, London, WC2A 1EL, and London House, 20–22 East London Street, Edinburgh EH7 4BQ
Australia	LexisNexis Butterworths, Chatswood, New South Wales
Austria	LexisNexis Verlag ARD Orac GmbH & Co KG, Vienna
Benelux	LexisNexis Benelux, Amsterdam
Canada	LexisNexis Canada, Markham, Ontario
China	LexisNexis China, Beijing and Shanghai
France	LexisNexis SA, Paris
Germany	LexisNexis Deutschland GmbH, Munster
Hong Kong	LexisNexis Hong Kong, Hong Kong
India	LexisNexis India, New Delhi
Italy	Giuffrè Editore, Milan
Japan	LexisNexis Japan, Tokyo
Malaysia	Malayan Law Journal Sdn Bhd, Kuala Lumpur
New Zealand	LexisNexis NZ Ltd, Wellington
Poland	Wydawnictwo Prawnicze LexisNexis Sp, Warsaw
Singapore	LexisNexis Singapore, Singapore
South Africa	LexisNexis Butterworths, Durban
USA	LexisNexis, Dayton, Ohio

First published in 1899

Published by LexisNexis

This is a Butterworths title

A CIP Catalogue record for this book is available from the British Library.

ISBN: 978 1 4057 6057 7

Typeset by Letterpart Ltd, Reigate, Surrey

Printed in the UK by CPI William Clowes Beccles NR34 7TL

Visit LexisNexis Butterworths at www.lexisnexis.co.uk

PREFACE

To improve your user experience as a valued subscriber of the Green Book, we have decided to position the Procedural Tables in a separate volume. The Procedural Tables show the steps to be taken in issuing proceedings and conducting other business in the courts, and cross-refer extensively to other sections in the book.

We would welcome and feedback on this, and any other aspects of this edition. Please contact us by e-mail at greenbook@lexisnexis.co.uk.

PROCEDURAL TABLES

TABLE OF CONTENTS

PREFACE TO THE TABLES

The definition of **legal representative and authorised person** includes barristers, solicitors and solicitors' employees, and also a manager of a body recognised under section 9 of the Administration of Justice Act 1985 and a person who, for the purposes of the Legal Services Act 2007, is an authorised person in relation to an activity which constitutes the conduct of litigation.

If all seems lost see *Hertsmere Primary Care Trust v Rabindra-Anandh* [2005] EWHC 320 (Ch), [2005] 3 All ER 274, per Lightman J: 'As part of the overriding objective the parties are required by r 1.3 to assist the court by co-operating with each other, which in this case included a duty to inform the other party of its omission.' This degree of co-operation does not appear to be expected where the error is not procedural; see *Thames Trains v Adams* [2006] EWHC 3291 (QB), [2006] All ER (D) 320 (Dec).

TABLE 1—START OF PROCEEDINGS UNDER PART 7

TAB 1

	Form No	CPR	PD
1. Preliminary			
Before issue, the claimant should:			
(a) comply with the Practice Direction (Pre-Action Conduct) and any relevant pre-action protocol (of which there are presently ten) The court **will** take this into account when it gives directions.		3.1(4)	Practice Direction (Pre-Action Conduct), para 4 Protocol 1, para 4.1–4.10
The Practice Direction (Pre-Action Conduct) (reproduced in full at **PRO 1**) is annexed to Part 3, the Court's Case Management powers. It came into force on 6 April 2009 and comprises: Section I – Introduction Section II – The Approach of the Courts Section III – The Principles Governing the Conduct of the Parties in cases not subject to a Pre-Action Protocol Section IV – Requirements that apply to all cases.			
There are three Annexes: A – Guidance on pre-action procedure where no pre-action protocol applies B – Information to be provided in debt claims where the claimant is a business and the defendant is an individual C – Guidance on instructing experts. Note in particular:			

	Form No	CPR	PD
(i) paragraph 7.4 and Annex B of the Practice Direction apply to business claimants seeking recovery of a debt from an individual defendant; (ii) Annex A para 2 requires disclosure of any funding arrangement in the letter before action as soon as possible.			
For a list of the CPR which provide for the consequences of, or impose sanctions for, non compliance with protocols see **PRO [5]**. The aims of the Practice Direction are: (i) early exchange of information; (ii) consideration of alternative dispute resolution; (iii) avoidance of litigation (iv) the efficient management by the court and the parties of proceedings that cannot be avoided.			PD (Pre-action Conduct), para 1.9(3)
Where there has been a failure by a party to comply with the Practice Direction or a relevant pre-action protocol when giving directions for the management of the claim or when making orders about who should pay costs the court may ask the party in default for an explanation.			PD (Pre-action Conduct), paras 4.1 and 4.2
When considering compliance the court will: (i) be concerned with whether there has been substantial compliance; (ii) consider proportionality; (iii) take into account the urgency of the matter.			PD (Pre-action Conduct), paras 4.3 and 4.4

	Form No	CPR	PD
The court will look at the overall effect of non compliance on the other party when deciding whether to impose sanctions. An increase in costs that can be shown to be as a result of the non-compliance and which is capable of assessment will have to be established before a costs order will be made or other penalty imposed: see *Green v Sunset + Vine Productions Ltd (Costs)* [2009] EWHC 1610 (QB) and for discussion see article 'Made to Measure' by Francesca Kaye in (2009) Sol Jo 22 December, page 23. A non-exclusive list of sanctions is set out at para 4.6 of the Practice Direction.			PD (Pre-action Conduct), paras 4.5 and 4.6
Where a claimant fails to comply with the provisions of a pre-action protocol it is appropriate for the court to grant a stay of proceedings commenced to facilitate compliance with the protocol: *Cunall Johnson & Partners LLP v Whipps Cross University Hospital NHS Trust* [2007] EWHC 2178 (TCC)			
Save in exceptional circumstances costs incurred by a defendant during the protocol procedure in dealing with issues that are subsequently dropped when the proceedings are commenced are not 'incidental to' those proceedings and are not recoverable by him: *McGlinn v Waltham Contractors Ltd* [2005] EWHC 1419 (TCC), [2005] 3 All ER 1126.			
For consideration of whether mediation can take place too soon and whether delaying mediation was reasonable see *Nigel Witham Ltd v Smith* [2008] EWHC 12 (TCC), [2008] All ER (D) 101 (Jan).			
It is customary for the parties to a mediation to make a written contract with the mediator which imposes express conditions of confidentiality; see article 'Mediation privileges' by Mr Justice Briggs in New Law Journal (2009) 3 April, page 506 and 17 April, page 550.			

	Form No	CPR	PD
For a case where it was decided that the mediator should give evidence and a witness summons was upheld see *Farm Assist (in liquidation) v Secretary of State for the Environment, Food and Rural Affairs (No 2)* [2009] EWHC 1102 (TCC), [2009] BLR 399 where it was held that the confidentiality was not absolute and that without prejudice privilege had been waived when the parties agreed that a witness statement should be taken from the mediator. A full consideration of the decision is made by Amanda Wadey entitled 'Mediator in the witness box?' in (2009) NLJ, 10 July, page 993.			
The question of whether mediation costs are recoverable is usually answered by the provisions of the mediation agreement itself; see on this point *National Westminster Bank plc v Feeney and Feeney* [2006] HC 90066 (Costs)			
In *Roundstone Nurseries Ltd v Stephenson Holdings Ltd* [2009] EWHC 1431 (TCC) there was a late withdrawal from mediation by the defendant; the court found he was wrong to withdraw and ordered the defendant to pay the costs thrown away by the late cancellation of the mediation.			
The Ministry of Justice has introduced two schemes to provide free or low-cost mediation to litigants: the **Small Claims Mediation Service** (**SCMS**) and the **National Mediation Helpline** (**NMH**) for fast and multi track cases. The SCMS (www.hmcourts_service.gov.uk/ems/14156.htm) is free and voluntary and the parties are invited to use the service by ticking a box in the allocation questionnaire. SCMS had conducted approximately 10,000 mediations in the year to October 2009. The NMH (www.nationalmediationhelpline.com) has created two schemes to provide free or low-cost mediation to litigants but in the year to October 2008 only 654 mediations were conducted albeit 432 of them resulted in settlements.			

	Form No	CPR	PD
(b) inform other potential parties if he enters into a funding arrangement. This must be done as soon as possible and in any event within 7 days of entering into the funding arrangement. If the funding arrangement was entered into before sending a letter of claim, in the letter of claim.		43.2(1)(k)	Practice Direction (Pre-action Conduct), para 9.3
(c) consider Alternative Dispute Resolution ('ADR') with particular reference to the Protocols Practice Direction at para 4.7 noting the statement that the court may 'require evidence that alternative means of resolving their dispute were considered' and that 'The Courts take the view that litigation should be a last resort'.			Practice Direction (Pre-action Conduct), 8 – Alternative Dispute Resolution
Note *Cowl v Plymouth City Council* [2001] EWCA Civ 1935, [2002] 1 WLR 803 where the paramount importance of avoiding litigation between public authorities and members of the public was stressed, and pay particular attention to the conjoined appeals of *Halsey v Milton Keynes General NHS Trust* and *Steel v Joy and Halliday* [2004] EWCA Civ 576, [2004] 4 All ER 920 where it was clearly stated that the court does not have jurisdiction to force parties to mediate against their will and that the burden is on the unsuccessful party to justify a departure from the general rule that costs follow the event. The Court of Appeal also listed eight factors to be checked when considering whether the refusal of ADR was reasonable or not.			

	Form No	CPR	PD
For strong criticism of this decision see a speech by Mr Justice Lightman, an edited version of which appears in the Law Section of The Times for 31 July 2007 and is reported in the Gazette (2007) 19 July and see also the report, in the Gazette for 24 April 2008 at page 1, of a speech by Lord Phillips, the Lord Chief Justice, strongly criticising the decision for 'significantly weakening' the costs sanction by placing the burden on the party seeking costs to show the other party had unreasonably refused to mediate.			
The decision in *Halsey* was amplified in *Burchell v Bullard* [2005] EWCA Civ 358, [2005] BLR 330; note in particular Rix LJ: 'the court is entitled to take an unreasonable refusal into account even if it occurs before the start of formal proceedings'; see CPR 44.3(5)(a).			
The decision in *Halsey* was further referred to in *Earl of Malmesbury v Strutt and Parker (a partnership)* [2008] EWHC 424 (QB), [2008] All ER (D) 257 (Mar). In the *Earl of Malmesbury* case it was held that a party who agreed to mediation but then took an unreasonable position in the mediation was in the same position as a party who unreasonably refused to mediate. For further discussion of this decision see (2008) NLJ 4 April, p 480.			
For cases where the court found the refusal to mediate was not unreasonable following *Burchell v Bullard* (above) see *Wethered Estate Ltd v Michael Davis* [2005] EWHC 1903 (Ch), [2006] BLR 86 and *Daniels v Metropolitan Police Comr* (2005) Times, 28 October, CA			

	Form No	CPR	PD
In *Hickman v Blake Lapthorn* [2006] EWHC 12 (QB), [2006] All ER (D) 67 (Jan) where a party had not been prepared to take a 'commercial view' and pay more than he thought the claim was worth, it was held the stance taken was not unreasonable. Useful guidance is given in this case.			
For a view of the stance of defendant's lawyers in personal injury claims see the report 'Twisting Arms' by a team led by Professor Dame Hazel Genn referred to in 104/22 Gazette for 31 May 2007, under the heading defendants personal injury lawyers 'Defeating Mediation'.			
For an attack on the 'downgrading of civil justice, the degradation of civil courts and the diversion of cases to private dispute resolution' copies should be obtained of three Hamlyn lectures delivered by Professor Genn in 2008. They are to be published in Spring 2009 and meanwhile see article 'Degradation and diversion' by Joshua Rosenberg in the Gazette for 18 December 2008, page 5.			
The rule against disclosure to the court of without prejudice negotiations applies on the determination of costs even if it prevents the court deciding whether a party had been unreasonable in refusing mediation; *Reed Executive plc v Reed Business Information Ltd (No 2)* [2004] EWCA Civ 887, (2004) Times, 16 July, CA			
(d) write a letter before action; in *Phoenix Finance Ltd v Federation International de l'Automobile* [2002] EWHC 1028 (Ch), (2002) Times, 27 June it was stressed that nothing in the CPR removed the necessity of doing so			Practice Direction (Pre-action Conduct), Annex A and Annex B for consumer debt claims

	Form No	CPR	PD
Failure to write a letter before action will not necessarily relieve an unsuccessful defendant of his liability for costs. If the court finds such a letter would have had no effect on the defendant's conduct it is not likely in the exercise of its discretion to refuse the claimant's application for costs; *Merial Ltd v Sankyo Co Ltd* [2004] EWHC 3077 (Pat), [2004] All ER (D) 272 (Dec) If such letters before action are 'oppressive and unacceptable' sending them is capable of amounting to harassment falling within the Protection from Harassment Act 1997: *Ferguson v British Gas Trading Ltd* [2009] EWCA Civ 46, [2009] All ER (D) 80 (Feb), (2009 NLJ, Civil Way, 27 February, page 304. Clearly, care should be taken as to the content of such letters. See further **TAB 24A**, para 8.10 below.			
(e) CPR 36.10 enables the Court, when making any order as to costs, to take into account any offer to settle made before proceedings. The offer must comply with CPR 36.10(2). A claimant who makes such an offer and betters it is prima facie entitled to indemnity costs; *Huck v Robson* [2002] EWCA Civ 398, [2002] 3 All ER 263			
(f) For the vulnerability of protective claims (i e issued with the imminent expiry of a limitation period fast approaching to safeguard a claimant's position) see *Nomura International plc v Granada Group Ltd* [2007] EWHC 642 (Comm), [2007] All ER (D) 404 (Mar) and the article 'A Canterbury Tale' that appears at NLJ 8 June 2007, p 273			

	Form No	CPR	PD
(g) Great care must be taken over the identity of the correct parties to proceedings because substitution of a party pursuant to CPR 19.5(2) will only be allowed if the person issuing the claim form made a mistake as to the name and not the identity of the party to be substituted: *Adelson v Associated Newspapers Ltd* [2007] EWCA Civ 701, (2007) Times, 18 July. See also *O'Byrne v Aventis Pasteur SA* [2007] EWCA Civ 966, (2007) Times 19 June			
(h) To avoid the danger of an application being made to strike out claims in a subsequent action as an abuse of process, claims against all defendants liable or considered to be liable for the damage suffered should be made in the original action; see *Aldi Stores Ltd v WSP Group plc (1) WSP London Ltd (2) and Aspinwall & Co Ltd (3)* [2007] EWHC 55 (TCC), [2007] BLR 11, and the cases there considered; also *Stuart v Goldberg Linde (a firm)* [2008] EWCA Civ 2, (2008) Times, 23 January where the Court of Appeal stated there is no legal principle that a claimant should use reasonable diligence to establish whether he has a further claim not yet asserted or to warn a defendant that an additional claim is contemplated. See articles by Dan Stacy and Alice Nash (2008) NLJ, 18 April, page 533 and Andrew Blair (2008 Sol Jo, 1 April. However, a claimant who is in a position to write such a warning letter may feel it expedient to do so. The Court of Appeal ruled in *Henley v Bloom* [2010] EWCA Civ 202, [2010] All ER (D) 8 (Mar) that a tenant's claim for disrepair should not have been struck out although he had kept it 'up his sleeve' when settling a possession claim.			

	Form No	CPR	PD
(i) In *Ashley v Chief constable of Sussex Police* [2008] UKHL 25, [2008] 3 All ER 573 the claimants, who were family relations of James Ashley who was shot and killed by a policeman who was charged with and acquitted of murder, were allowed to continue with a claim for assault and battery (amongst a number of claims). Their claim was held not to be a collateral attack on the acquittal but raised different issues which should proceed. (j) An injured party must sue for all the damage he has suffered or will suffer arising from a cause of action in one claim: see New Law Journal (2008) 1 February, page 177 (k) As to correcting errors in a claim form see *Evans v Cig Mon Cymru* [2008] EWCA Civ 390, 19 January. The claimant completed the section 'Nature of the claim' by stating 'loss and damage arising out of abuse at work' whereas it was a personal injury claim arising out of an accident. Arden LJ held it was a clerical error that could be corrected; Toulson LJ held the application to amend was merely to correct a formal error. The application to amend was granted and the Court of Appeal held that the amendment was not prohibited by CPR 17.4 (amendments to statements of case after the end of a relevant limitation period).			

	Form No	CPR	PD
(l) As to the creation of a binding contract of compromise by a chain of letters see *Thakrar v Jackson* [2007] EWHC 271 (TCC), [2007] All ER (D) 271 (Feb), (2007) NLJ 157, pp 331 and 483 – 'approach should not be too legalistic'. As to whether settlement communications before proceedings are 'without prejudice' see *Barnetson v Framlington Group Ltd* [2007] EWCA Civ 502, [2007] 3 All ER 1054.			
(m) Only people with causes of action vested in them at the time can validly commence proceedings and claims issued contrary to this basic rule fall to be struck out as an abuse of process: *Pickthall v Hill Dickinson LLP and Martindale* [2008] EWHC 3409 (Ch), [2009] BPIR 114 an appeal heard by CA on 11 June 2009. See Gazette (2009) 25 June, page 15. Further, the fact that the claimant had the intention to get in the cause of action and had good prospects of doing so made no difference.			

	Form No	CPR	PD
(n) For the availability of **'closed material procedure'** (which would be contrary to the principle that a litigant should be able to see and hear all the evidence seen and heard by the court) in respect of material regarded by the government as so secret that its disclosure to the claimants would be contrary to public interest see *Al Rawi v Security Service (Justice and Liberty intervening)* [2010] EWCA Civ 48, [2010] LS Gazette 20 May, (2010) Times, 7 May where it was held on appeal that it was not open to the court to order a closed material procedure in relation to an ordinary civil trial and further it would have no jurisdiction to do so in the light of the incompatibility of such a procedure with the provisions of the CPR. The court left open whether such a procedure could be allowed with the consent of all parties or where there was a substantial public interest issue. For discussion of the exceptional cases where the closed procedure might be adopted see [2010] NLJ, 2 July, p 939, an article 'Case Closed' by Kate Wellington. For the circumstances where **redacting reasons** for the judgment is in the interests of public security see *R (Mohamed) v Secretary of State for Foreign and Commonwealth Affairs* [2010] EWCA Civ 65, (2010) Times, 16 February; the application for redaction was refused and the Court confirmed it is axiomatic that a litigant should be entitled to see the reasoning of the Court in the absence of good reason to the contrary.			
2. The appropriate court – High Court or county court			
Restrictions on where proceedings may be started are set out in the relevant practice directions supplementing Part 7		7.1	7A

	Form No	CPR	PD
Subject to the provisions of the Practice Direction to CPR Pt 7, where both High Court and the county court have jurisdiction, the proceedings may be started in the High Court or a county court			7A, para 1
Claims which **must** be issued in the High Court: business from which county courts are excluded, e g admiralty, libel, slander, judicial review, patent infringement, human rights declarations of incompatibility, equity cases where the worth of the trust or estate is more than £30,000 *But note:*		58 (Commercial Court) 59 (Mercantile Courts)	7A, para 2.9 49 (specialist proceedings)
(a) as to Mercantile Courts – the Central London County Court		60 (Technology and Construction Court claims)	
(b) as to Technology and Construction Court Claims – county courts specified in the Practice Direction		61 (Admiralty claims)	
(c) as to Patent Court business – see Patents County Court		62 (Arbitration claims)	
But note also: Probate claims in the county court must only be brought where there is also a Chancery district registry or in the Central London County Court. See County Courts Act 1984 s 32 as to probate claims which may be heard in the county courts.		57.2	72.2.2
But note also that there is no monetary limit to the jurisdiction of the county court under the Trusts of Land and Appointment of Trustees Act 1996: see art 2(1)(a) of the High Court and County Courts Jurisdiction Order 1991.			
Claims which **should** be issued in the High Court: where the claimant believes that the claim ought to be heard by a High Court judge by reason of:			
(a) financial value and the amount in dispute, and/or			

	Form No	CPR	PD
(b) complexity of facts, legal issues, remedies or procedures involved, and/or			
(c) the importance of the outcome to the public in general			7A, para 2.4
Claims which **must** be issued in the county court:			
(a) proceedings whether for damages or a specific sum where the value is not more than £25,000			7A, para 2.1
(b) proceedings which include a claim for damages for personal injuries unless the value of the claim is £50,000 or more. For the definition of "value" see art 9 of the High Court and County Court Jurisdiction Order 1991 (SI 1991/724) as amended and note in particular that contributory negligence is not taken into account unless it is admitted (art 9(4)(b)) nor is interest unless it is contractual (art 9(2)(b))			7A, para 2.2
(c) where an enactment so requires			7A, para 2.3
2A. Jurisdiction by agreement			
(a) Actions other than those which if issued in the High Court would have been assigned to the Chancery Division or to the Family Division or involved the exercise of the High Court's Admiralty jurisdiction, see para **II CCA [10]**			
(b) As to those proceedings within the High Court's equity jurisdiction, see para **II CCA [12]**			
2B. Human Rights			
A claim under s 7(1)(a) of the Human Rights Act 1998 in respect of a judicial act can only be brought in the High Court. Any other claim under s 7(1)(a) may be brought in any court		7.11	

	Form No	CPR	PD
2C. Allocation to levels of Judiciary			
Judges, Masters and District Judges may exercise any function of the court except where an enactment rule or practice direction provides otherwise.		2.4	2B
3. The appropriate court – venue			
County Court proceedings may be issued in **any** county court unless:			
(a) there are restrictions in a relevant Practice Direction, or		7.1	
(b) the proceedings are for the recovery of land		55.3(1)	
Where a claim for a specific sum of money is issued other than in the defendant's home court and the defendant is an individual, then there will be **automatic transfer** to the defendant's home court on the filing of a defence. If such a claim is likely to be defended it is sensible to issue in the defendant's own court to avoid the inevitable delay caused by the court effecting the automatic transfer		26.2	
4. Completion of the claim form			
This applies whether the claim is started in the High Court or a county court. Similarly, it applies whether the claim is likely to be allocated to the multi-, fast or small claims track			7A
The **claim form** will be issued under CPR Pt 7 unless:		8.1(2)	
(a) it is unlikely there will be a substantial dispute of fact, or		8.1(2)(a)	
(b) a Rule or Practice Direction permits the use of the Part 8 procedure		8.1(2)(b)	
The claim form must normally be in the practice form N1 prescribed to start a Part 7 claim but exceptions include	N1		
(a) Admiralty	ADM1 and 1A		
(b) Arbitration	8		
(c) Probate	N2		

	Form No	CPR	PD
(d) Possession of land; Tab 22	N5 N5A N5B N119 N120 N121		
The claimant must lodge at or send to a court office a completed claim form together with a copy for sealing and copies for each defendant			
Particulars of claim must be contained in or served with the claim form, or be served on the defendant by the claimant within 14 days after service of the claim form (but in any event no later than the latest time for serving a claim form)		7.4(1) and (2)	
Where the particulars of claim are served separately, the claimant must file a copy within 7 days of service unless the PD 7C, para 5.2(4) or PD 7E para 6.4 apply.	N215	7.4(3)	7C and 7E
Where the claimant serves the claim form, the claimant:			
(a) must file a certificate of service within 21 days of service of the particulars of claim, unless all the defendants have filed acknowledgements of service within that time; and (b) may not obtain judgment in default under Part 12 unless a certificate of service has been filed		6.17(2)	
For contents of the certificate of service see		6.17(3)	
For bulk issue in a Production Centre see CPR PD 7C; there is a varying scale of discounts for claims, and a £10 discount for warrants issued through the Claims Production Centre		7.10	7C
5. Contents of the claim form			
For requirements for contents of the claim form, see	N1	16.2	16, para 2
Note:			

	Form No	CPR	PD
• A defendant may be identified by description rather than name: *Bloomsbury Publishing Group Ltd v News Group Ltd* [2003] EWHC 1205 (Ch), [2003] 3 All ER 736			
• The **name** of the court should be specified but the court office will insert the claim number			
In civil proceedings against the Crown for contents of the claim form see		16.2(1A)	
• For guidance as to the name and title of the claimant and of the defendant see "Notes for claimant on completing a claim form"	N1A		
• Where a partnership has a name, unless it is inappropriate to do so, claims must be brought in or against the name under which that partnership carried on business at the time the cause of action accrued		7.2A	7A, para 5A.3
• Where a person carries on business in a name other than his own ('the business name') the claim may be brought against the business name as if it were the name of a partnership		7.2A	7A, paras 5.1 and 5.1
• A written statement of the names and last known places of residence of all partners who were partners at the time when the cause of action accrued can be required (a 'partnership membership statement')		7.2A	7A, para 5B
• The claim form requires **brief details of the claim** and there should be inserted a concise statement of the nature of the claim and a statement of the remedy sought. These should be sufficient to identify the claim and inform the defendant of its nature and the remedy sought			

	Form No	CPR	PD
For example: "The claim is for damages for personal injuries and loss and damage caused by the **negligence** of the defendant in the driving of motor car [registration number] at [location] on or about [date and time] and interest thereon pursuant to [section 35A of the Senior Courts Act 1981] [section 69 County Court Act 1984]" "The claim is for damages for **nuisance** by noise from the defendant's house [address] and interest thereon ... (continue as above)" "The claim is for the price of **goods** [describe nature of goods] **sold** and delivered by the claimant to the defendant on [specify date] and interest thereon ... continue as above)"		16.2(1)(a) and (b)	
Note: The court may grant any remedy to which the claimant is entitled, even if that remedy is not specified in the claim form		16.2(5)	
• The claim form or the particulars of claim must contain a statement whether Sections III and IV of the Practice Direction (Pre-action Conduct) and any relevant protocol have been complied with.			Practice Direction (Pre-action Conduct), para 9.7
• Where the claimant is making a claim for money, he must state:			
(i) the amount of money he is claiming			
(ii) that he expects to recover not more than £5,000, more than £5,000 but not more than £25,000 or more than £25,000, or			
(iii) that the claimant cannot say how much he expects to recover		16.3	
The space opposite "value" can conveniently be completed:			

	Form No	CPR	PD
"The claimant expects to recover more than £5,000 but not more than £25,000 (or as the case may be) and, claims £X inclusive of £Y interest to the date of issue (when the claim can be so quantified)" This formula fits in appropriately with the calculation required in the claim form, where the only claim is for a specified sum, and on the form Notice of Issue (specified amount) when requesting judgment	N205A		
The matters to be disregarded by the claimant in calculating the amount he expects to recover are set out		16.3(6)	
In a claim for **personal injuries**, the claimant must also state in the claim form whether the amount the claimant expects to recover as general damages for pain, suffering and loss of amenity is or is not more than £1,000		16.3(4)	
• If the particulars of claim are not contained in or served with the claim form, there must be a statement in the claim form that **particulars of claim will follow**		16.2(3)	
• The claim form must also contain such matters as may be set out in a **Practice Direction**		16.2(1)(a)	
• Chancery business in the High Court should be marked in the top right hand corner of the claim forms "Chancery Division" and if issued in a county court, it should be marked "Chancery Business". If a chancery-type case is brought in a county court which does not coincide with a Chancery District Registry (usually described as a Chancery county court) and it needs specialist experience consideration will be given to its transfer to a Chancery county court for case management or trial or both.			7A, para 2.5

	Form No	CPR	PD
• Where a claim is for compensation for **mesothelioma** the claim form must be headed 'Living Mesothelioma claim' or 'Fatal Mesothelioma Claim'		3.1	3D, Mesothelioma Claims, para 3.1
• For the marking where a mercantile claim is intended to be entered in the business list of an authorised county court, see			59, para 2.2
• For the marking of a claim form in specialist proceedings generally, see		49	
• If the claim is to be served in Scotland, Northern Ireland or out of the United Kingdom where the permission of the court is not required the claimant must:			
(a) File with the claim form a notice stating the grounds on which the claimant is entitled to serve the claim form out of the jurisdiction; and (b) Serve a copy of that notice with the claim form. See **TAB 5** below.	N510	6.32–6.34	6B, para 2.1
• The claim form must be verified by a **statement of truth** whether or not separate particulars of claim incorporating a statement of truth are served			
The statement of truth can be signed by the claimant or his litigation friend or his solicitors, provided in each case they are duly authorised by the claimant to sign		2.3(1) 22	
Where a person is unable to read or sign a document to be verified by a statement of truth see			22, para 3A and Annex 1

	Form No	CPR	PD
Statements of truth are not simply formalities and witnesses must be made aware of the consequence that permission will be given for contempt proceedings to be brought against the maker of a false statement of truth: see *KJM Superbikes v Hinton* [2008] EWCA 1280, [2008] All ER (D) 200 (Nov) in particular per Moore-Bick LJ. The case is discussed in detail at (2008) NLJ 28 November at page 1679 in an article by Janna Purdie and reported in the same edition of the NLJ at page 1683			
As to the mechanical signature of a document, see		5.3	
As to **electronic communication and filing of documents** see PD 5B (Electronic Communications and Filing of Documents) which applies to claims in specified courts only. Section I of the Practice Direction provides for parties to communicate with the court and file specified documents by e-mail; Section II provides for parties to file specified documents electronically via an online forms service; and Section III contains general provisions that apply to sections I and II. For user guidance and protocols see PREMA (Preston E-mail Application Service). See also **TAB 1**, section 11, last para.		5.5	5B
As to the **electronic working scheme** (EWS) which came into operation on 1 April 2010 and will operate in the Admiralty, Commercial and London Mercantile Courts, the Chancery Division of the High Court at the Royal Courts of Justice (including the Patents and the Bankruptcy and Companies Court) see:		5.5, 7.12	5C
The EWS has an official website at www.electronic working.org.			

	Form No	CPR	PD
It is intended that the PD should continue to apply to these jurisdictions when they transfer to the Rolls Building and to the Bankruptcy jurisdiction of the Central London County Court. The scheme applies to all claims started on or after 1 April 2010 and to claims started or continued electronically under the pilot scheme which ran from 1 April 2009 to 31 March 2010.			
6. Other documents to be filed with the claim form			
(a) A party who seeks to recover an additional liability under a funding arrangement must give other parties information about this claim	N251		44, section 19
(b) Where the court is to serve a claim form a copy of any notice of funding should be filed with copies of it for service. Rule 44.15 deals with the provision of information about funding arrangements.		44.15	
Practice Direction (Pre-Action Conduct) provides that a party should inform any other party as soon as possible about any funding arrangement entered into prior to the start of proceedings			
(c) Where the claim is by a **child** (a person under 18 years old) or **protected party** (a party or intended party who lacks capacity to conduct the proceedings) a certificate of suitability and a certificate of its service must be filed if a person becomes a litigation friend without a court order. If, however, a deputy has been appointed by the Court of Protection under the Mental Health Act 2005 with power to conduct proceedings only an official copy of the order need be filed.	N235	21.1(2)(d), 21.5(3) and 21.5(4)(a) and (b)	21 paras 2.1–2.4

	Form No	CPR	PD
The certificate of service is as to service on a parent, guardian etc of the certificate of suitability.		21.5(4)(a) and (b)	
For the procedure where a person becomes a litigation friend by order of the court, see		21.8, 21.10	21 paras 3.1–3.4
For the ability for a litigation friend to recover expenses out of the child's or protected party's estate, see		21.12 and 48.5	21 paras 11.1 and 11.2
Where damages do not exceed £5,000 the litigation friend's recovery is limited to 25%; the court may increase this but not beyond 50%		21.12(6)	
For the court to adopt the **'show cause' procedure in mesothelioma cases** at the first case management conference, the claimant must file and serve any witness statements about liability as are available either at the time of serving the claim form and particulars of claim or in any even not less than 7 days before the case management conference. The relevant mesothelioma PD paras are • as to the filing of witness statements and starting proceedings • claimants with severely limited life expectancy • fixing case management conferences for cases that do not fall within para 4 • the 'show cause' procedure • setting trial date • evidence by deposition • pre-action protocols			 3D, para 3.2 3D, para 4 3D, para 5 3D, para 6 3D, para 7 3D, para 8 3D, para 7
Note that the present amount of a 'standard interim payment' is £50,000			3D, para 2(b)
(d) A response pack comprising (i) form for defending the claim (ii) form for admitting the claim (iii) form for acknowledging service should be provided for service with the particulars of claim	N9	7.8(1)	

	Form No	CPR	PD
7. Particulars of claim			
Particulars of claim must be served with the claim form or within 14 days thereafter, but in any event no later than the latest time for serving the claim form (generally 4 months, 6 months if served out of the jurisdiction)		7.4(1), 7.4(2), 7.5(2) and (3)	
If the particulars of claim are served separately from the claim form a copy must be filed within 7 days of service		7.4(3)	
The court does have a **discretion to extend time for service** of the particulars of claim where the claim form was served within the time prescribed: *Totty v Snowden* [2001] EWCA Civ 1415, [2001] 4 All ER 577. See also *Austin v Newcastle Chronicle and Journal Ltd* [2001] All ER (D) 243 (May)			
Where the application to extend time for service of the particulars of claim pursuant to CPR 3.1(2)(a) is made before the time for compliance has expired, the judge in deciding whether to exercise his discretion is not required to consider the checklist in CPR 3.9(1); *Robert v Momentum Services Ltd* (2003) Times, 13 February, CA. The prejudice to be considered is that arising from the failure to file the particulars not pre-existing prejudice. The rule 3.9(1) check list must be applied where the application to serve the particulars of claim out of time is made after the time for service has expired.		3.9(1)	
An extension of time may be granted subject to conditions; see *Price v Price* [2003] EWCA Civ 888, [2003] 3 All ER 911, where time was extended on conditions including a condition limiting the claim			

	Form No	CPR	PD
Powers in the CPR to extend time, remedy and error in procedure and dispense with service cannot be used to extend a statutory time limit or to avoid service required by statute unless the statute expressly provides: *Mucelli v Government of Albania* [2009] UKHL 2, [2009] All ER (D) 135 (Jan), (2009) Times, 27 January.			
The matters that must be included in the particulars of claim are set out in		16.4(1)	
There must be a **concise statement of the facts** on which the claimant relies. It must be constantly kept in mind that the circumstances in which an unpleaded issue would be considered by the court would be rare.			
If **interest** is claimed that must be stated and it must be further stated if it is claimed pursuant to statute (and if so which), pursuant to the contract or some other basis (and if so which)		16.4(1)(b), 16.4(2)	
If the claim for interest is for a specified amount of money, (i) the percentage rate claimed; (ii) date from which it is claimed; (iii) the date to which it is calculated (not being later than the date of issue); (iv) the total amount of interest claimed to the date of calculation; and (v) the daily rate must be set out			
No interest can be awarded on debts before proceedings			
Unless there is entitlement to interest by statute eg Taxes Management Act 1970, the award of interest is discretionary as to award, rate and period. The court has statutory power to award interest on debt and damages			
For interest in personal injury claims and its calculation, see Rodney Nelson Jones annual update, the most recent of which appears in the Gazette (2008) 2 October, p 23			

	Form No	CPR	PD
If a claim is for interest under the Late Payment of Commercial Debts (Interest) Act 1998 as amended see **CPR 16.4 [5.16]** and **CPR 16.4 [5.17]**, and for a precedent see **BCCP B[7]**. Note the ability to obtain a penalty as well as interest (£40 on a debt up to £1,000; £70 on a debt up to £10,000; and £100 above that figure). An error in an invoice does not prevent there being a liability for late interest: *Ruttle Plant Hire Ltd v Secretary of State for the Environment, Food and Rural Affairs (No 3)* [2009] EWCA Civ 97, (2009) Times, 4 March, (2009) Sol Jo, Lawbrief 10 March, page 27. For 'remittal' (reduction in whole or part) under s 5 of the 1998 Act see the judgment in *Ruttle* and Lawbrief, above.			
For a case where the contract rate of interest was allowed although it had been negotiated at a time (2001) when interest rates were considerably higher than those payable in the current climate, see *Taiwan Scot Ltd v The Master Golf Co Ltd* [2009] EWCA Civ 685, [2009] All ER (D) 221 (Jul).			
For the circumstances in which compound interest may be claimed see *Sempra Metals Ltd v IRC* [2007] UKHL 34, (2007) Times, 25 July and *Constantgreen v Customs Comrs* [2007] UKVAT V20303 where the test was expressed to be whether the taxpayer had to borrow to replace that which had been withheld. The effect of these decisions is not restricted to tax cases; for detailed consideration see article 'Bad pennies' by Crossley and Walsh in New Law Journal 14 September 2007, page 1254			
See further as to interest see **CPR 16.4[0]** to **CPR 16.4[17]** and articles in Gazette (2007) 18 October, page 29 and 25 October, page 29			
For interest on judgment debts in the county court see the County Courts (Interest on Judgment Debts) Order 1991, SI 1991/1184.			

	Form No	CPR	PD
If **aggravated damages, exemplary damages** or **provisional damages** are claimed, that must be stated and the ground for claiming them set out		16.4(1)(c) and (d)	
As a matter of pleading practice a claim for **disadvantage on the labour market** should be included in the particulars of injury but if omitted it will not be fatal where it is otherwise apparent from the pleadings: *Thorn v Powergen plc* [1997] PIQR Q71, CA; see also '*Smith v Manchester* awards', Butterworths Personal Injury Newsletter, October 2009, Vol 1, issue 8			
Any matters required to be set out in a **Practice Direction** must be included		16.4(1)(e)	
If the particulars of claim are separate from the claim form they must be verified by a **statement of truth**		22.1	
Besides the mandatory contents there are **additional requirements in particular cases:**			
personal injury claims – note that a schedule of details of any past and future losses claimed must be attached and the schedule of loss must be verified by a statement of truth. Further if the claimant is relying on the evidence of a medical practitioner the claimant must attach to or serve with his particulars of claim a medical report			16, para 4 and 22 para 1.5
fatal accident claims			16, para 5
hire purchase claims			16, para 6
injunction or declaration in respect of land, its possession, etc			16, para 7.1
return of goods			16, para 7.2
claim based on written agreement (unless claim issued from the Production Centre)			16, para 7.3 and 7, para 1.4(4)
claim based on oral agreement			16, para 7.4
claim based on agreement by conduct			16, para 7.5
consumer credit claim			16, para 7.6 7B, paras 7.1–7.4

	Form No	CPR	PD
It should be noted that where the agreement is regulated it is not appropriate to make an allowance for accelerated payment in the claim form. Judgment should be sought for the full amount; any refund will be given on settlement or enforcement of the judgment: *Forward Trust Ltd v Whymark* [1990] 2 QB 670, [1989] 3 All ER 915. For precedents see **BCCP K[1486]** and **BCCP K[1487]**			
where s11 or s12 of Civil Evidence Act 1968 is relied upon			16, para 8.1
where certain specific allegations, eg fraud or illegality are made			16, para 8.2
Besides the mandatory requirements and the additional requirement, the **particulars of claim may include**:			
(a) any point of law on which the claim is based			
(b) names of any witnesses			
(c) supporting documents (including an expert's report) attached			16, para 14.3
This provision enables particulars of claim to be "shaped" for the particular track to which the case is likely to be allocated. A small claim is given very little judicial case management and the particulars of claim can be drafted to cover, as much as is sensible of the claimant's statement, the aspects of which are supported by other evidence and the essential documents. If a point of law is involved this can also be dealt with. This will not be necessary on the fast track and on the multi-track, where disclosure and requests for information will be part of the normal procedure. The optional additions to the particulars of claim should be used sparingly on these tracks *Note*: *Morris v Bank of America National Trust* [2000] 1 All ER 954			
Contradictory statements are not permitted: *Clarke (Executor of the Will of Francis Bacon) v Marlborough Fine Arts (London) Ltd* [2002] 1 WLR 1731			

	Form No	CPR	PD
If the claim is to be served in Scotland, Northern Ireland or out of the United Kingdom without permission under rule 6.32 or 6.33 the statement required giving the grounds on which permission is not required must be filed with copies for service.		6.34	6B, para 2.1
8. Issue of the claim			
The claim form duly completed with notes for the defendant must be lodged at or sent to the court office with a copy for sealing and return and a copy for each defendant. If the particulars of claim are attached (as opposed to endorsed) a similar number of copies is required	N1		
Unless the claimant is entitled to full or part remission or applies successfully for remission of the fees by reason of undue hardship, the court fee on issue must be paid. For sanctions for non-payment of fees see			3B
For county court fees from 1 May 2008 see the civil Proceedings Fees Order 2008, SI 2008/1053, Schedule 1 at **FEE 1.8** below	EX50		
For full or part remission of fees see the Civil Proceedings (Fees) Order 2008, Schedule 2 at **FEE 1.9** below	EX160A		
The proceedings are issued on or started on the issue date entered by the court staff on the claim form, but where the claim form was received in the court office before the date it is issued by the court, the claim is brought for the purposes of the Limitation Act 1980 and any relevant statute on that earlier date		7.2	7A, para 5.1
See further *Barnes v St Helens Metropolitan Borough Council* [2006] EWCA Civ 1372, (2006) Times, 17 November, [2007] 3 All ER 525 and article by Andrew Williams in New Law Journal 1 December 2006 1826			
The court date stamps the claim form held on the court file or the letter that accompanied it with the date of receipt			7A, para 5.2

	Form No	CPR	PD
Where issue is shortly before the expiry of any relevant limitation period, the claimant is best advised to lodge the forms with the court for issue and make his own note of the time and date of lodgment and the name of the court clerk who received the documents			7A, para 5.4
9. Money claim online (**MCOL**)			
9.1 Preliminary – claimant			
Money Claim Online enables certain types of claim forms to be issued and other specified documents to be filed electronically via the Court Service website. Claims started using MCOL will be issued by Northampton County court (for address see CPR PD 7 MCOL, para 1.4 (at para **CPR PD 7E** above)) and will proceed in that court unless they are transferred to another court. Such claims can be issued electronically through MCOL when the particulars of claim are to be served separately. Judgment in default of acknowledgement of claim or defence and judgment on admission of the whole claim can be entered and a warrant of execution can be issued electronically. The electronic record of the progress of the claim may be viewed.		7.12	7E MCOL, para 1.4 and para 13
Practice Direction 5C deals with electronic issue of claims started or continued under the Electronic Working Pilot.			
9.2 Preliminary – defendant			
Defendants of claims issued by MCOL wishing to submit:			
(a) an acknowledgment of service of the claim form under CPR Part 10			
(b) a part admission under CPR 14.5			
(c) a defence under CPR Part 15 or			
(d) a counterclaim (if filed with a defence)			

	Form No	CPR	PD
may do so online. They can also view an electronic record of the progress of the claim			7E MCOL, para 1.3
9.3 Fees			
Fees can be paid by credit card or debit card; fees payable on issue are less for claims online than for claims issued in a court, the difference varies from £5 to £35 depending on the amount of the claim			7E MCOL, para 3.1
For security reasons persons using the service must register (creating for themselves a customer ID and password)			7E MCOL, para 2
A claimant who wishes to apply for exemption from or reduction of fees cannot use Money Claim Online			7E MCOL, para 3.2
9.3A Procedure on issue			
The procedure to be followed on issue of, and when responding to, a claim electronically are set out in the PD			7E MCOL, para 5–10
Since 6 April 2009 where MCOL is being used or issue is through a production centre if the particulars of claim are too long to fit into the space available electronically, i e they exceed 1,080 characters including spaces, it is possible to serve them separately but the claimant must state the detailed particulars of claim will follow and include a brief summary of the claim.			
9.3B Procedure after issue			
Service is deemed to take place 5 days after issue and note the requirements where the particulars of claim are served separately from the claim.			7E MCOL, para 6
For request to enter judgment or issue of a warrant see			7E MCOL, para 11

	Form No	CPR	PD
9.4 Availability			
The types of claims that may be started using MCOL are set out in para 4 of the PD but note in particular that the service is limited to Part 7 claims; that the only remedy claimed must be a specified sum of money less than £100,000 (excluding interest and costs); and that the defendant's address for service is within England and Wales			7E MCOL, para 4
An explanatory leaflet is available from county courts, there is a telephone helpline (0845 6015935), a fax facility (on 0845 601 5889) and an online guide at www.courtservice.gov.uk/mcol			
9.5 Filing			
The address for filing any document, application or request (other than one filed electronically) is Northampton County Court, St Katherine House, 21–27 St Katherine Street, Northampton, NN1 2LH, DX 702885 Northampton 7, Fax no 0845 601 5889			
9.6 Transfer out			
9.6.1 For transfer out when the defendant is an individual and Northampton County Court is not his home court see			7E MCOL, para 12.1
9.6.2 For transfer out to claimant's home court see			7E MCOL, para 12.2
10. Possession claims online			
See **TAB 22** below			
11. Electronic Communication and Filing of Documents and Service of Documents			
In specified courts litigants are able to **file** in specified county court forms via their home computers or by visiting agencies such as Citizens' Advice. The specified courts are those which have published an e-mail address for filing of documents on the Courts Service website (www.hmcourts-service.co.uk). The specified documents are also listed on this website.			

	Form No	CPR	PD
Para 15.1B of **CPR PD 52** provides for certain notices to be filed electronically at the Court of Appeal The document is merely filed by e-mail and other parties must be served in the normal way. But rules 6.3(1)(d) and 6.20(1)(d) permit **service by e-mail** in accordance with Practice Direction 6A. Rule 6.23(6) and para 4 of PD 6A set out the circumstances in which a party may serve a document by e-mail. See also **TAB 1** above, section 5, last para		5.5	5B
12. Supervening Insolvency			
Once a claim has been issued leave of the court is not required to continue the claim even though the individual or company against whom the proceedings were commenced was adjudicated bankrupt or became insolvent after issue: *Godfrey v Torpy* (2007) Times, 16 May			
13 Settlement or compromise before proceedings			
For requirements where the court's approval is sought to a settlement or compromise by or on behalf of a child or protected party reached before the issue of proceedings see		2.10	21A, paras 5.1–5.6
14 Striking out claims			
The court may exercise this power of its own initiative or on application. The court may strike out a statement of case or part of a statement of case where it appears to the court:			
(a) it discloses **no reasonable grounds** for bringing or defending the claim: see for example *Ikea Ltd v John Brown* [2009] EWHC 955 (Comm), [2009] All ER (D) 160 (May) where the counter claim was struck out as being 'incoherent and made no sense and therefore failed to disclose a reasonable cause of action';			

	Form No	CPR	PD
(b) it is an **abuse of the court's process** or is otherwise likely to obstruct the just disposal of proceedings. It is to be noted the fact that a matter could have been raised in previous proceedings does not necessarily give rise to an abuse if it is raised in later proceedings; see Bingham LJ in *Johnson v Gore Wood & Co (a firm)* [2002] EWHC 776 (QB), [2002] All ER (D) 52 (May) and see *Wellbrook Trustees (Jersey) Ltd v Fattal* [2009] EWCA Civ 297, [2009] All ER (D) 107 (Apr), Gazette Legal Update (2009) 15 October, page 16, where successive action on the same facts was found not to be an abuse of process in the particular circumstances; (c) there is a **failure to comply** with a rule, practice direction or court order.			
See further Sol Jo Litigation Focus 2009, September, article by Masood Ahmed and see **TAB 3** below for relief against sanctions.		3.4	3A

TABLE 2—START OF PROCEEDINGS FOR PART 8 CLAIMS

TAB 2

	Form No	CPR Rule	PD
1. Preliminary			
1.1 CPR Pt 8 provides an alternative procedure for use where:			
(a) the claimant seeks the court's decision on a question which is unlikely to involve a substantial dispute of fact, or		8.1(2)	
(b) where a Practice Direction permits or requires its use for the type of proceedings in question (although that Practice Direction may modify or disapply the Part 8 procedure and if so that Practice Direction must be complied with)		8.1(2) and (6)	

	Form No	CPR Rule	PD
1.2 'Schedule rules' means rules previously contained in RSC or CCR			8, para 1
1.3 CPR PD 8 para 3 is divided into sections A, B and C			8, para 2.1
(i) Section A contains general provisions about Part 8 claims and applications (paras 3.1–3.5)			
(ii) Section B comprises a table listing claims etc which **must** be made under Part 8			
(iii) Section C contains variations to the Part 8 procedure that apply to the claims and applications identified *Note:* • Practice Direction to CPR Pt 21, para 6.1 provides that a claim by or against a child or protected party or brought solely to obtain the approval of the court must be made using the Part 8 procedure			8, section A, para 3.1(1)
• CPR PD 8, Section A, para 3.1(2) provides that a claim for provisional damages which has been settled prior to proceedings but is to be the subject of a consent judgment, may be made under CPR Pt 8 (but see CPR PD 41 para 4.1)			8, section A, para 3.1(2)
• The court may at any stage order the claim to continue as if the claimant had not used the Part 8 procedure and give any directions it considers appropriate. The directions may include allocation to track. For the consequences of not so allocating see para **CPR 8 [8]**		8.1(3)	
• The defendant may object to the use of the Part 8 procedure and must state the reasons for his objection when he files his acknowledgment		8.8 and 8.8(1)	8, section A, para 5.3
2. The contents of the claim form			
A Part 8 claim form must be used and must state:			
(a) that CPR Pt 8 applies		8.2(a)	

	Form No	CPR Rule	PD
(b) (i) the question which the claimants wants the court to decide or		8.2(b)	
(ii) the remedy which the claimant is seeking and the legal basis for the claim to that remedy			
(c) if the claim is being made under an enactment, what that enactment is		8.2(c)	
(d) if the claimant is claiming in a representative capacity, what the capacity is		8.2(d)	
(e) if the defendant is sued in a representative capacity, what that capacity is		8.2(e)	
(f) if the claim is to be served in Scotland, Northern Ireland or out of the United Kingdom without permission under rule 6.32 or 6.33 the statement required giving the grounds on which permission is not required must be filed with the copies for service.		6.34	6B, para 2.1
(g) the claim form or the particulars of claim must contain a statement whether Sections III and IV of the Practice Direction (Pre-action Conduct) and any relevant protocol have been complied with.			Practice Direction (Pre-action conduct), para 9.7
The claim form must be verified by a statement of truth		Part 22	
Where the claimant seeks to recover an additional liability, information about the funding arrangement must be provided with the claim form and a copy of any notice of funding should be filed with copies for service.		44.15	6A, para 8.2

	Form No	CPR Rule	PD
3. Special provisions			
The claimant must use the Part 8 procedure if the claim, petition or application is listed in the table in Section B, para 9.3 but where the listed claim is identified as one to which particular provisions of Section C apply the Part 8 procedure shall apply subject to the additions and modifications set out in the relevant paragraph in Section C			
4. Issuing the claim			
The general provisions of CPR Pt 7 and the Practice Direction that accompanies it will apply to Part 8 claims where appropriate			8, para 4.1
The Part 8 claim form must be used	N208		
The claimant must file any written evidence on which he intends to rely when he files his claim form: this must be served on the defendant with the claim form unless an extension of time is granted		8.5(1) and (2)	8, paras 7.4 and 7.5
Information about funding arrangements must be filed with the claim form See also		44.15	6A, para 8.2
5. Defendant			
For the procedure to be followed by the defendant, see **TAB 7**			

TABLE 3—SANCTIONS, AVOIDANCE AND RELIEF

TAB 3

	Form No	CPR Rule	PD
1. Imposition of sanctions and types of sanction			
1.1 The long-standing power of the court to include in an order a sanction on default is reflected and repeated by CPR 3.1(3)(b) which provides that there is power to specify the consequences of non-compliance		3.1(3)(b)	
1.2 An order containing such a provision is frequently called an 'unless order'			

	Form No	CPR Rule	PD
1.3 The consequence of non-compliance is frequently that the case of the defaulting party be struck out or do stand struck out in whole or in part. This is not necessarily the sanction and it may be, for example, that a particular fact shall be taken to be admitted or that the defaulting party will not be permitted to adduce evidence on a particular issue. It has been described as 'one of the most powerful weapons in the court's case management armoury' (*Marcan Shipping (London) Ltd v Kefalas* [2007] EWCA Civ 463, [2007] All ER (D) 277 (May)) The court should not abuse its management powers by going to extremes and imposing sanctions that will result in claims being struck out for delay where a proportionate use of a more flexible power would be appropriate: *Marstons plc v Charman* [2009] EWCA Civ 719, (2009) 153 Sol Jo (no 18) 30, following *Biguzzi v Rank Leisure plc* [1999] 1 WLR 1926, CA.			3A
Coulson J held in *D Morgan plc v Mace and Jones* [2010] EWHC 697 (TCC), 23 March, that: (a) an unless order should only be made after the court has carefully considered whether it is appropriate in all the circumstances of the case; and (b) a court should satisfy itself that the party in question has a reasonable prospect of complying with the unless order.			
1.4 The sanction of striking out is not limited to breaches of court orders, rules of practice directions but can also be imposed when a statement of case discloses no reasonable grounds for bringing or defending the case or where there has been an abuse of the court process; see Sol Jo 'Litigation Focus' September 2009 for a full consideration.		3.4(2)	3A

	Form No	CPR Rule	PD
It is not essential for an order to strike out to be made for there to have been a preceding 'unless order'. The court in *Meldex International plc v Trevillion* [2010] 26 May (ChD) held that the failure by the claimant to comply with the provision in a consent order, requiring the provision of a substantial security for costs, with no adequate alternative proposal, was a gross breach and it was appropriate, on application by the defendant, to strike out the claim under CPR 3.4(2)(c).			
In the appeal *Masood v Zahoor* [2009] EWCA Civ 650, [2009] All ER (D) 33 (Jul) the Court of Appeal observed it must be a very rare case where it was appropriate for the judge at the end of a trial to strike out a claim on misconduct grounds rather than to dismiss it on its merits.			
2. Consequences of non-compliance			
2.1 In *Marcan Shipping* (see above) it was clearly stated a sanction should not be imposed unless the consequences can be justified			
2.2 Those consequences of default are that the sanctions will: • take effect if there is not complete compliance: *Jani-King (GB) Ltd v Prodger* [2007] EWHC 712 (QB), [2007] All ER (D) 505 (Mar) • take effect automatically without the necessity of a further order, see *E Group Ltd v Bay Baker* [2008] EWHC 2349 (TCC), (2008) 18 September, unreported (Coulson J) • prevent any argument that it is not an appropriate consequence of the non-compliance			3A, para 1.9
3. Avoidance of the sanction			
3.1 The sanction can only be prevented from taking effect by complete performance by the date specified. It is almost invariably the case that failure to comply with the date specified is the breach relied on			

	Form No	CPR Rule	PD
3.2 Besides the necessity of making a diary note of the date for compliance it is also necessary to note an earlier date when an assessment must be made of whether the time limit can be met. That earlier date must be sufficiently before the compliance date to allow steps to be taken to avoid non-compliance			
3.3 The most obvious step is to seek to agree with the opposing party an extension of time for compliance; if agreement is forthcoming the court should be informed		2.11	
If the time limit is part of a management timetable and the extension will necessitate a change in the date for delivery of the pre-trial check list, the trial window or the trial, an application, albeit by consent, will be necessary	N244	28.4 and 29.5	
3.4 If the opposing party refuses to agree the extension an application on notice should be made to the court for an extension supported by evidence of why it is required, the extra time required and how this has been calculated and the disproportionate effect of refusal taking into account the overriding objective. It is vital to seek a realistic extension of time for an extension to a date that will be insufficient to achieve complete compliance will be of no value to the applicant; it will merely be putting off the evil day.			
For forms of judgment for failure to comply with an 'unless' order see	PF 85A and 85B		
4. Review of the position where sanction is likely to take effect			
4.1 Where it is apparent that it is unlikely that it will be possible to comply with an unless order the party adversely affected should			

	Form No	CPR Rule	PD
(a) carefully consider whether the unless order was **defective** by reason of impossibility of performance when it was made, e g where the unless order is simply to comply with an earlier order within, say, 14 days of service. If the time specified for compliance had already passed when the unless order was made clearly the unless order would be defective and could be set aside. (b) consider an appeal for on an **appeal** it can be argued • the time for compliance is inadequate for the requirements cannot be satisfied by that time even with all proper efforts. The order as it stands is in reality equivalent to an order that judgment be entered. • the sanction (particularly if it is for striking out) for breach is not proportionate and if it came into effect it would be contrary to the overriding objective: see *Marcan Shipping (London) Ltd v Kefalas* above at para 1.3. A useful extract from the judgment of Keene LJ in *Marcan* at para 39 is: a conditional order striking out a statement of case or dismissing a claim … is one of the most powerful weapons … and should not be deployed unless its consequences can be justified. I find it difficult to imagine circumstances in which such an order could properly be made for 'good housekeeping' purposes.			

	Form No	CPR Rule	PD
See also *Lambeth Borough Council v Onayomake* (2007) Times, 2 November, CA. In this case the defendant made a counterclaim on substantial grounds in a possession action. The defendant's legal representative failed to file a check list on time. The defence and counterclaim were struck out and an application to re-instate refused. This was held to be disproportionate and the defendant's appeal allowed.			
4.2 If it is decided, at any rate, to consider an appeal permission should be sought at the hearing when the order was made and a careful note made of the reasons given by the judge whether he grants or refuses the permission sought. Pending the hearing of the appeal every effort should be made towards compliance and carefully scheduled.			
For the procedural aspects of such an appeal, see **TAB 37** and **TAB 3**8 below			
5. Where an unless order has not been complied with – application for relief			
5.1 See *Sayers v Clarke Walker (a firm)* [2002] EWCA Civ 645, [2002] 3 All ER 490, [2002] 1 WLR 3095 where Brooke LJ stated that in the event of non-compliance a defaulting party has to seek relief from the sanction by an **application under CPR 3.8** and in that event the court will consider all the matters raised in CPR 3.9 as far as they are relevant.			

	Form No	CPR Rule	PD
5.2 The court has power to dispense with the filing of an application notice and grant relief, see *Keen Philips (a firm) v Field* [2006] EWCA Civ 1524, [2007] 1 WLR 686 where the court did dispense with the application notice, granted relief against the sanction and extended the time for compliance. The duty of the court to act in this way 'is one which is likely to be exercised only rarely …' (Keene LJ in *Marcan* at para 33). The Court of Appeal in *Vernon v Spoudeas* [2010] All ER (D) 54 (May) (where an application for relief was dealt with on paper and dismissed) stated that the better course is to apply to the judge who made the order, seeking that it be set aside or varied; see further this TAB, para 6.2, final sub-para.			
5.3 In the case of *Supperstone v Hurst* [2008] EWHC 735 (Ch) after stating: 'If a party does not have a good explanation or the other side is prejudiced by the failure relief from sanctions will normally be refused. It is vitally important that rules of procedure are observed.' Mr Justice Floyd provided practical guidelines for those seeking or opposing an application for relief against sanctions imposed by the rules. Two points in particular are to be noted:			
(i) the exercise of the discretion in accordance with the rules to grant or refuse relief, which is not flawed, is not open to challenge by appeal; (ii) if the defendant maintains he has been prejudiced he must put in evidence to that effect. He cannot rely on the applicant's failure to prove there is no prejudice.			

	Form No	CPR Rule	PD
See also *Tarn Insurance Services Ltd (in administration) v Kirby* [2009] EWCA Civ 19, [2009] All ER (D) 211 (Jan) where it was emphasised that in a case of deliberate and persistent non-compliance the proper administration of justice required that sanctions imposed should take effect save in exceptional circumstances, and *Tomer v Atlantic Cleaning Services Ltd* [2008] EWHC 1652 (QB).			
In the *Tarn Insurance* case (see above) the Court of Appeal held that an order conditionally debarring a defendant from defending is only appropriate if it is made on the basis that there is no reason to believe that (in the absence of the order) the defendant would not be able to advance a defence with a real prospect of success. Accordingly the existence of such a real prospect could not be treated as a decisive factor for granting relief.			
It was held that the true test under CPR 3.9 is whether, notwithstanding that the unless order was a proper order to be made in the circumstances known at the time, it remained appropriate, at the time of the application for relief, to allow the sanction to take effect in the light of the facts then known.			
5.4 Where the sanction imposed was a stay of proceedings the claimant cannot avoid the stay by bringing fresh proceedings on facts that are not new and were capable of being pursued in the original stayed action. The second action would be struck out as an abuse of process: *Watson v Irwin Mitchell* [2009] EWHC 441 (QB), [2009] All ER (D) 113 (Mar).			

	Form No	CPR Rule	PD
5.5 In *Azeez v Momson* [2009] EWCA Civ 202, [2009] All ER (D) 193 (Mar) the application for relief again failed. One of the grounds was based on Article 6 of the European Convention on Human Rights but although the refusal of relief would deprive the Appellant of a trial the court held it served a 'legitimate claim' since the order was made to achieve a fair trial of the claim.			
The litigant in person claimant in *Serrano v Dan-Goor Ltd* [2008] EWHC 2323 (QB), [2008] All ER (D) 294 (Oct) appealed against an unless order for the filing of particulars of claim and complied with the order four years after it had been made. The appeal failed and the court stressed that the CPR applied equally to litigants in person and represented litigants.			
6. Service of the application for relief and evidence in support			
6.1 The filing, notice and service of the application must be in accordance with CPR 23; see **TAB 14**, para 3 below			
6.2 The application must be supported by written evidence and it is not open to the applicant to argue against the propriety of the terms of the order or the sanction; see para 4.1(b) above. The evidence should be prepared keeping in mind that the court will take into account the circumstances listed in CPR 3.9 and it is sensible to shape the evidence to deal with those considerations in turn: see, for example, the judgment of Mackay J in *Jani-King (GB) Ltd v Prodger* [2007] EWHC 712 (QB) at para 22. This was a case where the unless order was made and where having described an unless order as giving a 'last chance' the judge granted relief on terms.			

	Form No	CPR Rule	PD
The court, it must be borne in mind, will critically examine any prejudice which is alleged and weigh the prejudice which will be suffered by each party if relief was granted or relief was refused: *White v Greensand Homes Ltd* [2007] EWCA Civ 643, [2007] BLR 313 Where an unless order has been made in an order for security of costs and even if judgment has been entered as a result of the security having not been paid, if the party against whom the unless order was made, within a short period of time, has come to the court with the correct sum of money, the court should be willing to consider granting relief and setting the judgment aside: *Radu v Houston* [2006] EWCA Civ 1575, [2006] All ER (D) 295 (Nov)			
For cases where the court refused relief for sanctions by re-instating the action see *Marine Rescue Technologies Ltd and David Marshall Rescue Concepts LLC v Burchill* [2007] EWHC 1976 (Ch) and *Ethemi v Shiels* [2008] EWHC 291 (QB).			
In *Vernon v Spoudeas* [2010] All ER (D) 54 (May), 6 May 2010, where the application for relief from sanction was dealt with without a hearing and there was nothing to indicate the judge had considered the merits of the application, it was held that the order refusing relief could not stand and the matter was remitted for a proper hearing. The Court of Appeal indicated that where the order was made without a hearing and there was no right given to apply to vary it or set it aside the better course was not to appeal but to apply to the judge who made the order to vary it or set it aside. The application would be made under Part 3.			
6.3 The evidence should also make it clear what has been done in an attempt to comply with the order and what has so far been achieved. It should also set out any obstacles that have arisen since the making of the order which were not then envisaged.			

	Form No	CPR Rule	PD
6.4 The evidence should set out what time will be required to comply if relief is granted and should show how that period of time has been calculated.			
6.5 The evidence should include an apology for the failure to comply but stress that the default was not contumelous. Costs should in almost all cases be conceded			
7. Costs			
It is almost inevitable that the party in default will be liable for the costs			

TABLE 4—SERVICE OF CLAIM FORMS WITHIN THE JURISDICTION

TAB 4

	Form No	CPR Rule	PD
Preliminary			
It is important to remember that it is not necessary to serve particulars of claim, schedule of loss and medical report with the claim form. If the limitation period is about to expire and the documents to accompany the claim form are not available the claim form should be served and an application made pursuant to CPR 3.1(2)(a) for an extension of time for service of the particulars of claim. The court has greater flexibility on such an application than on an application to extend time for the service of the claim form under CPR 7.6		3.1(2)(a)	
The time limit for serving a claim form can be varied by written agreement of the parties: *Thomas v Home Office* [2006] EWCA Civ 1355, [2006] All ER (D) 243 (Oct). It is not necessary that the agreement be contained in a single document but may be comprised in or sufficiently evidenced by an exchange of documents. The agreement must be for an extension to a specific date. It will be seen that this decision predates the 1 October 2008 rules and would seem to be unaffected by them – see the new CPR 7.6.			

	Form No	CPR Rule	PD
The principle that a defendant may only be served or deemed to be served with originating process within the jurisdiction if he is present in the jurisdiction at the time of service was held not to have survived the CPR by the Court of Appeal in *City & Country Properties Ltd v Kamali* [2006] EWCA Civ 1879, [2007] 1 WLR 1219 where the defendant was served at his usual business address while he has temporarily out of the jurisdiction. The Court of Appeal also rejected arguments based on the Race Relations Act 1976 and on the Convention for the Protection of Human Rights.		6.5(6)	
Definitions 'bank holiday' see 'business day' see 'claim' see and note that claim form does not include particulars of claim where the latter document is not contained in or served with the former 'solicitor', includes any other person who, for the purposes of the Legal Services Act 2007, is an authorised person in relation to an activity which constitutes the conduct of litigation (within the meaning of that Act). Service of the claim form within the jurisdiction and service of other documents each have their own separate provisions with CPR rule 6, ie the former in Section II and the latter in Section III		 6.2(a) 6.2(b) 6.2(c) 6.2(d)	
1. Service by the court			
1.1 Unless a rule or Practice Direction requires service by the claimant or the claimant notifies the court that he wishes to serve, the court will serve the claim form unless the court otherwise orders or directs		6.4(1)	
Service must be within the jurisdiction unless it is being effected by service on a solicitor in any EEA state pursuant to r 6.7 or by a contractually agreed method pursuant to r 6.11 or unless the provisions for service out of the jurisdiction (see **TAB 5** below) are complied with.		6.6(1)	

	Form No	CPR Rule	PD
The court will decide upon the method of service which will normally be first class post.		6.4(2)	6A, para 8.1
Where the court is to serve the claimant must file a copy of the claim form for each defendant in addition to the copy for the court.		6.4(3)	
1.2 Where the court serves a claim for the court will send to the claimant a notice which will include the date of deemed service under rule 6.14; see para 4 of this **TAB** below.			
• Note where the claimant serves the claim form the claimant must file a certificate in accordance with rule 6.17(2) and (3), unless all defendants have filed acknowledgments within 21 days of service of the particulars of claim. Judgment in default of acknowledgment cannot be obtained unless a certificate of service has been filed.		6.17(2)	6A, para 7
1.3 Where the court serves the claim form by post and it is returned to the court the court will notify the claimant of its return but the claim form will be deemed to have been served unless the address for the defendant on the claim form is not the relevant address for the purposes of rules 6.7 to 6.10.		6.18	
1.4 Where the bailiff is to serve a claim form and is unable to do so the court will so notify the claimant.		6.19	
1.5 The court will not make further efforts to serve after it has notified the claimant of the outcome of postal service or given notice of non-service by the bailiff.			
2. Methods of service			
2.1 Must be within the jurisdiction – see further this TAB at 1.1 above		6.6(1)	
2.2 Personal service is mandatory where any other part, Practice direction or court order provides this method must be used.		6.3(a) 6.5(1)	

	Form No	CPR Rule	PD
Personal service of a claim form may be effected (except where rule 6.7, service on a solicitor, or rule 6.10, service no the crown, apply)		6.5(2)	
(a) on an individual by leaving it with that individual (b) on a company or other corporation by leaving it with a person holding a senior position (defined in Practice Direction 6A)		6.5(3)(a) 6.5(3)(b)	6A, para 6.2
(c) on a partnership where partners are being sued in the firm name by leaving it with a partner or a person who, at the time of service has control or management of the partnership business at its principal place of business.		6.5(3)(c)	6A, para 4
2.3 **First class post, document exchange** or other service providing for delivery on the next business day in accordance with Practice Direction 6A		6.3(1)(b)	
for 'document exchange' see			6A, para 2.1
2.4 **Leaving it** at (a) the business address of a solicitor within the jurisdiction or in any EEA state where the provisions of 6.7(a) or (b) are satisfied. These are (i) the defendant has given in writing the business address within the jurisdiction of a solicitor as an address at which the defendant may be served with the claim form; or (ii) a solicitor acting for the defendant has notified the claimant in writing that the solicitor is instructed by the defendant to accept service of the claim form on behalf of the defendant at a business address within the jurisdiction • Note the extended definition of solicitor in the preliminary paragraphs of this TAB		6.3(c), 6.7	

	Form No	CPR Rule	PD
• Note also that, subject to rule 6.5(1) above, where rule 6.7 applies service must be effected in accordance with its provisions and not in any other way. This reflects the decision in *Nanglegan v Royal Free NHS Trust* [2001] EWCA Civ 127, [2001] 3 All ER 793. The power that the court now has to make a retrospective order that steps already taken shall be good service under r 6.15(2) would, if exercised, rescue the claimant in the *Nanglegan* situation. The court's power is, of course, discretionary. See para 5 (3rd sub-para) below • Subject to r 6.5(1) above and Part IV of r 6 (service out of the jurisdiction) in the circumstances set out in 6.7(a) or (b) above the business address given may be within any EEA state and service must be effected at that address			
(b) Where rules 6.5(1) and 6.7 above do not apply, at an address within the jurisdiction that the defendant has given for the purpose of being served with the proceedings or (in a claim by a tenant) the address given by a landlord under s 48 of the Landlord and Tenant Act 1987		6.8	

	Form No	CPR Rule	PD
(c) where rules 6.5(1), 6.7 and 6.8 do not apply and the defendant does not give an address for service he must be served at the appropriate place for the defendant given by the table set out in rule 6.9(2); provided that if the claimant has reason to believe the defendant is an individual and no longer resides at the address shown in the table to the belief of the claimant, he must take reasonable steps to ascertain the defendant's current residence or place of business and serve there.		6.9(3)	
For 'usual or last known address' where the defendant spent only a small amount of his time in England but had a house here occupied by his wife and family, see *Varsani v Relfo Ltd (in liq)* [2009] EWCA Civ 560, [2009] All ER (D) 272 (Mar) where it was held service at that house was at a usual residence and accordingly it was unnecessary to consider the 'last known address' ground. It was further held that it was possible to have more than one such usual residence and that the critical test was the defendant's pattern of life (see *Levene v IRC* (1928) AC 217, HL).			
If the claimant is unable to discover the current address he must consider service by an **alternative method or at an alternative place** and if service can be so effected he must apply for an appropriate order. The application should be supported by evidence. If the claimant's enquiries are fruitless he may serve at the defendant's usual or last known address.		6.9(4)–(6)	
In *Lexi Holdings plc v Luqman* (2008) Times, 19 February it was held that when a person was known to be serving a substantial prison sentence 'his usual or last known residence' was the prison in which he was serving his sentence and not the place where he resided beforehand. (This case was under the rules in force prior to 1 October 2008.)			

	Form No	CPR Rule	PD
2.5 By **fax or other electronic means** in accordance with		6.3(d)	
Note the 'sufficient written indication' arising from the inclusion of a fax number in the letterhead of the legal representative, an e-mail address on such a letter included in such letterhead with a statement that the e-mail address may be used for service or a fax number, e-mail address or electronic identification set out in a statement of case or response to a claim filed with the court.			6A, para 4
For a failure to establish that service by fax was valid see *Brown v Innovatorone plc* [2009] EWHC 1376 (Comm), 153 Sol Jo (no 25) 27, (2009) Gazette, 3 September, page 14 and also *Thorne v Lass Salt Garvin (a firm)* [2009] EWHC 100 (QB), [2009] All ER (D) 218 (Jan) where the defendants were a firm of solicitors. This case applied *Kuenyehia v International Hospitals Ltd* [2006] EWCA Civ 21, (2006) Times, 17 February.			
Service by fax was held to be invalid although it was on solicitors for the defendant who included their fax number in letterhead used in writing to the claimant's solicitors in *Andrew Brown v Innovatorone plc* above. There had been no compliance with either of the alternatives in CPR 6.7. The claimant's cross application for the fax service to stand as good alternative service was dismissed.			
2.6 On a company by any method under CPR Part 6 or in accordance with the methods of service permitted under **Companies Act 1985** or the **Companies Act 2006**		6.3(2)	6A, para 6
2.7 A **limited liability partnership** may be served by any of the methods of service permitted by CPR Part 6 or by any of the methods of service permitted under the Companies Act 2006 as applied with modifications by regulations made under the Limited Liability Partnership Act 2000.		6.3(3)	

	Form No	CPR Rule	PD
2.8 For service on an **overseas company** under s 685 of the Companies Act 1985, s 685A of the Companies Act 1985 (inserted in 1992) or s 1139(2) of the Companies Act 2006, see CPR 6.3 [2]; to discover whether a person resident in the UK has been nominated to accept service on the company's behalf and if so the registered address of the person so nominated, communicate with Companies House which will supply the information on the telephone.			
2.9 **Special cases**:			
(a) in proceedings against the Crown see		6.10	
(b) by a contractually agreed method for the effect of a contractual term that service should be 'either delivered personally or …' see *Primus Build Ltd v Pompey Centre* [2009] EWHC 1487 (TCC), [2009] All ER (D) 14 (Jul).		6.11	
(c) in relation to a contract no an agent of a principal who is out of the jurisdiction see		6.12	
(d) on children and protected persons see		6.13	
(e) on members of the regular forces see			6A, para 5 and Annex
3. Place of service			
3.1 The claim form must be served within the jurisdiction: see further **TAB 4.1** above.			
Unless the court under rule 6.15, see below at para 5 of this **TAB**, specified the place or method of service the claimant must include in the claim form an address, complete with postcode, at which the defendant may be served.		6.6(2)	
4. Deemed service			
A claim form is deemed to be served on the **second business day** after completion of the relevant step contained in the table set out in rule 7.5(1):		6.14	
Method of service | *Step required*			

		Form No	CPR Rule	PD
First class post, document exchange or other service which provides for delivery on the next business day	Posting, leaving with, delivering to or collection by the relevant service provider			
Delivery of the document to or leaving it at the relevant place	Delivering to or leaving the document at the relevant place			
Personal service under rule 6.5	Completing the relevant step required by rule 6.5(3)			
Fax	Completing the transmission of the fax			
Other electronic method	Sending the e-mail or other electronic transmission			
For business day see the definition at rule 6.2(b)				
5. Service of the claim form by an alternative method or at an alternative place				
Where there appears to the court there is good reason to do so it may make an order for service of the claim form by an alternative method or at an alternative place.			6.15	
An order can be sought by application supported by evidence and may be made without notice.		N244	6.15(1)	
On an application under this rule the court may order that steps already taken to bring the claim form to the defendant's attention by an alternative method or alternative place is good service. It should be noted that this is a power to make a retrospective order.			6.15(2)	
An order under this rule must specify: (a) the method or place of service (b) the place of service (c) the period for filing, acknowledgment and admission or defence				6A, para 9

	Form No	CPR Rule	PD
Where service by an alternative method or at an alternative place is permitted by an order under rule 6.15 the fixed cost allowed for each individual served is £52.25.		45.5, Table 4	
6. Dispensing with service			
6.1 The court may dispense with service of a claim form in exceptional circumstances.		6.9	
6.2 An application seeking such an order should be made in accordance with CPR Part 23 and must be supported by evidence. See further paras 7.6 and 7.7 of this **TAB**	N244	6.16	
7. Time for service and extension of time for the service of claim form			
7.1 Service within the jurisdiction must be effected before 12.00 midnight on the calendar day 4 months after the date of issue (ie the time for service runs from the day after issue) but the period is extended where the claim is for service out of the jurisdiction to 'within 6 months of the date of issue'		7.5	
A table is set out in rule 7.5(1) showing the step required to effect service by each of the methods of service listed and is reproduced at para 4 above.			
Note particularly it is the taking of the step that has to be effected within the 4 month period.			

	Form No	CPR Rule	PD
7.1A It has been open to the parties to agree under CPR r 2.11 to extend the time for service of a claim form under r 7.5. The agreed extension and any extension of that extension had to be in writing; an exchange of letters being sufficient to satisfy this requirement. An oral agreement confirmed in writing by both parties was compliant: *Thomas v Home Office* [2006] EWCA Civ 1355, [2006] 42 LS Gaz R 35. This is a case decided before the amendments that took effect on 1 October 2008. No reference is made to an extension of time for service of the claim form by agreement but the mandatory terms of CPR 7.6(3) make it clear that it is preferable for the parties to obtain a consent order.			
7.2 The claimant may apply for an order to extend the time for serving a claim form. The general rule is that an application to extend time for compliance **must** be made within the period for serving the claim form under CPR 7.5 or when an order extending time has already been made, within the extended time allowed.			
The extension will be granted only if good reason for the failure to serve the claim form is shown: *Hashtroodi v Hancock* [2004] EWCA Civ 652, (2004) Times, 4 June and *Glass v Sarrendran* [2006] EWCA Civ 20, (2006) Times, 3 February (cases prior to the amendments made to this rule with effect form 1 October 2008) but see the statements of the Court of Appeal in *Hoddinott v Persimmon Homes (Wessex) Ltd* [2007] EWCA Civ 1203, [2007] All ER (D) 321 (Nov) and article by Gordon Exall in Sol Jo 21 December 2007, page 1615. Cases prior to the amendments made to this rule.	PF 3 and PF 4 or N244	7.6, 7.6(2), 7.6(3)	

	Form No	CPR Rule	PD
See more recently *Imperial Cancer Research Fund v Ove Arup Partners Ltd* [2009] EWHC 1453 (TCC), [2009] All ER (D) 282 (Jun) where general guidance was given as to the correct approach to applications under 7.6 and the leading cases explained. In this case the extension of time was granted to enable further investigations to be made. In *City and General (Holborn) Ld v Structure Tone Ltd* [2009] EWHC 2139 (TCC) the Court considered the decision in Imperial Cancer but came to a different decision. See also *FG Hawkes (Western) Ltd v Beli Shipping Co Ltd* [2009] EWHC 1740 (Comm), [2009] All ER (D) 207 (Jul) where little or nothing had been done to effect service and application for an extension of time was made just 7 days before the expiry of the permitted period, the application was granted but it was successfully challenged by the defendant. The Court stated that where there was no valid reason for non-service it was not an absolute bar to the grant of an extension of time but it was as strong reason for refusal.			
The Court of Appeal in *Drury v BBC* [2007] EWCA Civ 497, (2007) Times, 11 June, [2007] All ER (D) 384 (May). The court further said there was no duty on an employer to assist a claimant to serve proceedings on an employee and further a potential defendant was not obliged to help a claimant to serve proceedings upon him			
7.3 If the claimant applies to extend time **after the time for compliance under rule 7.5** or under an order under this rule, the court can **only** make an order under this rule if:			
(a) the court has failed to serve the claim form, or			
(b) the claimant has taken all reasonable steps to effect service in accordance with rule 7.5 but has been unable to do so, and			

	Form No	CPR Rule	PD
(c) In either case the claimant has acted promptly in making the application.			
These are mandatory requirements and in their absence the court has no discretion to extend time.			
7.4 Any application to extend time must be supported by evidence and may be made without notice. Rule 23.8 also permits the courts to deal with an application without a hearing. For the position where the application is refused or not granted in full on paper see *Leeson v Marsden, Glass v Surrendram and conjoined appeals* (2006) Times, 3 February, CA. The court stressed the danger of important applications made without notice being dealt with without a hearing		7.6(4)	
An order obtained without notice must be served on the other party (whether granted or dismissed) with the application notice and evidence in support. The order must contain a statement of the right of the party to apply to set aside or for review of the order		23.9 and 23.10	
7.5 The court in *Dickins v Solicitors Indemnity Fund* [2007] EWHC 2754 (Ch), [2007] All ER (D) 298 (Oct) at paragraph 26 stated that on a rehearing '… the proper question is whether the order under re-consideration should have been made at the time it was made'.			
For consideration of the guidance provided by previous authorities in assessing whether a court is likely to set aside an order extending time for service of proceedings obtained without notice see *Sodastream Ltd (in liquidation) v Coates* [2009] EWHC 1936 (Ch), [2009] All ER (D) 22 (Aug).			

	Form No	CPR Rule	PD
7.6 It was held in *Godwin v Swindon Borough Council* [2001] EWCA Civ 1478, [2001] 4 All ER 641, [2001] 1 WLR 997, CA that **the power to dispense with service pursuant** to CPR 6.9 (from 1 October 2008 replaced by CPR 6.16) should not be used to circumvent the restrictions on the grant of extensions of time imposed by CPR 7.6(3). See also *Mutifa Kuenyebia v International Hospitals Group Ltd* [2006] EWCA Civ 21 (para 26), (2006) Times, 17 February where the court considered *Godwin* and the case of Wilkey, see para 7.8 of this TAB above, and gave the following guidance: (a) an exceptional case will be required for the court to dispense with service where the time for service has expired; (b) the power is unlikely to be exercised save where either the claimant has made an ineffective attempt to serve in time or has served in a manner which involved a minor departure from one of those permitted methods of service; (c) it would not be possible to give an exhaustive list of the circumstances where an order dispensing with service could be properly made.		6.16 (formerly 6.9)	
7.7 In *Anderton v Clwyd County Council* [2002] EWCA Civ 933, [2002] 3 All ER 813 it was stated that generally applications for retrospective orders to dispense with service would be dealt with in accordance with *Godwin* (see 7.6 above) but exceptionally it might be appropriate to dispense with service. There were different considerations where the claimant had made no effort to serve as opposed to cases where the claimant had already made ineffective attempts to serve by one of the permitted methods.			

	Form No	CPR Rule	PD
7.8 In *Wilkey v BBC* [2002] EWCA Civ 1561, [2002] 4 All ER 1177 it was held that in cases involving late deemed service after the decision in *Anderton* ie after 3 July 2002 (see paragraph 7.6 above) the dispensing power will not ordinarily be exercised in the claimant's favour. For the power to be exercised in the claimant's favour the circumstances must be truly exceptional as perhaps for some very minor departure from the permitted method of service. For a case where the circumstances were considered to be exceptional and the power to dispense under CPR r 6.9 was exercised in favour of the claimant see *Olafsson v Gissurarson (No 2)* [2006] EWHC 3214 (QB), (2006) Times, 22 December following *Phillips v Nussberger* [2006] EWCA Civ 654, [2006] 3 All ER 838.			
7.9 It may well be that as a result of the new CPR 7.6(3) which came into force on 1 October 2008 that in cases involving late deemed service the dispensing power will not be exercised save where the court would be prepared to extend time under rule 7.6(1).			
7.10 The court's power to extend time, dispense with service and correct a procedural error cannot be used to extend a statutory time limit or requirement as to service: *Mucelli v Government of Albania* [2009] UKHL 2, [2009] 3 All ER 1035, [2009] 1 WLR 276			
7.11 An application can be made by a defendant for a claim to be served on him or the claim discontinued		7.7	

TABLE 5—SERVICE OF CLAIM FORM OUT OF THE JURISDICTION

TAB 5

	Form No	CPR Rule	PD
1. Preliminary			
1.1 The principle that a defendant can only be served with an originating process within the jurisdiction if he is present in the jurisdiction at the time of service or deemed service for which the authority was *Chellaram v Chelleram (No 2)* [2002] EWHC 632 (Ch), [2002] 3 All ER 17, [2002] NLJR 639 has been held not to have survived the CPR; see **TAB 4**, Preliminary, above			
• as to service of a claim form on an agent of a principal who is overseas see:		6.12	
1.2 Information concerning service out of the jurisdiction can be obtained from the Foreign Process Section, Room E02, Royal Courts of Justice, Strand, London, WC2A 2LL (tel: 020 7947 6691)			
1.3 CPR Part 6 Section IV contains rules as to:		6.30	
(a) service out of the jurisdiction;			
(b) obtaining permission of the court to serve out of the jurisdiction when that is required; and			
(c) the procedure for serving out of the jurisdiction			
2. Definitions			
2.1 For definitions generally see		6.31	
2.2 In particular note that for the purposes of CPR (and of this table):			
• 'the 1982 Act' means the Civil Jurisdiction and Judgments Act 1982		6.31(b)	
• 'claim form' includes petition and any application notice made before action or to commence proceedings		6.2(c)	

	Form No	CPR Rule	PD
• 'Civil Procedure Convention' means the Brussels and Lugano Conventions (as defined in s 1(1) of the 1982 Act) and any other Convention (including the Hague Convention) entered into by the UK regarding service out of the jurisdiction		6.31(c)	
• the 'Judgments Regulation' means Council Regulation (EC) No 44/2001 of 22 December 2000		6.31(d)	
• the 'Service Regulation' means Council Regulation (EC) No 1393/2007 on service in member states of judicial and extra judicial documents in civil or commercial matters		6.31(e)	
3. Service out of the jurisdiction where the permission of the court is not required – Scotland and Northern Ireland		**6.32**	
3.1 The claimant may serve the claim form on a defendant in Scotland or Northern Ireland where each claim is a claim **which the court has the power to determine under the 1982 Act** and:			
(a) no proceedings between the parties concerning the same are pending in the courts of any other part of the United Kingdom; and (b) (i) the defendant is domiciled in the United Kingdom; (ii) the proceedings are within para 11 of Sch 4 to the 1982 Act; or (iii) the defendant is a party to an agreement conferring the jurisdiction within para 12 of Sch 4 to the 1982 Act.		6.32(1)	
3.2 The claimant may serve the claim form on a defendant in Scotland or Northern Ireland where each claim is a claim which the court has the power to determine under **any enactment other than the 1982 Act** notwithstanding that:			

	Form No	CPR Rule	PD
(a) the person against whom the claim is made is not within the jurisdiction; or			
(b) the facts giving rise to the claim did not occur within the jurisdiction.		6.32(2)	
4. Service of the claim form where permission is not required out of the United Kingdom			
4.1 For claims that the court has power to determine under the 1982 Act or the Lugano Convention see		6.33(1)	
4.2 For claims that the court has power to determine under the Judgments Regulation see		6.33(2)	
4.3 For claims that the court has power to determine other than under the 1982 Act or the Lugano Convention or the Judgments Regulation see		6.33(3)	
5. Notice of statement of grounds where permission is not required for service			
5.1 Where a claimant intends to serve a claim under rule 6.32 (Scotland or Northern Ireland) or 6.33 (outside the UK) the claimant must: (a) file with the claim form a notice containing a statement of the grounds on which the claimant is entitled to serve the claim form out of the United Kingdom; (b) serve a copy of that notice with the claim form	N510	6.34(1)	6B, para 2.1
Until the claimant files the notice the claim form can only be served with the court's permission		6.34(2)	
6. Period for responding to a claim form when permission is not required			
6.1 The periods for filing and acknowledgment of service, an admission or a defence to a claim form served out of the jurisdiction under rules 6.32 and 6.33 (above) are (a) on a defendant in Scotland or Northern Ireland as set out in		6.35(2)	

	Form No	CPR Rule	PD
(b) on a defendant in a Convention territory within Europe or a Member State under rule 6.34 as set out in (c) on a defendant in a Convention territory outside Europe under rule 6.33 as set out in (d) on a defendant elsewhere as set out in		6.35(3) 6.35(4) 6.35(5)	
7. Service out of the jurisdiction where the permission of the court is required			
7.1 In any proceedings to which 6.32 or 6.33 above (service of the claim form) do not apply the claimant may serve a claim form out of the jurisdiction with the permission of the court if any of the grounds set out in para 3.1 of Practice Direction 6B apply.		6.36	6B, para 3.1(1)–(20)
7.2 There are 20 grounds set out in PD 6B, para 3.1, divided into 11 groups			
8. Application for permission to serve the claim form out of the jurisdiction			
8.1 The application must set out:			
(a) which paragraph of PD 6B, para 3.1 is relied on;			
(b) that the claimant believes the claim has a reasonable prospect of success; and			
(c) the defendant's address or, if not known, in what place the defendant is, or is likely to be, found		6.37(1)	
8.2 Where the application is made in respect of a claim referred to in para 3.1(3) of PD 6B (service on another person who is a necessary or proper party) the application must also state the grounds on which the claimant believes that there is between the claimant and the defendant a real issue which is reasonable for the court to try.		6.37(2)	

	Form No	CPR Rule	PD
8.3 The court will not give permission unless satisfied that England and Wales is the proper place to bring the claim			
• Guidance of the standard to be required by the court for it to be satisfied is provided by Christopher Clarke J in *Cherney v Deripaska* [2008] EWHC 1530 (Comm), [2008] All ER (D) 37 (Jul) (case decided before the 1 October amendments to the CPR)		6.37(3)	
• For the difficulties faced by a defendant in resisting an application for permission to serve out of the jurisdiction where the claimant is resident in this country and is suffering continuing loss, see *Cooley v Ramsey* [2008] EWHC 129 (QB), (2008) NLJ, 4 April, p 476 (a case prior to the amendments that took effect on 1 October 2008). See further *Lauren B v Mark B* [2008] QBD (Preston) 29 July, (2008) Gazette LR 16 October, page 20 as to the appropriate law in such cases in light of the general rule set out in s 11(1) of the Private International Law (Miscellaneous Provisions) Act 1995 that the applicable law is that of the country where the tortious act occurred. In this case the judge found on the facts that the general rule was displaced.			
8.4 Where permission is sought to serve a claim form in Scotland or Northern Ireland and it appears the claimant may also be entitled to as remedy there, in deciding whether to give permission the court will: (a) compare the relative costs and convenience; and (b) (where relevant) have regard to the relative powers and jurisdiction.		6.37(4)	

	Form No	CPR Rule	PD
8.5 When the court gives permission to serve a claim form out of the jurisdiction it will specify the periods within which the defendant may: (a) file an acknowledgment of service; (b) file or serve an admission; (c) file a defence; or			
(d) file any other response or document required by a rule in another Part, any other enactment or a practice direction			
and the court may (a) give directions about the method of service; and (b) give permission for other documents in the proceedings to be served out of the jurisdiction			
It was held in *Olafsson v Gissurarson* [2008] EWCA Civ 152, [2008] All ER (D) 11 (Mar) that the circumstances such that an order dispensing with service under CPR 6.9 (now CPR 6.16) in a Lugano convention case for the purpose of ensuring that an otherwise potential time bar would not defeat the claim, was one in principle that the court could properly make in a truly exceptional case (see **TAB 4**, para 7.7 above) but note this was a case decided prior to the amendment to the rules that came into force on 1 October 2008.			
9. Methods of service of a claim form on a party out of the jurisdiction			
9.1 Where a claim form is served n a party **in Scotland or Northern Ireland** he must be served by a method permitted in Section II of CPR 6 (serving a claim form within the jurisdiction)		6.40(2)	
9.2 Where a **defendant out of the United Kingdom** is to be served with a claim form it my be served: (a) (i) in accordance with the Service Regulations as provided by rule 6.41;			

	Form No	CPR Rule	PD
(ii) through foreign government, judicial authorities and British Consular authorities as provided by rule 6.44 (iii) CPR 6.27 (service on a State) or (b) by any method permitted by a Civil Procedure Convention; or (c) by any other method permitted by the law of the country in which it is to be served.		6.40(3)	
But it is specifically provided that nothing in rule 6.40(3) above or in any court order authorises or requires any person to do anything which is contrary to the law of the country where the claim form is to be served.		6.40(4)	
• Details of the Civil Procedure convention countries can be obtained form the Foreign and Commonwealth website, see the parenthesis at the end of rule 6.40.			
• Scotland and Northern Ireland – Sch 4 of the 1982 Act governs and allocates claims brought in one part of the United Kingdom against a person domiciled in other parts			
10. Service in accordance with the Service Regulation			
10.1 The Service Regulation is annexed to CPR PD 6B.			
10.2 Where the claimant wishes to serve the claim form under the Service Regulation the claimant must file:			
(a) the claim form; (b) any transaction; and (c) any other documents required by the Service Regulation. The court officer will seal a copy of the claim form and forward the document to the Senior Master			
Rule 6.47 (proof of service before obtaining judgment) does not apply to service in accordance with this Regulation.			

	Form No	CPR Rule	PD
The Regulation prevails over other provisions contained in any other agreement or arrangement concluded by Member States.		6.41 (parenthesis)	
11. Service through foreign governments, judicial authorities and British Consular authorities		6.42	
11.1 Where service of the claim form on a defendant is to be effected in any country which is a party to a Civil Procedure Convention see		6.42(1)	
11.2 Where service of the claim form on a defendant is to be effected in any country with respect to which there is no Civil Procedure Convention see		6.42(2)	
11.3 Where service of the claim form on a defendant is to be effected in: (a) any Commonwealth state which is not a party to the Hague Convention (b) the Isle of Man or Channel Islands, or (c) any British overseas territory			
The methods of service under 11.1, i e 6.42(1), and 11.2, i e 6.42(2), are not available and the claimant or claimant's agent must effect service direct unless PD 6B provides otherwise.		6.43(3)	
12. The procedure where service is through foreign governments, judicial authorities and British Consular authorities		6.43	
12.1 Rule 6.43 applies where the claimant wishes to serve a claim form under rule 6.42(1) or 6.42(2) (see 11.1 and 11.2 above)		6.43(2)	
12.2 The claimant must file: (a) a request for service of the claim form by one or more methods in rule 6.42(1) or 6.42(2); (b) a copy of the claim form; (c) any other document required by PD 6B, see (d) any translation required by rule 6.45			6B, para 4
12.3 The court on filing will seal the copy of the claim form and forward the documents to the Senior Master		6.43(3)	

	Form No	CPR Rule	PD
12.4 When service has been effected an official certificate will be issued pursuant to rule 6.43(5) which is evidence of the facts stated in the certificate		6.43(5)	
13. Service of a claim form on a State see		6.44	
14. Translation of Claim Form see		**6.45**	
14.1 Every copy of a claim form filed under rule 6.43 (service through foreign governments, judicial authorities, etc) or 6.44 (service on a State) must be accompanied by a translation of the claim form; but the translation is not required where the claim form is to be served:		6.45(2)	
(a) in a country of which English is an official language			
(b) on a British citizen unless a Civil Procedure Convention requires a translation		6.45(4)	
14.2 The claimant is not required to file a translation of a claim form under 6.44 (service of a claim form on a State) where English is an official language of the State in which the claim form is to be served.			
• The Service Regulation contains provision about the service of documents.		6.45(5)	
15. Undertaking to be responsible for expenses			
15.1 Every request for service under rule 6.43 (service through foreign governments, judicial authorities, etc) or 6.44 (service on a State) must contain an undertaking by the person making the request:			
(a) to be responsible for all expenses incurred by the Foreign and Commonwealth Officer or foreign judicial authority; and			
(b) to pay those expenses on being informed of their amount.		6.46	
16. Proof of service			
16.1 When:			

	Form No	CPR Rule	PD
(a) a hearing is fixed when the claim is issued (b) a defendant is served with the claim form out of the jurisdiction and (c) that defendant does not appear at the hearing			
the claimant may take not obtain judgment until he files written evidence that the claim form has been duly served in accordance with Part IV of CPR 6.			
This rule does not apply where service is effected under the Service Regulation. The 'receiving agency' is required to effect service and to complete and file a certificate at the court.			
17. Extension of time for service out of jurisdiction			
For the principles to be applied when an application is made for an extension of time for service outside the jurisdiction, i e 6 months from issue, see *Sodastream Ltd (in liq) v Coates* [2009] EWHC 1936 (Ch), [2009] All ER (D) 22 (Aug), 13 July, unreported.		7.5(2)	
It is essential that on each application all relevant material is brought to the court's attention, including whether, and if so how many, earlier applications have been granted and the evidence on which they were based.			
In *Duckworth* there had been 5 applications all of which had been dealt with on paper; two orders were set aside.			

TABLE 6—ACKNOWLEDGMENT OF SERVICE OF PART 7 CLAIM

TAB 6

	Form No	CPR Rule	PD
1. Preliminary			
A defendant may file an acknowledgment of service		10.1(3)	
• if he is not able to file a defence within the time allowed		15.4	

	Form No	CPR Rule	PD
• if he disputes the court's jurisdiction		Part 11	
2. Completion of the form			
The form of acknowledgment is included in the Response Pack served on the defendant	N9		
The defendant must set out his full name (if it is different to the name given on the claim form) and the address within the jurisdiction to which documents should be sent to him. Any reference and the telephone number are to be included and, if applicable, fax number, DX number and e-mail details			10, para 5.1
Where the defendant's name has been incorrectly stated in the claim, after stating his correct name the defendant should add "described as" and the incorrect name The defendant must "tick" the appropriate box from: "I intend to defend all of this claim" "I intend to defend part of this claim" "I intend to contest jurisdiction"			10, para 5.2
3. Signature of the forms			
The form must be signed by the defendant or the defendant's legal representative. Where the acknowledgment is signed by a legal representative, the address for service must be the legal representative's business address. Otherwise the address for service that is given should be as set out in r 6.5 and Practice Direction 6B (r 6.23).		2.3	
Where the defendant is a company or other corporation, a person holding a senior position in the company or corporation may sign the form on the defendant's behalf, but he must state the position he holds			10, para 4.2
For a "person holding a senior position", see			10, para 4.3
Where the defendant is a partnership:			

	Form No	CPR Rule	PD
(a) service must be acknowledged in the name of the partnership on behalf of all persons who were partners at the time the cause of action arose and			
(b) the acknowledgment of service may be signed by any of those partners or by any person authorised by any of those partners to sign it			10, para 4.4
Children or protected parties can only acknowledge service by their litigation friend or legal representative, unless the court otherwise orders			10, para 4.5
4. Period for filing			
Where the particulars of claim are served with the claim form the period for filing the acknowledgment of service is 14 days from service of the claim. If the particulars of claim are served subsequently, the time for filing the acknowledgment will be 14 days from their service		10.3(1)	
Note, however:			
(a) where service is effected on the agent of an overseas principal, or		6.12(3)	
(b) where claim form is served out of the jurisdiction without the permission of the court under CPR 6.32 or 6.33		6.35	
(c) where the claim form is served out of the jurisdiction with permission of the court see		6.37(5) and 10.3(2)(c)	
The court will give notice to the claimant that the defendant has filed an acknowledgment		10.4	
The court will also serve or deliver a copy of any notice of finding that has been filed with the acknowledgement of service provided copies were filed for service.			6A, para 8.2

	Form No	CPR Rule	PD
5. Effect of filing			
If an acknowledgment is filed in accordance with CPR Pt 10, the period for filing a defence is extended from 14 days after service of the particulars of claim to 28 days after service of the particulars of claim. Accordingly, the period before which the claimant can apply for judgement in default of defence (where CPR Pt 12 allows it) is extended		15.4	
Acknowledgment of Part 8 claim see **TAB 7**			
6. General			
(a) If two or more defendants to a claim acknowledge service of a claim through the same legal representative at the same time, only one of the acknowledgments of service need be used			
(b) An acknowledgment of service may be amended or withdrawn only with the permission of the court on application supported by evidence; such an application must be made in accordance with CPR Pt 23 and supported by evidence	N244	Part 23	
(c) As to the necessity of obtaining the consent of the claimant and permission of the court to file an acknowledgment out of time, see *Coll v Tattum* [2002] 03 LS Gaz R 26, NEUBERGER J			

	Form No	CPR Rule	PD
(d) If a defendant files an acknowledgment of service and does not within 14 days of filing it apply to the court for an order declaring that the court has no jurisdiction or should not exercise any jurisdiction it may have, he will be treated as having accepted that the court has jurisdiction to try the case. This remains the case even if the defendant has made an earlier application to set aside an order extending time for service. That application would be treated as abandoned (see *Hoddinott v Persimmon Homes (Wessex) Ltd* (2007) Times, 28 December, CA)			
A defendant who wishes to argue that service is defective or late should so indicate in the acknowledgment of service and within 14 days of filing the acknowledgment he should file an application under Part 11			

TABLE 7—ACKNOWLEDGMENT OF SERVICE OF PART 8 CLAIM

TAB 7

	Form No	CPR Rule	PD
Where Part 8 procedure applies			
(a) The provisions of CPR Pt 15 (defence and reply) do not apply when a Part 8 claim is served			8, section A, para 5.1
The defendant who wishes to respond to the claim must file an **acknowledgment of service** which should be in Form N210	N210		8, section A, para 5.2
(b) The general rule is that the acknowledgment must be filed not later than **14 days** after service of the claim form and a copy must be served on the claimant and any other party		10.3(1)	
The general rule under r 10.3(1) is subject to the exceptions listed at		10.3(2)	

	Form No	CPR Rule	PD
Where the particulars of claim are not served with the claim form, see		10.3(1)(a)	
If the claim form is served out of the jurisdiction, see		10.3(2)	
(c) The acknowledgment must state:			
(i) whether the defendant contests the claim, and			
(ii) if the defendant seeks a different remedy from that set out in the claim form, what that remedy is		8.3(2)	
It must be signed by the defendant or his legal representative and include the defendant's address for service		10.5	
If the defendant disputes the use of the Part 8 procedure he must state the reasons in writing when he files the acknowledgment of service. If the statement of reasons include matters of evidence, it should be verified by a statement of truth			8, section A, para 5.3
(d) An acknowledgment of a claim started by the Part 8 procedure must be verified by a statement of truth.		22.1	22 para 1.1
(e) A defendant who wishes to rely on **written evidence** must file it with the acknowledgment of service and at the same time serve a copy on the other party		8.5(3) and (4)	
If the defendant does not do so he can only rely on written evidence if the court gives permission		8.6(1)	
(f) If the defendant fails to file an acknowledgment, default judgment cannot be entered. The defendant may attend the hearing but not take any part in it unless the court gives permission		8.6	

	Form No	CPR Rule	PD
(g) As to filing an acknowledgment out of time, see *Coll v Tattum* at **TAB 6** para 6(c) and more recently *ESR Insurance Services v Clemons* [2008] EWHC 2023 (Comm) And discussion by Janna Purdie in (2008) NLJ, 5 September, page 1221. In this case a late acknowledgement by the defendant prevented a claimant obtaining a default judgment. The court extended the time for acknowledgement of service retrospectively to make this possible.			
(h) For subsequent procedure for Part 8 claims see CPR PD 8, Section A:			8, section A
(i) Managing the claim (para 6)			
(ii) Evidence (para 7)			
(iii) Hearing (para 8)			
(i) In the absence of specific allocation a Part 8 claim is deemed to be allocated to the multi-track			
(j) For the liability for costs where the defendant terminates the proceedings after filing an acknowledgment of service to the effect that he wanted a new lease see *Lay v Drexler* [2007] EWCA Civ 464, (2007) Times, 20 June, [2007] All ER (D) 318 (May) but note the costs decision in *Fox Gregory Ltd v Hamptons Group Ltd* [2006] EWCA Civ 1544, [2006] All ER (D) 47 (Oct) where, having achieved what it wanted the claimant filed notice of discontinuance		8.9(3)	

TABLE 8—ADMISSIONS AND JUDGMENT UPON ADMISSIONS

TAB 8

	Form No	CPR Rule	PD
1. Preliminary			
See General Notes to CPR Pt 14 (**CPR 14 [1]–CPR 14 [3]**) and in particular note that Part 14 applies in its entirety to Counterclaims (only certain provisions apply to other CPR Pt 20 claims)		20.3	
2. Making an admission after the commencement of proceedings			
A party may admit the truth of the whole or part of the other party's case by giving notice in writing		14.1 (1) and (2)	
Where the **only remedy sought is the payment of money**, the defendant can			
(a) admit the whole of a claim for a specified amount (by service direct to the claimant)	N9A	14.4	
(b) admit (by filing at the court) part of the claim for a specific amount	N9A	14.5	
(c) admit (by filing at the court) the whole of a claim for unspecified amount, or	N9C	14.6	
(d) admit (by filing at the court) liability to pay a claim for an unspecified amount and offer a sum in satisfaction of the claim	N9C	14.7	
Note: The defendant may also file a defence			15, para 3.3
3. Time for returning or filing an admission			
The period is 14 days after service of the claim if particulars of claim are served with it or if they are not 14 days after service of the particulars but if an admission is returned or filed late it will be effective if default judgment has not been entered. See as to 14 day period		14.2(3) and (4)	
(a) If the claim form is served out of jurisdiction under CPR 6.32 or 6.33		6.35	

	Form No	CPR Rule	PD
(b) If the court has specified a period for responding		6.12(3)	
4. Effect of an admission – general			
Any other party may apply for judgment on the admission; except where (a) the defendant is a child or protected party; or (b) the claimant is a child or protected party and the admission is of part of a claim for a specified sum of money or is of liability of a claim for an unspecified sum with an offer of a sum in satisfaction.		14.1(4)	
Judgment shall be such judgment as it appears to the court that the applicant is entitled to on the admission		14.3(1)	
This provision will be relied on only when the claim is for some other remedy or includes a claim for some other remedy than money		14.3(2)	
Where there is an admission of a specified sum of money, see para 6 of this Table "Any other party" includes a party under a Part 20 claim			
5. Effect of an admission – claim for unspecified sum of money only			
(a) The claimant may obtain judgment by filing a request if the defendant **does not offer a specified amount in satisfaction** of the claim	N226	14.6	
The court will serve a copy of the admission on the claimant and if the claimant does not file a request for judgment within 14 days the claim will be stayed until he does file a request for judgment		14.6(3), 14.6(5)	
Judgment will be for an amount to be fixed by the court plus costs. The court will, on entering judgment, give directions leading to the disposal hearing to fix the amount of the damages		14.6(7) and (8)	26

	Form No	CPR Rule	PD
The court will not normally consider it to be appropriate to allocate to track (other than the small claims track) unless the amount payable is disputed on grounds which appear to be substantial or the dispute is not suitable to be dealt with at a **disposal hearing**.			26 para 12.2 and 12.3
A disposal hearing is one			
(i) which will normally not last longer than 30 minutes, and			
(ii) at which the court will not normally hear oral evidence			26 para 4(1)
It will be only the most straightforward of disposals where the damages exceed the small claims limit that are not allocated to track			
(b) If the defendant not only admits the claim but **offers a sum in satisfaction of the claim**			
The court will serve a notice on the claimant requiring him to state whether or not he accepts the amount offered by the defendant in satisfaction of his claim. If the claimant does not file the notice in 14 days after its service on him the claim is stayed until he does so		14.7(3) and (4)	
If the claimant **accepts the amount offered** he can obtain judgment by filing the appropriate form payable by such date or instalments as he specifies. If no date or instalments are specified the judgment will be for payment immediately	N226	14.7(5) and (6)	
If the defendant makes **an offer acceptable but** makes a **proposal for instalment payments which is not,** judgment can be obtained for the amount offered and accepted and the rate of payment will be determined by the court as set out in para 8 of this Table	N226	14.9–14.12	
If the claimant **does not accept the amount offered** he can obtain judgment for an amount to be decided by the court and costs by lodging the appropriate form	N226	14.7(9) and (10)	

	Form No	CPR Rule	PD
6. Effect of admission of claim for specified amount of money only			
Where the admission is of **the whole amount claimed** the claimant may obtain judgment by filing the relevant form and, if the defendant has **not requested time to pay**, specify the date for payment or the time and amount of instalments. The judgment will be for the amount of the claim (less payments made) and costs	N225 or N205A	14.4(3) and (6)	
Where the **admission is of the whole amount but the defendant's proposal for payment is not acceptable to the claimant,** the claimant may obtain judgment for the amount claimed plus costs, and cause the rate of payment to be determined by the court by giving notice that the defendant's proposal is not acceptable	N225 or N205A	14.10	
Where the admission is of **part of a claim for a specified sum of money** the court will serve a notice on the claimant requiring him to return it stating whether:		14.5(3)	
(a) he accepts the amount admitted in satisfaction of the claim			
(b) he does not accept the amount admitted and wishes the claim to continue, or			
(c) if the defendant requests time to pay, he accepts the amount admitted in satisfaction but not the payment proposals			
The claimant must return the notice and serve a copy on the defendant in 14 days and if he does not, the claim will be stayed until he complies		14.5(4)	
If the claimant accepts the amount admitted and there is **no proposal for instalment payments** he can obtain judgment for the amount admitted (less payments made) and costs by such date instalments as he shall specify or, if none is specified, immediately	N225A	14.5(6) and (7)	

	Form No	CPR Rule	PD
If the claimant **accepts the amount admitted but not the instalments,** the claimant may obtain judgment for the amount admitted and costs and cause the rate of payment to be determined by so requesting in the notice returned	N225A		
If the claimant **does not accept the amount admitted** the proceedings continue and the procedure is that set out in CPR Pt 26			
7. Interest			
The judgment will include interest to the date of judgment if the particulars of claim include the details required by CPR 16.4 and the claimant's request for judgment includes a calculation of interest between the date of issue and that of the request for judgment. The rate of interest on judgment debts has been 8% since 1 April 1993; see CPR 14.4(1) ante		14.14	
8. Determination of rate of payment		**14.10**	
A court officer may determine the time and rate of payment where the amount outstanding (including costs) does not exceed £50,000. He must do so without a hearing			
Where a judge is to make the determination he may do so without a hearing. If he directs that there be a hearing, and the claim is for a specified sum of money, if the defendant is an individual the proceedings must be transferred automatically to the defendant's home court		14.12	
For exceptional cases where transfer is not automatically made, see		14.12(2)	
9. Redetermination			
Either party may apply for redetermination by a judge within 14 days after the service of the determination on him		14.3(2)	
On an application for redetermination the proceedings must be automatically transferred if the defendant is an individual		14.13	

	Form No	CPR Rule	PD
For exceptional cases where transfer is not automatically made, see		14.13(3)	
If the decision was made by a court officer, the redetermination may take place without a hearing unless a hearing is requested in the application notice			14, para 5.3
If the decision was made by a judge, the redetermination must be at a hearing unless the parties agree otherwise			14, para 5.4
In deciding the rate and time of payment the court will take into account: (a) the defendant's statement of means (b) the claimant's objections (c) any other factor			14, para 5.1
10. Withdrawal of admission			
The permission of the court is required to amend or withdraw an admission. But having regard to the decision in *Sowerby v Charlton* (see below) this would only be the case in a money claim. CPR 3.1(3) permits the court to attach conditions to the order. See *Soffit v DJ Broady* [2000] CPLR 259, CA and *Hamilton v Hertfordshire County Council* [2003] EWHC 3018 (QB), [2003] All ER (D) 260 (Dec) For the entitlement of the Court to receive from the applicant a full and frank account giving particulars as to why the admissions were made and justifying the application to withdraw them see *American Reliable Insurance Co v Willis Ltd* [2008] EWHC 2677 (Comm), (2008) 4 October, unreported, Civil Procedure News Issue 10/08, 2 December 2008, page 2			

	Form No	CPR Rule	PD
Valuable guidance on the exercise of the discretion is provided by Sumner J in *Braybrook v Basildon & Thurrock NHS Trust* [2004] EWHC 3352 (QB), [2005] All ER (D) 320 (Apr) and see *Lee Laboratories v Apotex Inc* [2007] EWHC unreported, Palfrey J and *White v Greensand Homes Ltd* [2007] EWCA Civ 643, (2007) Times, 19 July (a case to which CPR 14.1A has no application)		14.1(5)	14, para 7.2
A party to an action does not require the court's permission under CPR 14.1(5) to withdraw an admission of liability made before the action started (a pre-action admission) made before 6 April 2007: *Sowerby v Charlton* [2005] EWCA Civ 1610, (2006) Times, 5 January, CA and for discussion see article 'Resiling form admissions' by Andrew Williams [2006] NLJ 31 March, p 543 The status of a pre-action admission is evidential only and may not be sufficient to found an application for summary judgment after its withdrawal unless the facts are clear. Consideration should be given to an application to strike out the defence or part of it under rule 3.4; see dicta in *Stoke on Trent City Council v John Walley* (2006) Times, 25 August, CA			
11. Pre-action admissions made on or after 6 April 2007			
From 6 April 2007 pre-action admissions are governed by the CPR. A person may by giving notice in writing admit the whole or part of another party's case before the commencement of proceedings (a pre-action admission)		14.1A(1)	14, para 1.4
In proceedings to which any one of the protocols (a) for personal injury claims (b) for clinical disputes (c) for disease and illness claims applies, if a pre-action admission is made			

	Form No	CPR Rule	PD
(a) after the party making it has received a letter before claim in accordance with the Practice Direction (Pre-Action Conduct) or any relevant pre-action protocol (b) before such a letter before claim has been received but it is stated to be made under Part 14 it may be withdrawn by the party making it by notice in writing (i) before the commencement of proceedings with the agreement of the party to whom the admission was made (ii) after the commencement of proceedings if all the parties to the proceedings consent or with the permission of the court		14.1A(2) 14.1A(3)(a) 14.1A(3)(b)	14, para 1.1(2)
After the commencement of proceedings (i) any party may apply for judgment on the pre-action admission, and (ii) the party who made the admission may apply to withdraw it		14.1A(4)	
Either of the applications referred to in the last paragraph must be made by an application in accordance with Part 23 or may be by cross application		14.1A(5)	
When deciding whether to give permission for the withdrawal of an admission the court must have regard to all the circumstances including those set out in			14, para 7.2
A court will inevitably be significantly influenced by which of the parties will suffer the greater prejudice if the court does or does not allow the admission to be withdrawn when giving effect to the overriding objective to deal with the case justly: *White v Greensand Homes Ltd* [2007] EWCA Civ 643, (2007) Times, 19 July. But there remains the question, who suffers the greater prejudice? See article in Solicitors Journal, 18 May 2007, page 622			

TABLE 9—JUDGMENTS IN DEFAULT AND APPLICATIONS TO SET THEM ASIDE

TAB 9

	Form No	CPR Rule	PD
1. Preliminary			
See **CPR 12 [1]–CPR 12 [6]** and note in particular:			
(a) where judgment in default is wrongly obtained it must be set aside irrespective of merits		13.2	
(b) special provisions requiring an application for default judgment where claim is against a child or protected party, claim is by one spouse against the other or claim is against the Crown		12.11(3)	
(c) default judgment may be obtained in respect of **default of filing of defence to counterclaim** but not on claims between defendants for contribution or indemnity		12.3(2)	
(d) where the defendant is outside the jurisdiction and a judgment on the merits is required, see **CPR 12 [5]**			
(e) the procedure for obtaining default judgment is now the same in the High court and the county court			
2. Meaning and where it is not available			
"Default Judgment" means judgment without a trial where the defendant: (a) has failed to file an acknowledgment of service or (b) has failed to file a defence		12.1	

	Form No	CPR Rule	PD
It may include **interest** to the date of judgment where the particulars of claim include the details required by CPR 16.4 and any interest from issue to the date of request for judgment is calculated in the form of request. Interest may be added at the judgment rate, presently 8%, but if interest is sought at any higher rate the default judgment will be for an amount of interest to be decided by the court. It may also include **fixed costs**; if any other type of costs are sought, an application under CPR Pt 23 should be made for judgment and for the type of costs sought		12.6 12.9(1)	
If the claim is for a **specified sum of money,** judgment may be for the sum claimed less any sums paid in reduction. It will be payable by the date or at the rate specified by the claimant and if neither is specified it will be payable immediately		12.5(2)	
Default judgment cannot be obtained:			
(a) on a claim for delivery of goods subject to an agreement regulated by the Consumer Credit Act 1974		12.2(a)	
(b) where the claimant uses the Part 8 procedure		12.2(b)	
(c) in any other case where a Practice Direction provides default, judgment may not be entered, eg: (i) any mortgage claim in the High Court or in the county court for money secured by a mortgage unless, in either case, the permission of the court is obtained			12, para 1.3(5)
(ii) Admiralty claims (iii) Arbitration proceedings (iv) Contentious probate proceedings (v) Claims for provisional damages			12, para 1.3

	Form No	CPR Rule	PD
(d) on a claim for indemnity or contribution between defendants (e) Specialist proceedings where either: (i) there is no requirement for an acknowledgment of service, or (ii) special provision is made about obtaining default judgment		20.3(3) Part 49	
Note: CPR 20.11 as to Part 20 claims which are not counterclaims or contribution or indemnity notices			
3. Conditions to be satisfied			
For a salutary article see 'Service and Judgment in Default' by Andrew Butler in New Law Journal 23 March 2007, page 426, and also *Hart Investments Ltd v Fidler* [2006] EWHC 2857 (TCC), 109 Con LR 67, [2007] BLR 30			
Claimant may only obtain **judgment in default of an acknowledgment of service** if the defendant has not filed an acknowledgment of service or a defence to the claim (or any part of the claim) and the relevant time for doing so has expired		12.3(1)	
Claimant may only obtain **judgment in default of defence**:		12.3(2)	
(a) where an acknowledgment of service has been filed but a defence has not been filed			
(b) on a counterclaim made under CPR 20.4, where a defence has not been filed			
and, in either case, the relevant time for doing so has expired			
Default judgment may not be obtained:		12.3(3)	
(a) where the defendant has applied:			
(i) to have the claim struck out under CPR 3.4			
(ii) for summary judgment under CPR Pt 24			

	Form No	CPR Rule	PD
(b) where the defendant has satisfied the whole claim (including costs) on which the claimant is seeking judgment			
(c) in any other case where a PD provides that the claimant may not obtain default judgment			12, paras 1.1 and 1.3
(d) where the claimant is seeking judgment on a claim for money and the defendant has filed or served an admission with a request for time to pay			
In the absence of proof of valid service a claimant is not entitled to judgment in default under CPR 12.3 and the court has to set aside a judgment obtained where there is no such proof: *Shiblaq v Sadikoglu* [2003] hearing date 25 July (BLD 2807032773) Comm Ct			12 para 4.1
Where the claim form is served by the claimant, the claimant may not obtain default judgment unless a certificate of service has been filed.		6.17	
Where service is deemed to have been effected and judgment entered pursuant to the deemed service, the fact that the defendant had no actual knowledge of the issue of the claim does not give him an absolute right to have judgment set aside. Whether to set aside will be within the discretion of the Court: *Akram v Adam* (2004) Times, 29 December, CA.			
Where a claimant was in a position to enter judgment in default, due to a technical error or omission by the defendant, but knew the defendant had a real prospect of successfully defending the claim and of getting a default judgment set aside, he put himself at risk of an adverse costs order if he nevertheless entered judgment: *Roundstone Nurseries Ltd v Stephenson Holdings Ltd* [2009] EWHC 1431 (TCC), [2009] All ER (D) 72 (Jul).			

	Form No	CPR Rule	PD
4. Procedure where permission is required to obtain default judgment			
Applications in accordance with CPR Pt 23 will have to be made for **permission** to enter default judgment (rather than being able to obtain such judgment by filing a form of request) in the following circumstances:			
(a) where although the default judgment sought is for money or the delivery of goods, the claimant claims (and does not abandon) any other remedy		12.4(2)	
(b) where the default judgment sought is for costs other than fixed costs		12.9	
(c) claims against a child or protected person		12.10(a)(i)	
(d) tort claim by one spouse or civil partner against the other		12.10(a)(ii)	
(e) delivery up of goods where defendant not allowed alternative of paying value		12.4(2)	
(f) where judgment is sought for failure to file an acknowledgment of service against:		12.10(b)	
(i) defendant served out of jurisdiction without permission under CPR 6.32(1), 6.32(2) or 6.33(2) (ii) defendant domiciled in Scotland, Northern Ireland or any other Convention country or Member State (iii) a State (iv) diplomatic agent with immunity (v) persons or organisations having immunity			12, para 4.4
5. Procedure – permission not required			
Permission will not be required where claim is for only:			
(a) a specified sum of money			

	Form No	CPR Rule	PD
(b) an amount of money to be decided by the court			
(c) delivery of goods with alternative of paying their value			
Judgment in default is obtained by filing the relevant practice form in which the claimant may specify the date or rate of payment. If neither are specified the judgment will provide for immediate payment			
Where the sum of money is specified use	N205A or N225		
Where the sum of money is to be decided by the court use	N205B or N227		
Where the judgment entered is for an amount of money to be decided by the court, directions are likely to be given and allocation may be made to a track. Allocation to track is appropriate where the claim if defended would have been allocated to the small claims track or if the amount payable is genuinely disputed on substantial grounds or the dispute is not suitable to be dealt with at a disposal hearing	N154, N155, N157		26, para 12.3
All matters as to the quantification of damages including causation remain at issue at the disposal hearing; see *Lunnun v Singh* [1999] All ER (D) 718 and **CPR 12.7 [3]**.			
A 'disposal hearing' is a hearing which will not normally last more than 30 minutes and the court will not normally hear oral evidence and the court may either assess damages or give directions. Unless the claimant has served written evidence at least 3 days prior the court must not assess damages except where the claim has been allocated to the small claims track.			26, para 12.4
Where the claim is for delivery of goods or their value, the default judgment will be for delivery of the goods and in default for payment of their value to be decided by the court and for costs	N205B or N227	12.5(4)	

	Form No	CPR Rule	PD
Where the claim is against more than one defendant and default judgment is sought against one only, see		12.8	
Interest may be included to date of judgment (see **TAB 8** para 7) but if the necessary requirements have not been satisfied its amount will have to be decided by the court (see also para 2 above of this TAB)		12.6(1) and (2)	
Where in proceeding against **the Crown** a default judgment is sought see		12.4(4)	
6. Procedure where permission is required to obtain default judgment		**12.10**	
The application must be in accordance with CPR Pt 23 and judgment will be such as the court thinks the claimant is entitled to on his statement of case	N244	12.11(1)	
Any evidence relied on by the claimant in support of his application need not be served on a party who has failed to file an acknowledgment of service		12.11(2)	
For evidence required:			
(a) on application (or request), see			12, para 4.1
(b) on application against a child or protected party, or in tort between spouses or civil partners, see		12.11(3)	12, para 4.2 (as to child or patient)
(c) on application where service was outside without permission: (i) in Scotland or Northern Ireland in accordance with rule 6.32(1), or (ii) outside the United Kingdom in accordance with rule 6.33(1) or 6.33(2) And service has not been acknowledged (evidence must be by affidavit) see		12.11(4)	12, paras 4.3 and 4.5
(d) on application against a State (the evidence must be by affidavit), see		12.11(5)	12, para 4.4
(e) on delivery of goods (without alternative of payment), see			12, para 4.6

	Form No	CPR Rule	PD
Where the defendant is an individual the claimant must provide the defendant's date of birth (if known) in Part C of the application form		12.4(2)	
On all applications save for those referred to in (c) or (d) above, notice must be given in accordance with CPR Pt 23			12, para 5.1
7. Procedure for obtaining a default judgment for costs			
A default judgment for fixed costs may be obtained by filing a request in the relevant practice form		12.9(1)	
If any other type of costs are claimed, application must be made. On such an application judgment shall be for an amount to be decided by the court	N244	Part 23	
8. Setting aside or varying default judgment			
An application to set aside will be made by filing	N244		
If judgment has been **wrongly entered** the court **must** set it aside. It remains mandatory however long the delay before the application to set aside is made: *Credit Agricole Indosuez v Unicof Ltd* (2003) Times, 4 February)		13.2	

	Form No	CPR Rule	PD
If a defendant was not served or deemed by the CPR to have been served with the claim and had no knowledge of the proceedings, he would normally be entitled to have any judgment entered against him set aside. If the claimant, on being served with and application to set aside believed he could show the defendant had no real prospect of successfully defending he could cross-apply for an order dispensing with service of the claim form, granting permission to apply forthwith for summary judgment: *Nelson v Clearsprings (Management) Ltd* [2006] EWCA Civ 1252, [2007] 2 All ER 407, [2007] LHR 14, (2006) Times, 5 October. The court made it clear that the application to set aside in these circumstances is not governed by CPR 3.10(b) and 3.1(2)(m). In *Tombstone Ltd v Raja* [2008] EWCA Civ 1444, [2009] 1 WLR 1143 the Court of Appeal held that applications for setting aside orders made without notice are governed by CPR 23.10 and that rr 23.9 and 23.10 must be read together. It also considered the exercise by the Court of its inherent jurisdiction to set aside such orders. It should be carefully noted that if the claimant can show the defendant has been guilty of an inexcusable delay since learning of the judgment the court would be entitled to make 'no order' in the defendant's application			
In *Akram v Adam* (2004) Times, 29 December, CA it was held the judge had a discretion not a duty to set aside a judgment obtained in default of acknowledgement of service when the unrepresented defendant claimed he had never received notice of the proceedings but notice had been sent to him at his usual or last known address under r 6.5(b)			
In any other case the court may set aside or vary a judgment entered under CPR Pt 12 if:			

	Form No	CPR Rule	PD
(a) the defendant has a real prospect of successfully defending the claim or (b) it appears to the court that there is some good reason why: (i) the judgment should be set aside or varied, or		13.3(1)	
(ii) the defendant should be allowed to defend the claim		13.3(2)	
In considering whether to set aside or vary a judgment the matters to which the court must have regard include whether the application was made **promptly**			
Although damages have been assessed and final judgment entered the court still has discretion to set aside judgment in default but these facts would be highly relevant to the exercise of its discretion: *Strachen v The Gleaner Co Ltd* [2005] UKPC 33, [2005] 1 WLR 3204			
Note:			
• The burden of proof is on the defendant and that is 'the only significant difference' between the provisions of rules 24.2 (as to summary judgment) and 13.3(1)(as to setting aside judgment): *ED & F Man Liquid Products Ltd v Patel* [2003] EWCA Civ 472, [2003] 24 LS Gaz R 37			
• As to 'real prospect' – requires a case to be better than merely arguable before a default judgment can be set aside: *International Finance Corpn v Utexafrica Spr* [2001] All ER (D) 101 (May). See also cases at TAB 10, para 2.2 post			
• For the discretion to set aside for 'some other good reason' see *Berezovsky v The Russian Broasdcasting Co* [2009] EWHC 1733 (QB), [2009] All ER (D) 128 (Jul), (2009) NLJ, 24 July, Law Digest, page 1067.			

	Form No	CPR Rule	PD
• As to 'promptly' – 4 weeks after notification of decision not made promptly: *Regency Rolls Ltd v Carnall* [2000] All ER (D) 1417 (Oct), CA. See also para **CPR 13.3 [2]** and note that the inaction of the defendant's agent (in this case an insurance broker) must be treated as inaction by the defendant himself: see *Mullock v Price* [2009] EWCA Civ 1222, 15 October where the appeal was allowed and the default judgment allowed to stand.			
• The judge's discretion is to be exercised to further the overriding objective and not to punish a party for incompetence: *Hussain v Birmingham City Council* [2005] EWCA Civ 1570, [2005] All ER (D) 353 (Nov)			
For setting aside a judgment obtained by fraud or as a result of perjury see **CPR 13.3 [3]**		13.3(1)	
For setting aside a judgment obtained for failure to provide security as required by an unless order see *Radu v Houston* [2006] EWCA Civ 1575, [2006] All ER (D) 295 (Nov)			
For an application by a debtor to set aside judgment made only when faced with enforcement see *Nolan v Devonport (decd)* [2006] EWHC 2025 (QB) at **TAB 34**, section 1 'Preliminary', last para			
9. Application to set aside or vary judgment – procedure			
An application to set aside a default judgment can be made by a non-party if he is 'directly affected' by it; *Latif v Imaan Inc* [2007] EWHC 3179 (Ch), [2007] All ER (D) 241 (Dec).		40.9	
In all cases the application must be supported by evidence	N244	13.4(3)	
Unless the claim is started in a specialist list it will be transferred upon the making of the application to the defendant's home court when:			

	Form No	CPR Rule	PD
(a) it is for a specified sum of money (b) judgment was obtained in court other than defendant's home court (c) the claim has not been transferred to another defendant's court under CPR 14.2 or CPR 26.2, and (d) the defendant is an individual		13.4(1)	
If the court sets aside or varies, it may impose a condition with a sanction for failure to comply with the condition. See *CIBC Mellon Trust Co v Mora Hotel Corpn NV* [2002] EWCA Civ 1688, [2003] 1 All ER 564 as to payment into court of the costs of the application to set aside and of costs previously ordered to be paid but unpaid. The court found there were relevant differences between the two types of costs. See also as to the imposition of a financial condition *Redcliffe Close (Old Brompton Road) Management Ltd v Kamal* [2005] EWHC 858 (Ch) at **TAB 21**, section 4 (final paragraph)		3.1(3)	
For jurisdiction complications arising from setting aside a default judgment for an injunction by a master see *Richmond v Birch* [2006] EWHC 921 (Ch), [2007] 1 All ER 658.			
10. Setting aside default judgment on claimant's application			
See *Messer Griesheim GmbH v Goyal MG PVT Ltd* [2006] EWHC 79 (Comm), (2006) Times, 14 February where the default judgment was set aside and summary judgment granted. If judgment has not been entered, the claimant, having failed to give notice to the MIB, may validly discontinue the action to start a second action so that notice of it can be given: *Richardson v Watson* [2006] EWCA Civ 1662, [2007] PIQR P262, (2006) Times, 13 December			

TABLE 10—SUMMARY JUDGMENT

TAB 10

	Form No	CPR Rule	PD
1. Preliminary			
1.1 See paras **CPR 24** and **CPR PD 24**. Note in particular their availability to claimants and defendants and:		Part 24	24
• if a litigant wishes to **avoid allocation**, the application for summary judgment should be lodged prior to completion of the allocation questionnaire. The fact that it has been issued should be clearly stated in the reply to section D, with a request that allocation not take place prior to the hearing of the application The indication that there is an intention to apply for summary judgment in the immediate future may well not prevent allocation • the application notice should draw the attention of the respondent to the requirement that if he wishes **to rely on written evidence** he must file and serve it at least 7 days prior to the hearing of the application. This should be done prominently (see precedents **BCCP C[597]–BCCP C[600]**)		24.5(1)	24, para 2(5)
1.2 If the respondent fails to comply he can still rely on any document filed by him in the case that has been verified by a statement of truth		32.6	
1.3 The **court of its own initiative** may order an application for summary judgment to be made under its general powers of management		24.4(3) and 5(3) 3.3(1)	
1.4 For special provision where the claim is **for specific performance**, see para **CPR 24 [9]**			24, para 7.1
1.5 No application can be made for summary judgment against the Crown until after the period for filing a defence specified in r 15.4		24.4(1A)	

	Form No	CPR Rule	PD
1.6 Where the claimant has failed to comply with the Practice Direction (Pre-Action Conduct) or any relevant pre-action protocol an application for summary judgment will not normally be entertained before a defence has been filed or the time for doing so has expired			24, para 2(6)
2. Grounds			
2.1 The court may give summary judgment **against a claimant or defendant** on the whole of a claim or on a particular issue if:		24.2	
(a) it considers that: (i) the **claimant has no real prospect** of succeeding on the claim or issue, or (ii) the **defendant has no real prospect** of successfully defending the claim or issue, and (b) there is no other **compelling reason** why the case or issue should be disposed of at trial			
2.2 The test for summary judgment is not whether the case is bound to fail (*Peter Robt Crafft v Camden London Borough Council* (2000) LTL, 24 October, CA), but the court should not conduct a mini-trial to establish whether summary disposal is appropriate: *Swain v Hillman* [2001] 1 All ER 91, CA. The criterion to be applied by the judge is not one of probability but of the absence of reality: see *Supablast (Nationwide) Ltd v Story Rail Ltd* [2010] EWHC 56 (TCC), [2010] All ER (D) 133 (Jan) An application for summary judgment may be based on a point of law, the evidence (or lack of it), or a combination of both			24, para 1.3
As to "real", see para **CPR 24.2 [1]**			
Summary judgment is applicable to probate claims: for such a case where summary judgment was entered see *Griffin v Wood* [2007] HC Chancery 13 September, (2008) New Law Journal, 15 February, page 257			

	Form No	CPR Rule	PD
For an appeal concerning the entry of summary judgment by way of dismissal of a claim for contribution under the Civil Liability (Contribution) Act 1978 see *Charter plc v City Index Ltd* [2007] EWCA Civ 1382, [2008] Ch 313, [2008] 3 All ER 126			
A claimant resisting an application to strike out his claim will find the judgment of NEUBERGER J in *Chan U Seek v Alvis Vehicles Ltd* (2003) Times, 16 May of assistance. The basis of the decision was that if the court considered the claim had some prospect of success it was not just for the claimant to be prevented pursuing it			
3. Grounds – special cases			
• For **set-offs and counterclaims** as defences, see para **CPR 24 [7]** Where the claim is suitable for summary judgment but there is a defence of set-off which has a reasonable prospect a court may well grant summary judgment but subject to the decision on the defence of set-off with execution stayed until the trial of that defence or further order of the court • For **promissory notes, bills of exchange**, etc, see para **CPR 24.2 [3A]** • For **defamation**, see para **CPR 24.3 [2]**; CPR Pt 53 and the Practice Direction to that Part		Part 53	53
• For **area of expanding jurisprudence**, see *Douce v Staffordshire County Council* [2002] EWCA Civ 506, (2002) Times, 2 May			
4. Availability of summary judgment			
• The court may give summary judgment **against a claimant** in any type of proceedings		24.3(1)	

	Form No	CPR Rule	PD
• The court may give summary judgment **against a defendant** in any type of proceedings, except: (a) proceedings for possession of **residential premises** against: (i) a mortgagor, or (ii) a tenant or tenant holding over whose occupancy has protection within the meaning of the Rent Act 1977 or Housing Act 1988, and (b) proceedings for an Admiralty claim in rem For **defamation** proceedings, see para **CPR 24.3 [2]**; *Safeway Stores plc v Tate* [2001] QB 1120, CA; and more recently *Dee v Telegraph Media Group Ltd* [2010] EWHC 924 (QB) (where a part of the defendant's summary judgment application succeeded); and CPR Pt 53 and its Practice Direction			
Although the court has power under the CPR to permit an application for summary judgment before an outstanding challenge to jurisdiction had been decided it will be very rare for it to exercise that power: *Speed Investments Ltd v Formula One Holdings Ltd* (2004) Times, 10 September			
A challenge to the admissibility of evidence is best kept for the trial or substantive hearing rather than at a preliminary hearing; *Stroude v Beazer Homes Ltd* [2005] EWCA Civ 265, (2005) Times, 28 April			
The fact that the claim involves serious allegations of bad faith is not a compelling reason for a trial: *Wrexham AFC Ltd v Crucialmore Ltd* [2006] EWCA Civ 237, [2006] All ER (D) 199 (Mar)			
In an appropriate case the court can grant summary judgment on some aspects of a claim only, e g liability or a discrete issue which is part of the claim: *Datafind Services Ltd v Sugden* [2007] All ER (D) 145 (Nov)			

	Form No	CPR Rule	PD
Where on an application for summary judgment the issue raised was a pure point of construction the court held, in *BBC Worldwide Ltd v Bee Load Ltd* [2007] EWCA Civ 725, (2007) Times, 15 March that this could as well be decided on a summary application as at trial. The court accordingly proceeded with the summary application for a declaration; see also *ICI Chemicals and Polymers Ltd v TTE Training Ltd* [2007] EWCA Civ 725, [2007] All ER (D) 115 (Jun) where the court indicated that summary judgment would not be appropriate if it can be shown that there is evidence likely to exist which could affect the interpretation or construction. The mere possibility of such evidence being obtained would not be sufficient to make the cause unsuitable for a summary judgment application.			
The court, in *John D Wood & Co (Residential and Agricultural) Ltd v Craze* [2007] EWHC 2658 (QB), [2008] 06 EG 132, found that the Master should have determined the issues and granted summary judgment where the claim gave rise to a short point of law or construction and he had all the information necessary for summary determination. For a case on the other side of the line where it was held that the case necessitated a trial see *Apvodedo NV v Collins* [2008] EWHC 775 (Ch), [2008] All ER (D) 246 (Apr).			
Cases do not necessarily have to be straightforward to make them suitable for summary judgment; see, for example, *Webb v Macdonald* [2010] EWHC 93 where lawyers, who were defendants, successfully applied for summary judgment in a claim against them based on advice they gave which was alleged to have been negligent.			

	Form No	CPR Rule	PD
5. Procedure			
5.1 Timing			
An application for summary judgment should be made promptly, but leave of court is required to issue the application before the defendant against whom summary judgment is sought has filed: (a) an acknowledgement of service, or (b) a defence, unless a Practice Direction provides otherwise		24.4(1)	
If the claimant applies for summary judgment before the person against whom summary judgment is sought has filed a defence, that defendant does not need to file a defence before the hearing of the application		24.4(2)	
Where a claimant has not complied with any relevant pre-action protocol summary judgment cannot normally be sought until a defence has been filed or the time for so doing has expired			
5.2 Form of application			
Precedents of applications by claimant and defendant can be found at **BCCP C[597]** and **BCCP C[599]**. For practice forms of application see	PF 11 and 12		
The application notice must include a statement that it is an application for summary judgment made under CPR Pt 24 and why the applicant seeks the order			24, para 2(2)
The application notice or the evidence contained, referred to or served with it must: (a) identify any point of law or provision in a document on which the applicant relies, and/or (b) state that it is made because the applicant believes that on the evidence the respondent has no real prospect of succeeding on the claim or issue (as the case may be) or of successfully defending the claim			

	Form No	CPR Rule	PD
In either case state the applicant knows of no reason why the disposal of the claim or issue should await trial			24, para 2(3)
The application must identify any written evidence on which the applicant relies which is not contained in the application notice			24, para 2(4)
The application notice should bring to the respondent's attention the requirement of filing and serving any written evidence on which he relies at least 7 days before the hearing of the summary judgment application		24.5(1)	24, para 2(5)
5.3 Issue and service			
Upon issue (court fee £60), a date will be fixed for the hearing. The time allocated will usually be in accordance with the **time estimate** given by the applicant. It is important that sufficient time is allowed. If the time originally estimated becomes inadequate having regard to the evidence filed by the respondent, the court should be so informed and re-listing sought with an increased time estimate. Such re-listing may well require an application but the court should be asked to deal with it without a hearing. The delay caused by re-listing is well worth accepting to obtain adequate time to make the application			
The respondent (or the parties if the hearing is fixed of the court's own initiative) must be given at least **14 days' notice** of: (a) the date fixed for the hearing, and (b) the issues that the court will be asked to decide at the hearing		24.4(3)	
A copy of the application notice must be served as soon as practicable after filing and in time to give the notice required		23.7	

	Form No	CPR Rule	PD
Where the application for summary judgment is made much later than is normally the case the court will be especially vigilant in applying the 'no real prospect of success' test: *James E McCabe Ltd v Scottish Courage Ltd* [2006] EWHC 538 (Comm), [2006] All ER (D) 409 (Mar)			
5.4 Evidence			
The applicant's evidence will be filed as part of or with the application. The statement should be as concise as possible and the temptation to anticipate and answer the respondent's arguments should be resisted; that can be done by filing evidence in reply If the respondent wishes to rely on written evidence at the hearing he must: (a) file the written evidence, and (b) serve copies on every party at least 7 days prior to the hearing		24.5(1)	
If the applicant wishes to rely on written evidence in reply he must: (a) file the written evidence, and (b) serve a copy on the respondent at least 3 days before the hearing		24.5(2)	
• For the time for filing evidence where the hearing has been fixed on the court's initiative, see		24.5(3)	
• The Rules do not require evidence already filed to be filed again or evidence already served to be served again		24.5(4)	
• A party may rely on any statement of case or application notice as evidence provided it is verified by a statement of truth		Part 22	
6. The hearing			
6.1 Time is likely to be short and care must be taken to take up less than half the time available for the presentation of the application, leaving time for a short reply. In this way the respondent can be properly limited to his proper share of the allotted time. Time has to be left for the court's deliberation and delivery of judgment			

	Form No	CPR Rule	PD
6.2 A **skeleton argument** (with copies for each party and the court) will be appropriate in all but the most simple application. Copies of any authorities relied on should also be available as well as the original report The skeleton argument and authorities should be filed in advance of the hearing in the hope that the court will have the time to read them before the hearing Copies of the **order** sought should also be available			
6.3 The hearing will be before a Master or district judge but he may direct that the application be heard by a High Court Judge (in the High Court) or a circuit judge (in a county court). The court should avoid embarking on a mini-trial in advance of the trial particularly where the case involves the presentation of evidence and cross-examination to assess its strength: *Somerset-Leeke v Kay Trustees Ltd* [2002] BLD 0407022528, 3 July, Ch. See also *North East Lincolnshire Borough Council v Millennium Park (Grimsby) Ltd* (2002) Times, 31 October, CA.			24, para 3
The court may, perhaps must, have regard to considerations of efficient use of resources as is done in the delivery of every other public service: see *Sutradhar v Natural Environment Research Council* [2006] UKHL 33, [2006] 4 All ER 490 per Lord Hoffmann at 42.			
A factual dispute need not prevent summary judgment: *Miller v Shires* [2006] EWCA Civ 1386, [2007] PNLR 273 where summary judgment was given in professional negligence action arising out of a disputed road traffic claim			
For summary judgment in intellectual property legislation see *Bolton Pharmaceuticals Co 100 Ltd v Doncaster Pharmaceuticals Group Ltd* [2006] EWCA Civ 661, [2006] All ER (D) 389 (May)			

	Form No	CPR Rule	PD
6.4 For summary judgment at trial by the use by the trial judge of his powers under CPR 24.2(a)(ii) see *James v Evans* [2000] 42 EG 173, CA and **CPR 24 [4A]**			
7. The order			
7.1 The orders that the court may make include: (a) judgment on the claim (b) the striking out or dismissal of the claim (c) the dismissal of the application (d) a conditional order			24, para 5.1
7.2 The court may make a conditional order if it considers the claim or defence may succeed but it is improbable that it will do so. Such an order may require a party:			24, para 4
(a) to pay money into court, or (b) to take a specified step in relation to his claim or defence and will provide that the party's claim be dismissed or his statement of case be struck out if he does not comply			24, para 5.2
In the case of *Jacobs UK Ltd v Skidmore, Owings and Merrill LLP* [2008] EWHC 2847 (TCC), [2008] All ER (D) 258 (Nov) Coulson J gave very pertinent guidance as to the evidence required to obtain summary judgment in various different types of claims and as to the various heads of damage within such claims. He also stated that where applications do not succeed but a condition is made (see preceding paragraph) they could lead the way to settlement. For further guidance see article by Janna Purdie in (2008) NLJ 5 December, page 1713.			

	Form No	CPR Rule	PD
An application for summary judgment is capable of being made as a tactical step aimed at achieving an order whereby the defendant is given leave to defend, or to continue to defend, conditional on a payment into court and in the hope that a favourable judicial comment may be obtained on the likely outcome of the case. Such a tactical step has its risks, particularly as to costs, but may be fruitful. See *Antonio Gramsci Shipping Corpn v Recoletos Ltd* [2010] All ER (D) 241 (May) or for further consideration see article 'Early point scoring counts' by Catherine Reeves in 2010, NLJ, 25 June, at page 902.			
Conditions should not be imposed if a party has no prospect of complying with them: *Chapple v Williams* [1999] CPLR 731, CA			
7.3 If the case is to continue the court may give **directions** for the final hearing, the service of a defence and the management of the case, and in practice will do so		24.6	24, para 10
7.4 For **practice forms** of orders under CPR Pt 24, see	PF 13 and 14		
For **judgment** under part 24, see Forms (these are High Court forms but can be adapted)	No 44 and 44A		
8. Orders made in the absence of a party			
If a party does not appear and an order is made against him in his absence, he may apply for the order to be set aside or varied. On the hearing of the application the court may make such order as it thinks just Even if an application for summary judgment is unopposed the court has to be satisfied that it is appropriate to allow summary judgment to be entered: *Broderick and Broderick v Centaur Tipping Services* [2006] CL 27 July, 103/34 LSG 7 September at page 32			24, para 8.2

	Form No	CPR Rule	PD
9. Costs			
Where judgment is given for a specified sum, fixed costs may be awarded (£175 where judgment exceeds £25 but does not exceed £5,000; £210 where judgment exceeds £5,000). Where the court is disposed to give costs, other than fixed costs, the court is likely to summarily assess them. If the court is to be asked for costs, and not merely fixed costs, a costs schedule should be filed and served on the other party at least 24 hours before the date fixed for the hearing		45.4, Table 2 44.13(1)	24.9
If the order made does not mention costs no party is entitled to costs relating to that order			
10. Appeals			
See **TAB 34** but also note *Law Society v Southall* [2001] EWCA Civ 2001, (2002) Times, 7 January, [2002] BPIR 336, CA, per PETER GIBSON LJ: "… unless the judge on a Part 24 claim had made an error of principle the appellate court could not interfere. However if the judge was … plainly wrong … the appellate court could and was bound to, interfere"			

TABLE 10A—LOW VALUE PERSONAL INJURY CLAIMS IN ROAD TRAFFIC ACCIDENTS

TAB 10A

	Form No	CPR Rule	PD
1. Changes are made by the 52nd update to the Civil Procedure Rules with effect from 30 April 2010 by the insertion of:			
1.1 The Pre-Action Protocol for Low Value Personal Injury Claims in Road Traffic Accidents ('the RTA Protocol') setting out three stages.			
1.2 Practice Direction 8B – the RTA Protocol			
1.3 CPR 36, Section II (36.16–36.22 – RTA Protocol offers to settle) and CPR 45.27–45.40 (new fixed costs provisions)			

	Form No	CPR Rule	PD
1.4 Consequential amendments, in particular those to CPR 36.1, 36.2(2)(b) and 3.3(4) as to offers to settle.			
2. The **RTA Protocol** applies where: (1) a claim for damages arises from as road traffic accident (RTA) on or after **30 April 2010**; (2) the claim includes damages in respect of **personal injuries**; (3) the claimant's valuation of the claim on a full liability basis including pecuniary loss, but excluding interest, is **not more than £10,000** (the upper limit); and (4) if proceedings were started the **small claims track** would not be the normal track for the claim.			RTA Protocol, para 4.1
• A claim may include **vehicle-related damages** but these are excluded for the purpose of para 4.1			RTA Protocol, para 4.3
• As to **electronic communication** between the parties see:			RTA Protocol, para 5.1–5.2
2.1 Where the claimant gives notice to the defendant that the claims is unsuitable for the RTA protocol (eg complex issues) the claim will no longer continue under the Protocol. If, however, the court when considering costs considers that the claimant acted unreasonably it will award no more than the fixed costs under CPR 45.29.			RTA Protocol, para 7.67
• For action to be taken by the defendant when the claimant is unrepresented see:			RTA Protocol, para 5.10
3. The **aims of the RTA Protocol** are: (1) the defendant pays damages and costs using the process set out in the Protocol without the need for the claimant to start proceedings; (2) damages are paid within a reasonable time; and (3) the claimant's legal representative receives the fixed costs set out at the end of each stage in this Protocol.			RTA Protocol, para 3.1

	Form No	CPR Rule	PD
4. TIME TABLE STAGE 1			
4.1 The **start** of the process is when the claimant sends, duly completed: (1) the **claim notification form** (CNF) to the defendant's insurers; (2) the '**defendant only CNF**' to the defendant by first class post. • Where there is a claim for vehicle related damage see • Where the claimant is a child see • As to the statement of truth see • As to rehabilitation see	RTA 1 RTA 2		RTA Protocol, para 6.1(1) RTA Protocol, para 6.1(2) RTA Protocol, para 6.4 RTA Protocol, para 6.5 RTA Protocol, para 6.6 RTA Protocol, para 6.7
4.2 By way of response the defendant' insurer must send to the claimant an electronic **acknowledgement the next day after receipt of the CNF** and **within 15 days** and must send the duly complete **Insurer Response** section of the CNF ('the CNF response') to the claimant.			RTA Protocol, para 6.10 and 6.11
4.3 Before the end of stage 1 the defendant must apply to the Compensation Recovery Unit (CRU) for a certificate of recoverable benefits.			RTA Protocol, para 6.12
4.4 Where the defendant: (1) **alleges contributory negligence** (except for the claimant's admitted failure to wear a seatbelt); (2) **does not respond**; (3) **does not admit liability** (brief reasons must be given); (4) notifies the claimant there is inadequate mandatory information or that the small claims track would be the normal track for the claim the claim will no longer continue under the RTA Protocol but will proceed under the Pre-Action Protocol for personal injury claims.			RTA Protocol, para 6.1(1) RTA Protocol, para 6.1(2) RTA Protocol, paras 6.15 and 6.16

	Form No	CPR Rule	PD
4.5 Unless the claimant is a child, where liability is admitted or is admitted and the only contributory negligence relates to the admitted failure to use seat belts, **within 10 days** after sending the CNF response, the defendant must pay the Stage 1 fixed costs (CPR 45.29).			RTA Protocol, para 6.18
• For position of claimant in default of payment see			RTA Protocol, para 6.19
5. TIME TABLE – STAGE 2			
5.1 **Within 15 days of the claimant approving the final medical report** and agreeing to rely on the prognosis in that report the claimant should send to the defendant a **Stage 2 Settlement Pack** comprising: (a) the Stage 2 Settlement Pack Form; (b) a medical report or reports (see paras 7.1–7.7 and 7.24–7.25); (c) evidence of pecuniary loss; and (d) evidence of disbursements.			
If the defendant alleges contributory negligence because of the claimant's failure to wear a seatbelt the Pack must also contain a suggestion of the percentage reduction (which may be 0%) in the amount of damages.	RTA 5		RTA Protocol, para 7.26
• For **interim payments** see			RTA Protocol, paras 7.8–7.14 and 7.21–7.23
• For **vehicle-related damage – 'additional damages'** see			RTA Protocol, paras 7.16 and 7.46
• For request for **interim payment where the claimant is a child** see			RTA Protocol, paras 7.19–7.20
The defendant has **35 days – 'the total consideration period'** for the consideration of the Stage 2 Settlement Pack, made up of up to 15 days for its consideration (**'the initial consideration'**) and the remainder of the total consideration period for further negotiation (**'the negotiation period'**). These periods are capable of extension by agreement between the parties.			RTA Protocol, paras 7.28–7.29

	Form No	CPR Rule	PD
5.3 Where a party makes an offer 5 days or less before the end of the total consideration period and any agreed extension there will be a further period of 5 days after the end of the period for consideration. During this period (the further consideration period) no further offers can be made by either party.			RTA Protocol, para 7.30
5.4 Within the **initial consideration period** (or any agreed extension) the defendant must either: (a) **accept the offer** made by the claimant in the Stage 2 Settlement Pack; or (b) make a **counter offer** using that form.			RTA Protocol, para 7.31
For the required contents of the counter offer see:			RTA Protocol, paras 7.34–7.35
• For the position where the defendant gives notice within the initial consideration period that the small claims track would be the normal track or withdraws the admission of causation see			RTA Protocol, para 7.32
• For the position where the defendant does not respond see			RTA Protocol, para 7.33
5.5 Where a counter offer is made by the defendant (see para 5.4 above) the claimant has until the end of the total consideration period or further consideration period to accept or decline the counter offer.			RTA Protocol, para 7.36
5.6 Any offer to settle at any stage will automatically include and cannot exclude:			
(a) the Stage 2 fixed costs in rule 45.29; (b) an agreement in principle to pay disbursements; (c) a success fee in accordance with rule 45.31(1)			RTA Protocol, para 7.37
• For withdrawal of offers after the consideration period see			RTA Protocol, para 7.39
5.7 Upon **settlement** (except where the claimant is a child or where the provision as to deductible benefits in paras 7.41 and 7.42 applies) the defendant must pay:			

	Form No	CPR Rule	PD
(a) the agreed damages less any: (i) deductible amount which is payable to the CRU; and (ii) previous interim payment; (b) any unpaid Stage 1 fixed costs in rule 45.29; (c) the Stage 2 fixed costs in rule 45.29; (d) the relevant disbursements allowed in accordance with rule 45.30; and (e) a success fee in accordance with rule 45.31 for Stage 1 and Stage 2 fixed costs, within 10 days of the end of the relevant period in paragraphs 7.28 to 7.30 during which the parties agreed a settlement (7.40) or within 10 days of agreeing to pay the claim and additional damages (7.53).			RTA Protocol, paras 7.40 and 7.53
5.8 For situations where there are **partial settlements** – original damages not agreed but additional damages agreed, or original damages agreed and additional damages not agreed see			RTA Protocol, paras 7.49–7.50
In both instances provision is made for payment of the agreed part.			
5.9 Where the parties **do not reach agreement** on: (a) the original damages within the period specified (see 2.2 above); or (b) the original damages and where relevant any additional damages within the period specified, the claimant must send to the defendant the **Court Proceedings Pack** (**Part A and Part B**) which must contain: (a) the final offer and counter offer from the Stage 2 Settlement Pack Form; (b) supporting comments from both parties on disputed heads of damages; and (c) where relevant, the offer, and if made, the counter offer under paragraph 7.45 (vehicle-related damages – additional damages).	RTA 6 and RTA 7		RTA Protocol, para 7.55

	Form No	CPR Rule	PD
• Comments in the Court Proceedings Pack must not raise matters not raised in the Stage 2 Settlement Pack Form.			RTA Protocol, para 7.57
• If the defendant considers there is non-compliance in the Court Proceedings Pack it must be returned to the claimant within 5 days with an explanation of why it does not comply.			
• Where the defendant intends to nominate a legal representative to accept service he should give his name and address.			RTA Protocol, para 7.58
• For non-settlement payment by the defendant to the claimant (except where the claimant is a child see This effects an automatic interim payment.			RTA Protocol, paras 7.61–7.66
6. TIME TABLE STAGE 3			
Practice Direction 8B – RTA Protocol – Stage 3 Procedure			
6.1 The court is involved in the procedure for the first time at this stage which occurs where: (1) the parties have followed the RTA Protocol but have not been able to agree on the damages to be paid; or (2) the claimant is a child, settlement has been agreed but the approval of the settlement by the court is required; or (3) completion of the RTA Protocol is not possible before the expiry of the limitation period.		21.20(2)	8B, para 1
• A claim under this PD must be started in the county court and will normally be heard by a district judge.			
6.2 The claim is to be made under the Part 8 procedure, as modified by this PD, but the following provisions of Part 8 are disapplied: (1) rule 8.2A (issue of claim form without naming defendants); (2) rule 8.3 (acknowledgment of service);			

	Form No	CPR Rule	PD
(3) rule 8.5 (filing and serving written evidence); (4) rule 8.6 (evidence – general); (5) rule 8.7 (Part 20 claims); (6) rule 8.8 (procedure where defendant objects to use of the Part 8 procedure); and (7) rule 8.9(c).			
6.3 The application for the court to determine the amount of the damages must be started by claim form which must state: (1) that the claimant has followed the procedure set out in the RTA Protocol; (2) the date when the Court Proceedings Pack (Part A and Part B) form was sent to the defendant (this provision does not apply where the claimant if a child and the application is for a settlement hearing); (3) whether the claimant wants the claim to be determined by the court on the papers (except where a party is a child) or at a Stage 3 hearing; (4) where the claimant seeks a settlement hearing or a Stage 3 hearing, the dates which the claimant requests should be avoided; and (5) the value of the claim.			8B, para 2 8B, para 5
6.4 As to the filing and service of **written evidence** see			8B, para 6.1
Note in particular (save where the claim is for a child settlement hearing) that the Court Proceedings Pack (Part B) (which contains the parties' 'final offers') must be filed in a sealed envelope.			8B, para 6.1(2)
6.5 For **evidence – general** see para 7 of the PD and in particular note that if the court considers: (1) further evidence must be provided by any party; (2) the claim is not suitable to continue under the Stage 3 procedure, the court will order that the claim continue under Part 7, allocate to a track and give directions (in this event Stage 3 fixed costs will not be allowed).			8B, para 7.2

	Form No	CPR Rule	PD
6.6 The **acknowledgment of service** must state whether the defendant: (1) (a) contests the amount of the damages claimed; (b) contests the making of an order for damages; (c) disputes the court's jurisdiction; or (d) objects to the use of the Stage 3 procedure; (2) wants the claim to be determined by the court on the papers or at the hearing.			
• Where the defendant objects to the use of Stage 3 he must give reasons in the acknowledgment			
The acknowledgment of service must be filed **not more than 14 days after service of the claim form** and with: (1) any notice of funding; and (2) as soon as possible thereafter a certificate of recoverable benefits.	N210B	36.15(e)(1)	8B, para 8
6.7 For **dismissal of the claim** because of the defendant's opposition see			8B, para 9
For the **withdrawal of an RTA protocol** offer with the necessary permission of the court see			8B, para 10
6.8 **The court will assess the damages**: (1) on the papers; or (2) at **a Stage 3 hearing** where the claimant so requests in the claim or the defendant so requests in the acknowledgment of service or the court itself so orders.			
• The court will give the parties at least 21 days notice of the date of paper determination or the Stage 3 hearing.			
• An up to date certificate of recoverable benefits must be filed by the defendant at least 5 days prior to the hearing if the total of the benefits have increased since final offers.			8B, para 11

	Form No	CPR Rule	PD
The hearing will be confined to submissions and the court is unlikely to be greatly influenced by the citation of awards by county courts which of course are not in any way binding.			
6.9 As to **settlements** at Stage 2 and at Stage 3 where the **claimant is a child** see			8B, paras 12 and 13
7.1 As to **adjournments** see			8B, para 14
7.2 As to **appeals** where the determination has been on paper see			8B, para 15
7.3 As to **limitation** see			8B, para 16
8. OFFERS TO SETTLE			
8.1 An RTA Protocol offer must: (1) be set out in the Court Proceedings Pack (Part B) form; and (2) contain the final total amount of the offer from both parties.		36.17	
• It will be deemed to have been made on the first business day after this form (Parts A and B) is sent to the defendant.		36.18	
8.2 The amount of the RTA protocol offer must not be disclosed to the court until the termination of the case and any other offer must not be communicated to the court at all.		36.20	
8.3 The RTA offer is treated as exclusive of interest and is only of consequence for the costs of the Stage 3 procedure (see CPR 45.29) and not in respect of any appeal costs.		36.19	
8.4 The costs consequences are: (1) where the **judgment is less than or equal to** the defendant's RTA Protocol offer – the court will order **the claimant to pay** the fixed costs in CPR 45.38 (see below) and interest on those costs from the date of the offer; (2) where the judgment **is more than** the defendant's RTA Protocol offer **but less than** the claimant's RTA Protocol offer the court will order the **defendant to pay** the claimant's fixed costs in rule CPR 45.32 (see below);		36.21(2) 36.21(3)	

	Form No	CPR Rule	PD
(3) where the judgment is **equal to or more than** the claimant's RTA Protocol offer the court will order the **defendant to pay**: (a) interest on the whole of damages awarded at a rate not exceeding 10% above base rate for some or all of the period specified starting with the date specified in CPR 36.18 (the first business day after the Court Proceedings Pack (Part A and Part B) is sent to the defendant; (b) the fixed costs specified in CPR 45.32 and interest on those costs at a rate not exceeding 10% above base rate		36.21(4)	
• The amount of the judgment is less than the RTA Protocol offer where the judgment is less than that offer once deductible amounts identified in the judgment are deducted (see CPR 35.15(1)(d)).		36.22	
9. COSTS – CPR 45.27–45.40			
9.1 The only costs allowed are: (1) **fixed costs** in CPR 45.29; (2) **disbursements** in accordance with CPR 45.30; (3) **a success fee** in accordance with CPR 45.31.		45.28	
9.2 The amount of the fixed costs are:			
Stage 1 fixed costs £400			
Stage 2 fixed costs £800			
Stage 3 – Type A fixed costs (legal representative costs) £250			
Type B fixed costs (advocate's costs) £250			
Type C fixed costs (advice on child's claim) £150		45.29(1) and (2)	

	Form No	CPR Rule	PD
• The court will not award more or less than these amounts except where there is failure to comply with or election not to continue with the RTA Protocol.		45.29(4) and 45.36	
• Where the claimant lives in the area specified in the Costs PD and instructs a legal representative who practises in that area an addition of 12.5% will be recoverable in respect of Stage 1 and 2 and Stage 3A costs		45.29	Costs PD, para 25A.6
• VAT may be added when appropriate and will be recoverable in addition to the fixed costs		45.30	
9.3 The **disbursements** set out in CPR 45.30 may be allowed by the court which must not allow any other type of disbursement. Note in particular the costs of obtaining: (i) medical records; (ii) a medical report or reports as provided for in the RTA Protocol; (iii) an engineer's report; (iv) a search of the records of the Driver and Vehicle Licensing Authority, Motor Insurance Database. And also note the court fees in respect of the Stage 3 Procedure are all recoverable.		45.30(2)(a) 45.30(2)(d)	
9.4 A party who has entered into a funding arrangement in respect of any element of the fixed costs may recover a **success fee** on that element of the fixed costs in the circumstances set out in CPR 45.31 of the percentages thereby provided depending on the particular circumstances.			
For instance, where the court awards damages that are more than the defendant's RTA Protocol offer the amount of the claimant's success fee is: 12.5% of the Stage 1 and 2 fixed costs 100% of the relevant Stage 3 fixed costs			

	Form No	CPR Rule	PD
• Any additional amount included in the fixed costs pursuant to CPR 45.29(5) (claimant and legal representative in specified area – see above) will be ignored when calculating the success fee.			
9.5 Where the claimant obtains judgment for an amount **more than the defendant's RTA Protocol offer** the court will order the **defendant to pay**: (1) where not already paid by the defendant, the Stage 1 and 2 fixed costs; (2) where the claim is determined: (i) on the papers, Stage 3 Type A fixed costs; (ii) at a Stage 3 hearing, Stage 3 Type A and B fixed costs; or (iii) at a Stage 3 hearing and the claimant is a child, Type A, B and C fixed costs; (3) disbursements allowed in accordance with CPR 45.30; and (4) a success fee in accordance with CPR 45.31(6)		45.32	
• For the costs consequence of the claimant not complying with the RTA Protocol or electing not to do so see		45.36	
• For the position where the parties settle after a claim has been started under Part 8 in accordance with PD 8B see		45.37	
9.6 Where the claimant obtains judgment for an amount **equal to or less than the defendant's RTA Protocol offer** the court will order the **claimant to pay**: (1) where the claim is determined (i) on the papers, Stage 3 Type A fixed costs; or (ii) at a hearing, Stage 3 Type A and B fixed costs; or (2) disbursements allowed in accordance with CPR 45.30; and			

	Form No	CPR Rule	PD
(3) a success fee in accordance with CPR 45.31(4)		45.38	
9.7 For the costs position on the **adjournment** of a hearing see		45.39	
9.8 For provisions where the claimant is a **child** and: (1) there is a settlement at Stage 2, see (2) where there is a settlement at Stage 3, see (3) where the court orders the claim is not suitable to be determined under the Stage 3 procedure, see		 45.33 45.34 45.35	

TABLE 11—DEFENCE AND REPLY

TAB 11

	Form No	CPR Rule	PD
1. Preliminary			
See **CPR 15 [1]–CPR 15 [3]** and **CPR 16 [2]–CPR 16 [4]** *Note* in particular: • No defence is required where the claim is issued under Part 8 • No judgment in default of defence can be entered on a claim for delivery of goods subject to an agreement regulated by the Consumer Credit Act 1974 • The provisions of CPR Pt 15 apply subject to any special provisions in Rules or Practice Directions • Statements of case are essential to identify the issues and the extent of the dispute between the parties, per LORD WOOLF CJ in *McPhilemy v Times Newspapers* [1999] 3 All ER 775, CA • For the filing of a defence online to a claim issued through the online claims service Money Claim Online, see		 12.2 7.12	 7E, para 1.3
2. Defences – time for filing and service, consequences of not filing			
If a defendant fails to file a defence the claimant may obtain default judgment if CPR Pt 12 allows it		15.3	

	Form No	CPR Rule	PD
The **time for filing of the defence**: (a) 14 days after service of the particulars of claim (b) if the defendant files an acknowledgment under CPR Pt 10, 28 days after service of the particulars of claim		15.4	
But this is subject to: (a) CPR 6.35 – where claim form is served out of jurisdiction (b) CPR 11.7 – where defendant makes an application disputing the court's jurisdiction but the court does not make a declaration there is no jurisdiction (c) CPR 24.4(2) where claimant has filed an application for summary judgment (d) CPR 6.12(3) where court specifies period for defence having permitted service on agent of overseas principal Also note: (a) the defendant and claimant may agree to extend the prescribed time for service for up to 28 days. This is the totality of the time that the parties may agree for extension of the prescribed time		15.5	
The defendant must notify the court in writing of any such agreement (b) if a defence is filed out of time it will prevent a subsequent application for default judgment succeeding and will be valid (but see *Coll v Tattum* at **TAB 6** para 6(c) as to the requirement of permission to file out of time and the position where an acknowledgment or defence is filed out of time and after a request for judgment has been filed but not processed)			
Where an application for an **extension of time** for filing a defence it should be made pursuant to CPR 3.1	N244	3.1	
A copy of the defence must be **served** on every party		15.6	

	Form No	CPR Rule	PD
The Rules do not specify a time for so doing but good practice requires prompt service with details of the date of filing			
The Costs Practice Direction requires information about a funding arrangement to be provided with the defence when the defendant intends to recover an additional liability The court will serve or deliver a copy of any notice of funding filed with the defence provided copies were filed for service	N251		Costs PD, section 19 6A, para 8.2
3. "States paid" defence			
Where the only claim (apart from a claim for costs and interest) is for a specified amount and the defendant states he has paid the amount claimed, the court will send notice of this to the claimant requiring him to state in writing whether he wishes the proceedings to continue		15.10(1)	
The claimant must reply in 28 days or the claim will be stayed and an application to remove the stay required		15.10(3) and (4)	
When the claimant responds in the time prescribed he must serve a copy on the defendant. If the claimant wishes to proceed the proceedings will continue as a defended claim An unusual case of "states paid" is provided by *Cantor Index Ltd v Thompson* [2008] EWHC 1104 (QB) where the court decided that the presentation of a cheque sent in settlement is strong evidence of acceptance by conduct of the offer contained in the letter enclosing it so that a contract was concluded. This was held to remain the case if the cheque was not honoured.		15.10(2)	

	Form No	CPR Rule	PD
3.1 Defence of tender before action			
Where, before proceedings are started, the defendant makes a tender of a sum in settlement which the claimant refuses to accept, the defendant may rely on the tender as a defence provided he brings that amount into court and the claimant fails to establish that he is entitled to a larger sum. The procedure for bringing the money into court is set out in paragrpah 1 of CPR PD 37.		37.2	37, para 1
4. Contents of defence			
Where the defendant is an individual, and the claim form does not contain an address at which he resides or carries on business, or provides an incorrect address, the defendant must provide such an address for service, which must be within the United Kingdom, including a postcode. He must also provide his date of birth		16.5(8)	16, para 10.6
The defendant must state: (a) which of the allegations is denied and if so why, and his version of events if it is different (b) which allegations he is unable to admit or deny and requires the claimant to prove, and (c) which allegations he admits		16.5(1) and (2)	
The defendant must also: (a) if he disputes the claimant's statement of value, state why and, if he is able, give his own statement of value (b) if he defends in a representative capacity, state what that capacity is (c) if the defendant has not filed an acknowledgment of service, give an address for service The defence must be verified by a **statement of truth**			16, para 11.1

	Form No	CPR Rule	PD
If the claim is for **personal injuries** and the claimant has attached a medical report and/or a schedule of past and future losses, the defendant must comply with; a counter-schedule of expenses and losses must be verified by a statement of case			16, para 12.1 and 22 para 1.5
If the defendant relies on the expiry of any relevant **limitation period** he must give details of it: see			16, para 13.1
If the defence is one of **tender,** see		37.3	37, para 2
If the defendant relies on any provision or right arising under the **Human Rights Act 1998**, see			16, para 15.1
The **defence may include**: (a) any point of law on which the defence is based (b) names of any witnesses (c) supporting documents (including expert's report) This is the same right enjoyed by the claimant when drafting his particulars of claim, and for comment see **TAB 1** para 7, pre-penultimate paragraph			
5. Consequences of defence failing to deal with allegations			
A defendant who fails to deal with an allegation shall be taken to admit that allegation, save that:		16.5(5)	
(a) where the claim includes a money claim, a defendant shall be taken to require that any allegation relating to the amount of money claimed be proved unless he expressly admits the allegation		16.5(4)	
(b) a defendant who: (i) fails to deal with an allegation, but (ii) has set out in his defence the nature of his case in relation to the issue to which the allegation is relevant, shall be taken to require that allegation to be proved		16.5(3)	

	Form No	CPR Rule	PD
6. Effect of filing a defence			
Once a defence has been filed, judgment in default cannot be entered and the court will issue **Allocation Questionnaires** unless it dispenses with them		26.3(1)	
If the claim is for a specified amount and the defendant is an individual, the proceedings will be **automatically transferred** to the defendant's home court unless:		26.2	
(a) the claim was commenced in the defendant's home court			
(b) the claim has been transferred to another defendant's home court			
7. Reply			
If the claimant wished to file a reply to the defence he must:		15.8	
(a) file his reply when he files his **Allocation Questionnaire**, and (b) serve his reply on the other parties at the same time as he files it			
The claimant will wish to file a reply when the defence raises new issues, although if he fails to do so he will not be taken as admitting matters raised in the defence		16.7	

TABLE 12—COUNTERCLAIMS AGAINST CLAIMANT

TAB 12

	Form No	CPR Rule	PD
1. Preliminary			
See **CPR 20 [1]–CPR 20 [4]** and note that this Table does not deal with: (a) claims against a non-party (b) a defendant's claim for contribution or indemnity from co-defendant			
Additional claims under CPR Pt 20 fall into 3 categories and this Table deals with:		20.2	

	Form No	CPR Rule	PD
a counterclaim by a defendant against the claimant or against the claimant and some other person		20.2(1)(a)	
Claimants and defendants in the original claim are always to be referred to as such even if they subsequently acquire a new procedural status			20, para 7.3
'Additional claims' means any claim other than the claim by the claimant against the defendant		20.2(2)	
Note that a 'set off' is a defence only so that CPR 20 does not apply and no judgment can be obtained on the set off.			
For a detailed examination of the meaning of 'set off' including the difference between legal set-off and equitable set-off see *Gary Fearns (t/a Autoaint International) v Anglo-Dutch Paint & Chemical Co Ltd* [2010] EWHC 2366, (2010) Sol Jo, 2 October, 'Lawbrief', page 29.			
2. The Crown			
No counterclaim or set-off is possible against the Crown when the claim is for taxes, penalties or duties If the Crown is sued or sues in the name of a Government department and the subject matter of the counterclaim or set-off does not relate to that department, or if the Crown issued or sues in the name of the Attorney-General, permission of the court is required before a counterclaim or set-off may be made		66.4	
3. Permission to make a Part 20 counterclaim			
Permission is needed to bring a counterclaim against a claim brought under Part 8 but otherwise **no permission is required, provided the particulars of the counterclaim are filed with the defence.** Permission is required to bring a counterclaim after a defence has been filed		20.4(1) and (2)	

	Form No	CPR Rule	PD
If permission has to be sought the application under CPR Pt 23 will be necessary and it must be supported by evidence and an explanation for the delay	N244		20, paras 2.1–2.3
A copy of the proposed counterclaim must be filed with the application			20, para 1.2
4. Procedure			
The defence and counterclaim should be contained in the same document, as should any reply and defence to counterclaim	N211		20, para 6
The counterclaim is made by filing particulars with copies for service Guidance Notes are issued by the court A counterclaim will be treated as a claim for the purposes of CPR and must comply with the Part 16 "Statement of Case"		20.3(1)	20, para 3
A counterclaim must be verified by a statement of truth			20, para 4
A fee is payable to the court on the filing of a counterclaim as if it were a claim. It must be paid when the counterclaim is filed. For the sanction on failure to pay, or paying with a cheque that is dishonoured, the fee on filing or subsequent fees where the action proceeds on the counterclaim see		3.7A and 3.7B	3B, paras 1 and 2
Note: • If the Part 20 counterclaim is made against a defendant in addition to the original claimant, permission must be obtained (normally by application without notice) and CPR 20.12 must be complied with		20.5(2)	
5. Responding to a counterclaim			
The acknowledgment of service provisions in CPR Pt 10 do not apply to a claimant who wishes to defend the counterclaim, although the provisions do apply to any additional defendant to the counterclaim		20.4(3)	

	Form No	CPR Rule	PD
If the claimant wishes to defend, he must file a defence no later than 14 days after service of the counterclaim. The time allowed to an additional defendant to a counterclaim is 28 days from service if he has filed an acknowledgment		15.4(1)(a) and (b)	
Judgment may be obtained in default of defence to counterclaim		20.3(3)	20, para 3
6. Rules that do not apply to a Part 20 counterclaim			
The following Rules do not apply: (a) CPR 7.5 and CPR 7.6 – time for service of claim form (b) CPR 16.3(5) – statement of value where claim to be issued in the High Court (c) CPR Pt 26 – case management – preliminary stage			
7. Subsequent management			
The allocation of the claim will include the counterclaim and the court will give directions that the claim and counterclaim will, so far as practicable, be managed together		20.13	
8. Legal and Equitable set-off			
The law of set-off has been clarified by the decision in *Geldof Metaalconstructie NV v Simon Carves Ltd* [2010] EWCA Civ 667, [2010] All ER (D) 69 (Jan); for the distinction between legal set-off and equitable set-off and the advantages of set-off over a counterclaim see article 'Going places?' by Jonathan Arr in NLJ (2010) 16 July, page 1006.			

TABLE 13—ALLOCATION

TAB 13

	Form No	CPR Rule	PD
1. Preliminary			
The **Practice Direction – Automatic Orders Pilot Scheme** should be noted. This supplements CPR Part 26 (Case Management – Preliminary Stage) and CPR Part 28 (Fast Track) and will operate in county courts nationally and will apply to claims started on or after 1 October 2009.			51B
It is restricted to orders for a stay of one month where the parties request a stay in their allocation questionnaire and 'unless' orders arising out of failure to file an allocation questionnaire or a two-party fast track pre-trial check list. The period of 7 days will be given for compliance with strike-out in default.			
See **CPR 26 [1]–CPR 26 [6]** and note: An application for summary judgment or to strike out can be made prior to allocation if it is considered appropriate. Where such an application has been made the court will not normally allocate to track before the application has been decided	N244	24.2	26A, para 5.3(2)

	Form No	CPR Rule	PD
2. Allocation Questionnaires	N150 or N149 for claims having a monetary value within the small claims limit or N151 where the claim is for an amount to be decided by the court		
Revised forms of allocation questionnaires were introduced on 1 April 2008 (save in the West Midlands until a mediator is in post). Form N150 has the front page dedicated to settlement. In form N149 (small claims) the parties are asked if they wish to use the free court mediation scheme; the District Judge can refer the case to a mediator even if they do not. The mediation scheme does not apply to claims arising from road traffic accidents, concerning the DVLA, CSA or HM Revenue and Customs, claims concerning bank charges or water charges. In any event the allocation fee is payable and not refundable. See further NLJ, 11 April 2008, page 512 and NLJ, 6 June 2008, page 810.			
Unless CPR 15.10 (state paid defence) or CPR 14.5 (part admission) applies or the court dispenses with the need for a Questionnaire, when a defendant files a defence the court will serve an **Allocation Questionnaire** on all parties		26.3(1)	
Where there is more than one defendant see		26.3(2)	

	Form No	CPR Rule	PD
Each party must file a completed **Allocation Questionnaire** no later than the date specified and which much be at least **14 days after service** on the party in question. A copy should be served on the other parties The parties cannot by agreement vary the time for filing the allocation questionnaire		26.3(6) and (6A)	
No fee is payable on the allocation to track of a money claim of £1,500 or less, and where the claim is for money between £1,500 and £5,000 the fee payable is £35. For all other claims a fee, presently of £200, is payable. The fee is payable by the claimant. For the sanction for failure to pay this fee or paying with a cheque that is dishonoured see		3.7A and 3.7B	
Re-instatement after striking out for failure to pay the fee is not automatic		3.9	
Where a party does not file an allocation questionnaire within the time specified in Form 152 the court will serve notice on that party requiring it to be filed within 7 days from service of the notice.			
Where a party fails to comply with the notice within the period specified that party's claim, defence or counterclaim will be automatically struck out.			
The 7 day 'unless' order may, by virtue of the Automatic Orders Pilot Scheme – PD 51B – be made by staff in all county courts and the High Court.			26A, paras 2, 5(1) and (2) and 51B, para 2(2)
The parties may give additional information in their Questionnaires and should consult particularly as to proposed directions			26A, paras 2.2 and 3
A **costs schedule** must be filed and served with the allocation questionnaire unless the claim is within the limits of the small claims track or the fast track. A copy must also be served on the client by the solicitor acting for him. For the importance of compliance with this provision see PD 43, Section 6, particularly 6.5A			26A, para 2.1 and Costs PD, Section 6

	Form No	CPR Rule	PD
The requirement of a costs estimate has been deleted for Part 8 claims when a pre-trial checklist is filed.			
3. Allocation			
The court may order a **stay** for one month or for such period as it thinks appropriate to enable the parties to try to settle the case if it thinks it appropriate and will do so if both parties so request. The stay may be extended A party requesting a stay in his replies to the allocation questionnaire which is opposed or not consented to by the other party should ensure by annex to the form that the judge knows the reasons for the request		26.4	
If no stay is ordered, or a stay and any extension expires the court will **allocate** the claim to track: (a) when every defendant has filed an Allocation Questionnaire, or (b) the period for filing the Allocation Questionnaire has expired whichever is the sooner, unless it has dispensed with Allocation Questionnaires		26.5(1)	
For allocation after default judgment on request or judgment on admission the court will not normally allocate to track (other than the small claims track) unless the amount payable is disputed on substantial grounds or the dispute is not suitable to be dealt with at a disposal hearing see		12.7, 14.8	26A, paras 12.3 and 12.4
A disposal hearing is one:			
(a) at which the court will not normally hear oral evidence and			
(b) will not normally last more than 30 minutes			
Before deciding the track to which to allocate, the court may call for **further information** or hold an **allocation hearing**		26.5(3) and (4)	26A, para 6 and 27, para 2.3
The scope of these tracks is set out:			

	Form No	CPR Rule	PD
(a) the **small claims track** is the normal track for any claim which has a value of not more than £5,000. The forms giving notice of allocation are:	N157, N158, N159	26.6(3)	
These are respectively where there is a hearing date; where there is to be a preliminary hearing; and where there is no hearing			
but see: (i) for **personal injury** claims (value of claim for damages not more than £1,000)		26.6(1)(a)	
(ii) for certain claims **by a tenant of residential premises** against his landlord (cost of repairs and/or damages does not exceed £1,000)		26.6(1)(b)	26A, para 8.1(c)
(iii) for claims in respect of **harassment** or **unlawful eviction**		26.7(4)	
(b) the **fast track** is the normal track for any claim for which the small claims track is not the normal track which has a value if issued on or after 6 April 2009 of not more than £25,000 provided: (i) the trial is expected to last no longer than one day, and (ii) oral expert evidence is limited to two expert fields and only one witness per party per field	N154	26.6(4) and (5)	
(c) the **multi-track** is the normal track for any case for which the small claims track or the fast track is not the normal track	N155		
For an example of the type of case where the monetary value is not determinative of the appropriate track see *Low Velocity Impact Claims* at **TAB 16** paras 15 and 16 below			
The court will give notice of allocation		26.9	

	Form No	CPR Rule	PD
For allocation of assessment of damages after a "relevant order" has been made, see			26A, para 12.3
For "relevant order", see			26A, para 12.1
A Master or a district judge may decide the amount payable under a relevant order irrespective of the financial value of the claim and of the track to which the claim may have been allocated			26A, para 12.6
4. Allocation principles			
The court, in considering whether to allocation a claim, will have regard to the matters set out in CPR 26.8(1)(a)–(i)		26.8(1)	
The **financial value** of the claim is to be assessed by the court but it must disregard:		26.8(2)	
(a) any amount not in dispute (b) any claim for interest (c) any claim for costs (d) any contributory negligence Where the court believes the amount claimed is excessive it can make an order directing the claimant to justify the amount			26A, para 7.3(2)
The court will not allocate proceedings to a track if the financial value of the claim exceeds the financial value of the track unless the parties agree. Accordingly it can allocate to a higher track but not, without consent, to a lower track. The ability of parties to agree to allocation to a track even though the financial limits of that track are exceeded applies to both the fast track and the multi-track		26.7(3)	
When there is more than one money claim the court will generally regard the largest of them as determining the financial value of the claims. See			26A, para 7.7

	Form No	CPR Rule	PD
In deciding whether **any amount is not in dispute** the court will apply the following general principles: (a) any amount not admitted is disputed (b) any part of the claim for which judgment has been entered is not in dispute (c) any specific sum claimed as a distinct item which the defendant admits is not in dispute (d) any sum offered and accepted for a distinct part of the claim is not in dispute A claimant can limit his claim to bring it within the financial limits of the small claims track or even to reduce the court fees payable: *Khiaban v Beard* [2003] EWCA Civ 358, [2003] 3 All ER 362, [2003] All ER (D) 111 (Mar)			26A, para 7.4
5. Re-allocation			
Where a party is dissatisfied with the allocation order he may appeal or apply to the court to re-allocate. He should appeal if the allocation was effected at a hearing at which he was present or had notice; but otherwise should apply for re-allocation	N244		26A, para 11.1(1)
Where there has been a change of circumstances the court can re-allocate on application or on its own initiative. See *Maguire v Molin* [2002] EWCA Civ 1083, [2002] 4 All ER 325 as to the wide discretion enjoyed when deciding whether to reallocate and the matters to be taken into account. See also CPR 26.10[1] for further consideration of this case			26A, para 11.1(2)
6. Draft directions			
An attempt should be made by the parties to agree directions, with sensible time limits, for the court's consideration. For a comprehensive order for case management directions in the multi-track see Form PF 52			27, paras 9 and 10 (small claims), 28, para 9 (fast track)

	Form No	CPR Rule	PD
7. Costs on small claims and fast track			
Costs incurred before and after allocation shall be governed by the rules of the track to which the claim is allocated except where a court or a practice direction provides otherwise.		44.9(2)	
For a case where the relationship between a pre-action protocol and the entitlement to pre-allocation costs was considered see *Lee v Birmingham City Council* [2008] EWCA Civ 891, (2008) NLJ Law Reports, 15 August, page 1180 and NLJ 19 September, page 1293 'The Civil Way' by Stephen Gold			
This case fell within a protocol which required a claim to be made initially in accordance with its terms. The claim was put forward and the protocol procedure commenced; it was held that for the purpose of costs the claim was made when the protocol procedure commenced and not when the litigation was begun. The Court of Appeal held that fast track costs would be payable up to the time when the defendant carried out the repairs that were the subject matter of the claim although subsequently the claim for consequential damages was allocated to the small claims track.			

TABLE 14—APPLICATIONS

TAB 14

	Form No	CPR Rule	PD
1. Preliminary			
See **CPR 23 [1]–CPR 23 [12]** and in particular note: (a) an application should be made as soon as it becomes apparent that an application is necessary or desirable			23A, para 2.7

	Form No	CPR Rule	PD
(b) CPR PD 23: (i) requires parties, whenever possible, to make an application so that it can be considered at any hearing that has been fixed or is about to be fixed			23A, para 2.8
(ii) the parties should anticipate that, at the hearing of the application, the court may wish to review the conduct of the case as a whole and give any necessary directions and be ready to assist in so doing			23A, para 9
(c) all applications made before a claim is commenced should be made under Part 23			23A, para 5
(d) an application for **further particulars** under Part 18 will only be justified if they will narrow or dispose of an issue or help a court to do so In *Lexi Holdings (in administration) v Pannone and Partners* [2010] EWHC 1416 (Ch), 18 June the judge held that the appropriate tests on applications for further information are 'necessity' and 'proportionality' in relation to the applicant's ability to prepare its own case and to understand the case it has to meet.		18.1	

	Form No	CPR Rule	PD
(e) For applications for **interim remedies and security for costs** see CPR 25 and in particular for **interim payments** CPR 25.6 (general procedure) and CPR 25.7 (conditions to be satisfied). Useful guidance as to the proportion of the anticipated final judgment it is reasonable to award by way of interim payment is provided in *Spillman v Bradfield Riding Centre* [2007] EWHC 89 (QB) [200] AlL ER (D) 59 (Feb), 6 February. The 'reasonable proportion in that case was 75%. The determination of the amount must be in accordance with CPR 25.7(4) rather than a consideration of the purpose for which the payment is sought. The relationship between interim payments (IPOs) and the allocation of losses to periodical payments is considered in *Eeles v Cobham Hire Services Ltd* [2009] EWCA Civ 204, [2009] PIQR P273, Civil Procedure News, 7 April 2009 and see articles 'A clearer future' by Stephen Hazelton in Sol Jo (2009) 26 May, page 6 and 'Interim Solutions' by David Oldham in Sol Jo (2009) 16 December, page 15 Note most recently the application of the Eeles principles in *FP v Taunton and Somerset NHS Trust* [2009] EWHC 1965 (QB), 110 BMLR 164 and *Johnson (by her mother and litigation friend) v Compton-Cooke* [2009] EWHC 2582 (QB), [2009] All ER (D) 214 (Oct) and in *Brown v Emery* [2010] EWHC 388 (QB), 4 March		25.6 and 25.7	

		Form No	CPR Rule	PD
	Smith LJ in *Eeles v Cobham Hire Services Ltd* (above) stressed that although the power to make an interim order is discretionary it was not unfettered and there is no power to make an order for payment for more than 'a reasonable proportion of the likely amount of the final judgment'.			
	The Court of Appeal in *Eeles* recognised that there will be cases in which the claimant can clearly demonstrate a need to an immediate capital sum (typically for the purchase of a suitable house) which would be such that it would result in a reduction or postponement of periodical payments. This would be an exceptional situation but if there was no alternative source of funds to satisfy the claimant's needs the court would have no alternative but to so order. For detailed consideration and summaries of the cases where there have been such exceptional awards see (2010) NLJ, 12 June, page 374, article by Christopher Sharp QC.			
(f)	An application by a defendant for **security for costs** should be made using form N244 and written evidence in support is required. It is good practice to request security by letter before making the application.			
	The written evidence should have attached the request and any reply and also a bill of costs showing costs to date and costs to be incurred. The bill should preferably be in the form of Precedent H at CPR PD 48.			

	Form No	CPR Rule	PD
The court may make the order if having regard to all the circumstances of the case it is just to do so, and that either one of the conditions set out in CPR 23.13(2) applies or an enactment permits the court to require security.			
The court has a discretion whether to make an order (see *Sir Lindsay Parkinson & Co Ltd v Triplan Ltd* [1973] QB 609, [1972] 2 All ER CA) but the application should not be allowed if it is being used to stifle a genuine claim. The enactment most frequently relied upon is s 726(1) of the Companies Act 1985 where the claimant is a limited company.			
The amount of the security ordered and how and when it is to be provided is to be decided by the court in the exercise of its discretion.			
In *Michael Phillips Architects Ltd v Riklin* [2010] EWHC 834 (TCC), [2010] All ER (D) 164 (Jun) the court considered the effect on an application of the claimants having an after the event insurance policy which covered the claimant's liability for the defendant's costs. It was held that the presence of the policy did not preclude the making of the order but that in principle it would be taken into account when fixing the amount of the security.			
For the costs against someone other than the defendant see CPR 25.14 and for precedent see BCCP Division C, paras **C[56]** and **C[56A]**.			
For security for costs of an appeal see CPR 25.15 and BCCP Division F, para **F[204]** for a precedent.			

	Form No	CPR Rule	PD
(g) A Master or district judge may refer to a judge any matter he thinks should properly be decided by a judge. The judge may either dispose of the matter or refer it back to the Master or district judge			23A, para 1
(h) Although judges have wide case management powers these do not enable an individual judge or a court to make a general variation of the rules or practice directions; *Bovale Ltd v Secretary of State for Communities and Local Government* [2009] EWCA Civ 171, [2009] 3 All ER 340.			
2. Definitions			
"Application notice" means a document in which the applicant states his intention to seek a court order		23.1	
Practice Form N244 may be used and it is sensible to do so	N244		
"Respondent" means (a) the person against whom the order is sought and (b) such other person as the court may direct			
3. Filing, notice and service			
An application must be made by **filing an application notice** unless a Rule, Practice Direction or the court permits an application without such filing or dispenses with it		23.3	
A court fee is payable on the issue of an application; presently the fee is £75 where no other fee is specified; the fee is not payable if the application is by consent for an adjournment and is received at least 14 days before the day fixed for the hearing. On any other consent application the fee is £40 where no other fee is specified			
The application generally must be made **to the court where the claim was started** unless: (a) the claim has been transferred to another court			

	Form No	CPR Rule	PD
(b) if the parties have been notified of a fixed date for trial, the application must be made where the trial is to take place *Note:* If the application is made before the claim is started it should be made to the court where the claim is likely to be made unless there is good reason to apply to a different court			
Where an application must be made within a specified time it is so made if the application is received by the court within that time		23.5	
A copy of the application must be **served on each respondent** unless it may be made without such service by permission in: (a) a Rule (b) a Practice Direction, or (c) a court order		23.4	
Service must be effected as soon as possible after filing and, except where another time limit is specified in the CPR or a Practice Direction; must be served in any event **at least 3 days before** the application hearing (see r 2.8 for calculation of time expressed in days)		23.7	23A, para 4.1
Where there is to be a telephone hearing the application must in any event be served at least 5 days before the date of the hearing (see r 2.8 for calculation of time expressed in days)			23A, para 4.1A
Where a date for a hearing has been fixed and a party wishes to make an application at that hearing but there is insufficient time to serve an application notice he should inform the other party and the court (preferably in writing) as soon as possible of the nature of the application and the reason for it. The application should then be made orally at the hearing			23A, para 2.10

	Form No	CPR Rule	PD
If a copy of the application is to be served it must be accompanied by: (a) a copy of any written evidence in support, and (b) a copy of any draft order which the applicant has attached to his application If an application is served but the period of notice is shorter than required the court may direct that in the circumstances sufficient notice has been given and hear the application		23.7(4)	
4. Contents of application notice			
An application notice must state: (a) what order the applicant is seeking, and (b) briefly, why the applicant is seeking the order		23.6	
The formal matters set out in CPR PD 23 must also be included; note that where the applicant is not already a party address for service including a postcode has to be shown			23A, para 2.1
The application must be signed and be verified by a statement of truth if it is wished to rely on matters set out in the application notice as evidence		22.1(a)	
Except in the most simple case the applicant should bring a **draft order** to the hearing and it is good practice to attach a draft of the order to the application form	N244		
If the application is intended to be made to a judge the application should so state			23A, para 2.6
Where the hearing is not likely to last more than one day the parties must file and serve statements of costs on each other at least 24 hours before the time fixed for the hearing. This provision does not apply to mortgage possession proceedings	N260		Costs PD, para 13.5

	Form No	CPR Rule	PD
5. Evidence			
The evidence is generally given by **witness statements** unless the court, a Practice Direction or other enactment requires otherwise. If Form N244 is used, and only one statement is to be relied upon, it can conveniently be set out in Part C of the Form		32.6(1)	
A party may also rely at the hearing of the application on matters set out: (a) in his statement of case, or (b) in his application notice provided the statement or notice is verified by a statement of truth		32.6(2)	
If the respondent wishes to rely on evidence that has not yet been served he should serve it as soon as possible and in any event in accordance with any directions the court has given			23A, para 9.4
If the applicant wishes to file evidence in reply it should also be served as soon as possible and in accordance with any directions given			23A, para 9.5
The court will often need to be satisfied by evidence of the facts that are relied upon in support of or in opposition to the application			23A, para 9.1
6. Application without service of notice			
An application may be made without service only: (a) where there is exceptional urgency (b) where the overriding objective is best furthered by doing so (c) by consent of all the parties (d) with the permission of the court (e) where a date for hearing has been fixed and a party wishes to make an application and there is insufficient time: see final paragraph of part 3 of this Table, above (f) where a court order, Rule or Practice Direction permits			23A, para 3 23A, para 2.10

	Form No	CPR Rule	PD
Where the court has disposed of an application without service of the application notice, the application, any evidence in support and the order must be served			
The order must contain a statement of the right to make an **application to set aside or vary the order**		23.9	
The time for making such an application to set aside or vary must be made **within 7 days** after the date on which the order was served on the person making the application		23.10	
The duty to make full and frank disclosure on applications for ex parte relief means identifying all relevant documents and ensuring the judge is aware of the significance of what he is asked to read. The burden on the advocate is even greater where the application is by telephone to a judge who has none of the papers in front if him: *R (on the application of Lawer) v Restormel Borough Council* [2007] EWHC 2299 (Admin)			
For the attitude of the court to applications for injunctions of which no notice has been given and the only circumstances in which the court will entertain them see *National Commercial Bank of Jamaica Ltd v Olint Corpn Ltd* [2009] UKPC 16, [2009] 1 WLR 1405 where it was made clear that a judge should not entertain an application for an injunction where no notice has been given unless:			
(a) giving notice would enable the defendant to defeat the purpose of the injunction; or (b) there has been no time to give notice because the injunction is required to prevent the imminent threatened unlawful act.			
Short notice or telephone notice is better than none at all.			
At the interlocutory stage the court should take the course least likely to cause irremediable prejudice to one party or the other.			

	Form No	CPR Rule	PD
Note also the requirement as to an undertaking as to damages and see *Al Rawas v Pegasus Energy Ltd* [2008] EWHC 617 (QB), [2009] 1 All ER 346, [2009] 1 All ER (Comm) 393.			
7. Applications dealt with without a hearing			
The court may deal with an application without a hearing if: (a) the parties agree as to the terms of the order sought (b) the parties agree that the court should dispose of the application without a hearing, or (c) the court does not consider that a hearing would be appropriate		23.8	
Where the application is for an order in terms that have been agreed the provisions of CPR 40.6 (5)–(7) and PD 40B paras 3 and 11 must be observed		40.6(5)–(7)	40B, paras 3 and 11
Note: Under a court's duty to manage cases there is included "dealing with the case without the parties needing to attend court"		1.4	
When CPR 23.8(c) applies (i e the court considers a hearing not appropriate) the court will treat the application as if it were proposing to make an order on its own initiative. Accordingly, any party affected may apply within 7 days of service to have the order set aside, varied or stayed and the order must set out this right If the court does not agree to dispose of the application without a hearing the court will list the application for hearing and give any necessary directions			23A, para 2.4
If a witness statement for use at trial is not served within the time specified by the court the witness may not be called to give oral evidence at the trial without the permission of the court.		32.10	
8. The hearing			
It is essential for the applicant to have provided for a **sufficient time** allowance for his application to be property heard			

	Form No	CPR Rule	PD
Except in a simple application a **skeleton argument** should be used (a copy should be available for the respondent) If authorities are relied on a list should be filed and served in advance and copies of the cases attached to the court's list. A request should be made in the letter to the court that the skeleton argument and authorities be placed before the judge in the hope time will be available for him to read them prior to the application. Note *Goode v Martin* [2001] EWCA Civ 1899, [2002] 1 All ER 620 for 'extra tool ... to produce a fair result' discussed at CPR 1.2[1] The court can make a summary assessment of the costs or order a detailed assessment The court should assess summarily unless there is good reason not to do so. When the parties agree an order by consent without any party attending the parties should agree **a figure for costs to be inserted in the consent order** or agree there should be no order for costs. If the parties cannot agree the costs position attendance on the appointment will be necessary. No costs of that attendance will be allowed unless good reason for the failure to deal with costs is established		44.7	Costs PD, para 13.2 and 13.4
As to the costs of an application to amend, granted at a hearing, which the court finds should have been consented to by the respondent, see *La Chemise Lacoste SA v Sketchers USA Ltd* [2006] All ER (D) 348 (May)			
The exercise of the court's discretion to grant an **adjournment** is governed, not by old authorities, but by the CPR and in particular the overriding objective: *Albon (t/a NA Carriage Co) v Naza Motor Trading Sdn Bhd* [2007] EWHC 2613 (Ch), Lightman J [2008] 1 All ER 995, (2007) NLJ LR 16 November, page 1615. In this case the application to adjourn was refused			

	Form No	CPR Rule	PD
9. Judgment			
The judge may hand down his judgment in private giving permission for it to be reported: *JE v DE (by the official solicitor)* [2006] EWHC 3459 (Fam), [2007] 2 FLR 1150, [2007] Fam Law 1132, Mumby J			
In all proceedings other than family proceedings it is virtually invariable when granting an interim injunction to require a cross-undertaking in damages.			
10. Dismissal of totally without merit application			
If the court dismisses an application (including an application for judicial review or for leave to appeal) and it considers the application is totally without merit it must		23.12	
(a) record that fact (see *Bukhari v POW Trust* [2009] EWHC 19 (QB), [2009] All ER (D) 102 (Jan)), and			
(b) consider whether it is appropriate to make a civil restraint order (CRO) • For the circumstances in which the court has power to make a CRO see CPR 3.11(a) and PD 3C • For the procedure where a party applies for a CRO see CPR 3.11(b) and PD 3C • For the consequences of the court making a CRO see CPR 3.11(c) and PD 3C • For Limited Civil Restraint Order see PD 3C, para 2 and **CPR 3.11 [2]** • For Extended Civil Restraint Order see PD 3C, para 3 and **CPR 3.11 [3]** • For General Civil Restraint Order see PD 3C, para 4 and **CPR 3.11 [3]**	N19, N19A, N19B	3.11	3C

	Form No	CPR Rule	PD
Forrester Ketley & Co v David Brent [2008] EWHC 3150 (Ch) provides guidance in the judgment of Morgan J as to the highly relevant matters (including prospects of success) to be considered on an application to make applications subsequent to an ECRO and also illustrates the willingness of the court to use the court's inherent powers to supplement the powers set out in Practice Direction 3.			
For an ECRO to be made it is a precondition that there has been the 'persistent' issue of claims or making of applications which are totally without merit (see CPR PD 3C, para 31); three claims or applications without merit are the bare minimum to satisfy the requirement of persistence: *Re Ludlam (Bankruptcy)* [2009] EWHC 2067 (Ch), (2009) Times, 26 October.			
The applicant in *Supperstone v Hurst* [2009] EWHC 1271 (Ch), [2009] All ER (D) 77 (Jun) applied for an ECRO and sought to have included a term that the respondent be forbidden to communicate with him or with certain other specified people without the permission of the court. Held that the court under the ECRO procedure had no power to do so. The Protection from Harassment Act 1997 was capable of providing the relief sought in appropriate cases.			
11. Order requiring payment into court – compliance			
The effective date for compliance is the date of lodgment in the Court Funds office and that remains so whether it is a cheque (whether or not a sterling cheque) that is lodged: *Ene Kos Ltd v Petroleo Brasiliero SA* [2009] EWCA Civ 1127, [2009] All ER (D) 2 (Nov). It is open to the judge in his order to provide that cleared funds must be lodged by the date specified for compliance; see *Ene Kos* above per Arden LJ at paras [50]–[54], and if the order is so worded lodgment of a cheque will delay compliance to a date when the funds are cleared.			

TABLE 14A—TELEPHONE HEARING AND VIDEO CONFERENCING

TAB 14A

	Form No	CPR Rule	PD
1. General			
1.1 The court under the general powers of management **may**: 'hold a hearing and receive evidence by telephone or using any other method of direct communication,		3.1(2)(d)	23A, paras 6.1–6.8
1.2 The types of telephone hearings are: (a) a conference call when all parties and the judge communicate by telephone (b) where a party or parties communicate with those present by telephone or conference call			
1.3 Conference calls are arranged by a number of commercial providers and all judges have available a hands free telephone with a loudspeaker as an integral part (a speaker phone)			
1.4 Any request for a telephone hearing should be made in the application notice (there is a box to be ticked in Form N244) and if not at the earliest possible time, whether by the applicant or the respondent. Generally speaking a telephone hearing is regarded as inappropriate in the middle of a busy list rather than at the beginning of it. If a late request for a telephone hearing is granted the hearing may be adjourned for re-listing at a more convenient time.			
One hour seems to be the general maximum time that can be successfully dealt with by a telephone hearing within a general court list. Many courts will only list telephone hearings at the beginning of court lists, that is at 10 am or 2 pm, whilst some courts allocate certain days of the week for telephone hearings and others have telephone hearing lists.			

	Form No	CPR Rule	PD
Accurate time estimates are essential to avoid the injustice that can result from rushed hearings and in appropriate cases adverse costs orders where the hearing cannot be completed			
1.5 A '**designated legal representative**' means the applicant's legal representative (if any) or the legal representative of such other party as the court directs to arrange the telephone hearing A '**telephone conference enabled court**' means a district registry of the High Court or a county court in which telephone conference facilities are available. All district and county courts are now telephone conference enabled courts.			23A, para 6.1
1.6 Hybrid telephone hearings where one party is present are permissible; see			23A, para 6.9
1.7 The costs of the service provider are allowable as part of the application costs; the charge by BT or Cellnet is approximately £50 for 30 minutes.			
2. The court's discretion			
2.1 Unless PD 23 para 6.3 applies (see below at 2.2) at a telephone conference enabled court the following hearings **will** be conducted by telephone **unless the court otherwise orders** (i) allocation hearings; (ii) listing hearings; and (iii) interim applications, case management conferences and pre-trial reviews with a time estimate of no more than one hour			23A, para 6.2
2.2 The provisions of PD 23 para 6.2 (see 2.1 above) shall not apply (i) at the hearing of an application made without notice; (ii) if all the parties are unrepresented; or (iii) where more than four parties want to make representations (two parties represented by the same person count as one only)			23A, para 6.3

	Form No	CPR Rule	PD
2.3 The court may order the whole or part of an application, to which PD 23 para 6.2 (see 2.1 above) does not apply, to be dealt with by a telephone hearing either of its own initiative or at the request of the parties. The court will not normally make an order under para 6.5 unless all parties entitled to be heard consent.			23A, paras 6.5–6.8
If the court does make an order under para 6.5 it will give any directions which are necessary for the telephone hearing.			
2.4 A request that a hearing under paragraph 6.2 shall not be conducted by telephone			
(i) must be made at least 7 days before the hearing or such shorter period as the court may permit and (ii) may be made by letter			
The court will determine the application without a hearing			23A, para 6.4
3. Preparation for the hearing			
3.1 In the absence of any direction to the contrary the directions listed in para 6.10 of the PD will apply and in particular the designated legal representative is responsible for arranging the telephone conference			23A, para 6.10
3.2 Where a document is required to be filed and served the party or the designated legal representative must do so no later than 4pm at least 2 days before the hearing. It is good practice to mark the covering letter URGENT and specify the date and time of the hearing in bold type.			23A, para 6.11
3.3 A case summary and draft order must be filed and served in: (a) multi track cases; and (b) small and fast track cases if the court so directs. Any other document upon which a party seeks to rely must be filed and served in accordance with the period specified in paragraph 6.11.			23A, para 6.12 and 6.13

	Form No	CPR Rule	PD
4. The Hearing			
4.1 There can be no attendance before the judge on the hearing by a party or his representative unless the other parties to the application have agreed			23A, para 6.9
4.2 The hearing will be subject to the normal rules of procedure and the court will normally give a reasoned judgment at the conclusion of the telephone hearing and will deal with costs. The telephone charges will be treated as part of the costs of the application			
4.3 The basic provisions for the conduct of telephone hearings are set out in Practice Direction 23, paras 6.9 and 6.10 and BT Conferencing has made recommendations for the steps to achieve a successful telephone conference (email telephonehearings@bt.com)			23A, paras 6.9 and 6.10
4.4 The judge should keep by note or tape recording brief details of the proceedings including the date and a short statement of the decision taken			23A, para 8
5. Video conferencing			
5.1 Where a video conference is required and the court in question has such facilities application should be made to the Master or District Judge			23A, para 7
5.2 The court may allow a witness to give evidence through a video link or by other means and guidance for its use is given in Part 32, Annex 3. This is in part based on the protocol of the Federal Court of Australia		32.3	32, para 29.1 and Annex 3
5.3 For judicial statements as to evidence see: *Rowland v Bock* [2002] EWHC 692 (QB), [2002] 4 All ER 370 per Newman J at p 374; *Rowlands v Rentokil* [2003] EWHC 967 (QB), [2003] All ER (D) 111 (Apr); and *Polanski v Condé Nast Publications Ltd* [2005] Times, 18 February, HL			

	Form No	CPR Rule	PD
5.4 In *Pastouna v Black* [2005] EWCA Civ 1389, [2005] NLJR 1847 Brooke LJ stressed it was incumbent on legal advisers to take all steps possible in accordance with CPR 1.1 and 1.3 to reduce the cost of proceedings including taking advantage of such cost saving facilities as video conferencing when they were available.			
5.5 For discussion in the specialist court guides see Admiralty and Commercial Court Guide, section H3 and Chancery Guide, paras 14.14–14.17 and (telephone conference only) paras 7.12.8 and 7.12.11 of the Queen's Bench Guide.			

TABLE 15—DISCLOSURE AND INSPECTION

TAB 15

	Form No	CPR Rule	PD
1. Preliminary			
1.1 Normal disclosure is limited to 'standard disclosure' see para 2 below and the search for documents is limited to that which is reasonable and proportionate. The parties from the outset must decide what is proportionate and what are the real issues in the case and limit disclosure accordingly see CPR 31 [5]			
In civil proceedings a litigant's right to a fair trial under Art 6 ECHR entitles him to be given sufficient information of the evidential case against him to enable him to give effective instructions concerning the allegations against him: *Bank Mellat v HM Treasury* (2010) Times, 18 May, CA.			

	Form No	CPR Rule	PD
For detailed consideration of 'reasonable search' see *Nichia Corpn v Argos Ltd* [2007] EWCA Civ 741, [2007] All ER (D) 299 (Jul) where Jacob LJ stressed that the disclosing party should before making disclosure consider each document and not disclose a mass of background documents which do not really take the case one way or another. For a more detailed consideration of the guidance given in the judgment as to 'reasonable search' and 'standard disclosure' see article by District Judge Exton in Gazette, 5 June 2008, page 28. 'Lawyers should be encouraged at an early stage in the litigation process to consider the documents necessary to establish or defend the claim' per Jackson LJ in his review of costs in civil litigation. The duty to disclose extends to hard copy and electronic documents; electronic documents include data on portable devices, back-up systems and servers, and see PD 31B.			
1.2 Part 31 does not apply to small claims		27.2(1)(b)	
1.3 A party discloses a document by stating that document exists or has existed		31.2	
1.4 'Document' means anything in which information is recorded and **'copy'** means anything onto which information in a document has been copied by any means		31.4	

	Form No	CPR Rule	PD
1.4A The definition extends to electronic documents of which a non-exclusive list is contained in the Practice Direction to which reference should be made where **electronic disclosure** is being considered. It has been suggested, see Gazette (2007) 18 October, page 1, that judges need special e-disclosure training to equip them to interpret the broadly drafted rules. It may well be that the bulk of the judiciary agree with this view. For the vital importance of having the right 'tools' for e-disclosure and discovery and the costs considerations see article by Dr JC Scholtes 'Digging with the right tools' in Sol Jo (2009) 3 February, page 18 and article by Tracey Stretton 'Endless Possibilities' in Sol Jo Expert Witness Supplement, Spring 2009.			31, para 2A.1–2A.5
There is no duty on parties to preserve documents before proceedings are commenced but after that the situation radically changes. See *Earles v Barclays Bank plc* [2009] EWHC 2500 (QB), [2009] All ER (D) 179 (Oct), (2009) Times, 20 October as to this in relation to electronic data and CPR PD 31B, para 7.			31B, para 7
For 'reasonable search' for disclosure of electronic documents see *Digicel (St Lucia) Ltd v Cable & Wireless plc* [2008] EWHC 2522 (Ch), 23 October, Morgan J and article 'A shock to the system' by Sautter and Church, (2009) NLJ 23 January, page 111 and 'In search of reasonableness' by Chris Paley-Menzies (2009) NLJ, 29 May, page 792. It is to be noted that £2m and nearly 7,000 hours of legal time did not achieve a word search that was considered 'reasonable'. See also CPR PD 31B, paras 20–24.			31B, paras 20–24

	Form No	CPR Rule	PD
For a case where an application for e-disclosure (the application sought to require the defendant to search its back-up tapes for further electronic documents) was refused see *Fiddes v Channel 4 Television Corpn* [2010] EWCA Civ 516 and an article discussing the decision by Louise Buchanan in (2010) NLJ, 9 July, page 972 entitled 'E-utopia'. It is to be noted that Pill LJ upheld the decision at first instance on the basis of **reluctance to interfere with a management decision** of a first instance judge.			
For a case setting out the approach of the court where the parties cannot agree the terms on which a search of electronically stored information (ESI) should be made see *Goodale v The Ministry of Justice* [2010] EWCA Civ B40 (QB).			
For the disclosure of electronic documents for multi-track proceedings commenced on or after 1 October 2010 see PD 31B and para 1.17 below in this TAB.			
Those practising in civil courts are expected to know about and apply CPR PD 31, para 2A. Failure to do so is gross incompetence and will be taken into account when determining orders for costs: *Earles v Barclays Bank plc* above.			
In his final report on his **Review of Civil Litigation Costs**, Chapter 37, Lord Justice Jackson recognises that 'e-disclosure is inevitable in cases where the parties hold the relevant material electronically' and recommends that the judiciary familiarise itself with technologies which will whittle down the relevant documents. He makes it clear there will be no excuse for solicitors, barristers or judges who are ignorant on the subject.			

	Form No	CPR Rule	PD
For **claims started on or after 1 October 2010** allocated or likely to be allocated to the multi-track or where the court so orders **CPR PD 31B** will apply; see 1.17 below in this TAB.			
1.5 The duty of disclosure continues throughout the proceedings and see PD 31B, para 7 as to electronic documents.		31.11	31A, para 1.3
1.6 Only in a very exceptional case will a party be ordered to deliver witness statements before receiving disclosure from the other party: *Watford Petroleum Ltd v Interoil Trading SA* [2003] EWCA Civ 1417, [2003] All ER (D) 175 (Sep)			
1.7 The legal representative of a party giving disclosure must 'endeavour to ensure that the person making the disclosure statement … understands the duty of disclosure under Part 31'			31A, para 4.4
1.8 In a claim of privilege based on the **'without prejudice' rule** the crucial consideration is whether or not in the course of negotiations the parties contemplated or might reasonably have contemplated litigation if they could not agree: *Barnetson v Framlington Group Ltd* [2007] EWCA Civ 502, [2007] 3 All ER 1054. See also *Stax Claimants v The Bank of Nova Scotia Channel Islands Ltd* [2007] EWHC 1153 (Ch), [2007] All ER (D) 215 (May), [2007] LS Gazette, 2 August, page 28 and *Galliford Try Construction Ltd v Mott Macdonald Ltd* [2008] EWHC 603 (TCC), [2008] All ER (D) 30 (Apr).			

	Form No	CPR Rule	PD
For the exceptional circumstances where privileged communications will be admissible in evidence see *Unilever v Proctor & Gamble* [2000] 1 WLR 2436 where the three occasions on which 'without prejudice' statements can be referred to in evidence were stated by Longmore LJ to be: (a) to decide whether agreement to settle has been reached (b) to show that the agreement resulted from fraud or undue influence; or (c) where an estoppel is asserted. See further the *Oceanbulk Shipping* case at 1.14 below and article 'Keeping schtum' by Bryden Salter (2010) NLJ, 8 October, page 1363.			
For the practical aspects of the 'Without Prejudice' rule and its application see *Ofulue v Bossert* [2009] UKHL 16, [2009] 3 All ER 93 and detailed consideration of that decision in an article 'Lessons in Without Prejudice' by Crampin and Williams in New Law Journal (2009) 15 May, page 709. It was held that 'without prejudice' correspondence seeking to settle one case was not admissible in a subsequent case between the same parties save where it was wholly unconnected with the issue on those proceedings.			
1.9 For the consequence of revealing part of a privileged document or some privileged documents relevant to an issue see *Fulham Leisure Holdings Ltd v Nicholson Graham and Jones* [2006] EWHC 158 (Ch), [2006] 2 All ER 599 and 1.13 below.			

	Form No	CPR Rule	PD
1.10 For disclosure of without prejudice offers made by the parties during **mediation** see *Earl of Malmesbury v Strutt and Parker* [2008] EWHC 616 (QB), [2008] All ER (D) 339 (Apr) where the parties agreed the judge should know the offers made and *Cumbria Waste Management Ltd and Lakeland Waste Management Ltd v Baines Wilson* [2008] EWHC 786 (QB), [2008] BLR 330 where one party to the mediation would not waive privilege and the judge refused to order disclosure to preserve the freedom enjoyed by negotiators. For full discussion of the position see article by Tony Allen, 'Enforced Security', NLJ, 16 May 2008, page 688			
1.11 For **litigation privilege** see *London Pipeline & Storage Ltd v Total UK* [2008] EWHC 1729 (Comm), [2008] All ER (D) 294 (Jul).			
1.12 For **legal professional privilege** see *Three Rivers District Council v Bank of England (No 6)* [2005] 1 AC 610 as to the extent of the communication between solicitor and client covered by legal professional privilege.			
In *Prudential plc and Prudential (Gibraltar) Ltd v Special Commissions of Income Tax and Philip Pandolfo* [2008] EWHC 2494 (Admin) the court held that legal advice privilege does not extend to communications with accountants, even if they relate to legal advice. This decision is the subject of an appeal in which the Law Society has been given leave to intervene; see 'Practice points: legal professional privilege', Gazette, 13 May 2010, page 25.			
Legal professional privilege is the privilege of the client and only the client can waive it. See, for example, *Quinn Direct Assurance v Law Society* [2010] EWCA Civ 805, [2010] All ER (D) 134 (Jul) where the Court of Appeal upheld the High Court's decision that insurers could not have access to documents seized from a firm of solicitors during an intervention by the Solicitors Regulation Authority.			

	Form No	CPR Rule	PD
1.13 For the question of breach of **confidentiality** see *Napier and Irwin Mitchell v Pressdram* [2009] EWCA Civ 443, (2009) Sol Jo (no 20) 41, where the Court of Appeal refused to recognise it 'to protect' the interests of a solicitor against whom an adverse finding has been made by the Law Society adjudication panel. See further as to disclosrue of confidential documents *Croft House Care Ltd v Durham County Council* [2010] All ER (D) 12 (May).			
Under English law in-house lawyers are entitled to assert legal professional privilege over confidential communications with other individuals in the same corporate entity, but in EU law, legal professional privilege does not apply to legal advice given in these circumstances by in-house lawyers: *Akzo Nobel and Akoros Chemicals v Commission (Case C-550/107P)* (2010) Sol Jo, 21 September, page 4.			
1.14 The long established rule, that evidence of **pre-contract negotiation** is inadmissible when a contract is being interpreted was upheld but somewhat undermined by the obiter statements of the House of Lords in *Chartbrook v Persimmon Homes* [2009] UKHL 38, [2009] 3 WLR 267 which regarded them as *prima facie* admissible where they provide background which is potentially relevant. See further article 'Causing a stir' in Sol Jo (2009) 28 July, page 18 by Bramhall and Hodgson and 'The edifice begins to crack' in NLJ (2009), 16 October by John Pease.			
1.15 For **waiver of privilege** and the question of consequential further disclosure see *Fulham Leisure Holding Ltd v Nicholson Graham and Jones* [2006] EWHC 158 (Ch); *Dore v Leicester County Council* [2010] EWHC 34 (Ch); and article 'Selective disclosure' by Preece and Vannelli, (2010) Sol Jo, 23 March, page 13; and 1.9 above.			

	Form No	CPR Rule	PD
1.16 The 'long-established rule' (see 1.14 of this TAB above) was again upheld by the Court of Appeal in *Oceanbulk Shipping Corn v TMT Asia Ltd* [2010] EWCA Civ 79 but see the dissenting judgment of Ward LJ which underlines a degree of judicial disagreement. For detailed consideration see an article by Andrew Butler in (2010) Sol Jo 16 March, page 14 entitled 'Dubious privilege'.			
1.17 Practice Direction 31B is expressed to 'encourage and assist the parties reach agreement in relation to the **disclosure of electronic documents** in a proportionate and cost effective manner.			31B, para 2
Unless the court otherwise orders the PD only applies to:			
(a) proceedings that are (or are likely to be) allocated to **the multi track**;			31B, para 3
(b) proceedings started **on or after 10 October 2010** – paragraphs 2A.2 to 2A.5 of PD 31A continues to apply to proceedings issued before that date.			31B, para 4
For definitions, see:			
'Data Sampling'			31B, para 5(1)
'Disclosure Date'			31B, para 5(2)
'Electronic Document'			31B, para 5(3)
'Electronic Image'			31B, para 5(4)
'Electronic Documents Questionnaire' which means the questionnaire in the Schedule to the PD			
'Keyword Search'			31B, para 5(5)
'Metadata'			31B, para 5(6)
'Native Electronic Document'			31B, para 5(7)
'Optical Character Recognition (OCR)'			31B, para 5(8)
PD 36B requires the parties to keep in mind the general principles of: • efficient management to minimise costs;			31B, para 5(9)

	Form No	CPR Rule	PD
• use of technology for document management; • giving effect to the overriding objective; • making documents available for inspection in a way that it gives the other party the same ability to access etc the documents as the providing party; • only documents relevant to the proceedings should be disclosed.			31B, para 6
As soon as litigation is contemplated clients must be notified of the need to **preserve disclosable documents** including electronic documents that would otherwise be deleted.			31B, para 7
PD 31B makes further provision for: • discussions between the parties before the first CMC in relation to the use of technology and disclosure; • the Electronic Documents Questionnaire; • preparation for the first CMC; • the reasonable search; • keyword and other automated searches; • disclosure of metadata; • list of documents. Note in particular that the Form N265 may be amended to accommodate the sub-paragraphs CPR 31, paras 30(2)–(7); • provision of Disclosure Data in electronic form; • provision of electronic copies of disclosed documents. Note in particular that the parties should co-operate at an early stage about the format in which Electronic Documents are to be provided for inspection; • specialised technology.			31B, paras 8 and 9 31B, paras 10–13 31B, paras 14–16 31B, paras 20–24 31B, paras 25–27 31B, paras 28–29 31B, para 30 31B, para 31 31B, paras 32–35 31B, para 36
The **Electronic Documents Questionnaire** is annexed to PD 31B; the answers to the questionnaire must be verified by a statement of truth.			31B, para 11

	Form No	CPR Rule	PD
If the parties indicate that the cannot agree as to disclosure of Electronic Documents the court will give written directions at a separate hearing and when doing so will consider making an order for completion and exchange of all or part of the Electronic Document Questionnaire.			31B, para 15
The person signing the questionnaire should attend the first case management conference and any subsequent hearing at which disclosure is likely to be considered.			31B, para 16
Guidance notes are given at the end of the questionnaire			
• For a short form of questionnaire see article by Mark Clark in Sol Jo (2010) 20 April at page 18 (before the publication of PD 31B).			
2. Standard disclosure			
2.1 Standard disclosure requires a party to disclose only: (a) documents on which he relies and (b) documents which- (i) adversely affect his own case (ii) adversely affect another party's case (iii) support another party's case and (c) documents he is required to disclose by a practice direction		31.6	31A, para 1.1
2.2 An order to give disclosure is an order to give standard disclosure unless the court otherwise directs		31.3(1)	
2.3 The court, or the parties in writing may dispense with or limit standard disclosure. Any agreement between the parties has to be lodged with the court		31.5(2) and (3)	31A, para 1.4

	Form No	CPR Rule	PD
2.4 When giving standard disclosure a party must make **reasonable search** for documents within CPR 36.6(b) and (c): see para 2.1 above and see also the guidance given as to this by Jacob, Rix and Pill LJJ in *Nichia Corpn v Argos Ltd* [2007] EWCA Civ 741, [2007] All ER (D) 299 (Jul). For reasonable search and electronic documents see para 1, sub-para 4 above		31.7(1)	
The factors relevant in deciding reasonableness include: (a) the number of documents (b) the nature and complexity of the proceedings (c) ease and expense of retrieval (d) significance of documents likely to be located		31.7(2)	31A, para 2
2.5 The duty to disclose is limited to those documents which are or have been in a party's control		31.8	
2.6 For helpful guidance in preparing a disclosure list see Butterworths Personal Injury Newsletter (2010) Vol 2, Issue 3, March, pages 4–5			
3. Procedure for standard disclosure			
3.1 Each party must make and serve on every other party a list of documents in the relevant practice form	N265	31.10(2)	31A, para 3
The list is divided into 3 sections, which follow the enclosure statement: (a) first, documents which the party has within his control and does not object to produce; (b) second, documents which the party has within his control but objects to the other party inspecting; (c) third, documents that the party has had within his control but are no longer within his control.			

	Form No	CPR Rule	PD
3.2 The list must indicate: (a) the documents in respect of which it is claimed there is a right or duty to withhold inspect and (b) those documents which are no longer in the party's control and what has happened to them		31.10(4)	31A, paras 4, 5 and 6; 6.1 and 6.2
For the disclosure of copies that have been marked see		31.9	
For the disclosure of electronic documents see			31A, para 2A.1–2A.5
3.3 The list must include a **disclosure statement**. The solicitor for a party must try to ensure his client or the person signing on the client's behalf understands the duty of disclosure			31A, para 4.4
3.4 For the form of the statement see		31.10(6)	31A, para 4.2 and annex
For the ability to amend form N265 where a party is giving disclosure of documents see			31B, para 30
For the person by whom the statement is to be made see		31.10(6) and (7)	31A, para 4.2 and 4.3
For signature by an insurer or the Motor Insurers' Bureau see			31A, para 4.7
3.5 For withholding disclosure on the ground that disclosure would damage the **public interest** see		31.19(1) and(2)	
3.6 The parties may agree or the court may direct that disclosure or inspection, or both, shall take place in stages; typically where a split trial has been ordered		31.13	
4. The right of inspection of a disclosed document			
4.1 A party to whom a party has disclosed a document has a right to inspect it except where: (a) the document is no longer in the control of the party who disclosed it (see CPR 31.8)		31.3(1)(a)	
(b) the party disclosing the document has a right or duty to withhold inspection of it (see CPR 31.19)		31.3(1)(b)	

	Form No	CPR Rule	PD
(c) the party considers it would be disproportionate to the issues provided he has so indicated in his disclosure statement		31.3(2)	
4.2 For the right to inspect **documents referred to in statements of case etc** see		31.14(1)	
For the right to inspect a document referred to in a witness statement being displaced by a claim of privilege see *Expandable Ltd v Rubin* [2008] EWCA Civ 59, [2008] All ER (D) 148 (Feb), (2008) NLJ, 29 February, page 332 where the court held as to the sufficiency of 'mention' that the document in question doesn't have to be relied upon, referred to in any particular way or for any particular purpose. See also Civil Litigation Brief, Sol Jo (2008) 25 March, page 22.			
See further for disclosure of documents mentioned in witness statements the judgment of Nicol J in *Webster v Ridgeway Foundation School Governors* [2009] EWHC 1140 (QB), (2009) Sol Jo (no 22) 31, where limitations on the right to disclosure of such documents, including questions of proportionality, relevance, redaction, interference with private lives and Article 8 of the European Convention on Human Rights 1950, were fully considered.			
Exhibits attached to a witness statement were held not to be protected from discovery in *Accident Exchanges Ltd v Autofocus Ltd* [2009] EWHC 3304 (QB) because they comprised material collected by the witness on which he might be called to give evidence: see also note by Stephen Gold (2010) NLJ 19 February, page 261.			
4.3 For inspection of documents any document mentioned in an expert's report which has not already been disclosed in the proceedings etc see		31.14(2)	31A, para 7.1 and 7.2

	Form No	CPR Rule	PD
5. Specific disclosure or inspection			
5.1 The court may make an order for **specific disclosure** requiring a party to do one or more of (a) disclosing documents or classes of documents specified in the order (b) carrying out a search to the extent stated in the order (c) disclosing any documents located as a result of that search			
5.2 The court may make an order for **specific inspection** requiring a party to permit inspection of a documents referred to in CPR 31.3(2): (see para 4.1 above as to inspection considered disproportionate)		31.12	31A, para 5.1–5.5
5.3 The application will be made in accordance with Part 23 and even if the order is granted costs may be reserved until the court can evaluate the evidential value of material obtained (see CPR 31.12[1] and [2]	N244		
5.4 For a recent expression of the court's attitude to orders for specific discovery and the application of para 5.4 of CPR PD 31A and of the overriding objective see *Martin v Triggs Turner Barton (a firm)* [2008] EWHC 89 (Ch), (2008) Times, 5 February where an appeal against the making of a specific disclosure order was dismissed			
6. Inspection and copying of documents			
6.1 Where a party has a right of inspection he must give written notice of his wish to inspection and such inspection must be permitted and more than 7 days after the date on which the notice was received		31.15(a) and (b)	
6.2 A party may request a copy of a document and if he also undertakes to pay reasonable copying charges he must be supplied with a copy not more than 7 days after receipt of the request			
6.3 For the right or duty to **withhold inspection** see		31.15(c)	

	Form No	CPR Rule	PD
For discussion of refusal of inspection by reason of privilege see CPR 31 [2] –[15]		31.19(3)–(7)	
For use of **privileged documents inadvertently disclosed** see		31.20	
7. Relationship of disclosure and strike out			
A court will be reluctant to strike out the particulars of claim of a case arguably so speculative as to be an abuse of process before ordering disclosure under Part 31 so that the claimant can see if it has an arguable case; *Arsenal Football Club plc v Elite Sports Distribution Ltd* [2002] EWHC 3057 (Ch), [2002] FSR 450, [2003] 07 LS Gaz R 36.			
8. Disclosure before the start of proceedings			
8.1 This is now available in all proceedings see CPR 31.16[1] Where there has been a breach of the pre-action protocol, the defendant should be put on written notice that unless there is a compliance within, say, 14 days an application for pre-action disclosure will be made			
8.2 The application is made by application notice and must be supported by evidence; see *Lawrence v Metropolitan Police Comr* [2006] EWCA Civ 425	N244	25.4 31.16(2)	
The statement to be relied on should provide: (a) brief circumstances of the claim; (b) the date of the letter of claim and any acknowledgment; (c) the date of expiry of the protocol period and details of any breaches			
There should be attached to the statement (a) copy correspondence between the parties (b) a draft order requiring the defendant to file a statement with time limits for compliance and a schedule of the documents sought			

	Form No	CPR Rule	PD
(c) a statement of costs			
8.3 The court can only make an order for pre-action disclosure if there is a real prospect in principle of such an order being **fair to the parties** if litigation was commenced, or of assisting the parties **to avoid litigation** or of **saving costs** in any event; *Black v Sumitomo Corpn* [2001] EWCA Civ 1819, [2002] 1 WLR 1562 recently followed in *Hands v Morrison Construction Services* [2006] EWHC 2018 (Ch)		31.16(3)(d)	
Further the court can only make such an order where: (a) the respondent is likely to be a party to subsequent proceedings, and those proceedings are properly arguable, and that the applicant is also likely to be a party to those proceedings and (b) if proceedings were started the respondents duty by way of standard disclosure would extend to the documents or classes of documents of which the applicant seeks disclosure (c) pre-action disclosure is desirable to dispose fairly of the anticipated proceedings, assist the resolution of the dispute without proceedings or save costs It is only when all these matters are satisfied that the court can exercise its discretion to grant or refuse the order: *Independent Froebel Education Institute v Sodexho Education Services Ltd* [2007] EWHC 150 (QB), [2007] All ER (D) 51 (Feb)			
There is no power to order pre-action disclosure of medical records because it is too early to establish their relevance and determine if they would adversely affect either party's case. Further, they are private records protected under ECHR art 8 and 8(2); *OCS Group v Davina Wells* [2008] EWHC 919 (QB), [2009] 1 WLR 1895, 103 BMLR 17.			

	Form No	CPR Rule	PD
Issues of pre-action disclosure have frequently arisen in mis-selling litigation. In *Knowle v Barclays Bank* [2010] EWHC 1900 (Comm) on appeal the High Court held that to obtain an order for pre-action disclosure it is not necessary to establish a real prospect of success but the application must not be speculative and the applicant must raise a meaningful issue that requires an answer. In this case the application was found to be speculative. In *Pineway v London Mining Co Ltd* [2010] All ER(D) 208 (May) the Court held that where the application was for general pre-action disclosure (a fishing expedition) a real prospect of success had to be shown.			
8.4 When hearing an application for pre-action disclosure the courts should be hesitant about deciding substantive issues in the anticipated proceedings: *Rose v Lynx Express Ltd* [2004] EWCA Civ 447, (2004) Times, 23 April. See also *Total E & P Soudan SA v Edmonds* [2007] EWCA Civ 50, [2007] All ER (D) 303 (Jan) and *Hutchinson 3G (UK) Ltd v O2 (UK) Ltd* [2008] EWHC 50 (Comm), [2008] All ER (D) 80 (Jan), 18 January			
8.5 For the **form of the order** if granted see		31.16(4) and (5)	
8.6 For **precedents** see **BCCP D[21]** and **BCCP D[22]**			
8.7 For **costs** see CPR 48.1 at para CPR 48.1 and see also **CPR 31.16 [4B]** and *SES Contracting Ltd v UK Coal plc* [2007] EWCA Civ 791, (2007) Times, 1 October where the court confirmed that the respondent to such an application was ordinarily awarded his costs. A costs order against the respondent would only be appropriate where it was clearly unreasonable to oppose the application or where the manner of the opposition was so unreasonable as to make it appropriate to require him to bear the whole of both parties' costs. For a case where unreasonable opposition was found see *Bermuda International Securities Ltd v KPMG* [2001] EWCA Civ 26.			

	Form No	CPR Rule	PD
9. Orders for disclosure against a person not a party			
9.1 Such orders are now available in all proceedings see **CPR 31.17[1]** and, by way of example, *Ixis Corporate and Investment Bank v WestLB AG* [2007] EWHC 1748 (Comm), [2007] All ER (D) 276 (Jul) (see final para of 9.3 below)		37.17	
9.2 Application is made by application notice and must be supported by evidence	N244	25.4 31.17(2)	
9.3 The court may only make the order for disclosure against a non party where: (a) the documents of which disclosure is sought are likely to support the case of the applicant or adversely affect the case of one of the other parties to the proceedings and (b) disclosure is necessary to dispose fairly of the claim or to save costs		31.17(3)	
See *Three Rivers District Council v HM Treasury* (2002) Times, 4 October, CA where CHADWICK LJ indicated that 'likely' had the meaning 'might well' in r 31.17(3)(a)			
For the exercise of the court's discretion under *Norwich Pharmacal Co v Customs and Excise Comrs* [1974] AC 133 principles against third parties, who were mere witnesses innocent of any participation in the wrong-doing, being investigated as a remedy of last resort see *Mitsui Co Ltd v Nexen Petroleum UK Ltd* [2005] EWHC 625 (Ch), [2005] 3 All ER 51, ChD, per Lightman J; and *BNP Paribas v TH Global Ltd* [2009] EWHC 37 (Ch), [2009] All ER (D) 83 (Jan).			

	Form No	CPR Rule	PD
The court in *R (Mohamed) v Secretary of State for Foreign and Commonwealth Affairs (No 1)* [2010] EWHC 2048 (Admin), [2009] 1 WLR 2579, DC confirmed that the jurisdiction to grant such relief is an exceptional one and one which it will only exercise if necessary. In deciding whether it is necessary the court will have regard to all the circumstances.			
The applicant does not have to show that the information sought: (a) is vital to enable pleadings to be settled or that it could not be obtained by any other practicable means; (b) that all other avenues through which the information might be obtained have been exhausted.			
The court in *Mohamed* regarded the jurisdiction as 'flexible and open' and sought to remove artificial barriers to its use. In *Financial Times v UK (Application No 821/03 (FT))* however the ECHR found such an order to be in breach of the newspaper's human rights under Art 10 of the European Convention on Human Rights; for detailed discussion see article 'The big chill' by Anna FitzHerbert in (2010) NLJ, 26 February, page 307.			
Pre-action non party disclosure was the subject of the decision in *Yuri Nikitin v Richards Butler LLP* [2007] EWHC 173 (QB), [2007] All ER (D) 129 (Feb) where it was stressed that the person against whom the order is sought must be (a) mixed up in the wrongdoing or (b) likely to be able to provide the information necessary to enable the ultimate wrongdoer to be sued			

	Form No	CPR Rule	PD
For detailed consideration see article 'Mere Suspicion' by Sam Nafassi in New Law Journal [2007] 27 July, page 1076 The court held in *Ixis Corporate and Investment Bank v WestLB AG* [2007] EWHC 1748 (Comm), [2007] All ER (D) 276 (Jul) that the non party disclosure sought was necessary to fairly dispose of the case and made an order pursuant to r 31.17; concerns about privacy and confidentiality could be dealt with by proper redaction of the document disclosed. The party giving disclosure would be entitled to the costs of the disclosure exercise.			
For a full statement of the principles applicable see *Flood v Times Newspapers Ltd; Berezovksy v Comr of the Police of the Metropolis and Independent Police Complaints Comr* [2009] EWHC 411 (QB), [2009] EMLR 311, 5 March 2009 and note the importance attached by the court that this 'intrusive jurisdiction' is not used inappropriately even by consent. It was also stated that having for its consideration any submission made by a third party would be helpful. See article 'Balancing act' by Masood Ahmed (2009) Sol Jo, 26 June, page 10.			
9.4 For the **form of the order** see		31.17(4) and (5)	
9.5 For **precedents** see **BCCP D[23]-BCCP D[24]**			
9.6 For **costs** of non party pre-commencement disclosure and orders for disclosure see CPR 48.2 at para **CPR 48.2**			
10 For disclosure in **judicial review proceedings** see *Tweed v Parades Commission for Northern Ireland* [2006] UKHL 53, [2006] All ER (D) 175 (Dec) and articles by Charles Brasted in New Law Journal [2007] 16 February, page 257			

	Form No	CPR Rule	PD
10A For access to court documents filed in defence see *R (on the application of Corner House Research) v Director of the Serious Fraud Office* [2008] EWHC 714 (Admin), [2008] NLJR 556 and article by Francesca Richmond in (2008) NLJ 14 and 21 March, page 395. This case was the subject of appeals to the Court of Appeal and subsequently to the House of Lords. The decision of the Court of Appeal was overturned by the House of Lords who held that the SFO was entitled to end the investigation of BAE contracts with the Saudi government.			
11. Detailed assessment of costs and disclosure			
11.1 Disclosure is not ordered in detailed assessments, as it is in general litigation, because the documents in question are almost certain to be privileged. There is however a requirement in the Costs PD, para 40.11 to file the documents listed in the Costs PD, para 40.12 when filing a request for detailed assessment. If there is a dispute as to the receiving party's liability to pay costs to the solicitors who acted for him, the documents listed in the Costs PD, para 40.2 must be filed			Costs PD, para 40.2, 11 and 12
11.1A For disclosure of the relevant details of an additional liability see			Costs PD, para 32.5
11.2 The court may require the receiving party to produce any document which it believes is necessary for it to reach a decision. The court can require the party who produced the document to elect whether, if he wants to rely on the document as evidence, he will allow or refuse to allow disclosure of the document to the other party. If he refuses he cannot rely on that document as evidence but can rely on other evidence.			Costs PD, para 40.14
The question of costs privilege is fully dealt with by the Kings Chambers Costs Team in NLJ 14 September and 21 September 2007.			

	Form No	CPR Rule	PD
12. Subsequent use of disclosed documents and completed Electronic Documents Questionnaires			
12.1 The circumstances where a party may use documents that have been disclosed other than for the purpose of the proceedings are set out in CPR 31.22(1).		31.22	
12.2 If disclosure to a third party is sought in circumstances not covered by sub-para (1) an application must be made to the court. For the principles to be applied see *Sita UK Group Holdings v Serruys* [2009] EWHC 869 (QB), [2009] STC 1595 (Jack J), 29 April, and the cases considered by the judge; see also CPR 31.22(1) to (5).			
For the purpose of this rule an Electronic Documents Questionnaire which has been completed and served by another party pursuant to Practice Direction 31B is to be treated as if it is a document which has been disclosed.		31.22(4)	31B

TABLE 16—EXPERT EVIDENCE

TAB 16

	Form No	CPR Rule	PD
1. Preliminary			
1.1 See **CPR 35 [1]–CPR 35 [8]** and note in particular: (a) the only provisions of CPR Pt 35 that apply to **small claims** are: (i) CPR 35.1 – duty to restrict expert evidence (ii) CPR 35.3 – experts – overriding duty to the court (iii) CPR 35.7 – court power to direct evidence to be by a single joint expert (iv) CPR 35.8 – instructions to single joint expert			

	Form No	CPR Rule	PD
(aa) Practice Direction 35 – Experts and Assessors – was newly substituted by the Civil Procedure (Amendment) Rules 2009 in July 2009; the annex to it 'Protocol for the instruction of experts to give evidence in civil cases' has been retained. (b) the **pre-action protocol for personal injury claims** encourages and promotes voluntary disclosure of medical reports but failure to disclose the report of an expert instructed in accordance with the protocol (who is not a jointly instructed expert) does not constitute non-compliance with the protocol: *Carlson v Townsend* [2001] EWCA Civ 511, [2001] 3 All ER 663. In this case the expert was jointly selected by the parties but instructed by the claimant alone (c) a party who obtains expert evidence without an appropriate direction from the court does so at his own risk as to costs unless he has complied with the pre-action protocol (d) Practice Direction (Pre-Action Conduct) came into force on 6 April 2009 and Annex C comprises guidance on instructing experts The main tasks of experts in litigation have been neatly summarised in NLJ, 30 April 2010 by Mark Salon in an article entitled 'Working Relationship' as: • To prepare a written report for use in evidence by one or more parties and to assist the court in deciding the dispute (rule 35.5). • To answer written questions on the report for the purpose of clarification only (rule 35.6).			

	Form No	CPR Rule	PD
• To attend a discussion with an expert instructed by the other party if possible to narrow the area of disagreement and produce an agreed note for the parties and the court, if required by the court, under rule 35.12. • To give oral evidence and be cross-examined on the written report at trial if required by the court. (e) the aspiration to achieve equality of arms between the parties need not result in an absolute rule requiring each side to have an equal number of experts. Proportionality was one of the matters relevant and on some occasions it could be right to deviate from equality in number of experts; see *Kirkman v Euro Exide Corpn (CMP Batteries Ltd)* [2007] EWCA Civ 66, (2007) Times, 6 February, CA, particularly Lady Justice Smith: 'The desirability of equality of arms was not intended to result in an absolute rule … There may be circumstances in which the general rule should give way for the sake of achieving the overriding objective and dealing with the case justly'			
(f) at present expert witnesses enjoy immunity from action for negligence in relation to preparation for and taking part in a trial. The basis for the immunity is *Stanton v Callaghan* [2000] QB 75. Leave has, however, been given in *Jones v Kaney* [2010] EWHC 61 (QB), [2010] All ER (D) 131 (Jan) for appeal direct to the Supreme Court on the issue of expert witness immunity.			

	Form No	CPR Rule	PD
For discussion see NLJ (2010) 16 April, page 533, article 'All change' by Roddy Macleod; Sol Jo (2010) 11 May, page 26, 'Update: professional negligence' by Victoria Brackett and Katie Papworth and Sol Jo Expert Witness Supplement 2010, page 16, article by William Featherby QC and Henry Charles entitled ' A suit of armour'.			
(g) in *K/S Lincoln v CB Richard Ellis Hotels Ltd (No 2)* [2010] EWHC 1156 (TCC), [2010] All ER (D) 138 (Jun) it was decided that a judge at first instance should analyse a valuer's liability by consideration of the result arrived at rather than the methodology by which he arrived at the result. The court further stated that as a result of general principle the margin for error for valuations permitted is: (i) for a standard residential property – plus of minus 5%; (ii) for a one-off property – plus or minus 10%; (iii) where there were exceptional features of the property – plus or minus 15% or even higher in an appropriate case.			
1.2 The Legal Services Commission has published a consultation paper on 'the use of Experts Quality, Price and Procedure in Publicly Funded Cases'. The Judges' Council has responded to this. The Council considers (a) a requirement of compulsory accreditation as a pre-condition for providing expert reports or giving expert evidence in publicly-funded cases to be neither practicable nor desirable (b) providing guideline rates for fees for bands of cases in all frequently encountered areas of work to be desirable			

	Form No	CPR Rule	PD
(c) the fixing of fair and reasonable rates is essential if appropriate expertise is to be available to publicly-funded litigants so that there is no question of developing a second class of expert available to publicly-funded litigants			
In the short term the same rates are to be paid to experts in civil and criminal cases.			
1.3 The Justice Minister has indicated support for the mandatory accreditation of expert witnesses: Gazette, 13 November 2008, page 4			
1.4 The Law Society's 'Expert Witness Directory Helpline' 020 7393 7780 provides assistance in locating suitable experts			
An expert witness directory index in pull-out form is included in NLJ (2009) 26 June, after page 918 and Solicitor's Journal published in Summer 2009 an Expert Witness Supplement. See also article 'Selecting the Best' by Mark Salon (2008) NLJ, 19 September, page 1299 and 24 October, page 1496 and 'Decisions, decisions' (2009) NLJ, 26 June by the same author.			
When deciding on an appropriate expert it is prudent to consider his CV and also to ascertain what courses and professional training the expert has undertaken; see article 'Establishing expertise' by Graham Rogers in the Sol Jo Expert Witness Supplement for Spring 2009, at page 20 and article 'Medical attention' by David Oldham, (2009) Sol Jo, 16 June, page 15.			
1.5 A **clinical case manager** is not an expert but a witness of fact and is not subject to Part 35: he owes a duty only to the client: *Wright v Sullivan* [2005] EWCA Civ 656, [2006] RTR 116			
1.6 Lord Justice Jackson in his Final Report on the **Review of Civil Litigation Costs** considers five areas of possible saving:			

	Form No	CPR Rule	PD
(a) prolixity; (b) when experts should be instructed; (c) case management; (d) single joint experts; and (e) 'hot tubbing'.			
For detailed consideration see an article 'Expensive decisions' in (2010) NLJ 26 March, page 460.			
2 Powers and duties of the court			
No party shall call an expert to give oral evidence or put an expert's report in evidence without the **permission of the court**. A party can seek such permission by application in which he must identify:	N244	35.4(1) and (2)	
(a) the field in which expert evidence is required, and (b) when practicable, the name of the proposed expert			
An '**expert**' is a person who has been instructed to give or prepare expert evidence; for the purpose of proceedings where the instructions are given by two or more parties to the proceedings (including the claimant) he will be a '**single joint expert**'.		35.2(1) and (2)	
The court's order will relate only to the expert or expert field identified and it may limit the amount of the expert's fees and expenses that may be recovered from any other party		35.4(3) and (4)	
Where a claim has been allocated to the small claims track or fast track permission will normally be for only one expert on a particular issue		35.4(3A), 35.7	Protocol annexed to CPR 35, at para 7
Where an order requires an act to be done by an expert, or otherwise affects him, the party instructing the expert must serve a copy of the order on the expert. If the expert is jointly instructed the claimant must serve the order			35, para 8

	Form No	CPR Rule	PD
It is provided that expert evidence **shall be restricted** to that which is reasonably required to resolve the proceedings. This places a duty on the court and the court may exclude expert evidence if it would not be helpful in resolving any issue justly: *Barings plc v Coopers & Lybrand* (2001) Times, 7 March and *Clifford v Chief Constable of the Hertford Constabulary* [2008] EWHC 2549 (QB), [2008] All ER (D) 254 per Wyn Williams J. It is interesting to compare with that approach the course adopted by the court in *Stewart v Glaze* [2009] EWHC 704 (QB), 153 Sol Jo (no 16) 28 where it was stated that the expert accident reconstruction evidence provided a useful means of testing the factual evidence and the inferences to be drawn from it. That however was the limit of its use. This followed the principles set out in *Liddell v Middleton* [1996] PIQR P36. The Court of Appeal in *Heyward v Plymouth Hospital Trust* (2005) Times, 2 August held is was 'sensible and proportionate' to limit expert evidence to one consultant psychiatrist for each party in a relatively small claim for psychiatric injury.		35.1	
Exceptional circumstances are required before the court is likely to give permission for a party to adduce evidence of a second expert in the same discipline as the first. For a case where the circumstances were exceptional and such permission was granted see *S v Chesterfield and North Derbyshire Royal Hospital NHS Trust* [2003] EWCA Civ 1284, [2003] 38 LS Gaz R 34 but for a case where the circumstances were held not to be exceptional and permission was refused see *Beaumont v Ministry of Defence* [2009] EWHC 1258 (QB), [2009] All ER (D) 47 (Oct).			
Permission is not required if the evidence of the expert is evidence of fact only: *Gall v Chief Constable of the West Midlands* [2006] EWCA Civ 2638, [2006] All ER (D) 297 (Oct)			

	Form No	CPR Rule	PD
For the attitude of the Technology and Construction Court to a witness giving factual evidence (in this case an engineer) making statements of opinion based on his experience although not called as an expert see *Multiplex Constructions (UK) Ltd v Cleveland Bridge UK Ltd* [2008] QBD (TCC) (2008) Gazette LR 16 October, page 22 and article 'Expert evidences form witnesses of fact' by Janna Purdie in NLJ (2008) 17 October, page 1449 and 'Permission to Speak' article by Jonathan Raynes in Sol Jo Expert Witness Supplement, Spring 2009.			
A distinction must be drawn between the weight to be given to expert evidence and the competence of the witness to appear as an expert: *R (on the application of Doughty) v Ely Magistrates' Court* [2008] EWHC 522 (Admin), 172 JP 259.			
For the admission of video surveillance evidence for use in cross-examination of a claimant in a personal injury case see *Rall v Hume* [2001] EWCA Civ 146, [2001] 3 All ER 248			
3. Experts' reports			
Expert evidence is to be given in a **written report** unless the court directs otherwise and if a claim is on the small claims track or the fast track the court will not direct an expert to attend a hearing unless it is necessary to do so in the interests of justice		35.5	
The requirement for the **form and content of expert's reports** are set out in Practice Direction 35 and the provisions of the Rule. See also the Protocol for the Instruction of Experts to give Evidence in Civil Claims at **CPR (35) GUIDE**. In particular note that the experts' reports must contain statement that they: (i) understand their duty to the court and have complied and will continue to comply with it; and			

	Form No	CPR Rule	PD
(ii) are aware of the requirements of Part 35 and PD 35, the protocol for the instruction of experts to give evidence in civil claims and the practice direction on pre-action conduct.		35.10	35, para 3.1 and para 13.5 of the Protocol
When giving evidence at court an expert could be cross-examined as to his knowledge of the requirements and his understanding of his duty.			
As to the form of statement of truth for experts, see			35, para 3.3
The wording is mandatory and must not be modified. See also the Protocol for the Instruction of Experts to Give Evidence in Civil Claims, para 13 – Contents of Experts' Reports			
Solicitors who instruct experts must check reports to ensure the statement of truth and that of awareness exactly complies with the requirements of the rule and the PD.			
The expert's duty is to help the court on matters within his expertise; this is paramount and overrides any obligation experts owe to those from whom they have received instructions or by whom they are paid. The danger of an expert losing sight of this is provided by the decision of Roderick Evans J in *Williams v Jervis* [2008] EWHC 2346 (QB) in which he described the expert as looking at the claim 'through the prism of his own disbelief'. The expert's report must be addressed to the court. It has been suggested that the CPR seek to transform the role of experts from party champions to what are in effect court assistants. This is the subject of argument.		35.3	35, para 2.2

	Form No	CPR Rule	PD
The **experts' fees** should be proportionate to the case. See *Kranidiotes v Paschali* [2001] EWCA Civ 357, [2001] All ER (D) 342 (Mar) where accountants quoted a fee of £75,000 for valuing a shareholding which the judge restricted to £10,000. Experts' fees may be the subject of assessment at the conclusion of the case so time recording and detailed invoices are likely to be necessary. Cancellation fees will also have to be justified. For average charging rates for reports and court appearances see NLJ (2007) 26 October, p 1480, article by Dr Chris Pamplin and NLJ (2008) 25 January by Mark Salon. Avoiding disputes with experts about fees and the terms that should be included in the contract between expert and his client are helpfully reviewed and considered by Mark Solon in his article 'Fee simple?' published in NLJ (2009) 22 May, page 756. For the power of the court to limit the amount of an expert's fee and expenses that can be recovered from another party see		35.4(4)	
If a jointly instructed sole expert, who is to be paid equally by each of the parties as provided by a court order, cannot obtain payment from either party he is in a position to request a court under its management powers to stay the action until he is paid. There is also a right to sue in contract for payment.			
Where the parties have permission to instruct separate experts, the permission will normally be limited to one expert each in the same discipline. Where, however, the case is substantial and the issues complex permission may be given for more than one expert of the same discipline: *ES v Chesterfield and Northern Derbyshire Royal Hospital NHS Trust* [2003] EWCA Civ 1284			

	Form No	CPR Rule	PD
For the necessity of the court to avoid 'inequality of arms' see *Heyward v Plymouth Hospital NHS Trust* [2005] EWCA Civ 939, (2005) Times, 1 August, CA, per Smith LJ but see also para 1.1(d) of this TAB			
For the costs of an expert, acting for a litigant in person, for work done by him which would normally be done by a solicitor see *Agassi v Robinson (Inspector of Taxes)(Bar Council intervening)* [2005] EWCA Civ 1507, [2006] 1 All ER 900 where such costs were held to be irrecoverable			
4. Report by a single joint expert			
Where two or more parties wish to submit expert evidence on a particular issue, the court may direct that evidence on that issue is to be given by a single joint expert. The use of single experts is encouraged by the rules. The pre-action protocol for personal injury cases, at paras 3.17–3.19, requires a party to nominate a list of one or more experts he wishes to instruct and gives the other party 14 days to object to some or all of the experts nominated. On the **multi-track**, unless the parties agree, the court will not of its own initiative direct that there shall be a joint expert without holding a case management conference		35.7(1)	35, para 7 29, para 4.13
Machinery is provided by the rules for **selection of the joint expert** where the parties cannot agree		35.7(2)	
For the position where there is a relationship between the proposed expert and one of the parties, see *Liverpool Roman Catholic Archdiocesan Trust v Goldberg (No 2)* [2001] 4 All ER 950, Ch Div			
A single joint expert will typically be appointed in a claim of low value containing a simple issue on quantum or in a more complex case on a minor issue			

	Form No	CPR Rule	PD
If it is necessary to **challenge the report of a jointly instructed expert,** guidance has been provided by: LORD WOOLF CJ in *Daniels v Walker* [2000] 1 WLR 1382, CA and in *Peet v Mid-Kent Healthcare NHS Trust* [2001] EWCA Civ 1703, [2002] 3 All ER 688; and NEUBERGER J in *Cosgrove v Pattison* (2001) Times, 13 February and in *Layland v Fairview New Homes plc* [2002] EWHC 1350 (Ch), [2002] All ER (D) 102 (Jul)			
The report of an expert separately instructed without the permission of the court can be exhibited to an application seeking permission for a court order permitting instruction of a separate expert. Guidance is given for the court's consideration when deciding whether to order a single joint expert.		35.7	35, para 7
When seeking permission for expert evidence it is important to tailor submissions to the factors set out in the practice direction; see further article 'Bring your own' (2009) Sol Jo, 17 November, page 8 by Catherine Carter Shaw.			
For discussion see CPR 35.7 [2]; for precedent of application by party dissatisfied with the joint expert to instruct his own expert see **BCCP D[118]**			
Where a party is permitted to substitute one expert witness for another that party can be required, as a condition for the permission, to disclose the discarded expert's report: *Beck v Ministry of Defence* [2003] EWCA Civ 1043, (2003) Times, 21 July. Permission will only be required if the order permitting the obtaining of an expert's report named the expert to be instructed: *Vasiliou v Higigeourgiou* [2005] EWCA Civ 236, [2005] 3 All ER 17. If this is not done the way is open for **'expert shopping'**. For detailed discussion see (2007) NLJ 30 March, article by Mark Jones and (2007) Sol Jo, 30 November, article by Janice McMullen			

	Form No	CPR Rule	PD
5. Instructions to a single joint expert			
Any relevant "instructing party" may (provided the court has given a direction under r 35.7 for a single joint expert) **give instructions** to the expert and must at the same time send a copy of the instructions to the other relevant parties		35.8(1) and (2)	
The court may give directions as to the expert's fees and expenses and as to any inspection, examination or experiment which the expert wishes to carry out		35.8(3)	
The court may limit fees and expenses and give directions for the amount fixed to be paid into court by some or all of the relevant parties.		35.8(4)	
Unless the court otherwise directs the relevant parties are jointly and severally liable for the payment of the expert's fees and expenses		35.8(5)	
A conflict of interest does not automatically disqualify that expert's evidence but the conflict must be promptly disclosed so the court may decide whether it could act in reliance on the expert's evidence: *Toth v Jarman* [2006] EWCA Civ 1028, [2006] 4 All ER 1276, (2006) Times, 17 August. The court recommended that an expert's report should include statements that: (a) he has no conflict of interest other than as disclosed in his report (b) he did not consider any conflict disclosed adversely affected his suitability as an expert witness (c) he would advise the party instructing him of any change of circumstances in respect of (a) or (b)			
An expert's determination outside the scope of his authority as laid out in the contract has no effect between the parties: *Homepace Ltd v Sita South East Ltd* [2008] EWCA Civ 1, [2008] All ER (D) 18 (Jan)			

	Form No	CPR Rule	PD
6. Written questions to experts			
A party may put written questions about an expert's report, which must be proportionate, to: (a) an expert instructed by another party or (b) a single joint expert appointed under rule 35.7		35.6(1)	
This can only be done once, must be within **28 days** of service of the expert's report and be only for the purpose of clarification of the report, unless the other party agrees or the court gives permission: see *Mutch v Allen* [2001] EWCA Civ 76, [2001] All ER (D) 121 (Jan)		35.6(2)	
When questions are sent to the expert a copy of the questions should be sent to the other party			35, para 6.1
The party instructing the expert must pay the expert's fee for answering any question put under 35.6 but this does not affect who shall ultimately be ordered to pay the expert's fees			35, para 6.2
The answers when received will be treated as part of the report		35.6(3)	
If the expert does not answer the court may order: (a) that the evidence of the expert cannot be relied on, and/or (b) that the party may not recover the fees and expenses of that expert from any other party		35.6(4)	
The ordering of a pre-trial meeting of the experts has been held not to prejudice a fair trial and not to raise any question of breach of Art 6 of the Convention Rights and Freedoms (para **III HUM [28]**): *Hubbard v Lambeth Southwark and Lewisham Health Authority* [2001] EWCA Civ 1455, (2001) Times, 8 October			
Separate Experts **7. Discussions between experts**			
The court may direct that there be a discussion between the experts and may specify the issues to be discussed. Unless directed by the court discussions are not mandatory.		35.12(1) and (2)	35, para 9.1

	Form No	CPR Rule	PD
The court may also direct that after the discussion the experts prepare a statement for the court showing those issues on which: (a) they agree and (b) they disagree, with a summary of their reasons for disagreeing		35.12(3)	
To facilitate the discussion and to save costs the court will frequently order that the discussion be by telephone conference if that is feasible. In any event arrangments for discussion should be proportionate – in small and fast track claims a meeting will rarely be appropriate and a telephone discussion or even an exchange of letters will normally suffice. In multi-track cases video-conferences can often be a method of meeting the availability of busy experts. See article by Mark Solon 'A matter of protocol' (2010) NLJ, page 1305.			
Generally only the experts should attend. They can agree or disagree and need no authority from the client or lawyer to sign the joint statement which should be done promptly. If lawyers are present it will only be to answer questions for the experts.			
Where as a result of the joint discussion the expert of one party changes his mind so that the experts agree permission will only in a rare case be given to that party to instruct a new expert: *Stallwood v David* [2006] EWHC 2600 (QB), (2006) Times, 27 December, [2006] All ER (D) 286 (Oct)			
Cases in these circumstances where permission to instruct a new expert was refused include *Singh v CJ O'Shea* [2009] EWHC 1251 (QB), [2009] All ER (D) 230 (Feb) where the first expert's change of stance was for good reason.			

	Form No	CPR Rule	PD
A joint statement prepared by experts pursuant to a direction of the court pursuant to rule 35.12 is not privileged and its status remains unchanged although the report was ordered for the purpose of mediation: *Aird v Prime Meridian Ltd* [2006] EWCA Civ 1866. The parties can however, agree that it be privileged and if that is the case they should cause their agreement to be incorporated in the order. In this appeal May LJ stressed that the court cannot order the parties to engage in mediation and that the most the court can do is encourage For precedent of such an application, see **BCCP D[125]**			
8. Failure to disclose expert's report			
This will prevent the use of the expert's report at trial or calling the expert to give oral evidence unless the court gives permission. It is necessary that the client gives instructions for the report to be disclosed.		35.13	
There is no power to order the disclosure of an expert's draft report; it remains privileged and that has not been affected by CPR Part 35: *Jackson v Marley Davenport Ltd* [2004] EWCA Civ 1225, (2004) Times, 7 October			

	Form No	CPR Rule	PD
The court will not usually order a party to disclose an expert's report obtained pre-action (see *Carlson v Townsend* [2001] EWCA Civ 511) but when that expert has performed tests on the exhibit open justice and fairness would demand that the results of those tests be put before the court, particularly if there was some perception that the tests might have caused an alteration in the exhibit: *Carruthers v MP Fireworks* (26 January 2007, unreported), Bristol County Court. An extension of this principle occurred in *Pittalis v Ruzzala and Hendon Glazing* 19 September 2008 (unreported but see article by Emily Formby 'Tactical manoeuvres' Sol Jo Expert Witness Supplement, Summer 2009 at page 13) where a medical report 3.5 years old was not relied on by the claimant and was ordered to be disclosed to the defendant's expert, although it was privileged, so he would know the claimant's condition at the time of that report as well as at the date of his examination. A half-way house short of disclosure of the earliest report is an order for disclosure of objectively obtained medical facts and conditions.			
Where a party does disclose an expert's report but does not call the maker to give evidence or otherwise put the report in evidence the other party may use that report relying on the provisions for admissibility of hearsay evidence: *Shephard & Neame v EDF Energy Networks* [2008] EWHC 123 (TCC) and article by Gordon Exall in Sol Jo Civil Litigation Brief, 25 March 2008, page 22			
9. Expert's right to ask court for directions			
Experts may file written requests for directions to assist them in carrying out their functions and unless the court otherwise orders must provide copies of the proposed requests for directions: (a) to the party instructing them at least 7 days before filing; and			

	Form No	CPR Rule	PD
(b) to all other parties at least 4 days before filing.		35.14	
10. Joint Expert – attendance at trial There should be no need for the report of a single joint expert to be amplified or tested by cross-examination. His report was the evidence: *Peet v Mid-Kent Health Care Trust* [2001] EWCA Civ 1703, [2002] 3 All ER 688, [2002] 1 WLR 210. The court has a discretion to allow a joint expert to be cross-examined: see *Peet*, above and *Sara Austin v Oxford City Council* [2002] LTL, 14 June, QBD **11. Experts – difficulties as to trial date**			
See *Rollinson v Kimberly Clark Ltd* (1999) Times, 22 June, CA and *Matthews v Tarmac Brick and Tiles Ltd* (1999) 54 BMLR 139, CA		35.10(4)	
12. Costs liability of expert and his witness immunity			
In *Phillips v Symes* [2004] EWHC 2330 (Ch), [2005] 4 AlL ER 519, [2005] 2 All ER (Comm) 538 it was held that the Court had power to make a costs order against an expert who by his evidence caused significant expense by reckless disregard of his duties to the court			
This witness immunity from civil suit enjoyed by the expert does not extend to fitness to practice proceedings: *Meadow v General Medical Council* [2006] EWCA Civ 1390, (2006) Times, 31 October. By a majority, however, the Court of Appeal held that the evidence given by Sir Roy Meadow in the case of Sally Clark did not represent serious professional misconduct; see article 'Experts Exonerated' by Peter Gooderham (2007) NLJ, 21 September, page 1285			

	Form No	CPR Rule	PD
13. Instructions to experts – disclosure			
Once the expert's report is disclosed a court will not order disclosure of the instructions unless it is satisfied there are reasonable grounds for considering that the statement of instructions given to the expert was inaccurate: *Lucas v Barking, Havering and Redbridge Hospitals NHS Trust* [2003] EWCA Civ 1102, [2003] 4 All ER 720, [2004] 1 WLR 220		35.10(4)	
CPR do require the substance of all material on the basis of which the report was written to be disclosed and expressly provide that the instructions given to him are not privileged. An expert's earlier or draft reports remain privileged: *Jackson v Marley Davenport Ltd* [2004] EWCA Civ 1225, (2004) Times, 7 October		35.10(4)	
Where a party is given the court's permission to adduce expert evidence, but that expert is not named, he is entitled to reject the report of the expert first instructed, if he wishes to do so, and instruct another expert without any further permission from the court: *Vasiliou v Hajigeorgiou* [2005] EWCA Civ 236, (2005) Times, 22 March			
14. Protocols			
In particular note the Protocol for the Instruction of Experts to give Evidence in civil claims			35
Further note: (a) Pre-action protocol for personal injuries, paras 2.11, 2.12 and 3.14–3.21, also Annex C – "Letter of Instruction to Medical Expert" (b) Pre-action protocol for clinical disputes, paras 4.1–4.3 (c) Pre-action protocol for construction and engineering disputes, paras 3, 4.1 and 4.3.1 (d) Pre action protocol for professional negligence, paras B2.2, B7.1–B7.3 and C6.1–C6.4			

	Form No	CPR Rule	PD
(e) Pre-action protocol for housing repair cases, paras 9.11, 9.18 and Annex C 'Letter of Instruction to Expert' (f) The Practice Direction Pre-action Conduct, para 9.4 and Annex C			
15. The judge preferring lay evidence The Court of Appeal in *Armstrong v First York* [2005] EWCA Civ 277, [2005] 1 WLR 2751, (2005) Times, 19 January when dismissing the appeal stated there was no principle of law preventing a judge preferring lay evidence found to be honest to the directly conflicting evidence of a jointly instructed expert even if he could not identify any fault in that evidence. The Court also referred at para 33 to *Coopers Payen v Southampton Container Terminal Ltd* [2003[EWCA Civ 1223, [2004] 1 Lloyds Rep 331 and stressed that 'there is no rule that a judge has to explain why he cannot accept expert evidence at a technical level and on that evidence's own merits' However, where expert evidence is relevant the judge has to consider it when reaching his conclusions on the credibility of all the witnesses: *Hall v Jakto Transport Ltd* [2005] EWCA Civ 1327, (2005) Times, 28 November . See also *G and B (Children)* (2009) below in next paragraph.			

	Form No	CPR Rule	PD
15A. The judge rejecting the evidence of one expert			
The trial judge must explain why he has rejected the evidence of one of the experts. It is not sufficient to say that the other expert is highly reputable and represetntative of a responsible body of medical opinion: *Smith v Southampton University Hospital NHS Trust* [2007] EWCA Civ 387, 96 BMLR 79. See also *G and B (children) (fact-finding hearing)* [2009] EWCA Civ 10, [2010] 1 FCR 73, [2009] 1 FLR 1145 where it was held that there must be material on which the judge can safely found his disagreement with an expert and that the judge must exaplin fully the reasons for rejecting the expert's evidence.			
16. Experts' reports and personal injuries claimed to result from a low velocity impact In *Kearsley v Klarfeld* [2005] EWCA Civ 1510, [2006] 2 All ER 303 such a claim was allocated to the multi-track and it was stated that there was no requirement for a defence in such a case to include an allegation of fraud or fabrication; it is sufficient if the defence fully sets out the facts on which the judge will be asked to draw an inference See also 'Crash Course in LVI Claims' [2006] NLJ, 27 January, Boyd Morwood and Mathew Snarr and their further article 'Restoring Disorder' [2006] NLJ 1870 following the decision in *Casey v Cartwright* (see below) The Court of Appeal has most recently provide guidance in this sort of case in *Casey v Cartwright* [2006] EWCA Civ 1280, [2007] 2 All ER 78. A defendant wishing to raise causation in this type of case should: (a) within three months of receipt of the letter of claim notify all parties in writing that he regards the case to be one of low impact and intends to raise the causation issue; (b) expressly identify the issue in his defence; and			

	Form No	CPR Rule	PD
(c) within 21 days of filing a defence raising causation file at the court and serve on the other party a witness statement clearly identifying the grounds on which the issue is raised			
For a full discussion of these guidelines see All ER Annual Review 2007, para 19.43			
On the basis of the written statement the court will decide whether to give permission for the claimant to be medically examined by the defendant's expert and at a later stage after service by the defendant of his medical evidence decide whether to give permission for the defendant to rely on such evidence at trial. The guidance given by the Court of Appeal should be carefully considered by both parties in such cases for it is not set out fully in this TAB. A fuller summary can be seen in New Law Journal for 27 October 2006 in the 'Personal Injury Update' written by Roger Harris			
17. Supplementary reports			
Fresh evidence obtained after the expert's report may well make it necessary for him to update or supplement his original report. Each further report must be dated and signed and contain a statement of truth. It should be appropriately marked on the front sheet, e g 'First Supplementary Report'.			
18. Late reports			
If the time for delivery becomes impossible to meet and attempt should be made to agree an extension with the other party. If agreement cannot be achieved and application under Part 23 should be made for the required extension of time.			

TABLE 17—SMALL CLAIMS

TAB 17

	Form No	CPR Rule	PD
1. Preliminary			
See **CPR 27 [1]–CPR 27 [3]** and note in particular that a party may be represented by a **lay representative** provided the party is present throughout: Lay Representatives (Rights of Audience) Order 1999. For rights of representation generally, see *Avinue Ltd v Sunrule Ltd* (2003) Times, 5 December, CA where the party was a limited company and see the guidance given by the joint practice note issued jiontly by the President and the Master of the Rolls on 13 July 2010 (note in particular that whilst the McKenzie Friend may charge for the provision of reasonable assistance that charge is not recoverable from the opposing party).			27, para 3
A number of courts operate their own **small claims mediation schemes** but the Courts Service has decided to put an in-house small claims mediator in every court before April 2008. This is a result of a pilot scheme operated in Manchester since June 2005. See Gazette 19 July 2007, at page 3			
Annex B of the Practice Direction (Pre-Action Conduct) sets out the specific information that should be provided in a debt claim by a claimant who is a business against a defendant who is an individual. In appropriate cases this should be meticulously complied with			
For normal scope of small claims track see "Allocation" Procedural Table **TAB 13** and **CPR 26.6** and for allocation fees payable see **TAB 13** at part 2, 4th para		26.6	
The parties may **consent to the allocation** to the small claims track of a claim which exceeds the value limits for the track. The small claims track costs provisions will apply unless the parties agree that fast track costs provisions shall apply		26.7(3), 27.14(5)	

	Form No	CPR Rule	PD
Judicial case management of a small claim will usually comprise only the issue of Allocation Questionnaires and directions given by a district judge when allocating to track. There is considerable scope for case management by the parties			
On the claimant filing an allocation questionnaire or it being dispensed with or where there is automatic allocation the claimant (or defendant if the action is proceeding on the counterclaim alone) has to pay a fee of £35 if the claim is on the small claims track and exceeds £1,500.			
Before allocating the claim to the small claims track and giving directions for a hearing the court may require any party to give further information about that party's case. Further, a party may ask the court to give particular directions about the conduct of the case			27, paras 2.3 and 2.4
In deciding whether to make an order for the exchange of witness statements the court will have regard to:			
(a) whether either or both of the parties are represented; (b) the amount in dispute; (c) nature of dispute; (d) whether statements can be avoided by a request for information; (e) the need to avoid undue formality, cost or delay.			27, para 2.5
It should be noted that in Appendix A of the Practice Direction it is indicated that the court will normally require statements in road traffic cases			27, Appendix A
2. Preliminary hearing			
Notice of allocation will be sent out either with notice of a preliminary hearing or of a final hearing with directions for the parties to carry out. The court can give notice that it proposes to deal with the claim without a hearing but this is rarely done		27.4, 27.4(1)(c)	

	Form No	CPR Rule	PD
The court may hold a preliminary hearing only:		27.6	
(a) where: (i) it considers special directions are necessary to ensure a fair hearing, and (ii) it appears necessary for a party to attend at court to ensure he understands what he must do to comply with the special directions, or (b) to enable it to dispose of the claim on the basis that one or other of the parties has no real prospect of success at a final hearing, or (c) to strike out a statement of case or part of a statement of case which discloses no reasonable grounds for bringing or defending the claim			
The parties will be given 14 days' notice of the preliminary hearing and the court can, with the agreement of the parties, treat the preliminary hearing as the final hearing		27.6(3) and (4)	
The court must have regard to the desirability of limiting the expense to the parties of attending court		27.6(2)	
In practice a preliminary hearing will only very rarely be directed and then only because the complexity of the claim makes it unlikely that justice can be done between the litigants, especially if unrepresented, without explaining to them what will be expected of them in preparation and at the final hearing			
3. Directions			
At or after the preliminary hearing the court will fix the date of the final hearing, inform the parties of the time allowed for the final hearing and give directions		27.6(5)	

	Form No	CPR Rule	PD
Where a preliminary hearing is not held the court will give directions which will be sent out with the allocation notice. The parties will be informed, at the same time, of the date the hearing is to take place and the time allowed Alternatively, but rarely, the court having given special directions will consider what further directions are to be given no later than 28 days after the date the special directions were given		27.4	
The court will be concerned not only to give appropriate directions but to ensure that they are complied with prior to the hearing as the next occasion that the case is considered will almost certainly be the date of the hearing. The danger of adjournments and applications for costs because of unreasonable behaviour are all too apparent			
When giving directions, the court will have available details of the information and documentation the court usually needs in particular types of case set out in Appendix A of **CPR PD 27**. These are: (a) Road traffic claims (b) Building disputes, repairs, goods sold and similar contractual claims (c) Landlord and tenant claims (d) Breach of duty claims (negligence, deficient professional services and the like) The court will also have available the Standard Directions in Appendix B and Special Directions in Appendix C The Standard Directions include the encouragement of the parties to meet with a view to settling the claim or narrowing the issues			27

	Form No	CPR Rule	PD
If the parties have submitted proposed directions the court may well make those directions–perhaps with some additions or amendments, particularly if they are agreed by all parties. Otherwise it is virtually inevitable that the court will choose the most appropriate of the pro forma it has available, add special directions and, where the observance of a direction is vital either to doing justice or to dealing with the case in the time allotted, impose **sanctions for default**. If a Defence to Counterclaim, or more rarely a Reply, is necessary the court will order it			27, para 2.4
Sanctions to enforce compliance with the directions will vary depending on representation or otherwise. Where the parties are represented, a direction "that in default of due compliance the defaulting party's case do stand struck out and the other party be able to proceed accordingly" might well be appropriate but if the parties are unrepresented it is probably too draconian and a more appropriate direction would be that "default in compliance is likely to lead to an adjournment of the hearing and consideration by the court of an appropriate costs order"			
4. Parts of the rules that do not apply on small claims track			
The following parts of the CPR do not apply to small claims: (a) CPR Pt 25 – interim remedies (except interim injunctions) (b) CPR Pt 31 – disclosure and inspection (c) CPR Pt 32 – evidence (except CPR 32.1, power for court to control evidence) (d) CPR Pt 33 – miscellaneous rules as to evidence			

	Form No	CPR Rule	PD
(e) CPR Pt 35 – experts and assessors (except CPR 35.1 – duty to restrict expert evidence; CPR 35.3 – experts overriding duty to the court; CPR 35.7 – court's power to order evidence by a joint expert; and CPR 35.8 – instructions to single joint expert) (f) Subject to the court's right of its own initiative to order a party to provide further information (see 27.2(3), Part 18 – Further information (g) CPR Pt 36 – offers to settle (h) CPR Pt 39 – hearings (except the general rule that hearings are to be in public) **5. Expert evidence**		27.2	
No expert can give evidence, oral or written, without the permission of the court. If directing expert evidence the court will order joint instructions if possible. A specimen direction appears in Appendix C to the Practice Direction. Where the parties are both in person, letters of instructions may be beyond them and an additional direction may be necessary that they jointly seek the assistance of, perhaps, the Citizens Advice Bureau in complying with the direction		27.5	27, Appendix C, Form F
6. Disposal without a hearing			
This is only possible if all the parties agree		27.10	
7. The hearing			
The Rules provide: (a) the court may adopt any procedure it considers fair (b) the hearing will be informal (c) strict rules of evidence do not apply (d) the court need not take evidence on oath (e) the court may limit cross-examination, and (f) the court must give reasons for its decision		27.4	27, para 4.3

	Form No	CPR Rule	PD
A hearing fee is payable by the claimant (or the defendant if the action is proceeding solely on the counterclaim) varying in amount from £25 for a claim not exceeding £300 and £300 for a claim not exceeding £5,000. The fee will be refunded in full if at least 7 days before the hearing date the court received written notice of settlement or discontinuance			
For the place of hearing, whether the hearing be in public or in private, the putting of questions by the court, limiting cross-examination, recording evidence and giving reasons, etc, see			27, paras 4 and 5
Witness statements to stand as evidence in chief, **skeleton arguments** and the smallest possible, but properly paginated, **bundles of documents** are essential tools to enable an advocate, lay or qualified, to make the most of the limited time that will be allowed for presentation For the consequences of **a party failing to attend** a hearing without proper notice, see		27.9(2)–(4)	27 para 6
For the position where a **party does not attend but has**		27.9(1)	
(a) **given at least 7 days' notice to the court** and the other party that he will not attend;			
(b) has served on the other party at least 7 days before the hearing any other documents he has which he has filed with the court; and			
(c) in his written notice to the court has confirmed his compliance with paras (a) and (b) above			

	Form No	CPR Rule	PD
8. The court's powers on the small claims track			
The court may grant any final remedy which it could grant if the proceedings were in the fast track or multi-track. It can award damages (limited to £5,000, unless the parties have consented to allocation to this track under CPR 26.7(3)) and interest, grant an injunction or make a declaration. Its powers to award costs are limited		27.3, 27.14	
9. Costs			
The court may only award on the claim or any appeal: (a) court fees (in whole or part) (b) fixed costs on issue (c) where the claim includes a claim for an injunction or declaration, up to £260 for legal advice and assistance (d) expenses which a party or witness has reasonably incurred travelling to and from the hearing and staying away from home to attend the hearing (in whole or part) (e) loss of earnings or loss of leave for the party and his witnesses up to £50 per day each (f) experts' fees not exceeding £200 for each expert (g) such further costs as the court may assess by the summary procedure and order to be paid by a party who has behaved unreasonably		27.14	27 para 7
The limits on costs also apply to any fee or reward charged by a lay representative: Courts and Legal Services Act 1990 s 11		27.14(4)	
Any order for costs made before the allocation to the small claims track will not be effected by the allocation		44.11(1)	

	Form No	CPR Rule	PD
The cost of an engineer's report in a motor collision claim can only be recovered as damages if the extent of damage or the costs of repair is in issue but could in an appropriate case be recovered as costs: *Mistry v NE Computing* [1997] Current Law Digest May page 19: County Court			
Where a claim has not yet been allocated to track but would if allocated be appropriate for the small claims track the 'no costs' rule should apply prior to allocation: *Voice and Script International v Alghafar* (2003) LTL, 8 May, CA. This proposition had previously been accepted in *Woodings v BT plc* (2003) LTL, 17 March, but here the judge found although the case was of small value it was complicated and would have been allocated to the multi-track But see *Panchal v Maguire* [2006] 1 CL 59 where it was held disposal costs were in the discretion of the trial judge if there has been no allocation to the small claims track and *Lee v Birmingham city Council* [2008] EWCA Civ 891 at **TAB 13**, para 7 above.			
Where the parties have **consented to allocation to the small claim track** notwithstanding that the financial value of the claim exceeds the small claims limit, the claim will be treated as if it was in the small claims track unless the parties agree fast track costs shall apply. A hearing fee of £300 will have to be paid in either event			
Where the parties agree fast track provisions shall apply, the claim and any appeal will be treated for the purposes of costs as if it were proceeding on the fast track except that trial costs will be in the discretion of the court and shall not exceed the amount set out in rule 46.2		27.14(6)	
Where one of the parties has **behaved unreasonably** the court may order such further costs as it may assess summarily. If the claim is one where an application is to be made for costs on this basis there should be prepared:		27.14(2)(g)	

	Form No	CPR Rule	PD
(i) a schedule of the costs claimed (ii) schedule of the unreasonable behaviour A party's rejection of an offer in settlement will not of itself constitute unreasonable behaviour under para 2(d) but the court may take it into consideration when applying the unreasonable test		27.14(3)	
It will be rare that one particular failing will be enough to establish unreasonable behaviour and it is more likely to be the cumulative effect of an uncooperative attitude. The schedule may include, for example, some of the following: (a) failure to respond to a letter before action (b) failure to respond to a letter offering a choice of experts and to a suggestion that there be a joint instruction to an independent expert (c) failure to comply with directions (d) failure to provide requested information (e) failure to respond to an offer of settlement or rejecting it unreasonably (f) the fact that the party applying for costs achieved a better result than that proposed by him in his offer of settlement (g) failure to respond to the submission of proposed directions for the consideration of the court (h) failure to supply a copy of his Allocation Questionnaire and the documents attached to it (i) telephoning the night before the hearing with a suggestion that parties should talk about it (j) pursuing a hopeless case; see *Performing Right Society Ltd v Floravant* [2006] 1 CL 62 (k) failing to attend the hearing or to give notice of his intention not to attend			

	Form No	CPR Rule	PD
10. Setting aside judgment and rehearing			
A party who was not present or represented at the hearing and has not given written notice to the court may nevertheless apply to set aside the judgment and for the rehearing of the claim The application must be made not more than 14 days after the day on which the notice of judgment was served on him		27.11(1) and (2)	
The court may grant such an application only if the applicant: (a) had good reason for not attending or being represented at the hearing, and (b) he has a reasonable prospect of success at the hearing For 'good reason' see *Brazil v Brazil* [2002] EWCA Civ 1135, (2002) Times, 18 October, CA where the defendant's illiteracy was regarded a significant factor		27.11(3)	
If the judgment is set aside the court must fix a date for the rehearing or rehear it immediately. In practice the court will rarely have sufficient time to deal with the rehearing immediately		27.11(4)	
11. Appeal			
CPR Pt 52 and the accompanying Practice Direction deal with appeals; see in particular CPR PD 52, paras 5.8A–5.8D.			52 para 5.8A-5.8D
Where the court dealt with the claim subject to the appeal without a hearing or after the party gave notice under CPR 27.9 that he would not be attending and requesting the court to deal with the case in his absence, permission to appeal should be sought from the appeal court. If permission to appeal is sought by the unsuccessful party at the conclusion of the small claims hearing the court should give reasons if permission is not granted	N460		27 para 8.2
An appellant's notice in small claims must be filed and served in Form N164 (fee £100)	N164		27, para 8A

	Form No	CPR Rule	PD
Where permission to appeal is granted and the appeal itself allowed, the appeal court will, if it is possible, dispose of the case there and then. It may do so without hearing further evidence			27 para 8.3
The 'no costs' rule does now apply on an appeal		27.14(2)	
Hearings will be tape-recorded by the court. A party can obtain a transcript on payment of the proper transcriber's charges			27, para 5.1
For the provision of transcripts at public expense see			52, paras 5.17–5.18

TABLE 17A—SMALL PERSONAL INJURY CLAIMS ON THE SMALL CLAIMS TRACK

TAB 17A

	Form No	CPR Rule	PD
1. Procedural framework			
1.1 The small claims track is the normal track for any claim for personal injuries where: (a) the financial value of the claim is not more that £5,000 and (b) the financial value of any claim for **damages for personal injuries is not more than £1,000**		26.6(1)(a)	
The Lord Chancellor announced in April 2007 that the small claims limit for personal injury claims is to remain unchanged			
1.2 'Claim for personal injuries' is defined as proceedings in which there is a claim for damages for personal injuries to the claimant or any other person or in respect of a person's death		2.3(1)(c)	
1.3 'Personal injuries' include any disease and any impairment of a person's physical or mental condition		2.3(1)(c)	

	Form No	CPR Rule	PD
But damages for frustration, mental distress, injured feelings or annoyance cannot be recovered in a claim for damages for breach of contract (on whatever track it is proceeding) unless an important object of the contract was to provide peace of mind or freedom from distress: *Bliss v South East Thames Regional Health Authority* [1987] ICR 700; *Jarvis v Swan Tours Ltd* [1973] QB 233 (a holiday case); *Farley v Skinner* [2001] UKHL 49, [2001] 3 WLR 899			
1.4 'Damages for personal injuries' means damages claimed as compensation for pain, suffering and loss of amenity. Accordingly, damages for loss of earnings and for damage to property (i e special damages) are not to be taken into account in assessing the financial value of £1,000		26.6(2)	
For the approach of the Court to the quantification of **damages for distress and disappointment** in 'disaster holiday' claims see the judgment of Ward LJ in *Milner and Milner v Carnival plc (trading as Cunard)* [2010] EWCA Civ 389 where he indicated reliance could not be placed on the damages awarded in holiday cases alone and that comparables must be sought in awards of damages in other fields. For full discussion see (2010) Sol Jo, 27 April, pages 2 and 29 and NLJ (2010) 30 April, page 594. It is to be noted that diminution in the value of the holiday and damages for distress and disappointment fall to be assessed separately.			
In *Milner*, at para 37, Ward LJ grouped the awards of damages that were cited to him as follows: (a) cases involving marriage abroad – £4,360-£4,406; (b) honeymoon cases – £321-£1,890; (c) 'special' holidays – £264-£1,161; (d) 'run of the mill' – £83-£876.			

	Form No	CPR Rule	PD
Milner was regarded as an exceptional case being a 'holiday of a lifetime' and damages for disappointment were assessed at £4,000 for the husband and £4,500 for the wife in addition to damages for diminution of £3,500 and £2,000 towards the cost of the wife's gowns specially bought for the holiday cruise.			
Damages for care whether gratuitous or not would not fall to be taken into account in assessing the financial limit. See further section 2.7 below			
1.5 It is for the **court to assess the financial value** of a claim			
1.6 A claimant can **limit his claim** to bring it within the financial limits of the small claims track: *Khiaban v Beard* [2003] EWCA Civ 358, [2003] 3 All ER 362			
1.7 The **parties may consent to the allocation** of a claim exceeding the financial limit **to the small claims track** but in that event there are special rules as to costs: see **TAB 17** para 9, 5th section		26.7(3) 26.14(5)	
1.8 Notwithstanding the value of the small personal injury falls within the financial scope of the small claims track the other matters that the court has to take into account may nevertheless result in allocation to one of the other tracks.		26.8(1)	
2. Valuation			
2.1 The valuation of small personal injury claims is notoriously difficult because there are few reported cases where the Court of Appeal has fixed the quantification of the damages for such a claim. However, in *Oxley v BCH Ltd* (14 July 1998, unreported) the Court of Appeal reduced an award of damages to £1,000 where the claimant received a blow to the head which caused a cut over one of his eyes and headaches. Five months after the accident he had completely recovered save for an insignificant scar over his eye			

	Form No	CPR Rule	PD
2.2 The Judicial Studies Board's Guidelines for the Assessment of General Damages is of little help with small injuries but the figure given for the loss or damage to back teeth is £600 to £1,000 (£1,250 to £2,150 for the loss of one front tooth), the 'bracket' for an undisplaced fracture with full recovery is £1,000 to £1,400 and the 'bracket' for trivial scarring with minor effect only is £1,000 to £2,000.			
2.3 The tariff issued by the Criminal Injuries Compensation Board provides some help for multiple minor injuries. Three separate injuries of the type listed below (of which at least one has significant residual effects six weeks after the accident and at least two visits to a doctor have been necessary in the six week period) give an entitlement to a claim of £1,000: • grazing, cuts, laceration (no permanent scarring); • severe and widespread bruising; • severe soft tissue injury (no permanent disability); • black eye(s), a bloody nose; • hair pulled from the scalp; • loss of fingernail. These are not awards of damages but provide some guidance			

	Form No	CPR Rule	PD
2.4 The usual source of previous awards are those made in the County Court, usually by district judges, quoted in the monthly edition of Current Law and in Kemp & Kemp 'The Quantum of Damages' Vol 4 Section K – minor injuries and in its Release 91 'Low value awards special'. While these sources will provide numerous awards for most small injuries they must be treated with caution because they are published having been reported to the journal by advocates. Awards are usually only noteworthy because they are unusually high or low; nobody is likely to send in details of an award which is typical for the type of injury and for that reason unlikely to be of interest to readers. Current Law and Kemp & Kemp nevertheless are the source of many awards that are cited			
2.5 A medical report will be necessary if more than an extremely modest figure is being sought for personal injuries.			
2.6 For those cases where it is alleged that the claimant's injury, typically a 'whip-lash', must be fabricated or, at least, exaggerated because such a low velocity impact could not have caused it, see **TAB 16** para 15 Relevant aspects may include: (a) angle of impact (b) how the claimant was sitting in the car at impact (c) whether there was a delay in obtaining medical treatment (d) whether physiotherapy was 'hands-on' which would be more effective than the provision of an exercise programme (e) how an injury can be sustained just by missing a step in the home (f) the effect of the seat-belt.			

	Form No	CPR Rule	PD
Where a personal injury claim is tainted by falsehoods to a greater or lesser degree see *Kirk v Walton* [2008] EWHC 1780 (QB), [2008] All ER (D) 323 (Jul) and *Ul-haq v Shah* [2009] EWCA Civ 542, (2009) Times, 6 July 'Accident victims who made fraudulent claim can receive damages' and NLJ (2009) 19 June, page 897, Law Reports. Note in particular CPR 3.4(2) does not provide for a claim to be struck out in these circumstances unless it is not possible or has not been possible to hold a fair hearing. The judge could show his disapproval by his order for costs but could not deprive the claimant of what he had proved to be his entitlement. See also *Arrow Nominees v Blacklege* [2000] 2 BCLC 167, CA the leading authority (not a personal injury case) and *Masood v Zahoor* [2009] EWCA Civ 650, [2009] All ER (D) 33 (Jul). An article 'Dishonest litigants' (2009) NLJ, 6 November, page 1544 by Paterson and Keiller provides detailed consideration. These decisions do not affect the rule that in insurance contracts dishonest exaggeration will result in the whole claim being dismissed: *Axa General Insurance Ltd v Gottlieb and Gottlieb* [2005] EWCA Civ 112, (2005) 1 All ER (Comm) 445.			
2.7 Where there is a small claim for gratuitous care see *Giambrone v JMC Holidays* [2003] Birmingham District Registry, [2003] New Law Journal 100/44, 20 November where the parents had nursed children who were suffering form gastroenteritis while on holiday. The court held that this care gratuitously given fell to be compensated. As to amount of compensation, this should be related to the cost of professional care: see *Evans v Pontypridd Roofing Ltd* [2001] EWCA Civ 1657, [2002] PIQR Q61			

	Form No	CPR Rule	PD
3. Best course of action where the financial value of the personal injury only minimally exceeds the small claims limit			
3.1 The claimant will normally be able to obtain an order allocating the claim to the fast track if he wishes and so be able to seek an order for payment of his legal costs by the defendant			
3.2 The position merits careful analysis for there must be balanced against the advantage of having legal representation throughout any number of risk elements: (a) the claim may succeed but the damages could be £1,000 or less – there would be a real risk that fast track costs will not be awarded and the claimant left to pay his own costs at least (b) the defendant may make a Part 36 offer of a sum of money that the claimant can accept if he wishes. This Is not a procedure which is available in the small claims track		27.2(1)(g)	
If the Part 36 offer is not accepted and not beaten the claimant will be liable not only for his own costs but also for the defendant's costs from 21 days after the payment into court was made		36.14	
(c) the claim may be dismissed and the claimant will not be able to shelter behind a 'no costs' rule as he would on the small claims track, will almost certainly be ordered to pay the defendant's costs of the action as well as his own			
3.3 All the relevant factors have to be considered but if the case involves mainly the personal injury claim and the excess over £1,000 in the valuation of the personal injury claim is small the 'odds' may point to the client's best interest being served by advising that he should act in person and limit his claim for personal injuries to £1,000 (see para 1.6 above)			

	Form No	CPR Rule	PD
4. Personal Injury Protocol			
4.1 See the Practice Direction – (Pre-action Conduct) at **PRO 1** and the Pre-Action Protocol for Personal Injury Claims ('The PI Protocol') at **PRO 2**			PRO 2 para 2.2
4.2 The PI Protocol is intended to apply to all claims which include a claim for personal injury (except industrial diseases)			
4.3 It is primarily designed for those road traffic, tripping and accident at work cases which include an element of personal injury with a value of less than £15,000 which are likely to be allocated to the fast track			PRO 2 para 2.3
4.4 It provides useful guidance for the conduct of a case which is proceeding on the small claims track			PRO 1 para 4.1
4.5 Where a party proposes to instruct an expert, including a medical expert to report on personal injuries, the other party should be given a list of names of one or more experts, in the particular specialty, whom he considers are suitable to instruct			PRO 2 para 3.4
Even if it is obvious form the limited severity of the injury that a short report from the claimant's general practitioner is all that is appropriate it is wise to comply with **PRO 2** para 3.4 to avoid any later argument about the suitability of the expert instructed and the recovery of his fee			
The proposed defendant should indicate any objection in 14 days and for the resolution of any dispute as to the appropriate expert see the Protocol			PRO 2 para 3.16 to 3.18
4.6 As to putting written questions to the expert in his report see the Protocol			PRO 2 para 3.19
4.7 A specimen letter of claim is set out in the Protocol at			PRO 2 para 2.14
This will require to be adapted as necessary			
A letter before action is essential before the issue of proceedings: see **TAB 1** para 1(d) above			

	Form No	CPR Rule	PD
5. Specific requirements of CPR			
5.1 As to statement of value		16.3(3)	
5.2 As to claim for interest (note also **CPR 16.4 [5.11]** above)		16.4	
5.3 The requirements in personal injury claims are for contents of particulars of claim to contain or have attached: (a) the claimant's date of birth (b) brief details of the claimant's personal injuries (c) a schedule of any past and future expenses and losses (d) if the evidence of a medical practitioner is relied upon a medical report			16, para 4
A schedule of details of past and future expenses and losses must be verified by a statement of truth			22, para 1.4(3)
6. The right to compensation for the personal injury			
6.1 The claimant must establish liability in the same way as if the claim related to property damage, eg in a road traffic claim negligence must be proved: *Goundry v Hepworth* [2005] EWCA Civ 1738, 149 Sol Jo LB 1489 where it was stated 'a counsel of perfection should not be applied to a motorist so as to impose an unrealistically high duty of care upon him'			
There is normally no duty to guard a person against an obvious risk, see *Evans v Kosmar Villa Holidays plc* [2007] EWCA Civ 1003, [2008] 1 All ER 530 where the claimant who had dived into water at the shallow end or had dived into water of an unknown depth failed in his claim			
6.2 The claimant to recover damages for personal injury suffered will additionally have to prove that the defendant's wrongful act caused the personal injury complained of (to put it more technically the claimant will have to establish 'causation')			

	Form No	CPR Rule	PD
6.3 The general test of whether the damage was caused by the wrongful act is the consideration of whether it was 'reasonably foreseeable'. If it was not it will generally not be recoverable: see , for example, the decision in *Stewart v Glaze* [2009] EWHC 704 (QB), 153 Sol Jo (no 16) 28 where the defendant car driver was held not liable for the claimant's injury sustained after making an 'inexplicable charge into the road' when he was drunk.			
6.4 A claimant's damages may be reduced if he is guilty of contributory negligence (i e has failed to take due care for his own safety). If a claimant is faced by such an allegation see *Eva (Joseph) Ltd v Reeves* [1938] 2 KB 393 which was applied in *Knight v Wipes Supply Services Ltd* (1965) 109 Sol Jo 358 (driver who had entered a crossing against the lights failed to establish contributory negligence), Similarly *Davis v Hassan* (1967) 117 NLJ 72 where the defendant had jumped a red light.			
The Court of Appeal in *Armsden v Kent Police* [2009] EWCA Civ 631, 153 Sol Jo (no 26) 30 fully considered the contributory negligence of the drivers for the damage arising from a collision between them, one not keeping a proper look out and the other driving at a speed that was excessive when not using the siren fitted (the proportions found were 60/40).			

	Form No	CPR Rule	PD
The damages for personal injury suffered by a passenger in a motor car, who was not wearing an available seat belt, will be reduced by his contributory negligence up to a maximum of 25%: *Froom v Butcher* [1976] QB 286, [1975] 3 All ER 520. Permission to appeal against a finding that was made by a court bound by the decision in *Froom* was refused in *Gawler v Raettig* [2007] EWHC 373 (QB), [2007] All ER (D) 10 (Mar); see Gazette, 13 September 2007, page 30. See also article 'What seat belts have left behind' by Steve Parkin in Sol Jo Expert Witness Supplement, Spring 2009.			
The most recent attempt to persuade the Court that it was a 'rare and exceptional case' justifying the departure from 25%, where damage would have been entirely prevented, was made in *Stanton v Collinson* [2010] All ER (D) 276 (Feb). It was unsuccessful; the Court of Appeal stressed the strong public reasons why the guidelines in Froom were appropriate in most cases. For detailed discussion see article by Karen C Sullivan in NLJ (2010) 26 March, page 454 entitled 'Belt up'.			
It must be remembered that the burden in seat-belt cases is on the defendant who has to prove that damages should be reduced by the failure to wear a seat-belt. In substantial cases this is likely to require medical evidence: see article 'Clunk, no click' by Linda Jacobs in Sol Jo, Bar Focus, May 2010, page 14 and 'Update: road traffic seatbelts' by Stuart Andrews in Sol Jo (2010) 27 July, page 30.			
Where the claimant is faced with two allegations of behaviour which were successfully proved, eg not wearing a seatbelt and allowing himself to be driven by a driver he knew to be drunk, see *Gleeson v Court* [2007] EWHC 2397 (QB), [2008] RTR 10 where the damages were reduced by 30% in the circumstances set out in the example.			

	Form No	CPR Rule	PD
Where a defendant motorist seeks to establish contributory negligence against a claimant pedestrian see *Eagle v Chambers* [2003] EWCA Civ 1107, [2004] RTR 115, and note in particular per Hale LJ: 'It is rare indeed for a pedestrian to be found more responsible than a driver unless the pedestrian has suddenly moved into the path of an on-coming vehicle'			
For a case where the claimant's case was essentially that both drivers were equally to blame but the court found the defendant was not negligent see *Farley v Buckley* [2007] EWCA Civ 403, [2007] All ER (D) 54 (May), Gazette 104/21, 24 May 2007, page 26			
For recent road traffic cases on the apportionment of liability see *Hughes-Jukes v Etti* [2007] RTR 12 where a pedestrian tried to out-run' an oncoming car to a pedestrian crossing. The pedestrian's liability for the accident was assessed at 60% and also see *Buchan v Whiting* [2008] EWHC 2951 (QB), [2008] All ER (D) 122 (Nov) where a motorcyclist driving 'recklessly fast' (50–70 mph in a 30 mph zone) when a car drove into him was found to be 50% to blame and *Heating v Herzog* [2008] 13 Nov (2008) LTL 13 November where there was a finding of 75% contributory negligence.			
The court in *Smith v Finch* [2009] EWHC 53 (QB), [2009] All ER (D) 158 (Jan) would have been prepared to make a finding of contributory negligence against a cyclist not wearing a helmet (although not legally required to do so) but for the failure of the defendant to prove that the helmet would have made any difference; see article by Martin Porter QC in (2009) New Law Journal, 6 March, page 337.			

	Form No	CPR Rule	PD
An appropriate reduction for choosing to travel with a driver already affected by alcohol where that factor stands alone was held to be 20% in *Gleeson v Court* [2007] EWHC 2397 (QB), [2008] RTR 10. It is to be noted that if the claimant also contributed to the damage suffered in another way, e g not wearing a seat belt, it is not appropriate to add the two percentages together because that would amount to double accounting. The appropriate percentage reduction would be something less than the two 'stand alone' figures. For an unsuccessful attempt by insurers to re-coup compensation from its insured pursuant to s 151 of the Road Traffic Act 1988 that had been paid to him in respect of injuries suffered by him when travelling as a passenger in the vehicle he had allowed to be driven by a driver he knew to be uninsured see *Wilkinson v Fitzgerald and Churchill* [2009] EWHC 1297 (QB), [2009] All ER (D) 174 (Jun).			
6.5 Often coupled with a personal injury claim there is a claim for loss of use of a vehicle. Currently the appropriate daily rate for such loss is £15; *Mullins v Phillips* [2005] Current Law Digest Dec, para 141. See also Gazette, 26 March 2009, page 17, article 'Driving a hard bargain' by District Judge Pates.			

	Form No	CPR Rule	PD
6.6 As to the amount of car hire charges the only matter to be considered in respect of the rate charged is whether it was reasonable even if the claimant was indemnified against the charges by his insurer; see *Bee v Jenson* [2007] EWCA Civ 923, [2007] 4 All ER 791. An offer by a negligent driver's insurers to a claimant of a free replacement hire car must make it clear to the claimant the cost to the defendant of hiring the car: *Copley v Lawn* [2009] EWCA Civ 580, [2009] RTR 311. If the claimant is found to have unreasonably refused the offer he will at least be able to recover the cost that the defendant would have incurred. The normal rule where there is no such offer is that the recovery is limited to the 'spot' or market rate.			
6.7 Credit card charges incurred to enable a replacement car to be hired were held to be recoverable; *Lagden v O'Connor* [2003] UKHL 64, [2004] 1 AC 1067. This in effect overruled the decision in *The Leisbosh* [1933] AC 449 where it was held that a victim's impecuniosity was not foreseeable and accordingly loss resulting because of it was not recoverable.			
6.8 If the claimant alleges that as a result of the damage, after the repairs have been completed, there has been diminution in the value of the vehicle such loss can be the subject of a claim: see *Payton v Brooks* [1974] RTR 169. It will be for the claimant to prove the diminution in value and to do so evidence from an expert who has examined the vehicle after the repairs will be essential. Detailed guidance can be obtained from an article by Anthony John 'Measuring Loss', see NLJ, 16 May 2008, page 696.			
7. General matters arising including costs and appeals			
See **TAB 17** above			

TABLE 17B—DISTANCE SELLING AND COOLING OFF PERIOD ON SMALL CLAIMS TRACK

TAB 17B

	Reg No	CPR Rule	PD
1. Preliminary			
1.1 The Consumer Protection (Distance Selling) Regulations 2000 as amended by the Consumer Protection (Distance Selling)(Amendment) Regulations 2005 in this TAB called **the Regulations**.			
As a result of a preliminary hearing in *Pannon GSM Zrt v Gyorfi: C-243/08* [2009] All ER (D) 151 (Jun), ECJ the European Court of Justice ruled that **the national courts of their own accord** must apply the Unfair Terms Directive (93/13/EEC). Accordingly in a dispute between a commercial party and a consumer **fairness will automatically be a matter for the court's consideration** irrespective of whether it has been raised. If the court finds the terms to be unfair the whole contract is likely to be held invalid.			
1.2 The Regulations apply to certain contracts for goods and services to be supplied to a consumer where the contract is made exclusively by means of distance communication **'distance contracts'**. They must be between the consumer and a supplier under an organised distance sales or service provision scheme organised by the supplier. 'Consumer' means any natural person who is acting for purposes outside his business. The Regulations apply to any contract (other than one exempt under reg 5) made otherwise than in the physical presence of the parties. Some contracts are subject to part of the Regulations (reg 6).			
1.3 Where the Regulations apply a consumer has the right to cancel a distance contract by notice to the supplier during a specified **'cooling-off period'**.			

	Reg No	CPR Rule	PD
1.4 The length of the cooling off period depends on whether and when the supplier complies with the requirement to provide **required information** in the form specified by the rules.	7 and 8		
1.5 The Regulations are reproduced in full in Volume 2 of the Civil Court Practice at **III CON 125a-125z**.			
1.6 The Regulations, unless the parties otherwise agree, require performance by the supplier within a maximum of 30 days beginning with the day after the day the consumer sent his order to the supplier and the obligations to be fulfilled by the supplier who fails to do so are fully set out in the Regulations. The goods remain at the seller's risk until they are delivered to the consumer: Sale and Supply of Goods to Consumers Regulations 2002.	19		
1.7 Joint guidance on the Regulations has been issued jointly from the Office of Fair Trading and the Department of Trade and Industry in 'A Guide for Businesses on Distance Selling'. This is available at www.oft.gov.uk			
1.8 The relevant regulation numbers are set out in the column immediately adjoining this text			
1A. Checklist			
To establish a right to repayment under the Regulations the customer will have to be able to 'tick' all the items in the following list			
(i) The contract is a **distance contract**	3(1)		
(ii) The contract is **not exempt** from the Regulations. Where a contract is excluded it should be checked whether the Financial Services (Distance Marketing) Regulations 2004 of the Consumer Credit Act 1974 apply.	5		

	Reg No	CPR Rule	PD
(iii) If the contract is one which is **partly exempt** from the Regulations, the cancellation provisions under the Regulations are not disapplied	6		
(iv) The contract is not one of the **exceptional contracts** in respect of which there is no right to cancel	13		
(v) The **cancellation notice** complied with the formalities required as to form and service	10(3)–(5)		
(vi) The cancellation notice was given with the permitted **time limits**			
(a) as to goods	11		
(b) as to services	12		
2. Enforcement of refund of monies paid			
Regulation 14 requires the supplier to reimburse any sums paid by the consumer under the contract. If this is not paid within 30 days of cancellation a letter before action should be written and if this does not produce payment a claim may be issued; see **TAB 1**		7.1	
2A. Return of goods			
On cancellation the consumer is under an obligation to restore the goods to the supplier and meanwhile to retain possession of the goods and take reasonable care of them. The steps to be taken to return the goods are limited by sub-para (4) of reg 17.			
3. Entry of Particulars on Form N1			
When completing the claim form (form N.1) brief particulars of the claim have to be provided: Appropriate wording would be *'Repayment of monies paid by the claimant to the defendant under a distance contract under Regulation 14 of the Consumer Protection (Distance Selling) Regulations 2000 which was duly cancelled by the Claimant and interest on the monies due'*.			

	Reg No	CPR Rule	PD
The Particulars of Claim can be adapted from the following precedent relating to sale of goods – PARTICULARS OF CLAIM 1. On [specify date] the claimant contracted with the defendant for the purchase of [specify goods] 2. The contract was concluded [e.g. on the telephone] and is a distance contract within the Consumer Protection (Distance Selling) Regulations 2000 3. The claimant paid £ [specify price] to the defendant and the goods were delivered to the claimant on [specify date] 4. The claimant duly cancelled the contract by notice given in the letter dated [specify date] attached to these particulars 5. The defendant has failed to reimburse the said sum of £[specify] or any part of it although more than 30 days have elapsed since the cancellation notice was given and despite the claimant's written demand for reimbursement 6. The claimant therefore claims (i) £[specify] (ii)Interest under s69 of the County Courts Act 1984 calculated at the rate of [specify] per cent per annum and totalling £[specify] at the date of issue and continuing at the daily rate of £[specify] until judgment Statement of Truth I believe [the Claimant believes] that the facts stated in this claim Form and these particular of claim are true Dated etc. **4. The subsequent conduct of the small claim**			
4.1 A defence may be filed sometimes on grounds that display an ignorance of the regulations but otherwise on grounds such as:			
(a) the claimant has not complied with the prescribed procedure e.g. the cancellation notice was not given 'in writing or in another durable medium available to the supplier …'	10.3		

	Reg No	CPR Rule	PD
(b) the contract was for the supply of services and performance was begun with the consumer's consent before the end of the cancellation period and after the supply of the requested information	13(a)		
(c) the contract was for goods personalised e.g. a car number plate including the purchaser's initials and age (but is this supply of goods or services? i.e. is what is really being purchased the right to use such a number plate)	13(c)		
(d) etc, etc			
4.2 Allocation to the small claims track will be on the basis that the claim is less than £5000 and an Allocation Questionnaire will be sent to the parties for completion and return (Form N149 where claim is financially within the small claims limit – no allocation fee is payable if the claim is less than £1500)			
4.3 There is no right for a party to enforce the giving of further information but the court can require a party to do so. A request should be made in the Allocation Questionnaire for the court to require the defendant to give any details that the claimant specifies are required to enable him to accurately know the defence he faces (if that is not already obvious)		27.2(3)	
4.4 Part 31 as to disclosure and inspection does not apply to small claims but the Standard Directions given by the court include		27.2(b)	
'Each party must deliver to every other party and to the court office copies of all documents he intends to rely on at the hearing …' and			27, Appendix B
'The original documents must be brought to the hearing'			

	Reg No	CPR Rule	PD
There is a definition of 'document' in Rule 31.4 which extends to electronic documents, including e-mail and other electronic documents, word processed documents and databases. The Practice Direction to Part 31 at para 2A should be consulted if an issue arises about electronic documents. In many disputes over distance contracts relevant documents will include electronic documents and it must be ensured that copies are obtained and provided as the case may be Letters, telephone attendance notes and similar documents must, of course, also be copied and delivered in accordance with the court's direction.		31.4	31, para 2A
4.5 Witness statements			
The court may well not order the parties to prepare, file and serve witness statements. Nevertheless a prudent claimant will prepare a witness statement with a bundle of relevant documents annexed. The bundle should be arranged in chronological order and numbered. Copies should be available for the court and the opposing party.			27, para 2.5
If it is possible for the bundle of documents to be agreed with the other party that will obviously save time at the hearing.			
4.6 For the hearing, costs, setting aside judgment, rehearing and appeals See Table 17 paragraphs 7–11			

TABLE 17C—ESTATE AGENTS AND THE SOLE AGENCY AGREEMENT ON THE SMALL CLAIMS TRACK

TAB 17C

	Form No	CPR Rule	PD
1. Preliminary			
1.1 The contract between estate agents and property owners is typically one where remuneration will only become payable on the occurrence of a specified event. This will usually be finding a purchaser prepared to pay the required price or who exchanges contracts to do so. The remuneration is described as 'commission' and will be calculated by reference to the sale price. If the agent fails to achieve the specified event, unless the agency agreement specifically states otherwise, he is not entitled to any remuneration for the work he has done or to any reimbursement for the expenses he has incurred.			
1.2 The question of whether the agent has achieved the specified event will be determined by the construction of the particular agreement 'read in the light of the material circumstances of the parties in view of which the contract was made' per Lord Wright in *Luxor (Eastbourne) Ltd v Cooper* [1941] AC 108.			

	Form No	CPR Rule	PD
1.3 The Consumers Estate Agents and Redress Act 2007 received Royal Assent on 17 July 2007. It does not affect this TAB but an article setting out its effect appears in the Solicitors Journal for 14 September 2007. On 18 October 2007, s 53(1) and Schedule 6 were brought into force and this will enable redress schemes to be approved. It is also to be noted that it was decided in *Office of Fair Trading v Foxtons* [2009] EWCA Civ 288, [2009] All ER (D) 31 (Apr) that the estate agents could be prevented from enforcing certain terms in their standard letting agreement if they were unfair terms under the Unfair Terms in Consumer Contracts Regulations 1999 which apply to current as well as future agreements; see New Law Journal 10 and 17 April 2009, page 552. Mann J in *Office of Fair Trading v Foxtons* [2009] EWHC 1681 (Ch), (2009) Times, 29 July said that important terms should be flagged up and not hidden in small print. He found certain old terms as well as new terms used by the defendant to be unfair. The judgment applied the decision in *Office of Fair Trading v Abbey National* [2009] EWCA Civ 116, [2009] 2 WLR 1286.			
It was reported in The Times for 24 December 2009 that having regard to the success of the banks in the overdraft charges cases Foxtons are to appeal the High court decision against them in favour of the Office of Fair Trading. The report indicates that the appeal would not challenge rulings that provisions requiring landlords to pay a commission to the letting agent if the landlord sold the property let to the tenant were not enforceable.			
Subsequently the OFT has obtained a final order of the High Court preventing Foxton using certain renewal terms in its letting agreements with landlords; see NLJ (2010) 26 February, page 291.			

	Form No	CPR Rule	PD
1.4 All estate agents by 1 October 2008 have to belong to an approved redress scheme dealing with complaints from buyers and sellers of residential property. For 'estate agency work' and 'residential property' see Estate Agents Act 1979, ss 1 and 23C. The Estate Agents (Redress Scheme) (Penalty Charge) Regulations 2008, SI 2008/1713 came into effect on 1 October 2008 and specify the penalty charge that may be imposed by a local trading standards officer on a person in default.			
1.5 The Ombudsman for Estate Agents supervises an independent Code of Practice. It can grant compensation of up to £25,000. The National Association of Estate Agents is the main professional body for estate agents in the UK, but only 60% of agents are members.			
1.6 Estate agents marketing houses must belong to an approved redress scheme for HIP related complaints. The Ombudsman (see last sub-para) is an approved scheme.			
2. The Estate Agents Act and Regulations			
2.1 The Estate Agents (Provision of Information) Regulations 1991 SI 1191/859 (the '1991 Regulations') made under s18 of the Estate Agents Act 1979 require any estate agent using the term 'sole agency' or the like to explain to the client in writing what the term means, further the estate agent must use one of the forms of explanation contained in the regulations themselves.			

	Form No	CPR Rule	PD
2.2 Sole Agency			
'You will be liable to pay remuneration to us, in addition to any other costs or charges in each of the following circumstances: if unconditional contracts for the sale of the property are exchanged in the period during which we have sole selling rights, even if the purchaser was not found by us but by another agent or by any other person, including yourself if unconditional contracts for the sale of the property are exchanged after the expiry of a period during which we have sole selling rights, but to a purchaser who was introduced to you during that period or with whom we had negotiations about the property during that period'			
(1) reg 5(1) allows some modification of the statutory wording if necessary to prevent it being misleading in the context of the contract as a whole, and			
(2) the Schedule makes similar provision in the case of an agency which confers Sole Selling Rights			
2.3 The property owner will very frequently sign the sole agency agreement without legal advice and will only fully attempt to construe the effect of the clause after some dispute has arisen with the estate agent.			

	Form No	CPR Rule	PD
2.4 In *Foxtons v Bicknell* [2008] EWCA Civ 419, (2008) Times, 1 May the court considered the claimant's sole agency clause used by the majority of estate agents. The sale of the defendant's house was effected by other estate agents but the claimant argued it had introduced the purchaser after the signing of the sole agency agreement (although that introduction did not produce a sale) and that they were entitled to their commission. Lord Neuberger stated that Foxtons had to show that it introduced the purchaser to the purchase, i e not just to the house. To be entitled to their commission they had to show they were the effective cause of the sale and purchase. The claimant was held not to be entitled to commission. See NLJ, 13 June 2008, 'Civil Way' by Stephen Gold and NLJ, 11 July 2008, 'Sole Searching' by Michael Wilkinson, who considers variations that may be made by estate agents to their present form of agreement to 'avoid' the Foxtons situation.			
3. CPR and disputes over entitlement to commission under a sole agency agreement			
3.1 Defence			
3.1.1 Where the claim for commission is based on the exchange of contracts within the period of the agency even though the purchase has not been introduced by the agent, a valid defence to the claim for commission is unlikely unless the defendant has a counterclaim (see para 4 below) which will found a defence of set off See however s 18 of the Estate Agents Act 1979 as to the agents obligation under s 3(1) of the 1991 Regulations as to the time when the agent must give the client 'the requisite information'			

	Form No	CPR Rule	PD
3.1.2 Frequently the clause in the agreement between the parties whilst based on the clause in the 1991 Regulations deviates from it in various ways e.g. by providing that commission will become payable on introduction of an 'able and willing' purchaser rather than on exchange of contracts. When this is the case the agreement needs to be carefully construed to establish whether the agent has achieved the commission entitling event.			
3.1.3 If the agreement, whether it is comprised in a single document or an exchange of letters, is not attached to the particulars of claim, it should be attached to the defence. The defence should be drafted to divide up the commission entitling events to clarify the provisions and to assist the court in construction of the agreement.			
3.1.4 If the claim is based on the sale after the termination of the agreement to a purchaser introduced by the agent during the period of the agreement, the dispute is likely to be whether or not the agent did effect the introduction. The defendant must set out his case as to this in his defence but see also para 4.2 below as to further particulars of the claimant's case			
3.1.5 If the agreement excludes certain named persons from those to whom a sale will give a right to commission, any claim by the agent based on a sale to such a named person can be successfully defended [a house owner may well seek such an exclusion in the agreement if a potential purchase has been found by him before entering into the sole agency agreement]			

	Form No	CPR Rule	PD
Note: It will not be a valid defence to show that the fixed period of the sole agency agreement has expired prior to the sale if the agreement provides, as is usually the case, that it will continue after the fixed period until written notice of termination of a specified number of days is given. In these circumstances there will only be a defence if the sale was after the expiry of the requisite notice on the agent			
The sale to a purchaser found by the houseowner himself or by another agent after the sole agency agreement is terminated will not give rise to a valid claim for commission by the agent. The agent would have to show he introduced the purchaser *Harwood (Michael) (t/a RSBS Group) v Smith* [1998] 1 EGLR 5, CA discussed by John Murdoch in his text book 'The Law of Estate Agency'.			
For a case where the court found the former sale agent had introduced the eventual purchaser and was entitled to sale commission see *Shamas Charania v Harbour Estates Ltd* [2009] EWCA Civ 1123, (2009) Sol Jo, 3 November, page 28			
3.2 Particulars of the Claimant's case			
Although a party is not able to force another to give further particular of the case he faces voluntary further particulars can be sought. If they are not forthcoming the court can be asked in the Allocation Questionnaire to exercise its powers to request further particulars of the other party's case. This will be particularly important where there is a dispute about whether a sale outside the sole agency term was to a purchaser introduced by the agent. The court should be urged to require the claimant the specify the facts relied on to establish his introduction and to disclose any documents on which he relies in support of this contention. A copy of the letter requesting voluntary further particulars should be attached to the allocation questionnaire.			

	Form No	CPR Rule	PD
3.3 Preparation for the trial			
Paragraph 6 in Table 17 should be referred to for guidance but it is important to remember that whilst the 40th revision of the CPR has discouraged the court from ordering the exchange of witness statements in this type of case, it does not prevent a party from preparing a written statement. If the other party does not wish to exchange statement it can be read at the hearing (by the party or the court as the court prefers) a copy being provided for the court and the other party. Any comments which arise from the presentation of the claimant's case can be added by oral evidence.			27, para 2.5
Reference should be made to **TAB 17** paras 7–10 for further guidance as to the conduct of the hearing and the question of costs.			
4. Counterclaim			
The fact that the claimant agent proves his entitlement to commission does not prevent a counterclaim and perhaps a defence of set off being raised by the defendant. Complaint about general inefficiency will not help because whatever his faults the claimant has established he achieved the specified event i.e. the sale. But clearly there may be a counterclaim for example against an agent who breaks a valuable vase by over-enthusiastic pointing out of the view from the properly. This table is not designed, however, to embark on an exposition of things that an agent could do wrongfully that could cause damage to the householder and accordingly only the most obvious example has been given.		20.4	20, paras 6.1–6.7

TABLE 17D—SMALL CLAIMS: THE RECOVERY OF TENANT'S DEPOSITS

TAB 17D

	Form No	CPR Rule	PD
1. Preliminary			
1.1 In June 1998 the National Association of Citizens Advice Bureau (now Citizen's Advice) published 'Unsafe Deposits CAB'S experience of rental deposits' which stated that disputes over the non-return of rental deposits were among the most common issues of concern reported to CAB.			
1.2 A residential landlord receiving a deposit after 7 April 2007 from a tenant under an assured shorthold tenancy must place it in accordance with one of the government authorised **'tenancy deposit schemes'** (TDS) (there are two types of scheme: custodial, operated by an independent scheme administrator who will hold the deposit; and insurance, where the landlord keeps the deposit but pays a premium to the administrator. Currently there are 2 custodial schemes and 1 insurance backed.			

	Form No	CPR Rule	PD
A tenancy entered into after 1 April 1990 and where the rent exceeds £25,000 per annum cannot be an assured tenancy of any type (Sch 1, para 2 Housing Act 1988) and so is not subject to the Deposit Guarantee Scheme. However, on 1 October 2010 the figure of £25,000 was increased to £100,000 in England only; see the Assured Tenancies (Amendment) (England) Order 2010, SI 2010/908. The effect of the increase will be backdated so that all existing contractual tenancies that began on or after 28 February 1997 with an annual rent between £25,000 and £100,000 will become assured shorthold tenancies on 1 October 2010. If the tenancy began after 15 January 1989 but before 28 February 1997 it will become an assured tenancy. A previous assured tenancy which lost its security when the rent increased to over £25,000 will revert to being an assured tenancy. Any deposit taken in respect of a contractual tenancy which becomes an assured tenancy by reason of the increased limit will have to be protected under one of the schemes within 14 days of 1 October 2010.			
Both types of scheme offer Alternative Dispute Resolution but the deposit cannot be paid out or retained without agreement, adjudication or court order. The landlord may retain all or part of the tenant's deposit if he can demonstrate he suffered financial loss arising from the actions of the tenant			
The statutory basis for the scheme is contained in ss 212–215 and Schedule 10 of the Housing Act 2004. The Housing (Tenancy Deposit Schemes) Order 2007, SI 2007/796 has inserted new paras 4A, 4B and 4C into Schedule 10 and these set out procedures which apply after the determination of the tenancy where the parties fail to agree to whom the deposit, or part of it, shall be paid			

	Form No	CPR Rule	PD
The landlord who has received the deposit is also required by the Housing (Tenancy Deposits)(Prescribed Information) Order 2007, SI 2007/797, within 14 days of the receipt to give notice in the prescribed form to the tenant or the person paying the deposit on the tenant's behalf.			
Neither 'landlord' nor 'tenant' is defined but s 212(9)(a) states that the landlord shall include references to a person or persons acting on his behalf in relation to a tenancy.			
According to the Deposit Protection Service in November 2009, one in three of landlords fail to put tenants' deposits in a government accredited scheme.			
'**Deposit**' is defined in Chapter 4, Part 6 of the Housing Act 2004 as 'any money intended to be held … as security for … the performance of an obligation of the tenant'; see *UK Housing Alliance (North West) Ltd v Francis* [2010] EWCA Civ 117.			
If the landlord fails to comply with the requirements as to the deposit or the giving of notice, the court on finding he is in breach must order (a) the release of the deposit to the tenant or in the case of custodial schemes, payment of the deposit to the scheme's administrator (Housing Act 2004, s 214(3)); and (b) payment to the tenant of a sum equal to 3 times the value of the deposit (Housing Act 2004, s 214(4))			

	Form No	CPR Rule	PD
See however *Harvey v Bamforth* [2008] 46 EG 119, County Court, (2009) New Law Journal 27 February, page 306. In this case the court drew a distinction between a landlord's failure to comply with the scheme in its entirety and the much lesser fault of providing the prescribed information outside the time limits set out by the legislation. It held that the punitive provisions appropriate to complete failure should not be applied and that the landlord was not to be required to pay the penalty sum of three times the deposit.			
For a discussion of other county court decisions see article in NLJ 7 August 2009, page 1127 by West and Rivett entitled 'Deposit dilemmas'.			
The first **High Court decision** on the tenancy deposit protection schemes was made in *Draycott v Hannells Letting Ltd* [2010] EWHC 217 (QB), [2010] All ER (D) 136 (Feb) and NLJ (2010) 19 February, page 229. Tugendhat J held:			
(a) an agent can be held liable in place of the landlord (but what if the landlord holds the deposit?) (b) on the construction of the particular scheme's requirements it had not been established that 'the 14 days within receipt of deposit' for placing it with the scheme was made an 'initial requirement'. There remains the question of whether the payment of three times the amount of the deposit can be ordered if the deposit has been lodged with the scheme prior to the making of the order (even though late). The court took the view that it could not but that question may well be revisited.			

	Form No	CPR Rule	PD
The landlord who delays protecting the deposit will expose himself to an adverse costs order even if the tenant's action is defeated by late protection. Further, the landlord cannot recover possession during a period of non-compliance.			
The question of whether a set off can be made in favour of the landlord against the deposit that falls to be returned or the penalty is the subject of conflicting county court decisions (see NLJ 7 August 2009, page 1128 referred to above) and will probably only be resolved by a decision of a higher court.			
A further sanction is that no s 21 notice requiring possession may be served while the deposit is held other than in with the TDS. The tenant could wait until proceedings have been issued before taking the point			
Form N5B 'Claim for Possession of Property' has been amended to require evidence to be provided that any deposit has been dealt with under TDS			
For further reading see New Law Journal for 9 February 2007 (article by Mark Loveday) and for 9 March 2007 (article by Stephen Gold), for a review of the tenancy deposit scheme after one year form its inception see articles 'Money back guaranteed' by Daniel Dovar and Michael Walsh, NLJ for 14 and 21 March 2008, page 397 and also the article in NLJ for 7 August 2009 referred to above and for a detailed consideration of the decision in *Draycott* (above), article 'Whose deposit is it anyway?' by Tamsin Cox in NLJ (2010) 12 March, page 375.			
1.3 There is a Pre Action Protocol for Housing Disrepair cases which although not directly concerned with rental deposits provides some useful guidance.			

	Form No	CPR Rule	PD
1.4 Nevertheless disputes over the return of rental deposits frequently come before the court and are likely to continue to do so if the ADR service run with the Tenancy Deposit Schemes fails to resolve dispute between landlords and tenants. They both still have the option of seeking settlement through the court. Claims for the return of deposits are generally allocated to the Small Claims Track because the amount reclaimed is within the financial limits of that track.		27.1	
CPR Part 56 has been amended with effect from 1 October 2008 to provide for applications under the Housing Act 2004, s 214 (tenancy deposit schemes). In particular there has been added to r 56.1(1): '(f) section 214 of the Housing Act 2004'		56.1(1)(f)	
2. If the deposit is not returned after written request			
2.1 A letter before action should be written see **TAB 1** para 1(d). If TDS applies, not until the ADR process has failed			
2.2 If the letter before action does not produce payment a claim may be issued see **TAB 1**			
3. If a defence is filed			
3.1 The defence will most frequently allege-			
(a) arrears of rent – see **TAB 23** para 2 above and note the provisions of the tenancy agreements as to notices to quit and notices of intention to quit (b) failure to leave in a clean condition (c) failure to observe the covenants as to repair and decoration (d) missing or damaged chattels			
3.2 A request should be made for voluntary particulars listing each complaint and the alleged cost of replacement or remedial work			

	Form No	CPR Rule	PD
3.3 When completing the allocation form that will be sent out by the court (no fee payable if claim is for money of £1,500 or less). If the defendant has not given voluntary particulars ask the district judge to exercise his power to request further information by requiring the defendant to complete a schedule of which the following is an example and to file a copy at the court and serve a copy on the claimant within a specified time (the letter requesting voluntary particulars should be attached to the completed allocation form)	N149	27.2(f)	
Defendant's Complaints and cost to remedy each item of complaint	**Amount claimed and how calculated**	**Claimant's comments**	**For use by the court**
Copies of any purchase receipts, receipts for work done, estimates, valuations should be attached			
3.4 The claimant should be directed upon being served with his copy, to complete the column 'claimant's comments' and file the completed document and serve a copy on the defendant within a specified time.			
3.5 Although the court is discouraged from ordering the parties to file statements there is nothing to prevent the claimant preparing such a statement with relevant documents and photographs in a duly indexed separate bundle. The photographs should have been taken immediately before taking possession and immediately prior to leaving – the dates the photographs were taken should be capable of clear proof. An offer should be made to exchange statements but if this is not forthcoming a copy of the statement and bundle should be provided for the defendant shortly before the hearing date. A copy should of course be available for the court. There is no excuse for providing plain copies of coloured photographs when coloured photocopies can be easily obtained. The cost of obtaining them can be claimed as a disbursement if the claim is successful (this may or may not be allowed)		Disrepair Protocol PRO 9 HOU	

	Form No	CPR Rule	PD
3.6 If a proper inspection and a report on the condition of the house prior to the letting was obtained, leave should be sought in the allocation questionnaire to adduce expert evidence. This may be in the form of the inspection report or by the surveyor giving oral evidence whichever is proportionate.			
4. Conduct of the small claims hearing and costs			
See **TAB 17**, paras 7 and 8			

TABLE 18—FAST TRACK

TAB 18

	Form No	CPR Rule	PD
1. Preliminary			
The **Practice Direction – Automatic Orders Pilot Scheme** which supplements CPR Part 26 (Case management – preliminary steps) and CPR Part 28 (Fast Track) which will operate at the county courts at Chelmsford, Newcastle, Teesside, Watford and York and apply to claims started on or after 1 October 2008 should be noted.			
It must be continually borne in mind that the three most important effects of allocation to this track are: (a) the **length of time** will effectively be limited to **one day** – this will include the opening and, if any, closing speeches, judgment and summary assessment of costs. The court will use its powers to avoid loss of time, e g by dispensing with an opening or limiting cross-examination, but the parties will be anxious to ensure the case finishes in the day because the trial costs recoverable do not increase if the case runs into an extra day		35.7, 35.5(2)	27, para 7.2(4)(b)

	Form No	CPR Rule	PD
(b) besides the limitations on **expert evidence** contained in CPR 26.6(5) and (6) the court on this track will generally direct that expert evidence is given by a single joint expert. Further expert evidence will be by written report unless the attendance of the expert at the hearing is necessary in the interests of justice (c) **costs** will be summarily assessed at the conclusion of the case unless there is good reason not to do so. Generally the mere fact that costs are high will not be regarded as a sufficient reason. Summary assessment is unlikely to be generous in the face of arguments about proportionality and this has to be borne in mind in deciding how much work can be justified in the preparation of a fast track case. Success can be soured by a failure to recover the bulk of the costs incurred		35.5	Costs PD, paras 13.2 and 13.5
For fast track trials a party's statement of costs for summary judgment must be filed and served as soon as possible but not less than 2 days before the hearing.			
2. Scope of the fast track			
The fast track is the normal track for any claim for which the small claims track is not the normal track and which has a financial value of not more than £25,000, provided: (a) the court considers the trial is not likely to last longer than one day, and (b) oral expert evidence will be limited to: (i) one expert per party in relation to any expert field, and (ii) expert evidence in two expert fields *Note:*		26.6(5)	

	Form No	CPR Rule	PD
• Where there is a Part 20 claim to be tried with the claim, it is the total time that is likely for the trial of both claims that is determinative			26, para 9.1(3)(e)
• A claim may be allocated to and remain on the fast track although there is to be a split trial. Before a party seeks a split trial careful consideration should be given to the statements made by the court in *DHL Air Ltd v Wells* [2003] EWCA Civ 1743, (2003) Times, 14 November			
• As to allocation of claims in which judgment has been given for an amount to be determined by the court see **TAB 19** post, para 1			26, paras 12.1–12.6
3. Allocation and directions			
The same form of **Allocation Questionnaire** is appropriate for all levels of case and the information required is to enable the court to allocate to the appropriate track and to give appropriate directions. Completion of the form is particularly important on the fast track because in many fast track cases it will be the only contact between the litigants and the court until the completion of the Pre-trial Checklist shortly before the trial window. In some cases the court may direct that Pre-trial Checklist are dispensed with making the proper completion of the Allocation Questionnaire even more important	N150		

	Form No	CPR Rule	PD
The parties are, of course, required to help the court to further the overriding objective of dealing with cases justly but this does not prevent the different parties to a case having differing views of the appropriate track. It is understandably easier for the defendant, who is likely to be found to blame in some degree, to feel that justice requires the case to be dealt with on the fast track so that the time spent on the case will be less and the trial costs will be limited, than for a claimant, with an excellent prospect of success, who would wish for a greater length of time to be spent on the case with oral expert evidence and a longer time allowed for the trial			
The Allocation Questionnaire should be used by both parties to present their differing views to the court as persuasively as possible provided they fully discharge their duty to co-operate with the court and each other to achieve a trial of the issues in dispute in a manner that is consistent with the overriding objective		1.3, 1.4(2)(a)	
Obviously, if there is an issue as to whether the value exceeds £5,000 (£1,000 if the claim is for personal injuries) or £25,000, authorities on quantum with appropriate references should be sent with the Questionnaire			
The court may find it necessary to hold an allocation hearing but generally will be reluctant to do so and will allocate on the information it has available. Consequent upon the increase in the fast track limit to £25,000 allocation hearings may well increase as some claims will need to be allocated to the multi-track as the trial will take more than one day.			26, para 6
Upon the court allocating to the fast track, the court will give directions for the management of the case and will set a timetable for the steps to be taken between directions and the trial: (a) it will fix a trial date or a "trial window" of not more than 3 weeks. The standard time between directions and trial will not be more than 30 weeks		28.2(2) and (3)	

	Form No	CPR Rule	PD
(b) the matters to be dealt with in the directions given will include: (i) disclosure of documents (ii) service of witness statements (iii) expert evidence		28.3(1)	
Reference should be made to **CPR PD 28** for detailed guidance on directions on allocation and note should particularly be taken of para 3.2 which provides that regard will be had to the extent to which the Practice Direction (Pre-Action Conduct) or pre-action protocol has, or had not, been complied with			28.3
(c) if the court decides not to order standard disclosure it may: (i) direct no disclosure take place; or (ii) specify the documents or classes of documents that the parties must disclose		28.3(2)	
In the Appendix to CPR PD 28 the Fast Track Standard Directions are set out The allocation stage is the prime point in the case at which the court will exercise its powers of management. It is essential for justice to be achieved speedily, and with proportionate costs, for the preparation of the case to start properly and promptly and for a clear timetable to be set with achievable time limits which will result in the trial taking place not more than 30 weeks from the giving of directions The court will give careful consideration to directions submitted by the parties particularly if they are agreed. The solicitors for the parties are likely to know more about the facts of the case and to have a grasp of detail that the court cannot hope to achieve. The parties will be aware that the basic timetable the court will have in mind will be:			
(a) Disclosure 4 weeks (b) Exchange of witness statements 10 weeks			

	Form No	CPR Rule	PD
(c) Exchange of expert's reports — 14 weeks (d) Pre-trial Check Lists to be sent out by the court — 20 weeks (e) Pre-trial Check Lists to be filed — 22 weeks (f) Hearing — 30 weeks			
When considering the Allocation Questionnaires the district judge will have available to him a tick-box form to assist him to make the necessary directions quickly and to produce a degree of consistency and compliance with the Court Service technology (see **BCCP C[12]** for such a form) Proposed directions should be drafted keeping in mind the layout and order of the tick-box form which will be before the district judge. It must be made clear whether the directions are agreed or not and if not it will be useful to indicate why All necessary documents should be attached to the Allocation Questionnaire and copies of the completed Allocation Questionnaire and attachments should be served on the other parties. In a straightforward case it may be appropriate to seek a direction that Pre-Trial Check Lists be dispensed with			
Costs estimates must be filed and served with the Pre-Trial Check List but no longer with the Allocation Questionnaire; a copy must be served by each solicitor acting on his client's behalf; for the importance see *Leigh v Michelin Tyre plc* [2003] EWCA Civ 1766, (2003) Times, 16 December and PD 43 section 6, particularly 6.5A			Costs PD, paras 6.1–6.6
An allocation questionnaire fee of £200 is payable by the claimant except where the case is proceeding on a counterclaim alone, when it is payable by the defendant			
4. Expert evidence on the fast track			
For expert evidence generally see Procedural Table **TAB 16**		Part 35	35

	Form No	CPR Rule	PD
The section "Experts" in part D of the Questionnaire must be carefully completed and a copy of any report referred to attached. The Questionnaire asks whether it is thought that the attendance of the expert at trial to give oral evidence is necessary. If it is thought necessary this should be carefully answered. It is not enough merely to say that the report is not agreed as the court will expect to know what parts are in issue and what effect in money terms the disputed points will have. The court will have to consider whether it is proportionate to allow oral expert evidence bearing in mind that there is a real risk that such permission, if granted, will lengthen the trial and put allocation to the fast track in doubt The court will lean very strongly towards an appointment of a **single joint expert**. The PD states 'where possible matters requiring expert evidence should be dealt with by only one expert' and sets out the matters the court should take into account when considering whether to permit expert evidence and whether that evidence should be from a single joint expert. In a personal injury case hopefully observance of the relevant protocol will have resulted in the agreement of a suitable joint expert and a report from that expert enabling the court merely to order that expert's report shall be admissible as evidence and perhaps further ordering that the joint expert do update his report for the trial It is still unhappily the case that experts' reports are often obtained without observance of the relevant protocol or, if there is no applicable protocol, without observing the spirit of the protocols. If that is the case the argument that the report has unfortunately been obtained without observance of the protocol but is in existence and it would be a waste of money to instruct a further expert is unlikely to have a sympathetic reception			

	Form No	CPR Rule	PD
It is far more likely that the court will order that there be a joint expert's report and the costs of the original report obtained be not recoverable. In the same way if a defendant has studiously ignored invitations to join in the appointment of a joint expert but then makes application seeking permission to have his own expert's report, unless he can show good grounds for disputing parts of the report obtained by his opponent, he is likely to be left with the right only to ask questions of the expert who has already reported. Even if he is permitted to obtain his own report it is likely to be on terms that he bear the costs either of the original report or that he will bear the costs of obtaining his own report whatever the outcome of the case.			
The single joint expert is so vital to the fast track that parties who fail to seek such an appointment or to respond to proposals for such an appointment do so at their peril			
5. Applications			
Applications are often required to enforce compliance with directions and even if parties and their advisers are diligent in their preparation and observance of the timetable applications may be necessary. Further investigation may necessitate an application to add or substitute a party or to amend a statement of case; these are the sort of applications which the applicant will hope the court will deal with without a hearing, although the party not served may apply within 7 days to have the order set aside or varied	N244	Part 23, 23.10	28, para 5.1

	Form No	CPR Rule	PD
An adjournment because of failure to comply with directions is a matter of last resort and the court will be prepared to re-timetable on the tightest basis that is possible with sanctions for non-compliance to ensure the case can be heard and completed on the trial date. Even if this is impossible the court is likely to make as much progress as possible on the day fixed, perhaps by dealing with liability only or dealing with such issues as are ready on the basis that the costs of the necessary further hearing will be paid by the party in default. If postponement is necessary either in whole or in part, it will be for the shortest possible time. See *Elliot Group Ltd v Algeco SAS* [2010] EWHC 409 (TCC), 1 March 2010 (Coulson J).			28, para 5.4(1), (2) and (5)
The application for an adjournment by a litigant in person raises difficulties but useful guidance is available in *Fox v Graham Group Ltd* (2001) Times, 3 August, NEUBERGER J			
Useful guidance can be found as to an application to amend pleadings when such amendment will delay the trial, in the judgment of Walker J in *EDO Technology Ltd v Campaign to Smash EDO* [2006] EWHC 598 (QB), (2006) Times, 24 May although it is not a fast track case. See also *Davies v Wm Morrison Supermarkets plc* [2007] EWCA Civ 594 – again, not a fast track case			
6. Pre-trial Check List			
Unless they have been dispensed with, Pre-trial Check Lists will be sent out by the court and the parties are required to return them by the date specified in the directions which will not be more than 8 weeks before the trial date or the beginning of the trial period.	N170	28.5	

	Form No	CPR Rule	PD
Where a party (where there is only one claimant and one defendant) does not file a checklist the court will serve a notice on that party requiring the checklist to be filed within 7 days from service of the notice. If the notice is not complied with that party's claim, defence or counterclaim will be automatically struck out without further order of the court.	N171	28.5	28, paras 6.1–6.5 and 51B, para 2(3)–(5)
The pilot scheme (see below) enables staff in all county courts and the High Court to make the 7 day unless orders when any party has failed to file a pre-trial checklist questionnaire in a fast track case.			
For the extended period to 31 March 2011 in all courts rule 28.5 is amended by PD 51B (Automatic Orders Pilot Scheme). The preceding paragraph takes account of that amendment.			
The court has power to fix a listing hearing if it thinks a hearing is necessary to ensure proper preparation for the trial			
This will only be done rarely because of the proximity of the trial and the power of the court to control evidence by giving directions.		32.1	
For the sanctions that will apply on filing a pre-trail check list without the appropriate fee or with a cheque that is dishonoured see		3.7, 3.7A and 3.7B	3B
The rules do not require the parties to exchange copies of the check lists before they are filed but they may be encouraged to do so			28, para 6.4
If the directions given include permission to use expert evidence it will say whether that is to be by oral evidence or report and shall name the expert			28, para 7.2(a)

	Form No	CPR Rule	PD
If directions are not given the court must confirm the trial date, specify the place of the trial and give a time estimate all on the basis that the trial will be completed on the same day as it commences. Notice of the hearing will be sent at least three weeks before the hearing date unless the parties have agreed to accept shorter notice	N172		28, para 7.1
The parties should agree directions and file a draft of the proposed terms for the court's consideration. The agreed directions should include provision as to evidence, a trial timetable and time estimate, preparation of a trial bundle and any other matters needed to prepare the case for trial			28, para 7.2
If a party requires any order at this stage he must lodge an application, with the appropriate fee and a draft order, when returning the completed Check List	N244		
As to the requirement of a costs estimate with the pre-trial check list see final para of section 3 above			Costs PD, paras 6.1–6.6
As to the requirement for filing a statement of costs, which must be at least 2 days before the trial, see			Costs PD, para 13.5(4)
The fee payable is £100 on filing the Listing questionnaire. A hearing fee is payable by the claimant, unless the case is proceeding on a counterclaim, of £500. If the court receives notice in writing that the case is settled or discontinued the following percentage refunds will be made: (a) 100% more than 28 days before (b) 75% between 28 and 14 days before (c) 50% between 14 and 7 days (including the 14th day) before (d) Fewer than 7 days before, no refund		Civil Proceedings Fees Order 2008 (SI 2008/ 1053)	

	Form No	CPR Rule	PD
7. The trial			
Unless there are applications returnable after the court's consideration of the Pre-trial Check List, the only remaining opportunity for judicial management is at the commencement of the trial. Despite time restraints it is regrettably the case that either during the trial or immediately before it commences there are frequently last minute applications to amend, to adduce evidence not disclosed in accordance with the directions made on allocation or to introduce documents which have come to light at a late stage			
The court must deal with them but the applicant should be extremely cautious before taking up time allotted to the trial by making such an application. It may prevent the trial being completed within the time available and the costs arising from the case being adjourned part heard may well have to be paid by the applicant whether or not he is successful in the trial			
If a trial is not finished on the day it is listed the Rules contemplate that the judge will normally sit on the next court date to complete it. This is often impracticable where the trial is before a district judge who will already have a list for the following day			28, para 8.6
The judge will generally have read the trial bundle and may dispense with an opening address and the parties should anticipate that:			28, para 8.2
(a) the trial will be conducted in accordance with orders previously made		28.7	
(b) witness statements will stand as evidence in chief		32.3(2)	28, para 8.4(2)
(c) the court will exercise its power to control evidence and to restrict cross-examination		32.1	28, para 8.4(1)
(d) the court will confirm any timetable already given or, if there is not one, set its own			28, para 8.3

	Form No	CPR Rule	PD
These trial management directions form an essential part of the active management required by the judge to further the overriding objective		1.4	
The trial must not be allowed to "drift" and the completion of the evidence must be at such a time as will allow brief closing speeches, delivery of judgment and assessment of costs			
Save in the most exceptional case the judge should decide which party's case is more likely to be correct: *Cooper v Floor Cleaning Machines Ltd* [2003] EWCA Civ 1649, (2003) Times, 24 October where an appeal was allowed against a decision in a road traffic case dismissing both claim and counterclaim on the ground that neither had discharged the burden of proof			
8. Costs			
If an order for payment of costs is made, the judge will normally summarily assess the costs in accordance with CPR 44.7 and CPR Pt 46			
Note: • The advocate's fee for the trial is fixed depending on the size of the claim (these trial fees have been increased from 1 October 2007) They are presently: • Claim value not more that £3,000 – £485 • Claim value more than £3,000 but not more than £10,000 – £690 • Claim value more than £10,000 but not more than £15,000 – £1,035 • For proceedings issued on or after 6 April 2009 more than £15,000 – £1,650 These fees do not include VAT on the advocate's fee, nor any disbursements		46.2(1) and 46.1(2)(b)	

	Form No	CPR Rule	PD
• The fee for an instructing solicitor at the trial is also fixed but will be subject to the court's view of whether the attendance was necessary. It is presently £345		46.3	
• Parties must, at least 24 hours before the hearing, file and serve written statements of the costs claimed	N260		Costs PD, para 13.5
Fast track trial costs will not apply to a case dealt with at a disposal hearing (see **TAB 19**, para 1, penultimate sub-para) whatever the financial value of the claim			26, para 12.5(2)
For the position where the successful party forgets to ask for costs see **TAB 19**, para 10			

TABLE 19—MULTI-TRACK

TAB 19

	Form No	CPR Rule	PD
1. Preliminary			
See **CPR 29 [1]–CPR 29 [2]** and note in particular that: • the multi-track is the normal track for any claim for which the small claims track or the fast track is not the normal track		26.6(6)	
• Part 8 claims are treated as allocated to the multi-track and, accordingly, CPR Pt 26 does not apply (note, however, allocation of possession claims)		8.9, 55.9	55A, para 6.1
• the allocation fee payable is £200			

	Form No	CPR Rule	PD
• the fixing of a case management conference and/or a pre-trial review features frequently in judicial case management on this track. It is to be noted that, on 23 April 2007, Part 2 of the Compensation Act 2006 came fully into force and a whole range of claims-related activities came within the regulated sector for the first time. It is now an offence for a person to provide regulated claims management services in the course of a business unless he is authorised, exempt from the requirement or the requirement of authorisation has been specifically waived. For the regulation of claims management companies, see article by Gordon Exall, Sol Jo, 8 April 2008, page 20.			
Authorised claims management companies are required to pay an initial fee and an annual fee based on turnover, and at the time of writing (January 2010) the Claims Management Regulator regulates over 2,500 businesses. See article 'Clean up your act' (2009) Sol Jo, 27 October, page 12 by David Bywater.			
Solicitors are not allowed to purchase consumer credit claims from claims managers: Sol Jo (2009) 18 August, page 3.			
• where **damages are to be determined** by the court after the making of **a 'relevant order'** and the financial value of the claim exceeds the small claim limit it will not be allocated to track unless (a) the amount payable is genuinely disputed; or (b) the dispute is not suitable for disposal hearing			

	Form No	CPR Rule	PD
However, as a disposal hearing is not expected to take longer than 30 minutes and no oral evidence is expected to be taken, allocation will take place in all but the simplest case to either fast track or multi track whichever is appropriate. A master or district judge has jurisdiction irrespective of value			26, para 12.1–12.6
• for a review of the **bank charges litigation** and appeals to the High Court to lift a stay on the ground of hardship to a bank customer see *Rutherford v HSBC Bank plc* [2009] EWHC 733 (Blair J), 6 April 2009. The battle over unauthorised overdraft charges has been resolved now in favour of the banks; see *Office of Fair Trading v Abbey National* [2009] UKSC 6, [2009] 3 WLR 1215, [2009] NLJR 1702 leaving 'millions' of stayed cases to be resolved individually in the absence of settlement, withdrawal or admission.			
• parties concerned with claims arising because the claimant has or claims he has, contracted **mesothelioma** from exposure to asbestos dust would have been aware of the 'fast track' scheme operated by Senior Master Steven Whitaker at the Royal Courts of Justice, Strand, London WC2A 2LL. Most of the hearings were by telephone and the scheme covered the whole country. The scheme operated most of the provisions of the 'show cause' procedure that came into force on 6 April 2008 (see next sub-paragraph) and from that date the Masters of the QBD have operated the 'show cause' procedure			

	Form No	CPR Rule	PD
• for the 'show cause' procedure in claims for compensation for mesothelioma see as to issue and the procedure **TAB 1** section 6(c), last sub-paragraph above			
It is essential in asbestos cases to be aware of the various such conditions: pleura – thin membrane covering the lungs pleural plaques – thickening of lining of lungs; indicate asbestos exposure but are symptom free pleural thickening – can restrict the expansion of the lungs; can be due to various causes asbestosis – fibrosis of the lung due to exposure to asbestos mesothelioma – cancer of the pleura caused by exposure to asbestos lung cancer – can be due to a number of causes, frequently smoking, but can also be caused by exposure to asbestos.			
See generally article 'Smokescreen' by Christopher Moore (2009) Sol Jo Summer Expert Supplement, page 16.			
The Compensation Act 2006 which deals with damages for mesothelioma and the problem of multiple employments came into force on 26 July 2006. The Act restored the 'Fairchild principle' of joint and several liability between mesothelioma defendants.			
It is sufficient to show that tortious exposure materially increased the risk of contracting mesothelioma in the sense that the risk was more than minimal. Section 3 of the 2006 Act reflects the common law requirement of causation by reference to a material increase in risk: *Sienkiewicz v Greif (UK) Ltd* [2009] EWCA Civ 1159, 153 Sol Jo (no 44) 34, (2009) Times, 13 November; see also *Willmore v Knowsley Metropolitan Borough Council* [2009] EWCA Civ 1211 where the court stated 'the risk of exposure was a risk of harm'.			

	Form No	CPR Rule	PD
As to liability in mesothelioma cases arising on an exposure basis see *Durham v BAI (Run Off) Ltd* [2008] EWHC 2692 (QB), [2008] All ER (D) 220 (Nov) and article by Andrew Burns in NLJ 30 January 2009 entitled 'A sigh of relief'. Liability is triggered under an employer's liability policy at the time of inhalation although at that time there is no actionable injury.			
The range of damages for mesothelioma cases is given in the JSB Guidelines 9th edition as from £52,500 to £81,500, and for discussion see article by Simon Allan in)2010) Gazette, 11 June.			
The court in *Drake and Starkey (executrices of the estate of James Thomas Wilson decd) v Foster Wheeler Ltd* [2010] EWHC 2004 (QB) held the injured claimant could recover 'the reasonable value of gratuitous services rendered by voluntary care' and went on to hold that the recovery of hospice care was also recoverable – the damages for this aspect of the claim to be paid direct to the hospice; for a report see (2010) Sol Jo, 17 August, page 29.			
By its decision in *Rothwell v Chemical & Insulating Co Ltd, Re Pleural Plaques Litigation and Johnston v NEI International Combustion Ltd* [2007] UKHL 39, [2007] All ER (D) 224 (Oct) the House of Lords decided that pleural plaques after exposure to asbestos dust do not give rise to actionable damage. However, in his article in NLJ (2007) 9 November, Colin McCaul QC strongly argues 'Pleural plaques are still alive and kicking'.			
An Act of the Scottish Parliament makes pleural plaques a compensatory condition and an application for Judicial Review by a group of leading insurers has been successfully resisted in the Court of Session. This appeal decision is itself the subject of an appeal.			

	Form No	CPR Rule	PD
The government has issued a statement that it will not legislate to overturn the decision in *Johnston v NEI* (above) which upheld the finding that pleural plaques do not constitute damage.			
In February 2010 the Justice Secretary announced that anyone who has instigated a claim in respect of pleural plaques before the House of Lords decision in *Johnston* (above) in October 2007 will be entitled to a one-off payment of £5,000 but without additional payment for costs. Details have not as yet been published but see article in (2010) NLJ, 16 April, 'Unequal victims' by Richard Scorer.			
The Department for Work and Pensions has issued a consultation paper on setting up an Employees' Liability Tracing Office which will manage a database of employers' liability policy and has also set out plans for a compensation fund of last resort, the Employers' Liability Insurance Bureau.			
For the extremely unusual situation where the party who would normally be the defendant issues proceedings seeking **a** declaration of non-liability, ie a negative declaration, see *Toropdar v D (a minor by his litigation friend)* [2009] EWHC 567 (QB), 20 March 2009. Since 1 April 2005 courts have had the power to impose **periodical payments** rather than a conventional lump sum for all items of future care. Such awards should be linked to an earning based index rather than the Index of Retails Prices: *Thompstone v Tameside and Glossop Acute Services NHS Trust and other appeals* [2008] EWCA Civ 5, [2008] All ER (D) 72 (Jan). A model form is set out in the *Tombstone* case and the court's attitude to the costs of complying with the terms of the order is set out in *Long v Norwich Union Insurance Ltd* [2009] EWHC 715 (QB), 6 April. For an article on index linking and the discount rates see Gazette (2009) 18 June, page 22.			

	Form No	CPR Rule	PD
A claimant has the **right to pay for care** even when state funding is available and the cost can properly be included in a claim for damages: *Peters v East Midlands Strategic Health Authority* [2009] EWCA Civ 145, [2010] 1LR (QB) 48, [2009] PIQR Q1. It was made clear that this principle has nothing to do with mitigation of costs. For the consideration of the necessary machinery to prevent a subsequent application for public funding see the judgment of Dyson LJ, paras 57–16 and also article in Sol Jo Personal Injury Focus, April 2007, page 9, 'Victims Choice' by Jamie Clark.			
Damages for the cost of hospice care were held to be recoverable in *Drake v Foster Wheeler Ltd* [2010] EWHC 2004 (QB), [2010] All ER (D) 29 (Aug): these were to be held in trust for, or paid direct to, the hospice.			
2. Case management – general provisions			
When it allocates a case to the multi-track the court will: (a)give **directions for management and set a timetable** (normally in the type of case that would have been suitable for the fast track save for the value of the claim exceeding the fast track limit or the number of witnesses making it unlikely it will finish in a day), or (b) fix: (i) a **case management conference**, or (ii) a **pre-trial review** or both and give case management directions		29.2	
If the court decides only to give directions it can fix a case management conference or a pre-trial review subsequently at any time after allocation		29.3	
The court will **fix the trial date or trial period** as soon as possible		29.2(2)	

	Form No	CPR Rule	PD
Case management will generally be dealt with by: (a) a Master in cases proceeding in the Royal Courts of Justice (b) a district judge in cases proceeding in a High Court District Registry (c) by a district judge (usually) or by a circuit judge in cases proceeding in a county court			29, para 3.10
The conference will be held at the Royal Courts of Justice when the case is proceeding there but otherwise will normally be held at a Civil Trial Centre			29, para 3.1
The court may fix the conference hearing because it thinks it **necessary or desirable** and, when the necessity arises because of the deficiency of a party or his legal representative, will usually impose a **sanction** such as bearing the costs of all parties attending the hearing		3.8	29, para 3.6
A party in default would be advised to make good the deficiency that has occurred and seek to avoid the hearing by submitting agreed directions for the court's consideration, hopefully making the hearing unnecessary		29.4	
When a hearing of the conference is fixed the court will give the parties at least 3 days' notice (7 days if the hearing is a pre-trial review)			29, para 3.3
The parties should consider what directions should be sought and if a party requires a direction that is not routine and it is likely to be opposed he should **issue an application** to be heard at the case management conference. If the hearing of the application is likely to extend the time necessary for the hearing, that extra time should be sought even if this can only be at a fresh hearing date	N244		29, paras 3.5 and 5.8

	Form No	CPR Rule	PD
3. Directions			
The parties and their advisers are encouraged to agree directions and if the court thinks them suitable it will approve them and make directions accordingly			29, para 4.6
The **agreed directions** put before the court must: (a) set a **timetable** by reference to calendar dates (b) include a date or period for the **trial** (c) include provision for **disclosure** (d) include provision about **factual and expert evidence**; the provision about expert evidence may be that none is necessary			29, para 4.7(1)
It is specifically provided that disclosure may: (a) be limited to standard disclosure or less than that, and/or (b) be the supply of copies without a list and that a disclosure statement is dispensed with; but if it is not dispensed with it must provide that it be served			29, para 4.7(3)
If it is appropriate, the agreed directions should include provision for: (a) a reply or amended statement of case (b) dates for provision of further evidence and for questions to and replies by experts (c) disclosure of evidence (d) use of single joint expert or exchange (simultaneous or consequential) of expert evidence and discussion between experts			29, para 4.7(8)
Even if the court does not approve the agreed directions it will take them into account when giving its own directions, hopefully without a hearing			

	Form No	CPR Rule	PD
If the parties have agreed directions a covering letter can usefully seek to deal with any reservations or concerns of the court that can be anticipated. If a "split" trial is sought the covering letter should explain why it is appropriate, not simply that it will save costs but what costs will be saved and how the saved costs will exceed those of the extra hearing that may be necessary			
Where the court is giving directions on its own initiative without holding a case management conference see PD 29, para 4.10 and in particular note 4.10(a) as to requiring in appropriate cases that the parties consider ADR			29, para 4.10
Where the court is proposing of its own initiative to make a direction for a joint expert or to appoint an assessor, unless the parties have consented in writing, it must list a case management conference			29, para 4.13
For direction, in clinical negligence cases, for exchange of scholarly literature to be relied on see *Wardlaw v Farrar* [2003] EWCA Civ 1719, [2003] 4 All ER 1358n, (2003) Times, 5 December			
For the appropriate procedure and directions in **low velocity impact** cases see **TAB 15**, paras 15 and 16 above and *Casey v Cartwright* [2006] EWCA Civ 1280, [2006] All ER (D) 72 (Oct); in particular that the defendant who wishes to raise the causation issue should notify all other parties in writing, should raise the issue in the defence and within 21 days of the defence serve a statement showing the grounds and evidence on which the issue is raised			
The parties should raise any question of a **structured settlement** during case management			29 para 3A
4. Case management conferences			
must attend case management conferences and pre-trial reviews (a) familiar with the case (b) with sufficient authority to deal with issues that may arise			

	Form No	CPR Rule	PD
If a party has a legal representative, a representative:		29.3(2)	29, para 5.2
The court may require a party to attend		3.1(2)(c)	
These provisions must be kept foremost in mind when counsel or agents are being instructed to attend			
The inadequacy of the person attending or who has instructions will be likely to result in a wasted costs order			29, para 5.2(3)
The court will make arrangements to ensure that applications and other hearings "are listed promptly to avoid delay ..."			29, para 3.9
There may be hearings that can conveniently be heard by telephone conference but many case management conferences will not normally be suitable because of their length and complexity			
The **topics likely to be considered** at a case management conference include: (a) clarifying the claim (b) any necessary amendments (c) disclosure (d) the expert evidence reasonably required (e) disclosure of factual evidence (f) further information and questions to experts (g) split trials and preliminary issues			29, para 5.3
The court will also fix a timetable including, where appropriate, a further case management conference, a pre-trial review and a trial date or trial period			29, para 5.4
CPR PD 29 underlines that a party who obtains **expert evidence before obtaining a direction** does so at **his own risk as to costs**, except where the evidence was obtained in accordance with a pre-action protocol			29, para 5.5
To assist the court the parties and their legal advisers should:			29, para 5.6

	Form No	CPR Rule	PD
(a) ensure that all documents that the court is likely to want to see (including witness statements and experts' reports) are brought to the hearing			
(b) consider whether the parties should attend (c) consider whether a case summary will be useful, and (d) consider what orders each wishes to be made and give notice of them to the other parties			
Some courts issue with the notice of the case management appointment a letter setting out **the court's specific requirements** as to attendance, information, etc			
Where a split trial is being considered the court will be primarily concerned whether it will save costs without causing prejudice or unfairness: *Ajinomoto Sweeteners Europe SAS v Asda Stores Ltd* [2009] EWHC 781 (QB), [2009] FSR 687.			
A case summary: (a) should be designed to assist the court to understand and deal with the questions before it (b) should set out a brief chronology of the claim, the issues of fact which are agreed or in dispute and the evidence needed to decide them (c) should normally not exceed 500 words in length, and (d) should be prepared by the claimant and agreed with the other parties if possible			29, para 5.7
The case summary should be lodged in good time before the hearing; every effort should be made to ensure it is **before the district judge so that he can read it before the hearing**			
5. Variation			
A party dissatisfied with a direction or order should **appeal** (if he was present or had notice of the hearing) or apply to the court to **reconsider its decision**			29, para 6.3(1) and (2)

	Form No	CPR Rule	PD
If he does not do so (**within 14 days of service**) he will be assumed to be content with the direction			29, para 6.2(2)
Reconsideration will usually be by a judge of the same level as the judge who gave the directions or made the order. The court will give at least 3 days' notice of the hearing			29, para 6.3(4)
Where there has been a change of circumstances since the order the court may vary or set aside a directions on application or of its own motion			29, para 6.4
For procedure **where the parties agree about changes**, see		29.5	29, para 6.5
and note in particular an application to the court is necessary for varying a date fixed for: (a) a case management conference (b) a pre-trial review (c) the return of a Pre-trial Check List (d) the trial (e) the trial period or any date for doing any act which would necessitate the change of any of these dates.		29.5(2)	
On an appeal from an order made at a Case Management Conference the court will normally only interfere if the judge at first instance has exceeded 'the generous ambit within which reasonable disagreement is possible': *Clyde & Co LLP v New Look Interiors of Marlow Ltd* [2009] EWHC 173 (QB), [2009] All ER (D) 70 (Feb), NLJ Law Digest 20 February 2009, page 278.			
6. Pre-trial Check List			
The court will send out the Pre-trial Check Lists (unless it has been dispensed with by order or direction) for return by the date filed by the court. If one party fails to return the Check List properly completed or if the court considers it necessary it will fix a date for a listing hearing The fee on the filing of a Listing Questionnaire is £100	N170	29.6(1), 29.6(4)	29, para 8.1

	Form No	CPR Rule	PD
If no party files a Check List the court will order that the claim and any counterclaim will be struck out unless a Check List is filed within 7 days of service of the order		29.6(3)	29, para 8.3
On receipt of the parties' completed Check Lists the court may decide to hold a pre-trial review or cancel any pre-trial review that has previously been ordered that is considered unnecessary		29.7	
The parties should seek agreed directions and seek an agreed order. The agreed directions should include provision about: (a) evidence and in particular expert evidence (b) a trial timetable and time estimate (c) the preparation for a trial bundle (d) any other matter necessary to prepare the case for trial			29, para 9.2
A direction as to **expert evidence** will (unless it has been done previously) give permission to use expert evidence, indicate whether the permission is for oral evidence or reports or both and will name the experts concerned			29, para 9.2(4)
The court will fix or confirm the trial date or period, give a time estimate and fix the place of trial			29, para 9.1
The Pre-trial Check List assumes that each party required to complete it has complied with all directions that have been given and is ready for trial. If directions are required the party applying for them must send the appropriate application, with the fee payable and a draft order with the completed Check List	N244		
For the necessity of **costs estimates** and their service with both the allocation questionnaire and the pre-trial check list see			Costs PD, paras 6.1–6.6

	Form No	CPR Rule	PD
For the necessity of a statement of costs for the trial, which must be served as soon as possible and in any event not less than 24 hours before the time fixed for the hearing, see			Costs PD, para 13.5(4)
As to the consequences of serving inaccurate costs estimates see			Costs PD, para 6.5A
7. Trial bundles			
Unless the court otherwise orders, the claimant must file the trial bundle not more than 7 days nor less than 3 days before the start of the trial Unless the court orders otherwise, the trial bundle should include a copy of: (a) the claim form and all statements of case (b) a case summary and/or chronology where appropriate (c) requests for further information and responses to the requests (d) all witnesses statements to be relied on as evidence (e) any witness summaries (f) any notices of intention to rely on hearsay evidence under CPR 32.2 (g) any notices of intention to rely on evidence (such as a plan, photograph, etc) under CPR 33.6 which is not: (i) contained in a witness statement, affidavit or experts' report (ii) being given orally at trial (iii) hearsay evidence under CPR 33.2 (h) any medical reports and responses to them (i) any experts' reports and responses to them (j) any order giving directions as to the conduct of the trial, and (k) any other necessary documents See also as to trial bundles, para **CPR 39.5 [1]**, and *OJSC v Abramovich* [2008] All ER (D) 299 (Oct) per Clarke J as to 'deficiencies and the recurrence of failings'.			39A, paras 3(1) and (2) 39A, paras 3.3–3.10

	Form No	CPR Rule	PD
See also an article 'Benchmarks: good on paper' by Paul Waterworth (2009) Gazette 28 January, page 16 on the preparation an importance of trial bundles.			
Fro the preparation of a separate bundle, where that is appropriate, or the experts' reports and answers to questions to be included in the trial bundle see article by Mark Solon entitled 'Expert preparation' in NLJ (2010) 25 June, page 906.			
8. The trial			
Vacating a trial date that has been fixed is often described as a 'last resort' but that statement relates to a situation that has arisen because of failure to comply with case management directions: *Collins v Gordon* [2008] EWCA Civ 110, 21 January.			29, para 7.4(6)
For detailed consideration of appropriate principles to be applied by the court when considering applications to postpone a trial or adjourn a trial see *Elliott Group Ltd v GECC UK* [2010] EWHC 409 where Coulson J considered fully the earlier decisions in *Boyd and Hutchinson v Foenander* [2003] EWCA Civ 1516, 23 October and *Fitzroy Robinson Ltd v Mentmore Towers Ltd* [2009] EWHC 3070 (TCC), 26 November, an earlier decision of Coulson J. In *Elliott* some adjustments to the timetable were granted but the application to adjourn was refused as the case could properly and fairly be prepared in the time remaining before the trial date.			
A hearing fee of £1,000 is payable; the provisions for percentage refunds are the same as for cases on the fast track, see **TAB 18**, section 6, final paragraph.			
For the principles which the court will apply when faced with an application for an expedited or speedy trial see *Intervet (UK) Ltd v Merial* [2009] EWHC 1965 (Pat).			

	Form No	CPR Rule	PD
A case allocated to the multi-track can only be tried by a **Master or district judge**, subject to any Practice Direction: (a) In the High Court if (i) the case is proceeding under CPR Pt 8, or		8.9(c)	2B, para 11.1(a)
(ii) the case has been allocated under CPR Pt 26, with the consent of the parties *Note:* • The consent of the parties is required for the determination of a preliminary issue by a Master or district judge			2B, para 4.1
• A Master or district judge can assess the damages or sum due under a judgment without limit, but note *Sandry v Jones* (2000) Times, 3 August, CA			2B, para 4.2
• As to proceedings under the Inheritance (Provision for Family and Dependants) Act 1975 and s 14 of the Trusts for Land and Appointment of Trustees Act 1996, see			2B, para 3.2
(b) In the county court if: (i) the case is treated as being allocated to the multi-track under CPR 8.9(c) and Table 2 of the Practice Direction to CPR Pt 8 except those claims listed in para 11.1(a) of the Practice Direction to CPR Pt 2			
(ii) the proceedings are for the recovery of land			2B, para 11.1(b)
(iii) with the permission of the Designated Civil Judge			2B, para 11.1(d)

	Form No	CPR Rule	PD
Note: • The position as to assessment of damages is the same as in the High Court (see above) but subject to the approval of the Designated Civil Judge, in some circuits or areas at least, pursuant to CPR PD 26, para 12.6			2B, para 11.1(c)
• The position of proceedings under the Inheritance (Provision for Family and Dependants) Act 1975 and s 14 of the Trusts of Land and Appointment of Trustees Act 1996 is as in the High Court and see High Court and County Courts Jurisdiction Order 1991			
• A district judge may not hear appeals under s 204 of the Housing Act 1996 which deals with homelessness			2B, para 4.2
Trials on the multi-track are not subject to: (a) time limits (compare small claims track and fast track)		27.14 46.2	
(b) costs limits (compare small claims track and fast track)			26, paras 8.1 and 9.3
The rules of evidence apply to multi-track trials (compare small claims track)		27.8(3)	
The court will nevertheless seek to deal with cases **expeditiously and fairly** and may:		1.1(2)(d)	
(i) dispense with an opening address having read the papers in advance			29, para 10.2
(ii) enforce or set a timetable			29, para 10.3
(iii) direct statements and reports to stand as evidence		32.5(2)	29, para 10.4
(iv) control evidence and restrict cross-examination		32.1	29, para 10.4
where such steps would be **proportionate**			

	Form No	CPR Rule	PD
The greatest "blow" to the claimant's advocate will be the dispensing with an opening. The use and quality of a **skeleton argument**, lodged in advance of the trial, are vital. For the contents of a skeleton argument see *Tombstone Ltd v Raja* [2008] EWCA Civ 1444 at [125]–[128] per Mummery LJ and in particular that it should be used to aid advocacy and not as a substitute for it. In this case the skeleton argument extended to 110 pages with a further 64 pages of appendices! See also *Midgulf International Ltd v Groupe Chemique Tunisien* [2010] EWC Civ 66, [2010] All ER (D) 114 (Feb) where Toulson LJ expressed strong disapproval of the 'volume of papers' with which the Court was presented by the appellants. The original skeleton argument ran to 132 pages and there were over 100 authorities with 5 volumes of authorities! There was a supplemental skeleton of 30 pages.			
The first draft prepared will usually be improved if pruned by a half when it is finalised, a **list of any authorities** what will be referred to should be incorporated and copies of the authorities must be available. Note Practice Direction (citation of authorities) [2001] 1 WLR 1001 and dicta of May LJ in *Banton v Banton* (1989) Times, 4 April, CA ' Advocates should always be ready with authority in support of a submission and must not rely on their beliefs or opinions'.			
It is generally helpful for the skeleton argument to cross-refer to the evidence and to be accompanied by a chronology.			
In a trial where the order sought is complex, consideration should be given to annexing a **draft order**. Great care must be taken when so doing to avoid giving offence. If there is any doubt about its value it should be retained until after judgment has been delivered			

	Form No	CPR Rule	PD
In multi-track trials oral expert evidence will be more frequent than in fast track trials. In the case of *Clifford v Chief Constable of the Hertfordshire Constabulary* [2008] EWHC 2549 (QB), [2008] All ER (D) 254 Wyn Williams J refused to admit expert evidence as he did not see how it would assist in the determination of the main issue in the case which was one of pure fact to be determined by factual evidence. See also **TAB 16**, Expert Evidence, above.		35.5(2)	
An order will usually have been made for experts to meet and, if not agreed, to prepare a statement of the issues on which they agree and those in which they disagree and why. The **experts' statement** is vital in setting the parameters for cross-examination of the experts		35.12(3)	
Where the issue of **causation** is argued before the judge and the parties put to him two or more competing arguments as to the way the event occurred which might be uncommon but not improbable, the judge, having eliminated all causes of the damage save one, could properly ask himself on the balance of probabilities whether that one remaining cause was the cause of the action: *Ide v ATB Sales Ltd and Lexus Financial Services v Russell* [2008] EWCA Civ 424, [2008] AlL ER (D) 374 (Apr).			
For causation in clinical negligence actions where there are several possible causes of injury see *Bailey (by her father and litigation friend) v Ministry of Defence* [2008] EWCA Civ 883, [2009] 1 WLR 1052 and article in Sol Jo (2008) 21 October and (2009) 23 June, page 27			
In cases, such as tripping cases, where the precise location and physical defects are important **accurate sketch plans and photographs** can be crucial: see *Manning v Stylianou* [2006] EWCA Civ 1655 and article at (2007) Sol Jo, 25 May, page 662. See also *Hunte v Bottomley and Sons Ltd* (2007) Times, 21 November, CA			

	Form No	CPR Rule	PD
For the evidential value of plans already in existence in **boundary disputes** and for consideration of the relevant factors in that type of case see *Huntley v Armes* [2010] EWCA Civ 396, [2010] 12 May, Sol Jo, and for a detailed consideration see article 'The great divide' by Marc Glover in Sol Jo, Property Focus June 2010, page 8			
If there is an opportunity to prepare a typed **"skeleton closing"** it is prudent for the defendant's advocate to produce one. It is essential that this is brief, and leaves clear scope for fleshing out in closing speech			
Save in exceptional cases a party should not provide a document to the judge without the other party being provided with a copy or being given the opportunity to make representations about it; *Lloyds Bank plc v Cassidy* (2005) Times, 11 January, CA			
As to public perception of bias, **recusal** of himself by the judge and applications to the judge to withdraw see *AWG Group Ltd v Morrison* [2006] EWCA Civ 6, [2006] 1 All ER 967 and article by Louis Flannery [2006] 156 NLJ, 17 February, p 278 and also see *Howell v Lees Millais* [2007] EWCA Civ 720, [2007] All ER (D) 64 (Jul) where the judge concerned had had personal dealings with a firm of solicitors at to his taking up some form of consultancy. The judge declined to stand down but his refusal was overturned by the Court of Appeal. The case was subsequently referred to the Office for Judicial Complaints at the instance of the Lord Chief Justice. This case is the subject of a further article by Louise Flannery at [2007] 15 NLJ, page 2746. The judge was reprimanded by the Lord Chief Justice as a result of the reference to the OJC.			

	Form No	CPR Rule	PD
The court will not ordinarily uphold an objection based on the judge's receipt, whilst at the Bar, of instructions to act for or against any party, solicitor or advocate now before him: *Locabail (UK) Ltd v Bayfield Properties Ltd* [2000] 1 All ER 65, CA; and see also *Mireskandari v Associated Newspapers Ltd* [2010] EWHC 967 (QB), [2010] All ER (D) 06 (May).			
It is not part of counsel's duty nor is it appropriate for counsel to influence a decision by a lay client as to whether to waive his right to object to a judge in his case because of an appearance of bias; *Smith v Kvaerner Cementation Foundations Ltd* [2006] EWCA Civ 242, (2006) Times, 11 April, CA			
Where there is real ground for doubt that doubt should be resolved in favour of recusal: *Ansar v Lloyds TSB plc (No 2)* [2006] All ER (D) 277 (Jul)			
The court is unlikely to look favourably on claims of judicial bias after the complainant has awaited the outcome of the case and found it to be unwelcome: *Steadman-Byrne v Amjad* [2007] EWCA Civ 625, (2007) Times, 30 July, per Sedley J. The appeal in this case was nevertheless allowed, the judge having indicated a clear view having heard only one party to the case. There was no argument by the respondent that the appellant was estopped from filing an appeal notice by reason of his failure to take objection promptly upon the bias being apparent but the court obviously adverted to the possibility of an argument that an estoppel had arisen or that the apparent bias had been waived			

	Form No	CPR Rule	PD
A useful authority is to be found in the employment case of *Ezsias v North Glamorgan NHS Trust* [2007] EWCA Civ 330, [2007] 4 All ER 940 where the judge at a pre-hearing review expressed her view in such conclusive terms that it was reasonable for a fair-minded and informed observer to take the view that the judge had a closed mind as to the claimant's prospects of success. The Court of Appeal upheld the EAT's decision to set aside the decision, subsequently made by the judge, striking out the appeal on the basis that it had no reasonable prospect of success on the ground of bias, i e the possible perception by a fair-minded observer that the forum had already made up its mind.			
A clear manifestation of bias should be drawn to the attention of the court immediately to avoid any argument that the appearance of bias had been waived and in the interest of administration of justice: *Locabail (UK) Ltd v Bayfield Properties Ltd (leave to appeal)* [2000] QB 451; also *Baker v Quantum Clothing Group* [2009] EWCA Civ 566, [2009] All ER (D) 75 (Jun), where the application for re-hearing on the ground of apparent bias were made after the judgment had been reserved.			
For a case where the allegation of apparent bias 'plainly resulted from the extreme bitterness of the dispute between the parties' see *Thompson v Collins* [2009] EWCA Civ 525, [2009] All ER (D) 67 (Apr).			

	Form No	CPR Rule	PD
In *El Farargy v El Farargy* (2007) Times, 23 November, CA the judge made remarks in a directions hearing which resulted in an application for him to recuse himself. The applicant maintained that the remarks betrayed apparent bias. The judge refused to do so but his decision was reversed by the Court of Appeal which found the judge to have crossed the line between the tolerable and the impermissible. Ward LJ observed that it was invidious for a judge to sit in judgment of his own conduct. Where the circumstances permitted, first an informal approach should be made to the judge inviting recusal. This would provide a judge who denies the complaint with the opportunity either to pass the case to a colleague or to invite another judge to make the decision on the application.			
For criticism of Ward LJ's guidance see article 'The *El Farargy* postscript' by Craig Barlow and Jason Hadden, NLJ, 22 February 2008, pages 278–280.			
The Immigration Appeal case *Helow v Secretary of State for the Home Department* [2008] UKHL 62, [2008] 1 WLR 2416, (2008) Times, 5 November involved an allegation of bias and want of impartiality and was reported under the heading 'Partisan magazine did not influence judge'. The appeal failed but the speech of Lord Mance is of considerable interest			

	Form No	CPR Rule	PD
For guidance on circumstances which justify a **lawyer's withdrawal** from a case see *R v Ulcay* [2007] EWCA Crim 2379, [2008] 1 All ER 547; *R v O'Hare* [2006] EWCA Crim 471, [2006] All ER (D) 155 (Mar); and *Re Boodhoo (wasted costs order)* [2007] EWCA Crim 14, [2007] All ER 762n. In the case of *Ulcay* both counsel and solicitors successfully applied to withdraw from the case. Subsequently new counsel and solicitors appeared on behalf of the defendant but, after what they regarded as an adjournment for an inadequate time to prepare, they withdrew form the case because of insufficient time to prepare. Both counsel and solicitors followed advice given by their professional body but the advice was stated to be wrong by the court, which felt strongly that the lawyers were professionally obliged by their duty to the court to "soldier on" and do their best to comply with orders of the court. The judgment of the court was given by Sir Igor Judge and he made it clear that Code of Conduct 2007, rule 2.01(b) did not require a solicitor to refuse to act or cease to act in these circumstances			

	Form No	CPR Rule	PD
As to summary judgment at trial see *James v Evans* [2000] 3 EGLR 1, CA. As to a submission of **no case to answer** and whether an election as to the calling of evidence should be required see *Boyce v Wyatt Engineering* [2001] EWCA Civ 692, (2001) Times, 14 June and *Miller (t/a Waterloo Plant) v Cawley* [2002] EWCA Civ 1100, (2002) Times, 6 September; also *Youssif v Jordan* [2003] EWCA Civ 1852, (2004) Times, 22 January and *Sutradhar v Natural Environmental Research Council* [2004] EWCA Civ 175, (2004) Times, 19 March affd [2006] UKHL 33, [2006] 4 All ER 490. More recently *Benham Ltd v Kithira Investments* [2005] CLY 493 and *Graham v Chorley Borough Council* [2006] EWCA Civ 92, (2006) Times, 20 March As to the submission of no case to answer and the putting of the defence to its election see *Graham v Chorley Borough Council* [2006] EWCA Civ 92, (2006) Times, 20 March			
As to an application at trial to argue an **unpleaded point** see *Dupont de Nemours v St Dupont (No 2)* [2003] 05 LS Gaz R 32			
As to the effect of interference by the judge during the trial see *Alpha Lettings Ltd v Neptune Research and Development Inc* [2003] EWCA Civ 704, [2003] All ER (D) 273 (May), CA and the statement of Sir Thomas Bingham MR referred to that 'the English tradition sanctions and even encourages a measure of disclosure by the judge of his current thinking …'			
For the risk that arises from a judge's lengthy interrogation of witnesses see *Southwark London Borough Council v Kofi-Adu* [2006] EWCA Civ 281, (2006) Times, 1 June			

	Form No	CPR Rule	PD
The Court of Appeal in *Malik v Kalyan* (2010) Times, 1 April, per Rimer LJ, stated 'It is usually good practice for a judge trying a civil claim to see where a line of cross-examination was, or might be, going before stopping it.' The case was remitted to the judge for a retrial on the basis that he would hear further cross-examination from which he might reconsider his findings and conclusions.			
A hearing fee of £1,000 is payable by the claimant (or the defendant if the action is proceeding solely on the counterclaim). The provisions for refund on settlement or discontinuance are the same as on the Fast Track; see **TAB 18**, para 6, final sub-paragraph.			
It must be faced that there can be a degree of delay that can make a fair trial unachievable. The human rights argument can be followed from a consideration of the decision in *Lehtinden v Finland (No 2) Application No 4561804* [2009] ECHR 45618/04, Hg 31 March 2007. The proceedings lasted 9 years and 10 months which was found to be excessive and a breach of Art 6(1) of the Convention. An award of £4,000 pecuniary damage was made.			
8A. Judgment			
The requirement to make thorough **findings of fact** is such that failure to do so will result in a flawed judgment that requires re-hearing: *Gabriel v Kirklees Metropolitan Council* [2004] EWCA Civ 345, [2004] BLR 441, (2004) Times, 12 April			

	Form No	CPR Rule	PD
For the duty on judges to give reasons for their decisions see *Flannery v Halifax Estate Agency Ltd* [2000] 1 All ER 373 per Henry LJ. If at the end of a judgment it appears the judge has failed to deal with a material point it is the advocates' duty to draw the omission to the court's attention and request clarification or a supplemental judgment: *Re S (omission from judgment; duty of counsel)* (2007) Times, 2 July. See also *Re A (a child)(duty to seek reasons)* (2007) Times, 16 October, CA below			
A judge can alter his judgment at any time before it is perfected and entered; that is, in effect, by the sealing of the order giving effect to the judgment (which would now be pursuant to CPR 40.2(2)(b)): *Re Barrell Enterprises* [1973] 1 WLR 19, CA; *Pittalis v Sherefettin* [1986] QB 868, CA (decisions prior to CPR but unaffected by them); *Stewart v Engel* [2000] 3 All ER 518, CA and *Paulin v Paulin* [2009] EWCA Civ 221, [2009] All ER (D) 187 (Mar). Reference should be made to the judgments in *Pittalis* (see above) for the procedure to be adopted and to the judgment of Wilson LJ in *Paulin* above for a detailed consideration of those principles. See also New Law Journal 27 March 2009, page 475 and an article in the same journal on 17 July 2009 at page 1015 entitled 'Reverse gear' by Shantanu Majumdar.			
In *Earl of Malmesbury v Strutt & Parker* [2007] EWHC 2199 (QB), [2007] All ER (D) 103 (Oct) the court expressed the view that there should be 'strong reasons' before the judge's jurisdiction to alter his judgment was exercised. Earlier cases had made the existence of 'exceptional circumstances' as the pre-condition. The jurisdiction, on either pre-condition, should only be exercised where it was clear to the judge without prolonged enquiry that his conclusion was wrong.			

	Form No	CPR Rule	PD
A judge has an unlimited jurisdiction to amplify his reasons for the decision at any time: *Re T (a child: contact)* [2002] EWCA Civ 1736, [2003] 1 FCR 303 and *Paulin* (see above).			
A party cannot return to the trial judge and seek to have the re-opening of a final decision. In effect it would be asking him to hear an appeal from himself that he has no power to do. This remains the case if the judge's order was founded on a settlement agreed between the parties after advice: *Roult v North West Strategic Health Authority* [2009] EWCA Civ 444, [2009] PIQR P322.			
If a trial judge decides a claim on one of two or more points a party is not entitled to a decision on the other points that have been made academic by his finding: *Palfrey v Wilson* [2007] EWCA Civ 94, (2007) Times, 5 March			
Only in most exceptional circumstances should counsel ask a judge to reconsider a point of substance after the draft judgment has been sent out: *Egan v Motor Services (Bath) Ltd* [2007] EWCA Civ 1002, (2007) Times, 24 December, CA			
In *R (on the application of Edwards) v Environment Agency* [2008] UKHL 22, [2008] 1 WLR 1587 copies of draft speeches were provided in confidence with a request that counsel check them for 'error and ambiguity'. Lord Hoffmann said: 'The purpose of the disclosure of draft speeches to counsel is to obtain their help in correcting misprints, inadvertent errors of fact or ambiguities of expression. It is not to enable them to re-argue the case.'			

	Form No	CPR Rule	PD
Not only are draft judgments circulated in confidence but all communications in response are covered by the same principle; for the difficulties that arose when confidence was broken by one of the responses being circulated beyond the court see *R (Mohamed) v Secretary of State for Foreign and Commonwealth Affairs* [2010] EWCA Civ 158, 26 February, where the result was that the original paragraphs that had been circulated and subsequently amended, were made public on the Court waiving confidentiality.			
Besides circulating its draft judgment the court may also, on occasions, circulate a draft order and invite submissions on it: see for example *Owens v Noble* [2010] Gazette LR, 25 March, page 25 and 1 April, page 17, CA. An issue of fraud was remitted for determination and the issues included whether the remission should be to the original trial judge and as to the costs of the appeal. Remission to the trial judge was upheld there being no exceptional circumstances to the contrary.			
In *Owens v Noble* (above) the Court of Appeal clarified the correct procedure when it is alleged that a deceit had been practised on the court below. Where fresh evidence is adduced to the Court of Appeal tending to show the trial judge had been deliberately misled, the Court will only allow the appeal and order a retrial where either the fraud was admitted or was incontrovertible. If this is not the case the usual course would be for the issue of fraud to be tried before a decision was made on whether the established judgment should be set aside.			
For the Practice Direction as to Reserved Judgments given in:			
(a) Court of Appeal (Civil Division) and (b) Queen's Bench Division and Chancery Division at the Royal Courts of Justice see			40E (as substituted with effect from 1 October 2008)

	Form No	CPR Rule	PD
In *McKeowen v British Horse Racing Authority* [2010] EWHC 508 (Admin), 12 March 2010 (Stadler J) it was stated that although a judge had jurisdiction to make substantive changes to a judgment circulated to the parties in draft, even going so far as to reverse his decision, he would only exercise the jurisdiction to do so in exceptional circumstances following the case of *Robinson v Bird* [2003] EWCA Civ 1820.			
A judge who has sent a draft judgment to the parties still retains jurisdiction to alter its substance but should invite submissions on the point at issue; *Robinson v Bird* [2004] EWCA Civ 126			
See further CPR 40.3 [2] and the cases cited and considered there.			
Parties engaged in meaningful settlement discussions between the reserving and the delivery of judgment must tell the court of the discussions: *Gurney Consulting Engineers v Gleeds Health and Safety Ltd* [2006] EWHC 536 (TCC), (2006) Times, 24 April			
Although county court judges should be encouraged to give short judgments they must grapple with conflicts in the evidence of witnesses and sufficiently deal with the fundamental issues so as to explain how they arrived at their decision: *Baird v Thurrock Borough Council* [2005] EWCA Civ 1499, (2005) Times, 15 November			
A judgment takes effect from the date it was given or made or such later date as the court shall specify. An interesting use of the ability to defer the date the judgment takes effect is to be found in *Halabi v Camden London Borough Council* [2008] EWHC 322 (Ch), (2008) Times, 25 March, a case concerning an application to annul a bankruptcy order under the 'debts paid' provision.		40.7	

	Form No	CPR Rule	PD
CPR 3.1(7) does not empower a judge to hear an appeal from himself in respect of a final order nor permit any party to ask any judge to review his own decision because of the happening of some subsequent event: *Roult (by Angela Holt) v North West Strategic Health Authority* [2009] EWCA Civ 444, [2009] PIQR P322, where it was held the rule could not be used to revoke a judge's approval to a final settlement for the future care costs of the appellant. The court indicated that CPR 3.1(7) was essentially applicable to case management decisions.			
Similarly a court has no power to vary the terms of a settlement agreement in the schedule of a Tomlin order: *Community Care North East (a partnership) v Durham County Council* [2010] EWHC 959 (QB), [2010] All ER (D) 09 (Jun), (2010) NLJ, 18 June, page 877.			
8B. The advocate and the judgment			
As to advice given by an advocate at the door of the court, typically as to the acceptance or rejection of an offer, see *Moy v Pettman Smith (a firm)* [2005] 1 All ER 903, (2004) Times, 4 February, HL and *Walker v Chruszcz* [2006] EWHC 64 (QB), [2006] All ER (D) 224 (Jan) where an allegation by the client that he had been pressured into settling his claim at an undervalue at the door of the court failed; the availability of a detailed attendance note contributed significantly to the court's decision			
If an appeal is likely to be considered in cases of doubt counsel must ask the judge for amplification of the reasons where that could solve an issue: *Re A (a child)(duty to seek reasons)* (2007) Times, 16 October, CA			

	Form No	CPR Rule	PD
When considering an appeal it is salutary to bear in mind the standard of the court in *Vaughan v Vaughan* [2007] EWCA Civ 1085, [2007] All ER (D) 43 (Nov): "It is sometimes easy to think that an appeal is from a judgment. But it is not, it is from an order. A judgment may have contained an error and a change of circumstances may have invalidated some of its important assumptions but it does not follow that the order should be set aside upon appellate review."			
Advocates do not have immunity from suit in respect of acts concerned with the conduct of litigation: *Arthur JS Hall & Co (a firm) v Simons* [2002] 1 AC 615, HL, a decision which had retrospective effect: *Awoyomi v Radford* [2007] EWHC 1671 (Admin), (2007) Times, 23 July, QB and *McFaddens (a firm) v Platford* [2009] EWHC 126 (TCC), [2009] All ER (D) 257 (Jan) . In *McFaddens* the judge reviewed the roles and responsibilities of the barrister and solicitor and the question of whether the solicitor is entitled to rely on counsel's advice.			
8C. Retrial or fresh action			
If fraud is admitted or very clear evidence is found, an appeal on the ground that the trial judge was deliberately misled is the appropriate course rather than the commencement of a fresh action. The appeal will result in a new trial being ordered: see *Owens v Noble* [2010] EWCA Civ 224, 10 March. This is subject to the fresh evidence not being reasonably available to the party aggrieved at the time of the hearing: see *HJ Heinz & Co Ltd v EFL Inc* [2010] EWHC 1203 (Comm), [2010] All ER (D) 01 (Jun).			
Where the fresh evidence as to fraud is contested the appropriate course is for a trial of the issue to be ordered before the judgment obtained is set aside or the appeal dismissed.			

	Form No	CPR Rule	PD
8D. Personal injury interest rates			
• Damages for pain and suffering and loss of amentities – 2% (*Burkett v Hayes* [1982] 1 WLR 816, [1982] 2 All ER 710) • Special damage (special account rate). After 7 years at 6% fixed at: 1 February 2009 3% 1 June 2009 1.5% 1 July 2009 0.5% • Continuing special damages Half the appropriate rate from date of the injury until trial. There are conflicting decisions whether half the rate or the full rate is appropriate where the damage has ceased before trial. Benefits are disregarded when calculating interest on special damage. See article by John Nelson Jones in Gazette (2010) 16 September, page 28.			
9. Costs			
If costs are ordered the judge may order that they be subject to detailed assessment or may proceed to assess them summarily at the conclusion of the trial		44.7	
It is unlikely that the parties in a case of any substance will be eager for summary assessment, but schedules of costs should be prepared and, at any rate, brought to the trial even if they are not filed and exchanged			
If there is a trial on liability only the judge is not required to make an immediate decision on costs at that stage but may, at his discretion, postpone making a costs order until quantum has been finally determined: *Shepherds Investments Ltd v Walters* [2007] EWCA Civ 292, [2007] All ER (D) 40 (Apr). But for a different approach where the claim was not only for a sum of money see *Experience Hendrix LLC v Times Newspapers Ltd* [2008] EWHC 458 (Ch), [2008] AlL ER (D) 146 (Mar).			

	Form No	CPR Rule	PD
Where a party made an offer of settlement in accordance with CPR 36.21 and it was rejected but was more favourable than the eventual judgment of the court, the court will order costs on an indemnity basis and/or interest on damages at a higher rate from the date of rejection unless it is unjust to do so; *Mamidoil-Jetoil Greek Petroleum Co SA v Okta Crude Oil Refinery AD* (2002) Times, 27 December.			
For the court's attitude to costs where although the claimant has succeeded the court is satisfied he had exaggerated his personal injury claim; see *Painting v University of Oxford* [2005] EWCA Civ 161, (2005) Times, 15 February and *Hall v Stone* [2007] EWCA Civ 1354.		44.3(5)(d)	

	Form No	CPR Rule	PD
Where a personal injury claimant has exaggerated her claim but had still beaten the defendant's payment in (or Part 36 offer) the right order was held to be 'no order for costs' in *Widlake v BAA Ltd* [2009] EWCA Civ 1256, 153 Sol Jo (no 45) 29. See also the subsequent case *Sulaman v Axa and Direct Line* [2009] EWCA Civ 1331, [2009] All ER (D) 116 (Dec) where the decision in *Widlake* above was cited. In the circumstances of this case two thirds of the claimant's costs were disallowed, she being found to have lied during the trial. For discussion see NLJ (2009) 22 December, page 5 and note the appeal was dismissed with Sedley LJ dissenting expressing the view that it was disproportionate to deprive the appellant of two-thirds of her costs. For a discussion of the costs trends in such cases see article 'Spinning a yarn' by Gless and Goddard in (2010) NLJ, page 267 and for a review of the cases including those referred to above see article by Jonathan Upton entitled 'Lying litigants beware!' (2010) NLJ 19 March, page 418. See also an article 'Knocked down' by Andrew Trott in Sol Jo Personal Focus, (2010) April, page 12 and the consideration of the cases *Singh v CS O'Shea & Son Ltd* [2009] EWHC 1251 (QB) and *Kirk v Walton* [2009] EWHC 703 (QB) it contains. For the exceptional position of cases concerning an insurance contract see *Axa General Insurance Ltd v Gottlieb* [2005] EWCA Civ 112, [2005] 1 All ER (Comm) 445, [2005] Lloyd's Rep IR 369, (2005) Times, 3 March.			
If the claimant's 'exaggeration' was no more than to put his claim rather high, a defendant who had failed to make an effective and admissible offer could not be regarded as a winner.			

	Form No	CPR Rule	PD
For the court's attitude to the successful party's costs where it is found he was in breach of a pre-action protocol see *Straker v Tudor Rose* [2007] EWCA Civ 368, 151 Sol Jo LB 571. It is the responsibility of the claimant's solicitor to ensure the claim is not issued prematurely			
For the courts' attitude to costs involving fraud see *Cheltenham Borough Council v Laird* CA (Civ), 4 February 2010 where the defendant successfully defended an action for fraudulent misrepresentation but was awarded only 65% of costs as she failed on several issues.		44.3(4)(b)	
In a commercial case where each party has claims and asserts that there is a balance due to him, the party who is held to be entitled to a payment will generally be regarded as the winner and the starting point as to costs will be the general rule that a successful party is entitled to an order for costs : *Multiplex Constructions (UK) Ltd v Cleveland Bridge UK Ltd* [2008] EWHC 2280 (TCC), (2008) NLJ Law Digest 20 October, page 1473.			
For the effect of conduct on costs both as to disallowance in whole or part and as to the discretion to grant indemnity costs see *Bank of Tokyo-Mitsubishi UFJ Ltd v Baskian Gida Senayi Ve Pazarlama AS* [2009] EWHC 1696 (Ch), Briggs J, [2009] All ER (D) 159 (Jul), (2009) Law Digest 24 July, page 1066 and the cases referred to in the judgment.			
As to indemnity costs and the factors to be taken into account by the court when considering whether it is appropriate to award them see *Noorani v Calver* [2009] EWHC 592 (QB), 153 Sol Jo (no 13) 27, Coulson J and see also an article considering the Buncefield litigation in 2008 by Boylan, Francis and Brierly in NLJ (2009) 31 July, page 1081, entitled 'Counting the Total cost'.		44.3(4) and (5)	

	Form No	CPR Rule	PD
For consideration of **non-party costs** orders under Supreme Court Act 1981 see *Dymocks Franchise Supplies (NSW) Pty Ltd v Todd* [2004] UKPC 39, [2005] 4 All ER 195 where Lord Brown identified the principles and *BE Studios v Smith & Williamson* (2005) Times, 16 December where Evans-Lombe J held that impropriety was not a pre-requisite of liability and *Dolphin Quays Development Ltd v Mills* [2008] EWCA Civ 385, [2008] 4 All ER 58 where the court said such orders will always be exceptional and that the ultimate question will be whether or not it is just to make an order.			
The High Court in *Thomson v Berkhamsted Collegiate School* [2009] EWHC 2374 (QB), [2009] NLJR 1440 did find it just to make an order against the parents of the claimant who was seeking damages of nearly £1 million against his former school for failing to prevent him being bullied but dropped his case two weeks before the trial. The judge found there was evidence that the parents were not merely funders but directly concerned with the facts of the case. The judge followed the principles set out in *Dymocks* (above). Thomson is of considerable importance for the defendants obtained an order for disclosure of the correspondence between the claimant's solicitor and the third parties: see articles 'Once bitten twice shy' (2009) Sol Jo, 10 November, page 6 by Nick Gilkies and 'School of Thought' (2009) NLJ, 12 November, page 1571 by Nina Unthank. The third parties were joined in the action for the purpose of costs only.			

	Form No	CPR Rule	PD
It is good practice where it is likely that a third party costs order will be sought to give early notice of that to the third party: for a case where a third party costs order was made despite the failure to give such notice see *Farrell and Short v Birmingham City Council and Direct Accident Management Services Ltd* [2009] All ER (D) 172 (Jun), CA, the trial judge being satisfied that no prejudice had been suffered as there was no evidence that if notice had been given the third party would have acted differently.			
There is no formal procedure in relation to orders ancillary to applications for non-party costs. Blake J in *Thompson* above stated that ancillary orders that the court considered necessary, e g disclosure, skeleton arguments etc, are made pursuant to the courts' inherent jurisdiction with regard to the overriding objective.			
When the court has ordered a party to pay costs it may order an amount to be paid on account before the costs are assessed. The court has a broad discretion as to this: *Mars UK Ltd v Tecknowledge Ltd (No 2)* [2000] FSR 138, [1999] 2 Costs LR 44 (Ch) and *Dyson Ltd v Hoover Ltd* [2003] EWHC 624 (Ch), [2004] 2 All ER 1042, [2004] 1 WLR 126; see also article in Butterworths Costs Newsletter Vol 1, Issue 2, page 6.		44.3(8)	
For consideration of "exceptional" see *Lingfield Properties (Darlington) Ltd v Padgett Lavender Associates* [2008] EWHC 2795 (QB), [2008] All ER (D) 162 (Nov) where the court stated the meaning was 'no more than outside the ordinary run of cases which parties pursue for their own benefit and at their own expense'. See also **TAB 25**, part C, para 11.7 et seq below			

	Form No	CPR Rule	PD
It is interesting to note that in the *Dolphin Quays* case, see above, it was stated that an important factor in the exercise of the discretion to award costs against a non-party was the availability of **security for costs**. The discretion is likely to be exercised more readily in favour of the successful litigant if security was not available at all or only to an inadequate level			
It was held by the court in *Alan Phillips Associates Ltd v Dowling (Terence Edward) (t/a The Joseph Dowling Partnership)* [2007] EWCA Civ 64, [2007] BLR 151 that the third party director had conducted his affairs through the claimant company in such a way that it would be unjust for him to rely on the existence of two separate legal entities to avoid liability for costs.			
9A. Orders in respect of pro bono representation			
For orders under s 194(3) of the Legal services Act 2007 in respect of pro bono representation, see		44.3C	
10. Slip rule			
This has been held to cover forgetting to ask for costs; for a decision where its limits were considered see *SmithKline Beecham plc v Apotex Europe Ltd* [2005] EWHC 1655 (Ch), [2006] 2 All ER 53, [2006] 1 WLR 872 (the subsequent appeals in this case do not relate to the slip rule)		40.12(1)	
The provision in CPR 40.12 was considered in *R + V Versischerung AG v Risk Insurance and Reinsurance Solutions SA* [2007] EWHC 79 (Comm), (2007) Times, 26 February and the court made it clear that the rule cannot be used to correct errors of substance, nor in an attempt to add or detract from the order made. It does no more than to enable the correction of typing errors or matters that were genuine slips or mistakes			

	Form No	CPR Rule	PD
11. Vacating hearings			
Solicitors and counsel have a duty to inform the court as soon as it is known a hearing will not proceed. See *Tasyurdu v Immigration Appeal Tribunal* [2003] EWCA Civ 447, Times, 16 April			

TABLE 20—OFFERS TO SETTLE

TAB 20

	Form No	CPR Rule	PD
1. Preliminary			
1.1 From 6 April 2007 new rules came into force concerning offers to settle and Part 36 'Offers to Settle and Payments into Court' as it was in force **was substituted** by a new Part 36			
1.2 The position of offers and payments into court before 6 April 2007 is set out in Rule 7 Civil Procedure (Amendment No 3) Rules 2006 and the operation of those provisions is explained in the PD 36B see para **CPR PD 36B** above			36B
1.3 This **TAB** hereafter deals with the new Part 36 Offers to Settle only and the consequences where an offer to settle is made in accordance with Part 36		36.1(1)	
1.4 A party can make an offer to settle in any form he chooses but it will not have Part 36 consequences unless the Part 36 requirements are fulfilled. It will fall to be considered under CPR r44.3 if they are not		36.1(2)	
1.5 The party who makes an offer is the 'offeror' and the party to whom the offer is made is the 'offeree'		36.3(1)	
1.6 The provisions of CPR 36 do not apply to claims allocated to the small claims track		27.2(1)(g)	
1.7 For offers to settle where **the RTA protocol for low value personal injury claims** – Stage 3 procedure applies (see Practice Direction 8B) see **TAB 10A**, para 9.			

	Form No	CPR Rule	PD
2. Form and content of a Part 36 offer			
The requirements for an offer to have Part 36 consequences are that it **must:**	N242A (not mandatory)	36.2	36A, para 1.1 36B – Notice of offer to settle – Part 36
(i) be in writing		36.2(a)	
(ii) state it is intended to have Part 36 consequences		36.2(b)	
(iii) specify a period of not less than 21 days for acceptance		36.2(c)	
(iv) state whether it relates to the whole or part of the claim or to the whole or part of an issue		36.2(d)	
(v) state whether it takes into account any counterclaim		36.2(e)	
But note • requirement (iii) above as to at least 21 days being allowed for acceptance of the offer does not apply if the offer is made less than 21 days before the start of the trial		36.2(3)	
• additional information is required to be contained in an offer that relates to: (i) future pecuniary loss in a personal injury claim –see r36.5 (ii) offer to settle provisional damages claim – see r36.6 (iii) deduction of benefits see r36.15		36.2(4)	
• an offeror can make a Part 36 offer solely as to liability		36.2(5)	
• a Part 36 offer may be made by a defendant in respect of a claim and counterclaim and that remains the case even if the counterclaim has not yet been pleaded: *AF v BG* [2009] EWCA Civ 757, [2009] All ER (D) 249 (Jul). Acceptance will have Part 36 consequences.			
• where a party is legally represented notice of an offer, acceptance, withdrawal or change of terms must be served on the legal representative			36A, para 1.2

	Form No	CPR Rule	PD
• the 'relevant period' means: if the offer is made not less than 21 days before trial the period stated in the notice or such longer period agreed otherwise the period up to the end of the trial or such period as the parties agree		36.3(1)	
3. Time for making a Part 36 offer			
A Part 36 offer can be made: (i) at any time including before proceedings have been commenced (ii) in any appeal proceedings		36.3(2)	
4. Interest			
A Part 36 offer will be treated as inclusive of interest until the time given for acceptance expires or, if made less than 21 days before the start of the trial, a date 21 days after the offer was made		36.3(3)	
5. Costs of an appeal from a final decision			
A Part 36 offer will only have Part 36 consequences in respect of the proceedings in which it is made and not in relation to costs of an appeal from the final decision in the proceedings. A further Part 36 offer can be made in respect of the appeal.		36.3(4)	
6. Withdrawal of Part 36 offer or change of terms			
Withdrawal or the imposition of less advantageous terms requires the permission of the court within the relevant period (see last note in section 2 above) but outside the relevant period permission is not required provided the offeree has not previously served notice of acceptance. Written notice must be given to the offeree and should: (i) refer to the date on which the Part 36 offer was made; (ii) refer to the terms of the offer; and (iii) use words 'which bring home to the offeree that the offer has been withdrawn'.			

	Form No	CPR Rule	PD
For detailed discussion see articles by Christopher Gutteridge entitled 'Compromised position' in (2010) Sol Jo, 190 August, page 10 and by Pertoldi and McIntosh entitled 'Open 24 hours' in (2010) NLJ, 13 August, page 1146.			
A withdrawn offer loses the automatic costs protection of Part 36		36.3(5)–(7) 36.14(6)(a)	
Where the permission of the court is needed to withdraw or change the terms of an offer application should be made (other than to the trial judge) by Part 23 application or at a trial or other hearing.	N244		36A, para 2.2
6A. Multiple offers			
A party can make as many offers as he wishes and the making of a subsequent offer does not supersede any earlier offers that have not been withdrawn, They will all remain individually capable of acceptance even if the offeree has rejected the offer subsequently accepted: see *Gibbons v Manchester City Council and LG Blower Specialist Bricklayers Ltd (joined appeals)* [2010] EWCA Civ 726, [2010] All ER (D) 218 (Jun).			
7. Defendant's offer			
Save in personal injury claims for future pecuniary loss and in claims for provisional damages a Part 36 offer by the defendant to pay a sum of money must be an offer to pay a single sum of money and to be treated as a Part 36 offer it must be to pay it in not later than 14 days following the date of the acceptance. If a defendant is not able to pay within 14 days he will not be able to make an offer with Part 36 effect but he can make an open offer or an offer made without prejudice save as to costs to which the court must have regard under CPR 44.3 and CPR 44.5(3)(a)(ii)		36.4	

	Form No	CPR Rule	PD
8. Time when a Part 36 offer is made			
A Part 36 offer is effective when served on the offeree and a change of terms is effective from such service (provided any necessary permission has been obtained to make the change – see Section 6 above)		36.7	
9. Clarification of Part 36 offer			
Within 7 days of the offer being made the offeree may request clarification and if not given within 7 days, unless the trial has started, apply for an order that it be provided	N244	36.8(1) and (2)	
If the court makes an order it must specify the date when the Part 36 offer is to be treated as having been made		36.8(3)	
10. Acceptance of a Part 36 offer			
10.1 Unless the court's permission to accept (see 10.2 below) is required a Part 36 may be accepted at any time, by serving written notice of acceptance unless the offeror serves notice of withdrawal on the offeree. It has to be remembered that an offer not withdrawn can be accepted outside the relevant period. Express notice of withdrawal must be given if the offer is not to be left open for acceptance		36.9(1) and (2) 36.10(5)	36A, para 3.1
Further that remains the position even if the offer is first rejected; there can be subsequent acceptance (up to withdrawal) subject to agreement or a court ruling as to costs: *Sampla v Rushmoor Borough Council* [2008] EWHC 2616 (TCC), [2008] All ER (D) 335 (Oct).			
The necessity to withdraw offers immediately and in writing if the circumstances of a case change is stressed by Deborah Edwards in an article 'Seeking Settlement' in NLJ 16 January 2009, page 58			
For the acceptance of a claim for **provisional damages** see		36.6(5)	

	Form No	CPR Rule	PD
For the acceptance of an offer which includes the payment of any part of the **damages by periodical payments** see		36.15(7)	41B
• Acceptance out of time without permission will result in the default position as to costs applying so that the offeror will be entitled to costs from the end of the relevant period (defined in CPR 36.3(1)).If the default position is not to be accepted an application to the court will be necessary seeking some other costs order. It is likely that it will be difficult to persuade the court to depart from the default position: see *Matthews v Metal Improvements Co Inc* [2007] EWCA Civ 215, 151 Sol Jo LB 396. For consideration of whether the costs payable to the offeror in the default position should be on standard or indemnity basis see *Fitzpatrick Contractors Ltd v Tyco Fire and Integrated Solutions (UK) Ltd* [2009] EWHC 274 (Ch), 123 Con LR 69 (Coulson J), 20 February.			
• acceptance on behalf of a child or protected party is not valid unless the court has approved the settlement: *Brennan v ECO Composing Ltd* [2006] EWHC 3153 (QB), [2007] 1 WLR 773			
• acceptance is by service of written notice of acceptance on the offeror. A copy is to be filed with the court where the case is proceeding			
10.2 The court's permission to accept a Part 36 where:			
(i) where acceptance is by one or more, but not all, defendants and r36.12(4) applies			

	Form No	CPR Rule	PD
(ii) the relevant period has expired and further deductible amounts have been paid to the claimant since the date of the offer –see r36.15(3)(b)			
(iii) an apportionment is required between claims arising under Fatal Accidents Act 1976 and the Law Reform (Miscellaneous) Provisions Act – see r 41.3A or			
(iv) the trial has started			
Note Unless the parties agree a Part 36 offer may not be accepted after the end of the trial but before judgment is handed down		36.9(3)–(5)	
10.3 The court's permission is sought by application under part 23 or at a trial or hearing but not before the judge allocated in advance to conduct the trial	N244		36A, para 3.2
10.4 For consideration of whether the acceptance of a Part 36 claim creates an enforceable contract and the effect of the Law of Property (Miscellaneous Provisions) Act 1989, s 2, see *Orton v Collins* [2007] EWHC 803 (Ch), [2007] 3 All ER 863. The claimant tried to escape from the acceptance of a Part 36 offer on he ground that it amounted to a disposition of land and the acceptance by the defendant contravened s 2 of the 1989 Act. The argument was rejected by the court so that the claimant was bound by the acceptance.			
11. The acceptance of a Part 36 offer by one or more, but not all, defendants			
This is dealt with in		36.12	
12. Restrictions on disclosure of a Part 36 offer			
A Part 36 offer will be treated as 'without prejudice except as to costs'.			

	Form No	CPR Rule	PD
Its existence must not be communicated to the trial judge or to the judge (if any) allocated in advance to conduct the trial unless the case has been decided.		36.13(1) and (2)	
It follows that the existence of the offer (but not its amount) can be brought to the attention of the court on an interlocutory application			
The prohibition or disclosure to the judge does not apply (i) when the defence is one of tender before claim (ii) where the proceedings have been stayed following acceptance of a Part 36 offer (see r36.11 and section 13 of this TAB below) (iii) where the offeror and offeree agree in writing it should not apply			
13. The effect of acceptance of a Part 36 offer			
13.1 If a Part 36 offer is accepted the claim will be stayed		36.11(1)	
13.2 If the acceptance relates to the **whole claim** the stay will be upon the terms of the offer		36.11(2)	
13.3 If the offer accepted relates to only **part of the claim:**			
(i) that part of the claim will be stayed upon the terms offer and (ii) unless the claimant within the relevant period abandons the balance of the claim (see r36.10(2)), and unless the parties have agreed costs the liability for costs will be decided by the court		36.11(3)	
13.4 If the approval of the court is required before a settlement can be binding the acceptance of the Part 36 offer will take effect only when that approval has been given		36.11(4)	
13.5 Notwithstanding the stay the court can deal with the enforcement of the terms of the Part 36 offer and can deal with the costs (including interest on costs) of the proceedings		36.11(5)	

	Form No	CPR Rule	PD
13.6 Unless the parties otherwise agree a single sum of money offered and accepted must be paid within 14 days of acceptance and if not so paid the offeree can enter judgment for the same If the court makes an order for provisional damages or for periodical payments time for payment will be 14 days from service of the order, unless the court otherwise orders		36.11(6) and (7)	
13.7 Where a Part 36 offer accepted is not for payment of a single sum if it is not honoured the receiving party can apply to enforce the agreed terms and is not required to commence a new claim for this purpose. Where the settlement involves transfers of an interest in land, note *Orton v Collins* [2007] EWHC 803 (Ch), [2007] 3 All ER 863.		36.11(8)	
14. The costs consequences of acceptance of a Part 36 offer and costs consequences following judgment are set out in r 36.10 and r 36.14 respectively.			
14.1 If the acceptance is within the relevant period, unless the court otherwise orders, the claimant will be entitled to the costs up to the date the notice of acceptance was served on the offeror: this is in effect the equivalent of a costs order on a standard basis. This means the claimant is entitled to 100% of the costs allowed on detailed assessment. The costs judge has no power to vary the order but in an appropriate case he may disallow entire sections of the bill if the costs were unreasonably incurred: *Lahey v Pirelli Tyres* [2007] EWCA Civ 91, [2007] NLJR 294, [2007] PIQR P292. The costs consequences of a Part 36 offer do not apply to claims on the small claims track, but note CPR 27.14(2A)		36.10	
14.2 For the costs consequences of acceptance out of time see 10.1 above		36.10(4) and (5)	
14.3 Where upon **judgment being entered:**			

	Form No	CPR Rule	PD
(a) a claimant fails to obtain a judgment more advantageous than a defendant's Part 36 offer; or			
(b) a judgment against the defendant is at least as advantageous to the claimant as the proposals contained in a claimant's Part 36 offer the court will-			
• in the circumstances set out in (a) above order that the defendant is entitled to his costs from the date on which the relevant period expired and interest on those costs			
• in the circumstances set out in (b) above (provided that the offer has not been withdrawn, has not been changed to less advantageous terms that the offeree has beaten, and was not made less that 21 days before trial unless the court has abridged the relevant period) the claimant will be entitled to: interest on the whole or part of any sum awarded, excluding interest, at a rate not exceeding 10% above base rate for some or all of the period starting with the date on which the relevant period expired; his costs on an indemnity basis from the date on which the relevant period expired; and interest on those costs at a rate not exceeding 10% above base rate		36.14(1)–(3)	
For provisions where the court is considering whether it would be unjust for the consequence above to apply see		36.14(4)	
For the court's discretion and circumstances to be taken into account when exercising its discretion as to costs see		44.3	

	Form No	CPR Rule	PD
It was pointed out by the court in *Straker v Tudor Rose (a firm)* [2007] EWCA Civ 368, 151 Sol Jo LB 571 that 'beating' a Part 36 offer is not conclusive; it is a factor and will often be conclusive but the court must have regard to all the circumstances of the case.			
See *Carver v BAA plc* [2008] EWCA Civ 412, [2008] 3 All ER 911 as to the interpretation of the phrase 'more advantageous' and the ability of the court to take into account more than just the question of whether the offer had been 'beaten' in solely financial terms.			
The court's observations as to the obligations that fall upon the offeree and his obligation to respond must be given careful attention.			
Those observations can be important when determining whether the offer has been beaten or not. The test for 'more advantageous' is the same whether the Part 36 offer has been made in a money claim or a non-money claim. See further NLJ (2008) 9 May, PI Update at page 670 and NLJ (2008) 30 May 'Costs Law brief' at page 782, and note per Ward LJ in *Carver* at para 31: 'Litigation is time-consuming and it comes at a cost, emotional as well as financial. These are therefore appropriate factors to take into account in deciding whether the battle was worth it. Money is not the sole governing criterion.'			

	Form No	CPR Rule	PD
The Court of Appeal revisited the question of whether an offer was 'beaten' in two appeals heard together: *Gibbon v Manchester City Council and LG Blower v Reeves* [2010] EWCA Civ 726, [2010] All ER (D) 218 (Jun) and held that in most cases if the Part 36 offer is beaten costs should follow and only in rare cases would that be over-ridden. The amount by which the offer was beaten in *Carver* was as little as £51. For detailed discussion see articles 'Winning at what cost?' by Karen O'Sullivan in NLJ, 23 July 2010, page 1042 and 'Satellite litigation – has Part 36 spawned its own cottage industry?' by Caton and Arthurs in NLJ,30 July 2010, page 1073. Further see the judgment of *Bernard Livesey QC in Rowles-Davies v Call 24–7 Ltd* [2010] EWHC 1695 (Ch), [2010] All ER (D) 960 (Jul), (2010) NLJ LR, 23 July, page 1043.			
It is not proper to seek to use CPR 36.14 and in particular the phrase 'more advantageous' to obtain payment form a defendant of more than the sum to which the claimant is legally entitled. The court has made its attitude to such conduct clear in *D Pride & Partners (a firm) v Institute of Animal Health* [2009] EWHC 1617 (QB), [2009] All ER (D) 84 (Jul). The court made it apparent that such conduct was not in accordance with the overriding objective for courts to deal with cases justly.			
15. For the enforcement of the compromise resulting from the acceptance of an offer made before proceedings see CPR 36.9 [2]			

TABLE 21—APPLICATION TO SET ASIDE JUDGMENT AFTER FAILURE TO ATTEND TRIAL OR HEARING

TAB 21

	Form No	CPR Rule	PD
1. Preliminary			
This table does not apply to small claims, for which see **TAB 17**, para 10		27.11	

	Form No	CPR Rule	PD
Where a party fails to attend the trial, the court may proceed with the trial in his absence but:		39.3(1)	
(a) if no party attends the trial it may strike out the whole of the proceedings (b) if the claimant does not attend it may strike out his claim and any defence to counterclaim, and (c) if the defendant does not attend it may strike out his defence or counterclaim (or both)			
A claim should not be struck out by reason of the absence of the claimant if he is legally represented at the hearing: *Rouse v Freeman* (2002) Times, 8 January			

	Form No	CPR Rule	PD
Where a defendant fails to attend the trial but sends a message requesting an adjournment and the court hears the case and finds against him, his proper course is to apply to set aside judgment and not to appeal: *Tennero Ltd v Arnold* [2006] EWHC 1530 (QB), [2006] All ER (D) 61 (Jul) See also *Kampichler v Moore & Blatch (a firm)* [2008] EWHC 404 (QB), 152 Sol Jo (no 14) 29 where the claimant was held to be procrastinating but had written to the court that he would be in hospital at the date of the hearing of his application to set aside an order permitting the defendant to apply for a default costs certificate. The master nevertheless proceeded with the application in his absence and the default certificate was issued. On appeal the master's order was set aside because he was wrong to proceed and make the order when the claimant was in hospital and had so informed the court. For a case where the court did proceed despite a written application to adjourn on medical grounds see *Khudados v Hayden* [2007] EWCA Civ 131, [2007] AlL ER (D) 203(Dec) – 'enough was enough'. The court considered the case of *Dick v Piller* [1943] 1 All ER 627 and also dealt with the duty of the advocate opposing such an application. A check under CPR 3.9(i) should be carried out by the court when considering an application to adjourn; see *Primus Telecommunications Netherlands v Pan European Ltd* [2005] EWCA Civ 273, [2005] All ER (D) 359 (Feb) and *Albon (t/a NA Carriage Co) v Naza Motor Trading*, see **TAB 14**, para 8, final sub-para above For the different effects of a defendant's failure to attend the hearing when the proceedings had not been served on him and when the proceedings have been served but the hearing notice had not, see *Estate Acquisition and Development Ltd v Wiltshire* [2006] EWCA Civ 533, (2006) Times, 12 June and *Nelson v Mainsprings Management Ltd* [2006] EWCA Civ 1252, [2007] 2 All ER 407. See **TAB 9**, section 8 third para above			

	Form No	CPR Rule	PD
If the court's copy of the hearing notice has been endorsed to the effect that the notice was posted there will be a presumption that the notice has been posted if receipt is denied. In the absence of endorsement the evidence of non-receipt by the addressee is likely to be believed: see 'The Judicial Line', NLJ (2008) 29 February, page 336.			
For consideration of the question whether a limited company did not attend a trial and if so whether it had good reason for not attending see *Watson v Blue Moon Properties Ltd* [2002] EWCA Civ 1875			
Where the court strikes out the proceedings or part of them it can later restore them on application in accordance with Part 23	N244	39.3(2)	39A para 2.3
The Court of Appeal in *Forcelux Ltd v Binnie* [2009] EWCA Civ 854, [2009] All ER (D) 216 (Oct) held that the hearing of a landlord's possession claim against a tenant in the county court undefended possession list was not a trial for the purposes of CPR 39.3. However CPR 3.1(2) gives the court power to set aside if the interests of justice so demand and the court found the interests of justice did require it and set aside the possession order.			
Where the court gives judgment against or makes an order against an absent party that party can apply in accordance with Part 23 to set it aside		39.3(3)	39A para 2.3
An application to restore or to set aside can only be granted if: (a) it is made promptly (b) there was a good reason for the failure to attend, and (c) there is a reasonable prospect of success at the trial		39.3(5)	

	Form No	CPR Rule	PD
Note: The applicant needs to satisfy these three grounds in which there is no residual discretion: *Barclays Bank plc v Ellis & Ellis* (2000) Times, 24 October, CA but if the applicant did not attend the hearing because the proceedings were not served on him he is entitled as of right to have the judgment or order set aside because any judgment or order made by the court is a nullity: *White v Weston* [1968] 2 QB 647, CA.			
If the hearing of which the party was not given notice was an adjourned hearing and the party was present at the prior hearing, he will not have a right to have the judgment set aside if he does not attend the adjourned hearing but will have to satisfy the r 39.3(5) criteria: *Hackney London Borough Council v Driscoll* [2003] EWCA Civ 1037, [2003] 4 All ER 1205			
In *Sir John Fitzgerald Ltd v Macarthur* [2009] EWHC 265 the judge made observations on the proper procedure to be followed where an absent defendant's defence was struck out. The defendant in this case emigrated prior to the hearing date and did not appear; his defence was struck out and judgment given for the claimant. The judgment was set aside on application as it was decided the trial judge should have exercised his discretion in the defendant's favour. It was confirmed such an application should be made to the trial court pursuant to CPR 39.3(1)(c).		39.3(1)(c)	
If the applicant satisfies the three conditions but the party whose judgment is threatened seeks to argue there are "special grounds" that should prevent the judgment being set aside see: *Thakerar v Northwick Park and St Marks NHS* [2002] BLD 2404021487 hearing date 24 April, CA			
For **"good reason"** see *Brazil v Brazil* (2002) Times, 18 October, CA, a case where the defendant was acting in person, was illiterate and did not receive notice of the trial date			

	Form No	CPR Rule	PD
2. Procedure			
(a) the application must be supported by evidence	N244	39.3(4), Part 23	39A, para 2.4
(b) the application must be supported by evidence giving reasons for non-attendance and stating when the applicant found out about the order against him (c) the evidence should seek to show there are reasonable prospects of success, and (d) the application notice must be verified by a statement of truth if the applicant wishes to rely on it as evidence		Part 22	
Note: The application should be made to the court that entered judgment or made the order and, if execution had been issued, should seek a stay of execution until the hearing of the application. It is sensible to ask the court to deal with at least that part of the application without a hearing. There are circumstances where the application is so strong (eg notice of hearing specifying wrong hearing date) that the court can sensibly be asked to deal with the complete application without notice		23.8, 9 and 10	
3. Service			
Service must be effected at least 3 days before the court is to deal with the application on notice, a copy of the application, the draft order attached and the written evidence must be filed with the court for service (unless the applicant is proposing to serve himself). Where the respondent to an application wishes to rely on evidence he should serve it as soon as possible and file it		23.7(1)(b)	23A, paras 9.1–9.3 and 9.4
Note: Ensure a sufficient allocation of time is made for the appointment so that the evidence can be properly considered			
4. The hearing			
The court may, after hearing the parties:			

	Form No	CPR Rule	PD
(a) dismiss the application and deal with the costs of the application (b) set aside the judgment or order unconditionally, give directions and deal with costs, or (c) set aside the judgment or order subject to conditions, deal with costs and give directions to take effect if the conditions are satisfied *Note:* Consideration should be given to provision of a chronology and/or a skeleton argument An advocate should have instructions as to whether or not a condition requiring the payment of money into court could be satisfied and if so to what limit. A condition that the applicant cannot fulfil should not be imposed. But if a defendant is aware that conditions are being sought he should put in evidence of his financial position and if he fails to do so the imposition of such a condition cannot be criticised; *Redcliffe Close (Old Brompton Road) Managements Ltd v Kamal* [2005] EWHC 858 (Ch)			
5. Appeal			
Where a defendant has deliberately failed to attend and has not requested an adjournment he will almost certainly be unable to satisfy the r 39.3(3) requirements and the only path open would be to appeal. Before embarking on such a course reference should be made to the case of *Shocked v Goldschmidt* [1998] 1 All ER 372, CA			

TABLE 22—RECOVERY OF POSSESSION OF LAND – CLAIMS BY LANDLORD, MORTGAGEE, LICENSOR, PERSON ENTITLED TO POSSESSION AGAINST TRESPASSERS

TAB 22

See 1 below for general provisions applicable to **possession claims**

See 2 below for particular provisions for **residential tenanted property**

See 3 below for particular provisions for **land subject to mortgage**

See 3A below for particular provisions for **possession proceeding online** by landlords and mortgagees

See 4 below for particular provisions for **claims against trespassers**

	Form No	CPR Rule	PD
1. General provisions that apply to all such claims			
Interpretation For definition of:			
"a possession claim", see		55.1(a)	
"a possession claim against trespassers"			
note, in particular, this does not include a claim against a tenant or sub-tenant whether the tenancy has been terminated or not and see		55.1(b)	
"mortgage" note this includes a legal and equitable mortgage and see		55.1(c)	
"the 1985 Act" means Housing Act 1985, see		55.1(d)	
"the 1988 Act" means Housing Act 1988, see		55.1(e)	
"a demotion claim" means a claim by a landlord for an order under s 82A of the 1985 Act or s 6A of the 1988 Act ("a demotion order")		55.1(f)	
"a demoted tenancy" means a tenancy created by virtue of a demotion order		55.1(g)	
"a suspension claim" means a claim made by a landlord for an order under section 121A of the 1985 Act		55.1(h)	
1.1 The general provisions do not apply to: (a) claims for accelerated possession of property let on an assured shorthold tenancy		55.2(2)(b)	
(b) claims for an interim possession order made under the Criminal Justice and Public Order Act 1994, which are at present dealt with under CPR Pt 55 Section III except where the court otherwise orders or Section III so provides		55.2(2)(c)	
(c) where a claim is for a demotion claim only; Section III of Part 65 applies			

	Form No	CPR Rule	PD
(d) claims for possession of business premises but where the letting is of a mixed business and residential premises: see *Pirabkaran v Patel* (2006) Times, 19 July, CA and *Broadway Investments Hackney Ltd v Grant* [2006] EWCA Civ 1709, [2006] All ER (D) 304 (Dec), [2007] L&TR 11; *Thomas v Ken Thomas Ltd* [2006] EWCA Civ 1504, 151 Sol Jo LB 1396; and *Tan v Sitkowski* [2007] EWCA Civ 30, [2007] 1 WLR 1628. These cases strongly support the statement that such mixed tenancies will normally be governed by the Landlord and Tenant Act 1954. For detailed discussion, see NLJ 11 May 2007, page 669. *Note* that the general provisions apply subject to any enactment or Practice Direction setting out special provisions for a particular type of claim If a claim by a tenant of residential premises against the landlord seeks an order for repairs or other work to be done to those premises see CPR 16.3(4)–(7)		55.2(2)(a)	
1.2 High Court or county court			
The claim may only be started in the High Court if: (a) there are complicated disputes of fact (b) there are points of law of general importance or (c) the claim is against trespassers and there is a substantial risk of public disturbance or of serious harm to persons or property which properly require immediate determination *Note:* • Value of the property and the amount of any financial claim whilst relevant will not alone normally justify starting the claim in the High Court			55A, para 1.4

	Form No	CPR Rule	PD
• If a claim is started in the High Court the claimant must file with the claim a certificate, stating the reason for bringing the claim in that court, verified by a statement of truth		55.3(2)	
• If a claim is wrongly started in the High Court the court will normally either strike it out or transfer it to the county court			55A, para 1.2
• Where the claim form includes a demotion claim it must be started in the county court for the district in which the land is situated			55A, para 1.9
On starting possession proceedings the fee payable (unless PCOL is used) is: in the High Court £400 in the county court £150 **Possession claims should normally be brought in the county court** **1.3 Starting the claim**			55A, para 1.1
If the claim is started in the county court it must be the county court for **the district in which the land is situated** unless an enactment provides otherwise For the **electronic issue** of certain possession claims see The **claim form** must be in the form set out in Table 1 to **CPR PD 4** and be verified by a statement of truth	N5	55.3(1) 55.10A	55B 55A, para 1.5
The claim form or the particulars of claim must contain a statement notifying the court whether or not Sections III and IV of the Practice Direction (Pre-action Conduct) or any relevant protocol has been complied with.			Pre-action Conduct, para 9.7
Where the claim is for relief against forfeiture, the form to be used is:	N5A		
Where the claim is for a claim for possession of property held on assured shorthold tenancy the form to be used if using the accelerated procedure is	N5B		

	Form No	CPR Rule	PD
Possession Claims Online (PCOL) is now in operation nationally; it is a web-based method of seeking possession which will, it is anticipated, be used mainly by lenders, council and social landlords seeking possession of residential properties. Customers are able to set up direct debit arrangements for the payment of court fees. Unlike MCOL all possession claims will still have to have a hearing even if uncontested. The PCOL website sets out the 'specified courts' at which PCOL operates and the date from which it will be available in each specified court The PCOL website means the website www.possessionclaim.gov.uk which is accessed via the Courts Services website at www.hmcourts-service.gov.uk The relevant information and procedural requirements are set out in Practice Direction 55B Although the anticipated use is set out above PCOL may be used by any landlord or lender. See 3A below 'Possession Claims Online'			55B
1.4 Particulars of claim			
In a possession claim the particulars must:			55A, para 2.1
(a) identify the land to which the claim relates (b) state whether the claim relates to residential property (c) state the ground on which possession is claimed (d) give full details about any mortgage or tenancy agreement and (e) give details of every person who to the best of the claimant's knowledge, is in possession of the property See also CPR 16 "Statement of Case" – precise statement of facts, interest, etc The particulars of claim must be filed and served with the claim form	N119 (rented residential) N120 (mortgaged residential) N121 (trespassers)	55.4	

	Form No	CPR Rule	PD
1.5 The hearing date			
The court will fix a date for the hearing when it issues the claim form		55.1	
Where the **claim is against trespassers** service of the claim form, particulars of claim and any witness statement must be: (a) not less than 5 days before the hearing date where the property is residential (b) not less than 2 days before the hearing in the case of other land		55.5(2)	
In **all other possession claims:**			
(a) the hearing date will be not less than 28 days from the date of issue of the claim form		55.5(3)(a)	
(b) the standard period during issue of the claim form and the hearing will be not more than 8 weeks, and (c) the defendant must be served with the claim form and particulars of claim not less than 21 days before the hearing date		55.5(3)(b) and (c)	
Note: • The time may be extended or shortened by the court and particular instances when the exercise of this power should be considered are set out in: • The court will serve on the claimant or his solicitors **"notice of issue"**. This will specify the date of issue and details of the hearing. The notice draws attention to the time limits for service of the claimant's witness statements	N206B	3.1(2)(a)	55A, para 3.2
By reason of s 42 Finance Act 2003 the following changes have been in the effect of s 14 Stamp Duty Act 1891			

	Form No	CPR Rule	PD
(a) Courts should disregard the requirements of s 14 of the Stamp Duty Act 1891 in respect of any land transaction completed after 30 November 2003 except where it was pursuant to a contract entered into before 10 July 2003 (b) Except in the case of leases granted by Registered Social Landlords the requirements of s 14 of the Stamp Duty Act 1891 will continue to apply to all land transactions completed before 1 December 2003 (c) The requirements of s 14 of the Stamp Duty Act 1891 will not apply to any leases granted by Registered Social Landlords (RSLs) on or after 1 January 2000. The requirements of s 14 of the Stamp Duty Act 1891 will continue to apply to leases granted by RSLs before this date			
1.6 The defendant's response An acknowledgement of service is not required and CPR Pt 10 does not apply		55.7(1)	
For notes for defendant in claim for possession of rented residential premises see	N7A		
In a possession claim against trespassers the defendant need not file a defence		55.7(2)	
In any other possession claims where the defendant fails to file a defence within 14 days after service of the claim form he can nevertheless take part in any hearing but his failure is relevant as to costs		55.7(3)	
Default judgment is not available		55.7(4)	
For general form of defence to CPR Pt 55 claims, see	N11		
1.7 The hearing			
At the hearing the court may decide the claim or give directions		55.8(1)	

	Form No	CPR Rule	PD
Where the claim is genuinely disputed on substantial grounds the court will give directions that include allocation		55.8(2)	
Unless the court allocates to the fast track or multi-track or the court otherwise orders any fact that needs to be proved by **the evidence of witnesses** at the hearing, **may be proved by evidence in writing**. In a possession claim against trespassers all witness statements must be filed and served with the claim form and in other cases all witness statements must be filed and served at least 2 days before the hearing.		55.8(4) and (5)	
Where the claimant serves the claim form and particulars of claim there must be produced at the hearing a certificate of service of these documents and rule 6.17(2)(a) shall not apply		55.8(6)	
Where a claimant realises there is a genuine dispute on substantial grounds he should seek to avoid the expense of the first hearing which is only likely to have a time allocation of 5 minutes. If directions can be agreed dealing with allocation and management they should be submitted to the court in good time for consideration, with a request that the first hearing is vacated if the district judge is able to make the proposed directions or such other directions as he feels appropriate			
If the first hearing is to be effective to dispose of the claim, preparation should be such as to enable all relevant matters to be dealt with in the limited time available			
Each party should whenever possible include all the evidence he wishes to present in his statement of case verified by a statement of truth			55A, para 5.1
For the admission of hearsay evidence and reliance on it by the court at the hearing see *Solon South West Housing Association Ltd v James* [2004] EWCA Civ 1847, [2005] HLR 24			

	Form No	CPR Rule	PD
1.8 Allocation			
When the court decides the track for a possession claim the matters to which the court shall have regard include: (a) the matters in CPR 26.8 as modified by the relevant Practice Direction (b) the amount of any arrears of rent or mortgage instalments (c) the importance to the defendant of retaining possession of the land, and (d) the importance of vacant possession to the claimant (e) if applicable, the alleged conduct of the defendant		55.9(1)	
The financial value of the property will not necessarily be the most important factor and the court may direct a possession claim to be deal with on the fast track even though the value of the property exceeds £25,000			
The court will only allocate possession claims to the small claims track if the parties agree. If there is such agreement and allocation, costs shall be as if the claim were on the fast track save that the trial costs will be in the discretion of the court but shall not exceed the fast track trial costs applicable where the value of the claim is up to £3,000		55.9(2) and (3)	26, para 8.1(1)(c)
The parties can agree that the last provision as to costs shall not apply and that the costs shall be those recoverable on the trial of a small claim		55.9(4)	
2. Claims for possession of residential property let on a tenancy			
2.1 Preliminary			
It is essential for the efficient conduct of possession claims for residential tenancies to keep a set of the up-to-date version of all notices that have to be served. This is both to ensure that the claimant uses the appropriate form and also, when acting for the defendant, to check whether the landlord has used the correct form			

	Form No	CPR Rule	PD
Careful attention must be paid to the **Protocol for possession claims based on rent arrears** by local authorities, social landlords and housing administration trusts which have all since 2 October 2006 been required to give a tenant 5 chances to pay the arrears before the court makes a possession order. Additionally: the tenant must be kept informed of what is happening (para 4) the landlord must seek to obtain payment through the tenant's benefits (para 5) the landlord must work with the tenant to resolve benefit difficulties (paras 6 and 7)			
If a landlord fails to give notice to the tenant of an address in England and Wales at which notices (including notices in proceedings) may be served to the landlord by the tenant, any rent, service or administration charge otherwise due from the tenant to the landlord shall be treated for all purposes as not being due at any time before the landlord does comply with the requirement: Landlord and Tenant Act 1987, s 48. Oral notice is not sufficient but as to sufficiency of written notices see *Rogan v Woodfield Building Services Ltd* (1994) 27 HLR 78. [1995] 1 EGLR 72. Once 2 48 has been complied with the rent and other payments not previously due become payable in their entirety: *Dallhold Estate UK Pty Ltd v Lindsay Trading* [1994] 17 EG 148, CA.			
The agent of the landlord has no standing to bring proceedings: *Chesters v Abebrese* [1997] Lawtel, 18 July			
A claim which is not a claim for possession may be brought under Section I of Part 55 if it is started in the same claim form as a claim for possession which must be brought in accordance with Section I		55.2(1)	55A, para 1.7

	Form No	CPR Rule	PD
County courts have the power to accept undertakings as part of an order adjourning proceedings: *Hastings Housing Association v Ellis* [2007] EWCA Civ 1238, (2007) Sol Jo, 23 November, page 1475. Great care should be taken in drafting undertakings: see *Hiscox Syndicates Ltd v The Pinnacle Ltd* [2008] All ER (D) 193 (Jan), (2008) Times, 6 February as to degrees of endeavour and also article 'Best Endeavours' by Sara Partington and Kirk Page at (2008) NLJ, 10 October, page 1407 where the cases of *Rhodia International Holdings Ltd v Huntsman International LLC* [2007] EWHC 292 (Comm), [2007] 2 All ER (Comm) 577 and *Ryanair Ltd v SR Technics Ireland Ltd* [2007] EWHC 3089 (QB), [2007] All ER (D) 264 (Dec) are fully discussed.			
The common law of negligence imposes no general duty to warn another of impending danger and that remains the position where the relationship of landlord and tenant exists between the parties: *Mitchell v Glasgow City Council* [2009] UKHL 11, [2009] All ER (D) 182 (Feb).			
Care must be taken to distinguish service occupiers from tenants; the position has been clarified by the judgment in *Wragg v Surrey County Council* [2008] EWCA Civ 19, [2008] HLR 464 where countryside rangers were held to be service occupiers. See (2008) Sol Jo, 19 February, page 4, and 13 May, page 26.			
CLA Information Guide 'Dealing with rent problems' provides useful advice, phone numbers and website addresses: 'Community legal advice' is a free and confidential service paid for by Legal Aid – 0845 345 4 345; www.communitylegaladvice.org.uk.			
2.1A The following dates are important for **private sector tenancies**: (a) Only tenancies created **before 15 January 1989** can be tenancies protected by the Rent Act 1977 (**regulated tenancies**)			

	Form No	CPR Rule	PD
A regulated tenancy is any protected or statutory tenancy under the 1977 Act and is so defined in s 18(1) of that Act (b) Tenancies created on or after **15 January 1989** (**subject to satisfying the qualifying conditions**) are **assured or assured shorthold tenancies** depending whether the formalities required to create an assured shorthold were complied with (c) Since **28 February 1997** almost all new tenancies are **assured shorthold tenancies** unless the landlord deliberately creates an **assured tenancy** The annual rental threshold for assured shorthold tenancies was £25,000 but from 1 October 2010 has been increased in England only to £100,000; see Assured Tenancies (Amendment) (England) Order 2010, SI 2010/908. It is to be noted that it was held in *Hughes v Borodex Ltd* (2010) Times, 26 May that a tenant lost her protection by carrying out improvements which resulted in the rent of the property exceeding the assured protected tenancy limit. The requirement of compliance with s 20 of the Housing Act 1988 to create an assured shorthold tenancy has ceased since 28 February 1997 Useful guidance for tenants with private landlords who have tenancy difficulties is provided by Community Legal Advice Information Guide C1 'Dealing with rent problems if you rent privately'. CLA telephone number is 0845 345 4 345, and web address is www.communitylegaladvice.org.uk. *Note:* • The county court has no jurisdiction under s 7 of the 1988 Act to make a **possession order by consent** unless the judge is satisfied after investigation that the requirements are met: *Gil v Baygreen Properties Ltd* [2002] EWCA Civ 1340, (2002) Times, 17 July			

	Form No	CPR Rule	PD
2.1B Public sector lettings and pre-15 January 1989 housing association tenancies are generally secure tenancies governed by Housing Act 1985 and described as **secure tenancies** • Social landlords (such as local authorities, Registered Social landlords and Housing action Trusts) making a possession claim based solely on rent arrears must have regard to the Protocol for Possession Claims Based on Rent Arrears. The Protocol provides: 'Courts should take into account whether this protocol has been followed when considering what orders to make'			
2.1C "Tolerated trespassers" were **former secure tenants** allowed to remain in occupation after the date given for delivery of possession in an outright possession order or after the making of a possession order with its enforcement suspended on terms in Form N28 or who remained in possession because the order for possession had not been enforced by the landlord. From 20 May 2009 the Housing and Regeneration Act 2008, s 299 and Sch 11 and the Housing (Replacement of Terminated Tenancies) (England) Order 2009, SI 2009/1262 and a similar order for Wales (SI 2009/1260):			
(a) prevent tenants becoming tolerated trespassers by providing that tenancies (whether they be secure, assured, introductory or demoted) end only on **execution under a possession order**, unless the tenant has given notice to quit or surrendered the tenancy;			

	Form No	CPR Rule	PD
(b) give replacement tenancies to those who were tolerated trespassers on 20 May 2009 unless they had entered into any form of new tenancy with their landlord. The replacement tenancy will be of the same type as the original tenancy or as near to it as possible; (c) treat the possession order as applying to the replacement order;			
(d) enable the court when dealing with a claim arising from the breach of tenancy agreement or the breach of the statutory tenancy to treat the new tenancy and the original tenancy as being one continuous and uninterrupted tenancy.			
Consider the article 'Righting a housing wrong' by Francis Davey in NLJ, 9 May 2008, page 656 which deals also with the new 'replacement tenancies' for tolerated trespassers who remain in occupation, the provisions of the 2008 Act having come into effect.			

	Form No	CPR Rule	PD
The position of a potential successor to a deceased tolerated trespasser was not addressed by the Housing and Regulatory Reform Act 2008 but in *Austin v London Borough of Southwark* [2010] UKSC 28 it was unanimously decided that potential successors of deceased tolerated trespassers could apply to postpone the date of possession and revive the tenancy under s 85(2) of the Housing Act 1985. The application would have to be under the original possession proceedings and its success or otherwise would depend on the discretion of the county court judge. For consideration of the case of *Austin* and the background to it from the decision (now discredited) in *Thompson v Elmbridge Borough Council* [1987] 1 WLR 1425 to the judgment of Lord Hope and Lady Hale in *Austin* see article by Charlotte Collins and Giles Peaker in (2010) Sol Jo, 13 July, page 16 and see also (2010) NLJ, 2 July, page 914. If the tenancy is revived and the survivor satisfies the necessary conditions he will succeed to the tenancy.			
2.1D It should be noted that the survivor of a same-sex partnership has the same entitlement as a spouse to succeed on the tenant's death as a statutory tenant: *Ghaidan v Godin-Mendoza* [2004] UKHL 30, [2004] 2 AC 557			
But note the relationship must be one of 'mutual lifetime commitment': *Nutting v Southern District Housing Group Ltd* (2005) Times, 5 January, ChD			

	Form No	CPR Rule	PD
2.1E A clause in a tenancy agreement providing that the local housing authority could vary the terms of the agreement if the majority of the tenant's representatives agreed was held to be incompatible with the local authority's statutory right to vary tenancies unilaterally under the provisions of the Housing Act 1985, s 103; *R v Basildon District Council* [2005] EWCA Civ 475. It should be noted that a social landlord does not have the power to vary the terms of a tenancy unilaterally under s 103: *Peabody Trust (Governors of the v Reeve* (2008) Times, 9 June, Ch.			
2.1F For a case where a possession claim was brought by the claimant landlord, which had served a notice to quit on a disabled tenant because he had sub-let his premises see *Lewisham London Borough Council v Malcolm (Disability Rights Commission intervening)* [2007] EWCA Civ 763, (2007) Times, 28 August, CA and the Disability Discrimination Act 1995 (DDA 1995) It was held that the same considerations apply whether possession is claimed on a mandatory ground or a discretionary ground. The landlord will have to show that seeking an order for possession was not unjustifiably discriminatory treatment within DDA 1995, ss 22 and 24. If the tenant's disability is 'substantial' and the ground relied on by the landlord is 'related to' that disability the court would not make a possession order on the basis that a person may not rely on his own wrong. The position is the same for private sector landlords as for landlords of secure tenants. For case note and comment see New Law Journal 14 September 2007, page 1270.			

	Form No	CPR Rule	PD
The decision in *Malcolm* will be effected by the Equality Act 2010 which largely came into effect on 1 October 2010 in respect of conduct on or after that date. The new test for discrimination arising from disability will mean that the disabled person's case will not have to rely on a comparator. Section 15 of the Act provides a new cause of action where a person discriminates against a disabled person by treating that person unfavourably because of something arising in consequence of that person's disability. The government's express intention was to reverse the decision in *Malcolm*; see further article 'A framework for fairness' by Spencer Keen in (2010) NLJ, 1 October, page 1326.			
See also *Floyd v S* [2008] EWCA Civ 201, [2008] 1 WLR 1274, [2008] All ER (D) 264 (Mar) as to the inter-relation of the Housing Act 1988 and the DDA 1995 – Property Law Update, NLJ (2008), 25 April, page 588. An appeal by the local authority in the case of *Malcolm* was allowed by the House of Lords ([2008] UKHL 43, [2008] 3 WLR 194, Gazette, 10 July, page 23) because it had not been proved that (i) the fact of the disability was a motivating part in the discriminator's mind leading to the discriminatory treatment complained of and (ii) a secure tenant with no mental illness who had sublet would have been treated differently. Both of these points would have had to be satisfied before the possession order could be properly set aside. For detailed discussion see article 'Disability discrimination and possession after Malcolm' by Ann Bevington (2008) Sol Jo, 29 July, page 17 and for a more detailed consideration of the test for disability related discrimination see article 'Blame it on the dog' by Spencer Keen (2008) NLJ, 5 September and article by Rosenthal and Duckworth 'Disability v Possession (2008) NLJ, 19 September, page 1286.			

	Form No	CPR Rule	PD
In November 2008 the government issued a consultation paper 'Improving Protection from Discrimination'; for the discussion of this paper, responses to it and the Equality Bill see article 'The trouble with Malcolm' by Emma Williamson in (2009) NLJ 26 June, page 912.			
2.1G There can only be one succession to a secure tenancy (see Housing Act 1985, s 87) and s 88(1)(g) of the 1985 Act defines succession to include a joint tenant becoming the sole tenant: note *Birmingham City Council v Walker* [2007] UKHL 22, [2007] 2 AC 262 which makes it apparent that the provisions concerning secure tenants relate only to events that happened after the tenancy became secure			
2.1H Following a succession to a secure tenancy pursuant to s 89 Housing Act 1985 a landlord is entitled to seek possession under ground 18 of Sch 2 if the succession results in the under occupation of the property. For the conditions that have to be satisfied and that the date of trial is the relevant date see *Wandsworth London Borough Council v Randall* [2007] EWCA Civ 1126, [2007] 46 EG 176 (CS). In this case the successor's mother and half-sister moved into the property (a 4-bedroomed house) between succession and the hearing; as the hearing date was the relevant one a one-bedroomed flat was held not to be suitable alternative accommodation			
2.1I An express term in a document, described as a 'licence', that it does not create a secure tenancy will not of itself be sufficient to prevent the creation of a secure tenancy: *Langridge v Mansfield District Council* [2008] EWCA Civ 264, [2008] HLR 541.			
2.1J For the obligations of a local authority to provide housing for minors under s 20 of the Children Act 1989 and generally see article 'There's no place like home' by Bloom and Markus in NLJ (2009) 3 July, page 953.			

	Form No	CPR Rule	PD
2.1K For the fine distinction between 'notifying' and 'informing' see *Ali v Birmingham City Council* [2009] EWCA Civ 1279 and article by Nicholas Dobson in (2010) NLJ 29 January, page 133.			
2.2 Particulars of claim			
In addition to the general requirements (see 1.4, above) if the claim includes a **claim for non-payment of rent** the particulars of claim must set out:	N119	55.4	55A, para 2.1
(a) the amount due at the start of the proceedings			
(b) in schedule form, the dates and amounts of all payments due and payments made for a period of two years immediately preceding the date of issue, or if the first date of default was less than two years prior to issue from the first date of default and a running total If the claimant wishes to rely on a history of arrears for longer than two years he should state this in his particulars and exhibit a full or longer schedule to a witness statement (c) the daily rate of any rent and interest (d) any previous steps taken to recover the arrears of rent with full details of any court proceedings, and (e) any relevant information about the defendant's circumstances, in particular: (i) whether the defendant is in receipt of social security benefits, and (ii) whether any payments are made on his behalf directly to the claimant under the Social Security Contributions and Benefits Act 1992			55A, para 2.3 and 3A

	Form No	CPR Rule	PD
If the claimant knows of any person (including a mortgagee) entitled to claim relief against forfeiture as underlessee under s 146(4) of the Law of Property Act 1925 (or in accordance with s 38 of the Supreme Court Act 1981, or s 138(9C) of the County Courts Act 1984): (a) the particulars of claim must state the name and address of that person, and (b) the claimant must file a copy of the particulars of claim for service on him			55A, para 2.4
If the claim for possession relates to the conduct of the tenant, the particulars of claim must state details of the conduct alleged			55A, para 2.4A
If the claim for possession relies on a statutory ground or grounds for possession the particulars of claim must specify them			55A, para 2.4B
These are guidance notes on completing particulars of claim form (rented residential premises)	N119A		
2.3 Service of the claim form			
The general provisions as to service apply and note in particular the requirement of a certificate of service where the claimant serves the claim form		Part 6 55.8(6)	
2.4 The hearing date			
See general provisions, 1.5 above			
2.5 The defendant's response			
See general provisions, 1.6 above For form of defence see	N11R		
A landlord is not obliged to forfeit a lease for a fixed term to mitigate his loss by seeking a new tenant if the tenant stops paying the rent and vacates; *Reichman v Beveridge* [2006] EWCA Civ 1659, (2007) Times, 4 January, [2007] HLR 354. See article by Sebastien Kokelaar NLJ 2007, 20 April, page 545 for further discussion			

	Form No	CPR Rule	PD
2.6 The hearing			
The hearing date given on issue will be for a hearing in chambers generally before a district judge with a time estimate of 5 minutes. Whenever possible the parties should include the evidence they wish to give in their statements of case verified by a statement of truth			55A, para 5.1
Where relevant the **claimant's evidence** should include the amount of any arrears calculated to the date of the hearing (if necessary specifying a daily rate of arrears)			55A, para 5.2
If the case has not been allocated to fast track or multi-track unless the court otherwise orders any fact may be proved by written evidence		55.8(3)	55A, para 5.4
Witness statements must be served 2 days prior to the hearing but this does not prevent oral evidence or further written evidence on the day to update the position, e g typically last minute payments in reduction of arrears			55A, para 5.2
At the hearing there is no time or necessity for an opening address but **a "pro forma"** can be completed and handed to the court (a copy having been given to the defendant prior to the hearing) in a rent arrears case showing: (a) The date the tenancy commenced (b) The occupants (including ages of children) (c) The current rent (C/R) and if part of this is paid by Housing Benefit (H/B) the rebated rent (d) The current arrears (C/A) and if they include any arrears of H/B (e) The date and method of service of the notice (f) The order sought (g) The details known of the defendant's financial position Where relevant the **defendant's evidence** should include: (a) the amount of any outstanding housing benefit or social security payments and			

	Form No	CPR Rule	PD
(b) details of any claims for benefit made but not yet determined, and (c) details of any appeals or review applications against benefit refusal			55A, para 5.3
Where the court has to be satisfied that it is "**reasonable**" to make an order the defendant should include in his evidence the reasons the arrears have arisen, the effect that a possession order would have, the availability of any alternative accommodation and any proposals he has (and is financially able to maintain) to clear the arrears by instalments.			
For a recent judicial consideration of 'reasonableness' see the judgment of Rimer LJ in *Whitehouse v Lee* [2009] EWCA Civ 375, [2009] 31 EG 74, a case on the Rent Act 1977 in which the test under s 98 is 'reasonableness' and see also the article 'Listening to reason' by Julian Sidoli del Ceno in (200() Sol Jo, 28 July, page 8.			

	Form No	CPR Rule	PD
The court has to be satisfied it is reasonable to make the order for possession where the ground on which the order is sought is a discretionary ground i e for secure tenancies the grounds 1–8; see Housing Act 1985, s 84, or for assured tenancies grounds 8–17 in Schedule 2, Housing Act 1988 A case which strongly underlines the importance of the court itself being satisfied on this point is *London Borough of Hounslow v McBride* [1999] 31 HLR 143, CA. The simple assent to a suspended possession is not an admission of the landlord's grounds and any such order obtained 'by consent' will be set aside. Setting aside may be achieved on appeal or on an application for judicial review. An instructive case where the court held that the tenant's breaches of the tenancy agreement (conviction for drug offences) were not such as to make it unreasonable for a possession order to be made in respect of the defendant's tenancy of sheltered accommodation: see *North Devon Homes Ltd v Batchelor* [2008] EWCA Civ 840, 152 Sol Jo (no 30) 31.			
For the balancing exercise to be performed when the tenant's right to buy competes with the landlord's possession claim, see *Basildon District Council v Wahlen* [2006] EWCA Civ 326, (2006) Times, 7 April, CA. See also *Manchester City Council v Benjamin* [2008] EWCA Civ 189, [2008] All ER (D) 185 (Mar), (2008) Gazette, 28 March, page 20 a case where the landlord's notice seeking possession was on the ground that the property was more extensive than the tenant reasonably required. Here the balancing exercise came down in favour of the local authority. The court noted that if the tenant became a secure tenant of an alternative property she would have a right to buy the new property.			

	Form No	CPR Rule	PD
It was held in *Islington London Borough Council v Honeygan-Green* [2008] UKHL 70 that on the revival of a secure tenancy, after the tenant had become a tolerated trespasser but before possession was given, its covenants were to be treated as having been continuously in existence even during the limbo period. This included an accrued right to buy under s 124 of the Housing Act 1985 and the tenant did not need to begin the right-to-buy process again by service of a fresh notice. If this gives the tenant an unfair advantage (e g a purchase price well below the market price) the court could in the exercise of its discretion under HA 1985, s 85 make it a condition of discharging the possession order that the tenant could not pursue the right to buy. This would leave the tenant to serve a fresh notice.			
The relevant parts of the Housing and Regeneration Act 2008 have been brought into effect, so that former tolerated trespassers, in the main, will be given replacement tenancies which the court may treat as one continuous tenancy. It may still be possible to prevent giving the tenant and unfair advantage from his delay; probably the fall in property prices had made the problem academic, however.			
For the effect of the Disability Discrimination Act 1995 on the question of whether it is 'reasonable' for the court to make an order see *North Devon Homes Ltd v Brazier* [2003] EWHC 574 (QB), [2003] 22 EG 141, [2003] NLJ 153 No 7085 P 944 and para 2.1F of this **TAB** above. On 1 October 2010 the Equality Act 2010 was in the main brought into force in respect of conduct on or after this date and pre-Act decisions will need to be reconsidered in the light of the new test it provides for 'discrimination arising from disability'. Section 15 of the Act creates a new cause of action in respect of such discrimination and it is clearly intended to reverse the decision in *Malcolm* which was the government's expressed intention.			

	Form No	CPR Rule	PD
It is only in exceptional circumstances that the power to adjourn a hearing to enable a tenant to reduce his rent arrears below 8 weeks so that Ground 8 of Part 1 of Sch 2 to the Housing Act 1988 will not apply. The fact that the arrears were due to maladministration by a housing benefit authority was not such an exceptional circumstance: *North British Housing Association Ltd v Matthews* [2004] EWCA Civ 1736, (2005) Times, 11 January			
An uncleared cheque can be treated as payment for the purpose of arrears calculations: *Day v Coltrane* [2003] EWCA Civ 342, [2003] All ER (D) 210 (Mar)			
2.7 Directions			
If the court is satisfied that the claim is **genuinely disputed** on substantial grounds the court will not decide the claim but will give case management directions including allocation		55.8	
2.8 Orders			
For forms of order, outright and suspended and postponed, see	N26, N28, N28A		55A, para 10
Where an order for possession is made on a mandatory ground this should be noted on the court file: *Diab v Countryside Rentals 1 plc* [2001] All ER (D) 119 (Jul)			
Note *Norwich City Council v Famuyiwa* [2005] EWCA Civ 1770, (2005) Times, 24 January where it was stated where the judge found it reasonable to make a possession order he should consider whether the position could be controlled by postponing the date for possession on appropriate terms			
Note also the order and suspended order for possession on forfeiture for rent arrears	N27, N27A		

	Form No	CPR Rule	PD
As to the effect of possession orders against **secure tenants suspended** in the terms of N28 (in contrast to the pre-CPR form N28) see *Harlow District Council v Hall* [2006] EWCA Civ 156, [2006] 1 WLR 2116 where it was held that the effect of a suspended possession order in the existing form terminated the tenancy so that the tenant became a tolerated trespasser even if he kept to the terms of the suspended order In *Bristol City Council v Hassan* [2006] EWCA Civ 656, [2006] 22 EG 176 (CS) the Court of Appeal concluded nothing in Housing Act 1985 s 85 fettered the court's discretion to make such order for **postponement** as it thought fit and that a judge was not obliged to set an absolute date to be specified in the order This was particularly significant when the arrears are paid by Housing benefit which in practice is paid 4 weekly Brooke LJ stated it was lawful to make an order in terms that are now set out in form N28A Subsequently the House of Lords held in *Knowsley Housing Trust v White* [2008] UKHL 70, [2009] 1 AC 636 that the position of assured tenants was not the same as that of secure tenants as their tenancy did not come to an end on breach of a suspended order but only when that order was executed. The discrepancy between the two types of tenancy was put to an end on 20 May 2009 when the provisions considered in para 2.1C above were brought into effect.			

	Form No	CPR Rule	PD
As a result of the coming into force of the Housing and Regeneration Act 2008 (see 2.1C above of this TAB) tenancies, whether they be secure or assured and whether the possession order be suspended or postponed, remain in force until execution. Which of the two alternative orders should the court be urged to make? From the tenant's point of view a postponed order will be preferable because the landlord will have to apply to the court for a date to be fixed which gives the court the opportunity to consider whether to fix a date or list the application for a hearing. From the landlord's point of view a suspended order will be preferable for a warrant can be issued upon default and it is up to the tenant to apply to suspend it.			
2.9 Orders fixing a date for possession where the court has made an order postponing the date for possession of a secure or an assured tenancy	N28A		55A, section IV
It must be remembered on making a possession order that the court may impose an additional condition, e g that the defendant comply with the tenancy conditions until possession is given up. See further article in New Law Journal, 13 April 2007, page 505, 'Re-thinking possession orders' by Holbrook and Billingham			
The tenancy will remain in being notwithstanding the making of an order for possession postponing the date for possession, until execution under the possession order			
If there is default at least 14 days and not more than 3 months before applying for an order the claimant must give written notice to the defendant			55A, para 10.3
For the contents of the notice see			55A, para 10.4
In his reply to the notice the defendant must: (a) where he disputes the stated arrears, provide details of payments or credits made;			

	Form No	CPR Rule	PD
(b) where he agrees the stated arrears, explain why payments have not been made			55A, para 10.5
The claimant's application for an order fixing the date upon which the defendant has to give up possession must be made by Part 23 application notice. The application must state whether the defendant has any outstanding housing benefit claims			55A, para 10.6
The documents to be filed with the application are listed in			55A, para 10.7
The rules dealing with applications without notice, service and the right to set aside do not apply			55A, para 10.8
The application will be referred to the District Judge who will normally determine the application without a hearing by fixing the date for possession as the next working day but otherwise will fix a hearing date and direct service of the application and supporting evidence but for a case where the court found there was a triable issue as to breach of one or more of the conditions of the postponement see *Wandsworth London Borough Council v Whibley* [2008] EWCA Civ 1259, (2008) Times, 25 November			55A, para 10.9
The court cannot review the finding that it was reasonable to make the order			55A, para 10.10
2.10 Costs			
Unless the court otherwise orders, the order will be for fixed costs where one of the grounds for possession is arrears of rent, whether or not the order for possession is suspended, if the defendant has not delivered a defence or counterclaim nor otherwise denied liability or has delivered a defence limited to his proposals for payment of the rent arrears		45.1(2)(c), (d) and (f)	

	Form No	CPR Rule	PD
The fixed costs at present are £276.75 (£150 court fee; £69.25 commencement costs and £57.50 costs on entry of judgment); see article 'Short Changed' [2007] NLJ 4 May by Francis Davey. The tenancy agreement may provide that the tenant will pay the landlord's costs and this will normally entitle the landlord to recover reasonable costs (but not more than reasonable costs) and not fixed costs: *Church Comrs v Ibrahim* [1997] 1 EGLR 13, [1997] 03 EG 136, CA		45.2A and 45.4A	
2.11 Human Rights			
For consideration of the infringement of the right to respect for a person's home, pursuant to Article 8 ECHR, by the making of a possession order in respect of a public sector tenancy (a secure tenancy) see *Harrow London Borough Council v Qazi* [2003] UKHL 43, [2004] 1 AC 983, [2003] 3 All ER 461 as explained in *Lambeth London Borough Council v Kay* [2006] UKHL 10, [2006] 2 AC 465 and the conjoined appeal *Leeds City Council v Price* [2006] UKHL 10, [2006] 2 AC 465 where *Connors v United Kingdom* [2004] 40 ECHR 189 was distinguished. An appeal on the article 8 ground was refused in *Doherty v Birmingham City Council* [2006] EWCA Civ 1739, [2007] LGR 165 (a case concerning a gypsy caravan site). a decision reversed by the House of Lords in part where it was decided that the defendant was able to raise a public law gateway (b) defence (see below), that the decision to evict was an improper exercise of the power of the local authority, in a county court – see further para 2.12.			

	Form No	CPR Rule	PD
The position established by these cases is that the right of a public landlord to enforce a claim for possession under domestic law would in most cases automatically supply the justification required by Article 8(2) ECHR. This is subject to the proviso that a challenge could be made to the making of a possession order in the county court, so far as the limits on the jurisdiction permitted, if the defendant could exceptionally show: (a) a seriously arguable point is raised that the law that enables the court to make the possession order is incompatible with its jurisdiction under the Human Rights Act 1998; (b) if the defendant wishes to challenge the decision of a public authority as an improper exercise of its powers on the ground that it was 'a decision that no reasonable person would consider justifiable' per Lord Hope in *Kay* (see above) Lord Bingham has indicated that where a serious arguable issue on one of those grounds is raised the court itself should decide the issue unless on consideration it would be appropriate to refer the proceedings to the High Court.			

	Form No	CPR Rule	PD
The local authority in the case of *McCann v United Kingdom (Application No 19009/04) ECHR* (2008) Times, 23 May did not seek to evict the applicant under the statutory scheme governing secure tenants but obtained from the former wife and co-tenant a common law notice to quit. This immediately terminated the applicant's right to remain in the house. A possession order was obtained in proceedings in which the applicant's right to respect for his home was not considered. It was held that the applicant's rights under Article 8 had been violated and he was awarded damages for pecuniary loss and costs. For a detailed consideration of this case and its implications see 'Human Rights Updater' published by LexisNexis, Issue 78, June 2008, pages 14–16. The House of Lords in *Doherty v Birmingham City Council and the Secretary of State for Communities and Local Government (Intervenor)* [2008] UKHL 57, (2008) Times 14 August allowed an appeal in part on Human Rights grounds and held a gateway (b) defence could be raised by these particular appellants, who did not have a private law defence, in the county court. However, their unease with the decision in *McCann* above by ECHR was clear to the extent that one of the Law Lords expressed the view that the decision was based on a mistaken understanding of how possession claims by public bodies were dealt with in the United Kingdom. The House of Lords stated the county court judges should continue to follow the guidance given in *Kay* above as more fully explained by Lord Hope in *Doherty* when considering a human rights defence.			

	Form No	CPR Rule	PD
The decision in *Kay* is further supported by *Taylor v Central Bedfordshire Council* [2009] EWCA Civ 613 where the Council's decision to seek a possession order against a trespasser in circumstances similar to those in *Kay* was held to be not capable of valid challenge on public law grounds; see per Waller LJ, paras 43–44. It was made clear in *Doherty* that gateways (a) and (b) above were modifications made to the decision in *Qazi* by the majority in *Kay* to accommodate the decision in Connors (for all three of these cases see above). For an extremely informative note and commentary on the case of *Doherty* see Human Rights Updater published by LexisNexis UK (2008) October, Issue 81 at page 13 and note 'the Lords were careful to restrict their conclusions to cases involving gypsies' in para 9			

	Form No	CPR Rule	PD
The present (2010) position is that the courts at district and circuit level continue to follow *Qazi* and *Kay* (see above) as explained in *Doherty* (see above) and *Liverpool City Council v Doran (Secretary of State for Communities and Local Government intervening)* [2009] EWCA Civ 146, [2009] All ER (D) 28 (Mar) but they will have to face the pressure of statements and decisions by ECHR as to breaches of Article 8 as for example in the *Cann* case (see above) when the court stated: 'The loss of one's house is the most extreme form of interference with the right to respect for her home. Any person at risk of an interference of this magnitude should in principle be able to have the proportionality of the measure determined by an independent tribunal.' More recently in *Cosic v Croatia* Application No 28261/06 [2009] EWHC 28261/06, the European Court held that a possession order against an occupier whose lease had expired and who had no security was in violation of Article 8. This underlines the conflict between the domestic courts and the European Court. The degree of conflict is considered by Annette Cafferkey in her article 'Seeking Possession' in (2009) NLJ, 27 November, page 1651. Most recently (September 2010) the ECHR in *Kay v United Kigndom* (App No 37341/06) has in effect rejected the argument that the Gateway (b) defence is limited to conventional public law grounds (i e no reasonable person would consider it justifiable) or whether personal circumstances should be taken into account (the minority view in *Kay* in the House of Lords). The ECHR allowed the appeal on the basis that the county court was wrong to strike out the article 8 defences put forward by the claimants.			

	Form No	CPR Rule	PD
The court said that in *McCann* it had agreed with the minority of the House of Lords in their ruling on *Kay v Lambeth London Borough Council* in 2006: 'In conclusion, the *Kay* applicants' challenge to the decision to strike out their article 8 defences failed because it was not possible at that time to challenge the decision of a local authority to seek a possession order on the basis of the alleged disproportionality of that decision in light of personal circumstances.' The only relevant decision of the UK courts on the point since *Kay* to account for the use by the ECHR of the words 'at that time' is the decision in *Doherty* (see above). That decision however did not approve the minority view in *Kay* or hold the Gateway (b) defence should be based on personal circumstances in a proportionality consideration. Pending clarification, the view expressed above as to the present (2010) position is likely to remain accurate. Clarification may be provided by the Supreme Cour when it delivers judgment in *Manchester City Council v Pinnock* (see para 2.12 of this TAB below) at or shortly after the end of this year. A detailed assessment of the present position is to be found in the article 'An ongoing saga' by Lindsay Johnson in (2010) NLJ, 8 October, page 1365.			

	Form No	CPR Rule	PD
The *Birmingham City Council* case (see 2.11 above, second para), established that a public sector defence can be raised in the county court. Doubts as to whether a registered social landlord is to be treated as a functional public authority were resolved by the decision of the Court of Appeal in *R (on the application of Weaver) v London and Quadrant Housing Trust (Equality and Human Rights Commission intervening)* [2009] EWCA Civ 587, [2009] 25 EG 137 (CS). This decision means that registered social landlords ('registered providers') are public authorities for the purposes of s 6 of the Human Rights Act 1998 when acting as landlords, albeit there will be some such bodies which exceptionally are not by reason of not meeting the criteria set out by Lord Nicholls in *Aston Cantlow and Wilmcote with Billesley Parochial Church Council v Wallbank* [2004] 1 AC 546. See generally article by Louise Curtis 'All Change' (2009) New Law Journal 17 July, page 1019.			
The Supreme Court has refused permission to appeal the decision of the Court of Appeal in the *Weaver* case, see last para above; Sol Jo (2009) 19 November, page 5. The effect of *Weaver* on the exchange of tenancies can be seen in *R (on the application of McIntyre) v Gentoo Group* [2010] EWHC 5 (Admin), [2010] All ER (D) 01 (Jan), (2010) Sol Jo, 12 January, page 2 and 19 January, page 29 where it was held that the requirement of clearance of 'elderly' rent arrears before the Housing Association's consent could be given was unlawful in public law. The tenant's application for judicial review was dismissed because judicial review is a remedy of last resort and other remedies were available and had not been used. For further consideration and discussion see article by Giles Parker in (2010) Sol Jo, 16 February, page 6 entitled 'Who holds the keys?'.			

	Form No	CPR Rule	PD
The group legal chairman of the Equality and Human Rights Commission is quoted in the Gazette (2009) 26 June, page 208, as saying: 'It is only correct that RSLs, who are providing these public functions, be treated as a public authority and be subject to the Human Rights Act. This will require social landlords to consider the proportionality and reasonableness of their actions.' It is understood that leave to the House of Lords is being sought.			
2.12 Human rights – homelessness housing, demoted and introductory tenancies			
In so far as persons in **homelessness accommodation** are concerned it is clear form the House of Lords decision in *Doherty* (see para 2.11 above) that they must present their cases under gateway (b) in the county court which will determine them in accordance with the guidance in *Kay*. see further the decision of the Supreme Court in *Ali v Birmingham City Council and Secretary of State for Communities and Local Government (Intervenor)* [2010] UKSC 8, (2010) Sol Jo, 23 February, page 38 as to homelessness and human rights.			
The position of **demoted tenants** is presently uncertain because the Supreme Court is due to consider the decision in *Pinnock v Manchester City Corporation* [2009] EWCA Civ 852 which relates to demoted tenancies (ss 143A-143M of the Housing Act 1996) and the impact of the Human Rights Act 1998, Art 8 on the right of such tenants who enjoy only limited security. The Supreme Court has asked counsel for written submissions on the impact on *Pinnock* of the ECHR ruling in *Kay v United Kingdom* (App No 37341/06) in September 2010. The Supreme Court's judgment in *Pinnock* is expected by the end of 2010.		65.11–65.20	

	Form No	CPR Rule	PD
In respect of introductory tenancies (Housing Act 1996, ss 124–138) the Court of Appeal has given interim guidance in relation to gateway (b) defences in *Salford City Council v Mullen* [2010] EWCA Civ 336 with conjoined appeals.			
It establishes that at present: (a) these arguments have to be presented in the Administrative Court (not the county court); (b) it will only be in highly exceptional circumstances that a county court will adjourn a matter so that an application for judicial review can be made; (c) there is no right to a proportionality review and the consideration will be whether in the circumstances the decision was one that 'no reasonable person would consider justifiable'; see per Lord Hooper in *Kay* and see *Doherty* above; (d) gateway (b) can be applied to any decision of the local authority relevant to seeking possession which could be the subject of judicial review (see per Waller LJ at paras 73 and 74 of *Salford City Council v Mullen* above).			
For detailed consideration see articles 'Housing Focus' by Annette Cafferkey (2010) NLJ, 18 June, page 861 and 'A new gateway' by Burton and Gask (2010) NLJ, 9 July, page 964.			

	Form No	CPR Rule	PD
2.13 Homeless			
Intentionally homeless families are entitled to temporary accommodation for a period of time that gives 'a reasonable opportunity to find their own accommodation'; s 190 Housing Act 1996. That period should take into account the particular needs and circumstances of the individual and not the cost and other demands on the resources of the local authority: *R (on the application of Colville) v Richmond-on-Thames London Borough Council* [2006] EWCA Civ 718, [2006] 4 All ER 917, [2006] 1 WLR 2808			
When considering the suitability of accommodation offered to homeless people regard should be had by the court to any proposed adaptations or alterations: *Boreh v London Borough of Ealing* [2008] EWCA Civ 1176, [2008] All ER (D) 291 (Oct).			
In *Manchester City Council v Moran* [2009] UKHL 36, [2009] 1 WLR 1506 it was held that women living in a refuge, whether or not they were evicted, and families living in overcrowded accommodation awaiting council housing, were to be regarded as homeless (as opposed to intentionally homeless) within the provisions of the Housing Act 1996. The definitions of homelessness are contained in ss 175 and 177 of that Act.			
Accommodation provided under s 192 of the Housing Act 1996 in a women's refuge or similar is a staging post along the way to permanent accommodation and in the light of this finding in *Moran* (see above) the court was 'inclined to accept' that the decision in *R v Ealing London Borough Council, ex p Sidhu* [1982] 8 LGR 534, 2 HLR 45 that a women's refuge was not 'accommodation' could not stand in the light of the decisions in *R v Hillingdon Borough Council, ex p Puhlhofer* [1986] AC 484 and *R v Brent London Borough Council, ex p Awua* [1996] AC 55.			

	Form No	CPR Rule	PD
3. Mortgage possession claims relating to residential property			
3.1 Preliminary			
On 19 November 2008 a pre-action protocol for residential mortgage possession claims was brought into force. It covers: (i) first mortgages (ii) subsequent mortgages whether or not regulated under the Consumer Credit Act 1974			
Para 1.1 of the Preamble to the protocol states that the Protocol describes the behaviour the court will normally expect of the parties prior to the start of a possession claim within its scope			
Its provisions include: (i) a possession order being postponed where the borrower has taken or will take steps to market the property at an appropriate price in accordance with professional advice (ii) the parties to discuss the cause of the arrears, the borrower's financial position and proposals for payment of the arrears (iii) where appropriate lender to refer the borrower to independent debt advice (iv) the lender to give written reasons within 10 days for rejecting any proposal by the borrower for payment			
The protocol gives good reasons for not starting possession proceedings in paragraph 6 of the Protocol and it is provided at 6.4: 'Where the lender decides not to postpone the start of a possession claim it should inform the borrower of the reasons for this decision at least 5 business days before starting proceedings.'			
For consideration of the effectiveness of this protocol see article 'Stemming a rising tide?' by Bailey and Williams in NLJ 13 February 2009, page 221 and 'Vulture funds prey on hard-up homeowners' by James Charles (2009) Times, 4 July, page 72			

	Form No	CPR Rule	PD
The Government has introduced the following schemes to advise and assist borrowers: (a) Support for Mortgage Interest (SMI) whereby homeowners receiving Income Support or certain other benefits can claim an additional element, called Support for Mortgage Interest, on eligible capital up to £200,000 after 13 weeks from claiming benefit. (b) Mortgage Rescue Scheme (MRS) for homeowners who would be eligible for help under the homeless legislation from their local authority on repossession. (c) Homeowners Mortgage Support (HMS) which is a Government guaranteed scheme enabling deferment of a proportion of mortgage interest on experiencing a substantial loss of income. The deferment can be for up to 2 years and the income deferred will have to be paid by the borrower eventually. The eligibility requirements are numerous and detailed. The total principal amount of loans secured on the home must not be more that £400,000. More information about the schemes can be obtained from www.direct.gov.uk.			
The Administration of Justice Acts 1970 (s 36) and 1973 (s 8) give powers to the court where the principal sum can be paid by the mortgagor by instalments or otherwise be deferred in whole or in part. See **III REA [22]–III REA [23.6]** in Volume 2. The powers are not available where the principal sum is to be paid on a fixed date or on demand (subject to any collateral agreement to accept instalment payments)			

	Form No	CPR Rule	PD
If the mortgage is one to **which the Consumer Credit Act 1974** applies, the defendant may make an application for a time order in his defence or by application on notice. The £25,000 ceiling for regulation under the CCA 1974 having been abolished from 6 April 2008 agreements, including second mortgages of residential property, made by an individual after 6 April 2008, will be covered by the Act irrespective of the amount borrowed. The time order provisions under s 129 accordingly apply to such second mortgages. An agreement for business purposes for over £25,000 will be exempt from regulation under CCA 1974, s 16. It is to be noted in respect of mortgages and agreements governed by the CCA that 'Rule 78' clauses whereby on early redemption a calculation is made of the total interest to the end of the original term and only a partial rebate given are void by reason of the Unfair Terms in Consumer Contracts Regulations 1999, SI 1999/2083. Overpayments can be reclaimed: *Evans v Cherrytree Finance Ltd* (13 April 2007, unreported). For further discussion see article 'Unfair Windfalls' by Paul Beevers, NLJ, 28 February 2008, page 317. For an unsuccessful attempt to invoke the CCA see *Southern Pacific Mortgage Ltd v Heath* [2009] EWCA Civ 1135, [2009] NLJR 1581, (2009) Times, 20 November where the then limit of £25,000 was exceeded by the payment off of a previous mortgage in favour of another lender of about £19,000 and the provision of £9,000 to the defendant. The Court of Appeal held they were not to be treated as two separate agreements. See further the article 'Time to wipe the slate clean?' by Paul Healey in NLJ (2010) 30 April, page 614. Buy to let mortgages will be exempt form the provisions of the CCA 1974. Regulation and administration of first residential mortgages will continue to be dealt with by the Financial Services Authority under the provisions of the Financial Services and Markets Act 2000 and not the CCA 1974. See further NLJ, 14 and 21 March 2008, page 411.			55A, para 7.1

	Form No	CPR Rule	PD
The effect of a **forged legal mortgage over jointly owned property** (i e where the signature of one but not both of the borrowers is forged) is to vest in the lender an equitable charge over the interest of the borrower who did genuinely sign. The remedy available to the lender is to apply as an equitable chargee for an order for sale under s 14 of the Trusts of Land and Appointment of Trustees Act 1996: *Edwards v Bank of Scotland* [2010] EWHC 652 (Ch).			
Where the re-mortgage of a jointly owned property is vitiated by the undue influence of the husband, it nevertheless operates as an equitable charge under s 14 (see immediately preceding para above) on the husband's share: see *Hewett v First Plus Financial Group Ltd* [2010] EWCA Civ 312.			
This table does not deal with **chattel mortgages** obtained by use of a security bill of sale. The relevant statutes are the Consumer Credit Act 1974, the Bills of Sale Act 1878 and the Bills of Sale (Amendment) Act 1882. It is vital to appreciate that in the event of default and the expiry of a default notice no court order is required before the chattel (usually a car) is seised and the lender has only to wait five days before selling the chattel. There is a very useful article by Paul Beevers in NLJ, 11 April 2008, page 507 which sets out the possible steps open to the borrower and above all stresses the urgency of acting appropriately.			7B
Where, to avoid a possession order in favour of the lenders, the owner sells pursuant to a 'sell to rent back' arrangement and is subsequently faced with a claim for possession see **TAB 23** section 4 below.			

	Form No	CPR Rule	PD
3.2 Particulars of claim			
In addition to the general requirements (see 1.4, above) and in particular the necessity of the lender dealing with protocol compliance including handing to the judge two completed copies of form N123 with the statement of truth duly completed and providing an explanation for any failures to comply with the protocol apparent from the answers to the questions in the form.	N123		55A, para 2.1
If the claim is a possession claim by a mortgagee, the particulars of claim must also set out:	N120		55A, para 2.5
(a) if the claim relates to residential property whether: (i) a land charge of Class F has been registered under s 2(7) of the Matrimonial Homes Act 1967 (ii) a notice registered under ss 2(8) or 8(3) of the Matrimonial Homes Act 1983 has been entered and on whose behalf, or (iii) a notice under s 31(10) of the Family Law Act 1996 has been registered and on whose behalf, and if so, that the claimant will serve notice of the claim on the persons on whose behalf the land charge is registered or the notice or caution entered (b) the state of the mortgage account by including: (i) the amount of: the advance any periodic repayment, and any payment of interest required to be made			

	Form No	CPR Rule	PD
(ii) the amount which would have to be paid (after taking into account any adjustment for early settlement) in order to redeem the mortgage at a stated date not more than 14 days after the claim started specifying the amount of solicitor's costs and administration charges which would be payable (iii) if the loan which is secured by the mortgage is a regulated consumer credit agreement, the total amount outstanding under the terms of the mortgage, and (iv) the rate of interest payable: at the commencement of the mortgage immediately before any arrears referred to in paragraph (3) accrued at the commencement of the proceedings (c) if the claim is brought because of failure to pay the periodic payments when due: (i) in schedule form, the dates and amounts of all payments due and payments made under the mortgage agreement or mortgage deed for a period of two years immediately preceding the date of issue or if the first date of default was less than two years before the date of issue from the date of default and a running total If the claimant wishes to rely on a history of arrears longer that two years he should state this on his particulars and exhibit a full (or longer) schedule to a witness statement (ii) give details of:			

	Form No	CPR Rule	PD
any other payments required to be made as a term of the mortgage (such as for insurance premiums, legal costs, default interest, penalties, administrative or other charges) any sums claimed and stating the nature and amount of each such charge; and whether any of these payments is in arrears and whether or not it is included in the amount of any periodic payment (d) whether or not the loan which is secured by the mortgage is a regulated consumer credit agreement and, if so, specify the date on which any notice required by ss 76 or 87 of the Consumer Credit Act 1974 was given (e) if appropriate details that show the property is not one to which s 141 of the Consumer Credit Act 1974 applies (f) any relevant information about the defendant's circumstances, in particular: (i) whether the defendant is in receipt of social security benefits, and (ii) whether any payments are made on his behalf directly to the claimant under the Social Security Contributions and Benefits Act 1992 (g) give details of any tenancy entered into between the mortgagor and mortgagee (including any notices served), and (h) state any previous steps which the claimant has taken to recover the money secured by the mortgage or the mortgaged property and, in the case of court proceedings, state: (i) the dates when the claim started and concluded, and			

	Form No	CPR Rule	PD
(ii) the dates and terms of any orders made (i) unless it is included in the claim form a statement explaining the steps that have been taken to comply with the Protocol for Possession Claims based on Mortgage or Home Purchase Plan Arrears in respect of Residential Property and dealing with compliance with any other relevant protocol including sections III and IV of the Pre-Action Conduct protocol.			
3.3 Service of the claim form			
The general rules as to service apply:			
If a class F land charge has been registered or a notice entered, service must also be effected on the person who caused this to be registered or entered		Part 6	
Where the claimant serves, a certificate of service must be produced at the hearing and CPR 6.14(2)(a) as to the filing of a certificate of service does not apply		55.8(6)	
3.4 Hearing date			
The general rules apply (see 1.5, above) and the date given on issue will be for a hearing in chambers generally before a district judge with a time estimate of 5 minutes			
The claimant must send a notice to the property addressed to 'the tenant or occupier' to the housing department of the relevant local authority and to any other registered proprietor (other than the claimant) of a registered charge over the property within 5 days of receiving notification of the date of the hearing by the court giving the prescribed information and produce a copy at the hearing and prove service. The notices must contain the information set out in sub-ss (3) and (3A) respectively.		55.10(1)–(4)	

	Form No	CPR Rule	PD
An unauthorised tenant of residential property may apply to the court for the order for possession to be suspended: see 3.6A of this TAB.		55.10(4A)	
3.5 Defendant's response			
See general provision, 1.6 above For form of defence, see	N11M		
For notes for defendant in mortgage possession claim of residential premises see	N7		
3.6 The hearing			
The date given on issue will be for a hearing before a district judge in chambers Wherever possible the parties should include their evidence in a statement of case verified by a statement of truth The **claimant's evidence** should include the amount of mortgage arrears and interest on those arrears. These amounts should if possible be calculated up to the date of the hearing (if necessary by specifying a daily rate or arrears and interest) Such evidence can be brought up to date orally at the hearing			55A, para 5.1 55A, para 5.2
Subject to this updating, if the case has not been allocated to fast or multi-track, any fact may be proved by written statements		55.8(3)	
Witness statements must be served 2 days prior to the hearing.		55.8(4)	
The claimant **must** bring to the hearing two copies of **form N123** as to compliance with the mortgage arrears pre-action protocol. One of these is to be handed to the defendant and the other to the judge at the hearing. No documents are to be attached to the form and none are required at the hearing. The object of the document is to avoid the court having to look beyond it unless it is challenged. The claimant or their solicitor has to complete a statement of truth.	N123		

	Form No	CPR Rule	PD
At the hearing there is no time or necessity for an opening but **a "pro forma"** can be completed and handed to the court (a copy having been given to the defendant prior to the hearing) showing: (a) the date of the mortgage and the amount advanced (b) any further advance (c) the date of notice to the occupiers (d) the current instalment (and whether any part is paid by social security) (e) the amount of arrears (f) the balance outstanding (g) any information as to the value of the property (h) details of the occupants (i) the order(s) sought The court will have before it the claimant's statement of case, the form N123 and any witnesses' statements and will expect the production of: (a) **clear search** under the Land Charges Acts (unregistered land) or the Land Registration Acts (registered land) showing that no class F land charge has been registered under s 2(7) of the Matrimonial Homes Act 1967 or notice registered under s 2(8) or 8(3) of the Matrimonial Homes Act 1967 or under s 31(10) of the Family Law Act 1996, and (b) an official copy of the register			
If it is relevant the defendant should give evidence of: (a) the amount of any social security or housing benefit payments relevant to the mortgage arrears, and (b) the status of: (i) any outstanding claims for social security or housing benefit and (ii) any outstanding applications to appeal or review social security or housing benefit decisions The defendant should also give evidence of:			

	Form No	CPR Rule	PD
(a) his ability to pay the current instalments (b) his proposal for clearing the arrears – with a supporting financial statement showing it is a realistic proposal (c) why the court should be satisfied he is likely to pay the arrears of instalments within a reasonable time 'Reasonable' can extend to the whole of the remaining period of the mortgage term: *Cheltenham and Gloucester Building Society v Norgan* [1996] 1 All ER 449; *Solon South West Housing Association Ltd v James* [2004] EWCA Civ 1847 The court does not have to take formal evidence from the defendant: *Cheltenham and Gloucester Building Society v Grant* (1994) 26 HLR 703 The court does not have the power to alter the contract between the borrower and the lender and for that reason will only very rarely make an order postponing possession on terms that do not provide for payment of the current monthly instalments. It is the case that the court has power to do so for it is not altering the contractual requirements but merely postponing the date for possession under the Administration of Justice Acts 1970 and 1973. The court may: (a) grant an **outright possession order**, or (b) grant a **suspended possession order** and in either case	N26		
(c) grant a **money judgment** for the balance outstanding but if the possession order is suspended the will stay execution of the money judgment on terms	N31		

	Form No	CPR Rule	PD
(d) **adjourn** the proceedings under CPR 3.1 or the court's inherent jurisdiction but before doing so the court would require adequate evidence of the borrower's proposed means of repayment: *Cheval Bridging Finance v Bhasisn* [2008] EWCA Civ 1613, [2009] All ER (D) 143 (Apr) and see article 'Beg, borrow or steal' by Edward Peters in New Law Journal, 13 March 2009, page 381. District judges are prepared to adjourn to ensure the protocol is properly followed: see feature in Sol Jo (2009) 8 September, page 2.			
The claimant is **not** likely to seek an order for **costs** but will prefer to rely on its contractual rights to costs. The CPR are believed to preserve the legal position as set out in *Gomba Holdings (UK) Ltd v Minories Finance Ltd (No 2)* [1993] Ch 171, [1992] 4 All ER 588, CA. See further *Marchmont Investments Ltd v BFO SA* [2006] EWHC 1990 (Ch), [2006] All ER (D) 49 (Jul) where an order was made for the borrower to pay the lender's costs in accordance with the terms of the mortgage deed: see also *Adamson v Halifax* [2002] EWCA Civ 1134, [2003] 4 All ER 423		48.3	
If the claim is not made out it will be dismissed			
3.6A Possession claims by a mortgagee against persons other than the mortgagor			
Where private landlords have their property repossessed, their tenants are normally evicted with very little notice. The government has the intention to give such tenants 'an extra layer of protection' under government plans: 'Lender Repossession of Residential Property: Protection of Tenants'.			

	Form No	CPR Rule	PD
For the difficulties facing the mortgagee claiming possession against an occupier who is not a mortgagor, see article by Robin Powell entitled 'Repossession claims against third parties' Sol Jo, 17 June 2008, page 8 and the cases referred to in it.			
The **Mortgage Repossessions (Protection of Tenants) Act 2010** which was enacted on 8 April 2010 was brought into effect on 1 October 2010 together with the Dwelling Houses (Execution of Possession Orders by Mortgagees) Regulations 2010, SI 2010/1809. Limited protection is given to assured or Rent Act **tenants whose tenancy is not binding upon the lender**. The court will on the application of the tenant be able to stay or postpone the delivery of possession for up to 2 months from (it would appear) the date of the tenant's application.		55.10	
The court has to have regard to the circumstances of the tenant and whether the tenant is in breach of his tenancy agreement and the reason for any breach. The court may make the suspension conditional upon payments being made to the lender during the period of suspension.			
The insertion of a new rule 4A in CPR 55.10 enables the unprotected tenant to make the application for suspension of the lender's order for possession.			
3.7 Directions			
If the court is satisfied the claim is genuinely disputed substantial grounds it is unlikely to dispose of it but then give case management directions including allocation		55.8(2)	
3.8 Sale of the property			
For the lender's general duty to take reasonable care to obtain the best reasonably available price, see *Michael v Miller* [2004] EWCA Civ 282, [2004] 2 P & CR D12, [2004] 2 EGLR 151 and article entitled 'Fair play' in (2009) Sol Jo 11 August, page 19 by Christopher Berry.			

	Form No	CPR Rule	PD
Where the borrower relies on a prospective sale to avoid a 28 day possession order he will find useful authority in the decision in *Target Home Loans v Clothier* [1994] 1 All ER 439, CA and the statement of Nolan LJ: "… is there a prospect of an early sale? If so is it better in the interests of all that it be effected by the defendant and his wife or by the mortgage company?" He concluded an order for possession in 3 months was appropriate. In Royal Trust of Canada v Markham (1975) 1 WLR per Sir John Pennycuick 'likelihood' was said to be a question of fact to be determined by the judge on the evidence			
For a case where there was a sale to a closely connected company see *Bradford & Bingley plc v Ross* [2005] EWCA Civ 394, (2005) Times, 2 May			
For consideration of a bank's position when it is a mortgagee see *Francis v Barclays Bank plc* [2004] EWHC 2787 (Ch), [2004] 51 EG 88 (CS)			
For a case where the lender had mixed motives for exercising the power of sale see *Meretz Investments v ACP Ltd* (2006) Times, 27 April, CA and also see *Meretz Investment NV v ACP Ltd* (2008) Times, 2 January, CA where an attempt was made to pursue a cause of action in the tort of conspiracy. This failed, the lender's exercise of its power of sale was lawful and further there were no unlawful means employed			
The exercise of a power of sale after default by the borrower was held not to infringe the borrower's rights under art 1 of the First Protocol to the European Convention on Human Rights in *Horsham Properties Group Ltd v Clark and another (Secretary of State intervening)* [2008] EWHC 2327 (Ch), [2008] All ER (D) 58 (Oct), (2008) Times, 29 October			

	Form No	CPR Rule	PD
For a case where the lender's security was extinguished under the provisions of the Limitation Act 1980 see *Ashe v National Westminster Bank plc* [2007] EWHC 494 (Ch), [2007] All ER (D) 227 (Mar). [2007] 2 P & CR 525. This was a case where the mortgage deed gave the lender an immediate right to possession which was not dependent on any default by the borrower or restricted by any term of the deed. Further, more than 12 years had elapsed since any payment had been made by the borrower. For useful discussions of this case see article 'Watching the Clock' by Sarah Greer, NLJ, 18 April 2008, page 548 and article 'Lenders beware – do not delay or you will pay', Sol Jo, 15 April 2008, page 12. Where a borrower sought to dispute the validity of a suspended possession order after 15 years the judge was held on appeal to have been correct in dismissing the application: *Abbey National plc v Miller* [2007] EWCA Civ 138, [2007] All ER (D) 118 (Feb)			

	Form No	CPR Rule	PD
A lender (mortgagee) can sell the mortgaged property in the exercise of the power of sale contained in the mortgage deed and the statutory power of sale, with the effect of over-reaching the borrower's rights, without any court order. In *Horsham Properties Group Ltd v Clark* (see preceding paragraph) the lenders appointed a receiver who sold the property to the claimant who claimed possession from the defendant borrower who was in default of the mortgage covenants. It was held that s 36 of the Administration of Justice Act 1970 did not apply as its provisions only affect claims for possession by lenders and the claimant was not a lender. This procedure is common in buy-to-let mortgage enforcements. See articles in NLJ by Tony Poole, 2 and 9 January 2009 and by Sarah Greer, entitled 'Urgent Review' 20 February 2009; also by James Charles referred to at 3.1 of this TAB, fifth paragraph. It is to be noted that where the sale realised a sufficient sum to discharge the mortgage debt the mortgage ceased to subsist. A human rights defence also failed. The decision in *Ropaigealach v Barclays Bank plc* [2000] 1 QB 26 was followed.			
Statutory reform of the position has been prepared, being in draft form at the time of writing (January 2010).			

	Form No	CPR Rule	PD
3.9 Recovery of shortfall			
For the purposes of ss 8 and 20 of the Limitation Act the date at which a building society's right accrued to recover the shortfall from the borrowers after the sale of the security was the date when the borrowers defaulted in monthly instalment payments so that the right to recover the monies (i e the principal) accrued; s 20(1)(b) Limitation Act 1980. Mortgage deeds commonly provide the principal becomes due upon 2 months default in repayments; *West Bromwich Building Society v Wilkinson* [2005] UKHL 44, [2005] 4 All ER 97, [2005] 1 WLR 2303			
Section 29(5) of the Act provides that a fresh limitation period will arise from the date the debtor 'acknowledges the claim' but s 29(7) provides that once the limitation period has expired acknowledgement will not revive the debt. As to what amounts to an acknowledgement see *Bradford & Bingley plc v Rashid* [2006] UKHL 37, (2006) Times, 14 July, HL and note the views expressed there of acknowledgements in without prejudice correspondence; and *Ashcroft v Bradford & Bingley plc* [2010] EWCA Civ 223 where monthly payments in reduction of mortgage shortfall debt (made during the period of primary limitation) would amount to a part payment and start time running afresh. See also article by Daniel Lewis 'Owning Up' Sol Jo, 23 November 2007, page 1484. Mortgage interest paid by the Benefit agency revived the limitation period as the agency was acting as the agent for the borrower within the statutory framework even though the borrower had no direct control over the agency: *Bradford & Bingley Building Society v Cutler* (2008) Times, 22 February, CA.			

	Form No	CPR Rule	PD
3.10 Clearance of arrears and subsequent default			
If in mortgage possession proceedings where a suspended order for possession has been made the borrower clears the arrears but later again falls into arrears on a strict construction of the form of possession order and on the authority of *Greyhound Guarantee v Caulfield* [1981] CLY 1808 a claimant may simply apply for a warrant but it may be considered more appropriate to apply for permission to enforce the possession order or to start fresh proceedings based on the new default although this will give the borrower the opportunity to apply in good time for the opportunity to remedy the breach			
3.11 The effect of bankruptcy of the borrower			
If his interest in the home does **not exceed £1,000** no sale may be ordered or charge imposed on the property If **no charge** is obtained or other action taken **within 3 years** the property reverts to the bankrupt If a **charge** is applied for and obtained or other action taken **within 3 years** any increase in value after that date will accrue to the bankrupt and not his estate For detailed discussion see article by Professor Gareth Miller [2006] NLJ, 31 March, p 535			
3.12 Where a charge has been imposed on a bankrupt's home an application by the trustee more than 12 years later is not statute barred: *Doodes v Gotham* [2006] EWCA Civ 1080, (2006) Times, 14 August, CA			
3.13 For the application of s 33A of the Insolvency Act 1986 on an application by a trustee under s 14 of the Trusts of Land and Appointment of Trustees Act 1996 see *Nicholls v Lan* [2006] EWHC 1255 (Ch), (2006) Times, 4 August, CA			

	Form No	CPR Rule	PD
3A. Possession proceedings online by landlords and mortgagees			
3A1. Preliminary			
The ability to start certain possession cases under CPR 55 electronically by use of the 'Possession Cases Online' (PCOL) website is limited to 'specified county courts'. Where the claim has been so started further steps in the claim may be taken electronically.			55B, para 1.1
'**PCOL website**' means the website www.possessionclaim.gov.uk which may be accessed through the courts service website www.hmcourts-service.gov.uk '**Specified court**' means a county court specified on the PCOL website as one for which Possession Cases Online is available.			55B, para 1.2
As to payment of **fees and exemption** from payment of fees see			55B, para 4
Presently the fee on starting proceedings for the recovery of land in county court brought by PCOL is £100, i e a discount of £50 per claim			
As to '**statement of truth**' see CPR PD 55B para 8 in particular note any statement of case must be verified by a statement of truth and this applies to online claims, defences and application notices.			55B, para 8
As to **signature** note CPR PD para 9 that provides this may be a person entering his name on an online form.			55B, para 9
3A2. Claims which may be started using PCOL			
A claim under section 1 of part 55 which includes a claim for possession of residential property within the district of a specified court which is brought by:			
(a) a landlord against a tenant solely on the ground of arrears of rent (but not a claim for forfeiture of a lease) or			
(b) a mortgagee against a mortgagor solely on the ground of default in payment of sums due under a mortgage.			

	Form No	CPR Rule	PD
The claim cannot seek any remedy, other than possession, except for arrears of rent or money due under a mortgage, interest and costs and the defendant must have an address for service in England and Wales.			
Note: (i) the claimant must be able to specify the postcode of the property			
(ii) a claim against a child or protected person under PCOL			55B, para 5
3A3. Starting a claim using PCOL			
3A3.1 A claimant can start a claim by (a) completing an online claim form at the PCOL website (b) paying the issue fee electronically at the PCOL website or by other means approved by the court's service (c) the particulars of claim **must be included in the online form** but it is not necessary to file a copy of the tenancy agreement, mortgage deed or agreement.			55B, paras 6.1 and 6.2
3A3.2 The particulars of claim must include a **history of tenancy or mortgage account** in schedule form setting out the information required by PD 55B para 6.3(2) and (2) but if the claimant has provided the defendant with: (a) the information required by MCOB (Mortgagees: Conduct of Business Rules) 13.4.1 and 11.4.4 or (b) in schedule form the information required by PD 55B para 6.3A(2) the claimant instead of complying with PD 55B para 6.3 may include in the particulars of claim **a summary only** of the arrears containing the information required by PD 55B para 6.3B(1)–(3).			
Note: MCOB provisions may be found at www.fsahandbook.info/FSA/html/handbook/MCOB/13			55B, paras 6.3A and 6.3B

	Form No	CPR Rule	PD
3A3.3 Where the particulars of claim include a summary only (see above) the claimant must (a) serve on the defendant not more than 7 days after issue a full , up to date history of arrears containing at least the information required by para 6.3 of PF 55B (see above) **and** (b) either (i) make a witness statement confirming that he has complied with 6.3A(1) or (2) (see last preceding sub-para of this TAB) including and exhibiting the full arrears history or (ii) verify by way of oral evidence at the hearing that he has so complied and produce and verify the full arrears history			55B, para 6.3C
Note: • CPR 55.8(4) requires all witness statements to be filed and served at least 2 days prior to the hearing		55.8(4)	
• for requirement of the claimant if history of arrears of more than 2 years is relied upon see			55B, para 6.4
• the claim shall be deemed to be served on the fifth day after the claim was issued whether or not that day is a business day			55B, para 6.5
• for date the claim is brought for purposes of Limitation Act 1980 see			55B, para 6.6
• for the action to be taken by the court on issue see			55B, para 6.7
3A4. Defence and counterclaim			
3A4.1 A defendant wishing to defend or make a counterclaim to a claim issued using PCOL may file a written defence or defend or make a counterclaim (to be filed with the defence) by (a) filing the relevant written form, or			

	Form No	CPR Rule	PD
(b) completing the relevant online form at the PCOL website and, if the defendant is making a counterclaim, paying the appropriate fee electronically at the PCOL website or other approved means.			55B, para 7.1(1)
The defendant who completes the relevant online form must not send a hard copy to the court.			55B, para 7.2
Note: • as to effect of acknowledgement of receipt sent to the court by the defendant see			55B, para 7.3
• as to date of filing of the defence form and steps that will be taken by the court see			55B, paras 7.4 and 7.5
3A5. Communication with the court electronically			
When a claim is brought using PCOL the parties may communicate with the court messaging service electronically but the provisions of PD 55B, para 10 must be observed			55B, para 10
3A6. Electronic application			
Certain applications in relation to a possession claim started online may be made ('online applications'); the provisions of PD 55B, para 11 must be observed			55B, para 11
3A7. Viewing the case record			
There are facilities for the parties or their representatives to view the case record; for the provisions see			55B, para 14
4. Claims against trespassers			
4.1 Preliminary			
A claim against trespassers is one for recovery of land which the claimant alleges is occupied only by a person or persons who entered or remained on the land without the consent of the person entitled to possession of the land It **does not include a claim against a tenant or sub-tenant** whether his tenancy has been terminated or not		55.1(b)	

	Form No	CPR Rule	PD
In the case of *Bradford v James* [2008] EWCA Civ 837, 152 Sol Jo (no 30) 32 Mummery LJ observed 'calamitous neighbour disputes ' should be made the subject of mediation because by the time neighbours get to court it is often too late for court-based ADR and mediation schemes to have much effect.			
Where the claimant does not know the name of a person in occupation or possession of the land the claim must be brought against **"persons unknown"** in additions to any named defendant		55.3(4)	
The claim form must be in the form annexed to the Practice Direction	N5	55.3(5)	
This table does not deal with applications for **"interim possession orders"**. These were introduced by the Criminal Justice and Public Order Act 1994 (ss 75–76) and are dealt with under CPR 55, Section III. See **TAB 24**			
Although the defendant (in a claim for possession against trespassers) is not required to file a defence, a form of defence should be served with the claim form so he can do so if he wishes: see CPR 55.3[3], ante		55.7(2) 55.3(5)	
A possession order by reference to an anticipated trespass can only be made in exceptional circumstances: *Secretary of State for the Environment, Food and Rural Affairs v Drury* [2004] EWCA Civ 200, (2004) Times, 15 March			
The Court of Appeal in *Secretary of State for Environment, Food and Rural Affairs v Meier* [2009] UKSC 11, [2009] 1 WLR 2780, [2009] 49 EG 70 (CS) held that possession orders can only be made in respect of a plot of land occupied by the defendant and not in respect of separate plots not occupied. It did uphold injunctions preventing the defendant occupying these plots. The case of *Drury* above was relied on by the unsuccessful claimant but rejected as incorrect. For discussion see (2009) NLJ 8 December, page 4.			

	Form No	CPR Rule	PD
Where a landowner is seeking damages for temporary trespass see *Sinclair v Gavaghan* [2007] EWHC 2256 (Ch). The approach of the court in such cases is to assess what payment would have been arrived at between the parties for the temporary use of he claimant's land. The court will invariably grant an injunction requiring the defendant to stop trespassing			
In *JA Pye (Oxford) Ltd v United Kingdom (Application No 44302/02)* (2007) 23 BHRC 405 it was held that Art 1, 1st protocol of the ECHR (right to peaceful enjoyment) was not infringed by domestic law enabling a squatter to obtain title by 12 years' adverse possession. Note, however, the Registered Land Act 2002, which does not have retrospective effect, which gives the squatter the right to apply for registration after 10 years' adverse possession but on notice to the registered owner who then has 2 years to regularise the position			
4.2 Start of proceedings and particular of claim			
In addition to the general requirements (see 1.3 and 1.4, above) the particulars of claim must state the claimant's interest in the land or the basis of his rights to claim possession and the circumstances it has been occupied without his licence or consent	N121		55A, para 2.6
4.3 The hearing date			
See 1.5 above and the court's power to extend or shorten time		3.1(2)(a)	55A, para 3.2
4.4 The defendant's response			
An acknowledgment of service is not required and the defendant need not file a defence. Form N11 should be used if a defence is filed	N11	55.7(1) and (2)	
4.5 Service			
Where a possession claim against trespassers the claim has been issued against persons unknown:		55.6	

	Form No	CPR Rule	PD
(a) the claim form (b) the particulars of claim and (c) any witness statements			
must be served by: (a) attaching them to the main door or some other part of the land so that they are clearly visible and if practicable, inserting copies in a transparent envelope addressed to "the occupiers" through the letter box, or (b) placing stakes on the land in places where they are clearly visible and attaching them in a transparent envelope addressed to "the occupiers"			
The transparent envelopes and the stakes will have to be supplied by the claimant			55A, para 4.1
See below under 4.6 as to shortening the time for service			
4.6 The hearing			
All witness statements on which the claimant relies must have been filed and served with the claim form		55.8(5)	
The time periods for service may be shortened, particularly where there have been assaults, threats or damage			55A, paras 3.1 and 3.2
Where the claimant effected service he must produce at the hearing a certificate of service		55.8(6)	
At the hearing the court may decide the case or give case management directions			
The court does not have power under s 89 Housing Act 1980 nor under any other provision in that Act to give trespassers time to vacate: *Boyland and Son Ltd v Rand* [2007] EWCA Civ 1860, (2007) Times, 18 January			

	Form No	CPR Rule	PD
4.7 Enforcement			
A judgment or order of a county court for possession of land made in a possession claim against trespassers may be enforced in the High Court or county court: High Court and County Courts Jurisdiction (Amendment No 2) Order 2001			
4.8 Liability for injury suffered by a trespasser			
See the judgment of the House of Lords in *Tomlinson v Congleton Borough Council* [2003] UKHL 47, [2004] 1 AC 46, [2003] 3 All ER 1122 where the claimant was willingly running an obvious risk.			

TABLE 23—ACCELERATED POSSESSION PROCEDURE – HOUSING ACT 1988 S 21

TAB 23

	Form No	CPR Rule	PD
1. Availability			
(a) The claimant may bring a possession claim under this section of this Part where: (i) the claim is brought under s 21 of the 1988 Act to recover possession of residential property let under an assured shorthold tenancy (an AST), and (ii) all the conditions listed in CPR 55.12 are satisfied (b) The claim must be started in the county court for the district in which the property is situated (c) The claim must be brought by the landlord and not, for example, by the landlord's letting agent: *Chester Accommodation Agency Ltd v Abebrese* (1997) Times, 28 July, CA		55.11	
For notes for claimant in an accelerated possession claims see	N5C		
2. Conditions in CPR 55.12 (a) the tenancy and any agreement for the tenancy were entered into on or after 15 January 1989			

	Form No	CPR Rule	PD
(b) the only purpose is to recover possession and no other claim is made (c) the tenancy did not immediately follow an assured tenancy which was not an assured shorthold tenancy (d) the tenancy fulfilled the conditions provided by ss 19A or 20(1)(a) to (c) of the 1988 Act (e) the tenancy: (i) was the subject of a written agreement (ii) arises by virtue of s 5 of the 1988 Act but follows a tenancy that was the subject of a written agreement, or (iii) relates to the same or substantially the same property let to the same tenant and on the same terms (though not necessarily as to rent or duration) as a tenancy which was the subject of a written agreement, and (f) a notice in accordance with ss 21(1), terminating an AST on the expiry of a fixed term, or 21(4), terminating a periodic AST which has arisen on the expiry of the original fixed term, of the 1988 Act was given to the tenant in writing The **notice under s 21(1)** must be in writing and give to the tenant not less than two months notice that the landlord requires possession of the house. It may be given at any time during the currency of the tenancy including the last day or more frequently at the beginning of the tenancy. It is not necessary to specify a date for possession but a notice that contains one is not invalidated. Possession cannot be sought before the expiration of the 6 month period and the landlord cannot serve a notice if he has not complied with the Tenancy Deposit Scheme			

	Form No	CPR Rule	PD
The **s 21(4) notice** must be in writing and specify a date after which possession is required. The date specified must be in the last day of a period of the tenancy and be not earlier than 2 months after the date the notice was given. As to 'the last day of a period of a tenancy' see *Fernandez v McDonald* [2003] EWCA Civ 1219, [2003] 4 All ER 1033. However the decision in *Lower Street Properties Ltd v Jones* (1996) 28 HLR 877, CA remains good law (see *Notting Hill Housing Trust v Roomus*, below) so that a formula for ascertaining the date can be used to ensure if the date is wrong the landlord will be entitled to possession. An appropriate formula is 'this notice will expire at the end of the period of your tenancy that will end next after the expiry of 2 months from the service of this notice upon you'. The Court of Appeal in the case of *Bradford Community Housing Ltd v Hussain and Kauser* [2009] EWCA Civ 763 held a notice containing both a date and a 'catch-all' provision was just as good at law as a notice properly calculated in accordance with the provisions of the tenancy. For detailed discussion see article 'Terminating assured shorthold tenancies' New Law Journal 13 October 2006, page 2001, by Andrew Williams and an article by Michael Walsh in (2008) NLJ, 24 October, page 1482 entitled 'Section 21 or bust'. The use of such a clause, however, will not assist the claimant who issues the claim before the notice has, as a matter of law, expired It must always be remembered that if the first day of the period is on, say, the 14th, the period will expire one day before that date, i e on the 13th See *Notting Hill Housing Trust v Roomus* [2006] EWCA Civ 407, [2006] All ER (D) 432 (Mar), [2007] HLR 2 where it was held that 'at the end of the tenancy' means 'after the end of the tenancy' so that the s 21 notice was valid			

	Form No	CPR Rule	PD
See also *Church Commissioners v Meya* [2006] EWCA Civ 821, [2006] All ER (D) 234 (Jun) where the importance of when rent was last payable under the fixed term, in establishing the periods of the periodic tenancy, was confirmed by the court *Note* • As to condition (d) section 19A relates to tenancies entered into on or after 28 February 1997 and section 20(1)(a)-(c) to those assured tenancies not within s 19A (because they were entered into before 28 February 1997) • If the tenancy is a demoted shorthold tenancy only the conditions in 1(b) and 1(f) need to be satisfied • Arrears of rent cannot be claimed in accelerated possession proceedings		55.12(1)(b)	
3. The claim form			
(a) must be in the form set out in the relevant Practice Direction, and (b) (i) must contain such information and (ii) must be accompanied by such documents as are required by that form All relevant sections of the form must be completed. The form is such that if correctly completed all the requirements of CPR 55.12 will be addressed The court will serve the claim form by first class post or an alternative service which provides for delivery the next working day It should particularly be noted that section 7B of form N5B sets out requirements as to the multiple occupancy lettings and as to any deposit taken and calls for evidence that those requirements have been satisfied.	N5B	55.13	
4. The defence			
Any defence should be in the form set out in the Practice Direction	N11B	55.14	

	Form No	CPR Rule	PD
Where the assured tenancy was granted to the tenant as part of a 'sell to rent back' arrangement where the tenant had entered into the arrangement to avoid a possession order in favour of lenders, the availability of a defence of proprietary estoppel should be considered: see article by Rawdon Crozier in (2009) Gazette, 14 May, page 27.			
A defendant must file his defence within 14 days after service of the claim form if he wishes: (a) to oppose the claim (b) seek a postponement of possession in accordance with CPR 55.18 On receipt of the defence the court will: (a) send a copy to the claimant, and (b) refer the claim and defence to a judge		55.15(1)	
Where the period for filing a defence has expired and no defence has been filed:		55.15(2)	
(a) the claimant may file a written request for an order for possession, and (b) the court will refer that request to a judge If the defence is out of time but received before the landlord's written request is received the court may still consider the defence		55.15(3)	
5. Consideration of the claim			
After considering the claim and any defence, the judge will: (a) make an **order for possession without a hearing**	N26A	55.16 55.17	
(b) where he is not satisfied as to service of the claim form or that the claimant has established his right to possession under s 21 of the Housing Act 1985 the judge will:		55.16(1)(b)	
(i) direct that a date be **fixed for a hearing**, and (ii) give any appropriate case management directions, or		55.16(1)(c)	

	Form No	CPR Rule	PD
(c) **strike out the claim** if the claim form discloses no reasonable grounds for bringing the claim			
The court will give all parties not less than 14 days' notice of a hearing Where a claim is struck out: (a) the court will serve its reasons for striking out the claim with the order, and (b) the claimant may apply to restore the claim within 28 days after the date the order was served on him		55.16(3) 55.16(4)	
6. Postponement of possession		55.18	
Where the defendant seeks postponement of possession on the ground of **exceptional hardship** under s 89 of the Housing Act 1980, the judge may direct a hearing of that issue		55.18(1)	
Where the judge directs a hearing: (a) the hearing must be held before the date of which possession is to be given up, and (b) the judge will direct how many days' notice the parties must be given of that hearing		55.18(2)	
Where the judge is satisfied on a hearing directed that exceptional hardship would be caused by requiring possession to be given up by that date in the order of possession, he may vary the date on which possession must be given up		55.18(3)	
In a claim in which the judge is satisfied that the defendant has shown exceptional hardship, he will only postpone possession without directing a hearing under CPR 55.18(1) if:			55A, para 8.1
(a) he considers that possession should be given up 6 weeks after the date of the order or, if the defendant has requested postponement to an earlier date, on that date, and (b) the claimant indicated on his claim form that he would be content for the court to make such an order without a hearing			

	Form No	CPR Rule	PD
In all other cases if the defendant seeks a postponement of possession under s 89 of the Housing Act 1980, the judge will direct a hearing under CPR 55.18(1) If at that hearing, the judge is satisfied that exception hardship would be caused by requiring possession to be given up by the date in the order possession, he may vary that order under CPR 55.18(3) so that possession is to be given up at a later date That later date may be no later than 6 weeks after the making of the order for possession on the papers (see s 89 of the Housing Act 1980)			
7. Setting aside or varying		55.19	
The court may: (a) on application by a party within 14 days of service of the order, or (b) of its own initiative, **set aside or vary any order made** under CPR 55.17			
8. Court fee and costs			
The court fee payable is £150. Unless the court otherwise orders, which is unlikely, the costs will be fixed costs, presently £79.50		45.2A(2)	

TABLE 24—INTERIM POSSESSION ORDERS – RECOVERY OF POSSESSION OF LAND FROM TRESPASSERS

TAB 24

	Form No	CPR Rule	PD
1. Preliminary			
1.1 An **interim possession order (IPO)**is one made under rules of court for the bringing of summary proceedings for possession of premises which are occupied by trespassers; s75 (4) of the Criminal Justice and Public Order Act 1994 (the 1994 Act)			
1.2 A person who is **present on premises as a trespasser at any time during the currency of an IPO** commits an offence unless:			

	Form No	CPR Rule	PD
(a) he leaves the premises within 24 hours of the time of service of the IPO and does not return or (b) a copy of the order was not fixed to the premises in accordance with rules of the court; s76(2) and (3) of the 1994 Act			
1.3 A person who leaves the premises after service of the IPO commits an offence if he **re-enters or tries to re-enter within the period of one year** beginning with the date of service of the IPO s 76(4) of the 1994 Act			
Notes • The claim must be started in the county court in which the land is situated unless there are circumstances which justify starting the claim in the High Court see TAB 22 paras 1.2 and 1.3 • Where claimant does not know the name of a person in occupation the claim must be brought against person unknown see TAB 22 para 4.1 • For full text of ss 75 and 76 see CPR 55.20[2] and 55.20[3] A constable in uniform may arrest without warrant any person is or whom he reasonable suspects to be, guilty of an offence under s76 • The offences are **criminal offences** • For the penalties see s75(3) and 76(5) of the 1994 Act			
2. Conditions for use			
2.1 An application for an IPO can be made if: (a) the only claim is against trespassers for recovery of possession of premises (b) the claimant has an immediate right to possession and has had such a right throughout the period of alleged unlawful occupation, and			

	Form No	CPR Rule	PD
(c) the claim is made within 28 days of the date the claimant first knew or ought to have known that the defendant (or one of them) was in occupation (d) the defendant did not enter the premises or remain on them with the consent of a person who, at the time the consent was given, had an immediate right to possession			
Note • **premises** means a building, a self-contained part of a building or the land ancillary to it		55.21	
3. The application and its issue			
3.1 The claimant must file:			
(a) claim form in specified form	N5		
(b) application in specified form	N130	55.22(2)	55A, para 9.1
(c) written evidence *Note* • **the written evidence must be by the applicant** or if the applicant is a body corporate a duly authorised officer • a statement of truth by the maker is necessary • it must be stated in the claim form whether Section III and IV of the Practice Direction (Pre-action Conduct) or any relevant protocol have been complied with		55.22(3) 55.22(4)	55A, para 9.2 Pre-action Conduct, para 9.7
3.2 The court will issue the claim form and the application and set a hearing date after the hearing of the application. This will be as soon as practicable but **not less than 3 days after the application.**		55.22(5)	
4. Undertakings			
The claimant on issue will have set out the undertakings he gives in support of his application. These will be considered by the court on the hearing.		55.25(1)	

	Form No	CPR Rule	PD
These undertakings are set out in CPR 55.25(1) (a) and (b) and are for the benefit of the defendant against whom the claim does not succeed			
5. Service			
5.1 Within **24 hours of issue** the claimant must serve on the defendant: (a) the claim form (b) the application form with evidence in support (c) a blank form of defendant's witness statement		55.23(1)	
5.2 Service must be served in accordance with CPR 55.6(a) see TAB 22 para 4.5		55.23(2)	
5.3 At or before the hearing the claimant must file a certificate of service of the documents set out in 5.1 above		55.23(3)	
6. Defendant's response			
The defendant can at any time before the hearing file a witness statement in response to the application	N133		55A, para 9.2
7. The hearing of the application			
7.1 The court will **make an IPO** if	N134		55A, para 9.2
(a) the claimant has – (i) filed a certificate of service (para 5.3) (ii) proved service to the satisfaction of the court and (b) (i) the conditions set out in r 55.21(1) are satisfied (see para 2.1 above) and (ii) any undertakings given by the claimant as a condition of making the order are adequate		55.25(2)	
Note The IPO will require the defendant to vacate the premises specified in the claim form within 24 hours of service	N134	55.25(3)	
7.2 On making the IPO the court will **set a date for the hearing of the claim for possession** which will be not less than 7 days after the date the IPO was made		55.25(4)	

	Form No	CPR Rule	PD
7.3 When the court **does not make an IPO** the court will (a) set a date for the hearing of the claim (b) give directions for the future conduct of the claim and (c) subject to such directions the claim shall proceed in accordance with Section II of CPR 55 (see TAB 22 para 4)		55.25(5)	
8. Service of the IPO			
8.1 Within 48 hours after it is sealed the claimant must serve the IPO with copies of the claim form and the written evidence in support. Service must be effected in accordance with CPR 55.6(a) (see TAB 22 para 4.5)		55.26(1) and (2) 55.26(3)	
8.2 If not served in accordance within the 48 hour time limit, the claimant can apply to the court for directions for the claim for possession to continue under Section I of Part 55		55.26(4)	
9. Application to set aside the IPO			
9.1 If the defendant has left the premises he may apply on grounds of urgency for the IPO to be set aside before the date of the hearing of the claim. The application must be supported by a witness statement		55.28(1) and (2)	
9.2 The court will give directions as to service and hearing of the application		55.28(3)	
9.3 The application to set aside will thereafter be dealt with by the court in accordance with CPR 55.28 (4) –(6)		55.28(4)–(6)	
9.4 Where notice of the application to set aside is ordered to be given the court may treat the hearing of the application to set aside as the hearing of the claim		55.28(7)	
10. The hearing of the claim			
10.1 Before the hearing the claimant must file a certificate of service of the documents specified in CPR 55.26(2)		55.27(1)	
10.2 The IPO will expire on the date of the hearing		55.27(2)	
10.3 At the hearing the court can make any order it considers appropriate, in particular may			

	Form No	CPR Rule	PD
(a) make a final order for possession (b) dismiss the application for possession (c) give direction for the claim to continue under CPR 55 section I (d) enforce any of the claimants' undertakings		55.27(3)	
Note • the claimant must serve any order or directions unless the court otherwise orders		55.27(4)	
• a warrant for possession (see TAB 35 may be issued at any time after the making of the order for possession to enforce the order see CCR Ord 24 r6			
• the warrant for possession will be executed by the bailiff (county court) or the sheriff (High Court) contrast the IPO which is enforced as a criminal offence by the police			

TABLE 24A—ANTI-SOCIAL BEHAVIOUR ORDERS UNDER THE CRIME AND DISORDER ACT 1998

TAB 24A

	Form No	**CPR Rule**	**PD**
1. Preliminary			
1.1 The insertion made by the Police Reform Act 2002 in the Crime and Disorder Act 1998 enables applications for an **anti-social behaviour order** (ASBO) to be made in the county court. Previously jurisdiction to make such orders was conferred only on magistrates courts		65.21(1)	
1.2 The amendments came into force on 1 April 2003 and further amendments have been made by the Anti-Social Behaviour Act 2003.			
1.3 Applications to the court for such orders can only be made by **relevant authorities** and are made pursuant to s 1B of the 1998 Act. Applications for interim orders are made pursuant to s 1D.			

	Form No	CPR Rule	PD
A district judge has jurisdiction to make an order under s 1B or s 1D of the Crime and Disorder Act 1998 (anti-social behaviour) **Note** that a **freestanding application** cannot be made (s 1B(1)) and there must be principal proceedings in existence to which the person against whom the order is sought is a party or is joined as a party (freestanding applications would have to be made in the Magistrates' Court) **Note** A relevant authority cannot seek an anti-social behaviour order on behalf of individuals: *Dalichi UK Ltd v Stop Huntington Animal Cruelty* (2003) Times, 22 October and for a precedent of particulars of claim where the individuals are second claimants and the first claimants claim under the Protection from Harassment Act 1997 see **BCCP L[907]**		65.21(1)	65, para 8.1A
Note In *W v DPP* [2005 EWCA Civ 1333, (2005) Times, 20 June it was held that a clause in an anti-social behaviour order prohibiting the defendant from 'committing any criminal offence' was too wide and accordingly unenforceable			
In *R (Stanley) v Metropolitan Police Comr* [2004] EWHC 229 (Admin), (2004) Times, 22 October it was held publicity was necessary for an anti-social behaviour order to operate and that photographs, names and at least partial addresses were a necessary part of such publicity Further in *R (on the application of Lonergan) v Lewes Crown Court* [2005] EWHC 457 (Admin), [2005] 2 All ER 362 it was held that the inclusion of a curfew term in an anti-social behaviour order was not legally objectionable as it was prohibitory in nature and necessary for prevention and protection			
In *Hewlett v Holding* (2006) Times, 8 February it was held that secret surveillance can be harassment. It would seem likely it would also be considered anti-social behaviour			

	Form No	CPR Rule	PD
In *Conn v Sunderland City Council* (2007) Times, 23 November, CA, (2007) NLJ, 16 November, page 1613 (a claim under the Protection from Harassment Act 1997) the court indicated that the boundary between unattractive and unreasonable conduct and oppressive and unacceptable conduct is whether the conduct was of such gravity as to justify the sanction of criminal law			
In *R v Gowan* [2007] EWCA Crim 1360 the court held an ASBO could not be used to protect a wife with whom the offender had been living and in future would be cohabiting as she lived in the same household as him			
Note There is inevitably overlap with the power to grant an anti-social behaviour injunction (ASBI) under Housing Act 1996 s 153A			
In most cases a local authority should seek to restrain anti-social behaviour by use of its powers under the 1998 Act (ASBO) rather than under s 222(1)(a) of the Local Government Act 1972 by way of injunction: *Birmingham City Council v Shafi* [2008] EWCA Civ 1186, [2009] 3 All ER 127.			
2. Definitions			
'the 1998 Act' means the Crime and Disorder Act 1998		65.21(2)(a)	
'relevant authority' means: (a) the council for the local government area (aa) in relation to England, a county council (b) the chief officer of any police force maintained for a police area (c) the chief constable of the British Transport Police Force (d) any person registered under section 1 of the Housing Act 1996 as a social landlord who provides or manages any houses or hostels in a local government area or			

	Form No	CPR Rule	PD
(e) a housing action trust established by order in pursuance of s62 of the Housing Act 1988 There is a power to add other bodies by statutory instrument		65.21(2)(b)	
'the principal proceedings' means any proceedings in a county court		65.21(2)(c)	
'relevant persons' see s1(1B) of the 1998 Act			
Note • **premises** means a building, a self-contained part of a building or the land ancillary to it **3. Conditions to be established for grant of an Anti-Social Behaviour Order**		55.21	
3.1 The following conditions have to be fulfilled by virtue of s1 of the 1998 Act with respect to a person aged 10 or over: (a) that person has acted, since 1 April 1999, in an anti-social manner, that is in a manner that caused or was likely to cause harassment, alarm or distress to one or more persons not of the same household as himself and (b) that such an order is necessary to protect relevant persons from further anti-social acts **3.2** The application for an order must be accompanied by **written evidence** that must **include evidence** that the **consultation requirement** of s 1E of the 1998 Act has been complied with. There are different requirements for councils and for local authorities (s 1E(2)), the police (s 1E(3)) and other relevant authorities (s 1E(4)); see **III ANSB [15]** and *McC v Wigan Metropolitan Borough Council* [2004] Legal Action, 31 January. A consultation certificate duly signed will be sufficient evidence of compliance		65.25	

	Form No	CPR Rule	PD
3.3 Where an anti-social behaviour order is sought against a child the best interests of the child are a primary consideration but not the primary consideration see *R (Kenny and M) v Leeds Magistrates Court* [2003] EWHC 2963 (Admin) and *R (A) v Leeds Magistrates Court* (2004) Times, 31 March (But see below at the next paragraph as to the expiry of the pilot scheme)			
At present an order can be sought in the county court only against an adult. In courts within a pilot scheme that commenced on 1 October 2004 and operated until 30 September 2006 applications could be made to join a child in existing proceedings and if the child was joined an order under s 1B(4) could be made against him. The courts within the pilot scheme are Bristol, Central London, Clerkenwell, Dewsbury, Huddersfield, Leicester, Manchester, Oxford, Tameside, Wigan and Wrexham The scheme has not been extended and the result of the pilot is being evaluated			65, para 13
3.4 The court must ignore any behaviour prior to 1 April 1999 and any act which the defendant shows was reasonable in the circumstances: s 1(5) of the 1998 Act.			
3.5 Evidence of anti-social behaviour after the making of the application is admissible: *Birmingham City Council v Dixon* [2009] EWHC 7612 (Admin), (2009) Times, 13 April, Div Ct.			
4. Application where the relevant authority is party to the principal proceedings (Crime and Disorder Act 1998, s 1B(2))			
4.1 Where the relevant authority is the claimant in the principal proceedings and considers that another party to the proceedings is a person against whom an application for an ASBO could reasonably be made, the application must be made in the claim form		65.22(1)(a)	

	Form No	CPR Rule	PD
4.2 Where the relevant authority is a defendant in the principal proceedings the application must be made by application notice (Part 23) filed with the defence		65.22(1)(b)	
4.3 Where the circumstances that lead to the application only becoming known after filing the claim form or the defence the application must be made by application notice issued as soon as possible.		65.22(2)	
4.4 The application made by application notice must normally be on notice to the person against whom the order is sought		65.22(3)	
5. Application by relevant authority to join a party in the principal proceedings (Crime and Disorder Act 1998, s 1B(3A) and (3B)			
5.1 Such an application under 1B(3B) of the 1998 Act by a relevant authority who is a party in the principal proceedings and considers the person's anti-social acts are material in he principal proceedings must be made - (a) in accordance with Section 1 of CPR 19		19.4	
(b) in the same application notice as the application for an order under 1B(4) of the 1998 Act (an anti-social behaviour order) and (c) as soon as possible after the relevant authority considers the criteria for making the anti-social behaviour order are met	N244	65.23(1)	
5.2 The application notice must contain - (a) the relevant authority's reasons for claiming that the person's anti-social behaviour acts are material in relation to the principal proceedings and (b) the details of the anti-social acts alleged		65.23(2)	
5.3 The application should normally be made on notice to the person against whom the order is sought		65.23(3)	

	Form No	CPR Rule	PD
5.4 A person must not be joined unless his anti-social acts are material to the principal proceedings: s 1B(3C)			
6. Applications where the relevant authority is not a party in the principal proceedings (**Crime and Disorder Act 1998, s 1B**(**3**))			
6.1 An application to be made a party by a relevant authority, that considers it would be reasonable to apply for an ASBO against a person who is a party, may be made in accordance with Part 19 and the application for an anti-social behaviour order must be made in the same proceedings	N244	65.24(1)	
6.2 The application must be made as soon as possible after the authority became aware of the principal proceedings and should normally be made on notice to the person against whom the order is sought		65.24(2)	
6.3 An application by a relevant authority to join a person to the principal proceedings may only be made against a person aged 18 or over			65, para 13.2
7. Procedure for claims			
(see paras 4, 5 and 6 above)			
7.1 The application will be by claim form or, if the case falls within para 5 or para 6 above, by application notice			
7.1A Unless the nature of the principal proceedings requires those proceedings to start in another court, it is appropriate to commence proceedings in the defendant's home court			
7.2 The application for an order under s 1B(4) of the 1998 Act must be supported by written evidence which must include that s 1E of the 1998 Act (that is the consultancy requirements) has been complied with. The evidence must be verified by a statement of truth		65.25	
7.3 A hearing date will be given on issue and the court will prepare notices of the hearing for all parties			

	Form No	CPR Rule	PD
7.4 The defendant must be served with the application, the notice of the hearing and a copy of the witness statement not less than 3 clear days before the hearing and because of the serious nature of the application personal service should be effected			
7A. Application for an Interim Order (Crime and Disorder Act 1998, s 1D)			
7A.1 Such an application must be made in accordance with CPR Part 25			
7A.2 The application should normally be made in the claim for or application notice seeking the order and on notice to the person against whom the order is sought		65.26	
Note *R (on the application of M) v Lord Chancellor* [2004] EWCA Civ 312, [2004] 2 All ER 531, (2004) Times, 31 March where it was held that an interim anti-social behaviour order made without notice when necessary for a limited period did not contravene the right to a fair trial under Art 6 of European Convention on Human Rights. The order is not effective until served personally and the fact that the defendant could apply for review or discharge and further that the order would contain provision for a return date or a date fixed for hearing the full application made it impossible to say it affected human rights. See also *R (on the application of Stanley, Marshall and Kelly) v Metropolitan Police Comr* [2004] EWHC 2229 (Admin), 168 JP 623			
7A.3 The order must be for a fixed period and, if still in force, end with the determination of the main application (s 1D(4) of the 1998 Act)			

	Form No	CPR Rule	PD
7A.4 The comments of the Court of Appeal in *Moat Housing Group South Ltd v Harris* [2005] EWCA Civ 287, [2005] 2 FLR 551 give guidance and a clear call for caution when dealing with applications that were not on notice and were of an intrusive nature. Without notice applications should be made only in wholly exceptional circumstances			
8. The hearing and the order made			
8.1 The court must be satisfied that the defendant acted in an anti-social manner (see the notes to para 1 and para 3.1 of this table). The court must be satisfied to a criminal standard although not necessarily that the acts were done with intent to cause harassment alarm or distress: *R (on the application of McCann) v Crown Court at Manchester* [2002] UKHL 39, [2003] 1 AC 787, [2002] 4 All ER 593. See also **III ANSB [13.4]** for further discussion but note that the civil standard of proof has been held to be appropriate to injunction applications under s 3 of the Harassment Act 1997: *Jones v Hipgrave* [2004] EWHC 2901 (QB), (2005) Times, 11 January, albeit a different view was expressed in *Birmingham City Council v Shafti* (see this TAB, 1, preliminary to the final paragraph) by a majority of the Court of Appeal in respect of an application for an injunction under s 222(1)(a) of the Local Government Act 1972.			

	Form No	CPR Rule	PD
8.2 The civil rules of evidence apply and note May LJ's judgment in *R (on the application of Cleary) v Highbury Corner Magistrates' Court* [2006] EWHC 1869 (Admin), [2007] 1 All ER 270. Although this is a decision of the Divisional Court it is likely to be relevant in any proceedings where anti-social behaviour is the basis of the claim and the evidence relied on to prove the behaviour is, in whole or in part, anonymous hearsay evidence. The judgment cautioned the courts as to the weight to be given to such evidence and stressed the value of credible direct evidence. See further [2007] NLJ 22 June 'Fighting Back', an article by Chris Cuddihee, and the response to it by Robin Denford in [2007] NLJ 17 August, page 1184 where reference is made to *Solon South West Housing Association v James* [2004] EWCA Civ 1847, [2004] All ER (D) 328 (Dec) **8.3** An anti-social behaviour order shall have effect for a period (not less than 2 years) specified in the order or until further order; s 1B(7) of the 1998 Act The terms of the order must be pronounced in open court and a written order must accurately set out the order pronounced **8.4** Except with the consent of the parties no anti-social behaviour order shall be discharged before the end of the period of 2 years beginning with the date of service of the order s 1B(6) of the 1998 Act. A person for whose benefit an ASBO has been obtained cannot waive it, in this case by inviting the defendant into the house, because the order was also for the benefit of others: *Anthony Lee v Accent Foundation Ltd* [2007] 151 Sol Jo LB 806			

	Form No	CPR Rule	PD
8.5 Subject to the last provision (no discharge for 2 years unless by consent of parties) the applicant or defendant may apply for the anti-social behaviour order to be varied or discharged by s 1B(5) of the 1998 Act An application to extend the order for less than 2 years can only be appropriate if it is the applicant's case that it is not necessary to have a further period as long as the minimum period of 2 years: *Leeds City Council v RG* [2007] EWHC 1612 (Admin), [2007] All ER (D) 114 (Jul), (2007) Times, 11 September, QB, Div Ct **8.6** A modified form of **Penal Notice** must be endorsed on the order made warning the defendant that any breach of the terms of the order will be a criminal offence. The order must be clear and specific in its terms and be both necessary and proportionate **8.7** Careful drafting of the order is essential as to the terms of the prohibition, duration and the definition of any specified area. Consideration should be given to attaching a plan showing any area specified			
8.8 An example of an anti-social behaviour order being too wide to be enforced is provided by *W v DPP* [2005] EWCA Civ 1333, (2005) Times, 20 June, Div Ct; the ban was against "committing any criminal offence" **8.9** It was held in *R (on the application of Gosport Borough Council) v Farnham Magistrates Court* [2006] EWHC 3047 (Admin) that if nobody was present to be harassed, alarmed or distressed an order could not be made.			

	Form No	CPR Rule	PD
8.10 The PD on pre-action conduct sets out permitted behaviour by a business creditor seeking repayment of a debt due to it from the debtor. It may inform the debtor of how the money claimed can be paid and can contact the debtor to discuss possible repayment options and provide contact details of agencies that provide free independent advice. In *Ferguson v British Gas Trading Ltd* [2009] EWCA Civ 46, [2009] 3 All ER 304 it was held on appeal, against the refusal to strike out, that letters threatening to terminate gas supply, to start legal proceedings and to report to credit agencies were capable, if sufficiently grave, of amounting to harassment. The court rejected the argument that a large corporation could not be guilty of harassment.			
In *S&D Property Investments Ltd v Nisbett* [2009] EWHC 1726 (Ch) the judge accepted that, in this debt recovery case, calling at the debtor's house and shouting abuse amounted to harassment and awarded damages of £7,000; see article 'Run for your money' by Roddy MacLeod in Sol Jo, 3 August 2010, page 6.			
8.11 It was held in *Mitchell v Glasgow City Council* [2009] UKHL 11, [2009] All ER (D) 182 (Feb) that public authorities who take action against perpetrators of violence and anti-social behaviour are safeguarded from legal proceedings arising from their failure to warn those who might be at risk of a criminal attack in response to the local authority's actions. See also Human Rights Updater (2009) Issue 85 (March), page 5.			
9. Service			
An interim anti-social behaviour order must be personally served on the defendant and may be varied or discharged at any time			65, section IV, para 13.1
An anti-social behaviour order must be served on the defendant personally			

	Form No	CPR Rule	PD
10. Offence			
10.1 If without reasonable excuse a person does anything which he is prohibited from doing in an anti-social behaviour order he is guilty of an offence – see s 1(10) of the 1998 Act			
10.2 On summary conviction the maximum term of imprisonment is 6 months and on conviction on indictment the maximum term is 5 years. In either case the defendant can be fined as an alternative or additionally			
10.3 Proceedings may be brought by - (a) a council which is a relevant authority (b) the council for the local government area in which the person resides or appears to reside: s 1(10A) of the 1998 Act See also section 2 of this **TAB**			

TABLE 25—COSTS

TAB 25

For the costs of solicitors pursuant to the **Protocol for Low Value Personal Injury Claims in Road Traffic Accidents** see **TAB 10A**, para 9.			
For the scale of costs for claims in a **Patents County Court** see Section VIII, **CPR 45.41-CPR 45.43**.			
The Practice Direction which supplements Parts 43 to 48 us known as the 'Costs Practice Direction'.			
Costs estimates may be own client estimates or inter partes estimates: for practice notes see Butterworths Costs Newsletter September 2009 Volume 1, Issue 2. Costs estimates are not required in small claims.			
The court has, at any stage, explicit power to order any party to file and serve an estimate of costs. This power may be exercised of its own initiative		3, paras 1(2)(ll) and 3(i)	Costs PD, para 6

Where a party, other than a litigant in person, in any claim, save for a small claim or claim proceeding on the fast track, files an allocation questionnaire checklist he must file an estimate of costs and serve a copy on every other party and on his client.			Costs PD, para 6.4
Where a claim is being dealt with on the fast track or multi track or under Part 8 and a party files a pre-trial checklist (listing questionnaire) he must also serve a copy of his estimate of costs on every other party and his client.			
For a precedent of a costs estimate see Precedent H in the schedule of costs precedents. For guidance on completing a costs estimate see the newsletter referred to in the first paragraph of this TAB.			Costs PD, para 57
Inadequate **costs estimates**: see PD to part 43, section 6 (in particular 6.2(1) and 6.5A). If there is a difference of 20% or more between the base costs claimed on a detailed assessment and the costs shown in the estimate of costs filed by that party, the receiving party must provide a statement of the reasons for the difference between the estimate and the bill of costs			Costs PD, paras 6.1–6.6

In *Mastercigars Direct Ltd v Withers LLP* [2007] EWHC 2733 (Ch), [2007] NLJR 1731, [2008] 3 All ER 417 it was stated that there is no legal principle that estimates of costs result in the capping of costs entitlement by the application of a margin. In the same way there is no principle which gives a solicitor an entitlement to the full extent of the margin on top of the estimated figure. Solicitors are entitled to reasonable costs and the estimate provides a useful yardstick in measuring what is reasonable. Where it is found that there was reliance on an under-estimate the court should decide whether there should be a reduction because of this and if so by how much. For an article inspired by this decision see (2008) NLJ, 4 January, page 12 and Gazette, 6 March 2008, page 33 and see also an article 'An end to estimates?' by Howard Dean in Sol Jo (2009) 5 May, page 8. The first official report of Morgan J's judgment in 2007 is published in *Mastercigars Direct Ltd v Withers LLP* (Practice Note) [2007] EWHC 2733 (Ch), (2009) 1 WLR 881.			
For a case where solicitors were held to their original costs estimate (subject to a 15% increase on the authority of *Wong v Vizards* ([1997] 2 Costs LR 46, QB) and their client's liability, see *Reynolds v Stone Rowe Brewer (a firm)* [2008] EWHC 497 (QB), 152 Sol Jo (no 14) 29. The court found no significantly unusual development before a revised estimate and found it was an attempt to correct an earlier under-estimate (this case contrasts strongly with the decision in the *Mastercigars* case above). It may be that the presence of the original erroneous estimate in Reynolds enables these cases to be reconciled.			

A further decision in the *Mastercigars v Withers* saga this time [2009] EWHC 651 (Ch), 153 Sol Jo (no 14) 28, Morgan J, in effect terminated the 'percentage margin' which had become standard practice after the decision in Wong (see above): 'It can never be right for costs to be expressed by reference to a margin', per Morgan J. In a case where the client satisfied the court that the inaccurate estimate deprived him of an opportunity to act in a different way which would have been more advantageous that was a relevant matter in assessing costs. See (2009) Sol Jo, 14 April, pages 4 and 28 and note in particular that *Leigh v Michelin Tyres plc* [2003] EWCA Civ 1766, (2004) 1 WLR 846 was followed.			
The costs obligations of solicitors towards their clients are set out in the Solicitors' Code of Conduct 2007, at para 2.07.			
The Practice Direction contains no compulsion to update estimates given to the client or the other side but it does insist that if the court requires a new estimate to be served in accordance with r 44.15(3), if that party is represented, the legal representative must in addition serve the estimate on the party he represents			Costs PD, para 6.4(2)
For the effect of the **failure of a solicitor to give a costs estimate** to a client who is subsequently successful in a claim see *Garbutt v Edwards* [2005] EWCA Civ 1206, (2005) Times, 3 November; this case is of considerable importance where there is a conditional fee agreement in existence. See also *Gover v Propertycare Ltd* [2006] EWCA Civ 286, [2006] 4 All ER 69 from which it will be seen that the effectiveness of costs estimates as a brake on the escalation of costs has been significantly undermined			

A court can exercise its discretion to make a costs order in favour of an unsuccessful claimant but only where the successful defendant, being a substantial public body, had acted so unreasonably in refusing to negotiate a settlement that it should be deprived of its costs or some of them: *Daniels v Metropolitan Police Comr* (2005) Times, 28 October, CA			
A positive case must be put forward for departing from the general rule that the successful party is entitled to his costs. The court has to take into account all the circumstances; see *Perrins v Holland (as executor of the estate of Perrins, dec'd)* [2009] EWHC 2558 (Ch), 153 Sol Jo (no 41) 30 as to this and its application to contested probate cases.		44.35	
For the effect of any payment into court or admissible offer to settle made by a party which is drawn to the court's attention which is not one to which Part 36 costs consequences apply, see			Costs PD, para 8.4
For the costs implications for a party who pursues bad points but succeeds on other points see *Kew v Bettamix Ltd* (2006) Times, 4 December, CA			
The fact that the defendant was successful in keeping the damages below the sum sought by the claimant will not necessarily make him the winner or even a partial winner; accordingly the defendant should not be entitled to costs or to reduction in the percentage of costs payable to the claimant in such circumstances: *Hall v Stone* [2007] EWCA Civ 1354, (2008) Times, 1 February, [2007] All ER (D) 260 (Dec). For discussion see the Civil Way, NLJ 25 January 2008, page 143			

Note *Earl of Malmesbury v Strutt and Parker* [2008] EWHC 424 (QB); see **TAB 1** at 1.1, 12th sub-para, a case where the unsuccessful defendant was awarded 15% of the costs of the action because of the claimant's failure on one issue (the joining of a third party) and the claimant was awarded only 70% of the balance of the liability costs and 80% of the balance of the costs on damages. The damages awarded were a fraction only of the damages the claimant was seeking. Exaggeration is a factor to which the court is directed to have regard in deciding what order (if any) to make about costs.		44.3(4)(d)	
By virtue of the Legal Services Act 2007 s 194, from October 2008 the courts can make costs orders in all civil cases where the successful party was represented wholly or in part by a **pro bono lawyer**; for further information see the website of the Access to Justice Foundation at www.accesstojusticefoundation.org.uk (enquiries@atjf.org.uk).			
Generally the costs will be summarily assessed and will not exceed the amount that would have been awarded had the legal services not been provided pro bono.			
The costs paid by the paying party will be paid to the nominated charity the Access to Justice Foundation			
For orders in respect of pro bono representation see		44.3C	Costs PD, para 10A.1 and 10A.2
For discussion and assessment see NLJ (2010) 30 April, page 899 'Accessing justice' by George Gordan.			
When the costs of a litigant in person are to be paid pursuant to an order of the court by any other person, see CPR 48.6: 'Note that for the purpose of the rule a litigant in person includes a company or corporation which is acting without a legal representative' (CPR 48.6(6)(a))		48.6	

The Association of Law Costs Draftsmen: SI 2006/333 designated the Association as an authorised body for the purposes of the Courts and Legal Services Act 1990, ss 27–28 under which an authorised body can grant rights of audience and the right to conduct litigation but see further Legal Services Act 2007.			
The court will not assess any **additional liability** – defined by r 43.2(o) as any percentage increase, insurance premium or provision by a membership organisation – until the conclusion of the proceedings or part of the proceedings to which the **funding arrangement** defined by r 43.2(k) relates.		44.3A	
The circumstances in which a party may not recover an additional liability, without an order of the court		44.3B(c)-(e)	
Other parties **must** be informed of a funding arrangement as soon as possible and in any event within 7 days of entering into the funding arrangement or, where the claimant enters into a funding arrangement before sending a letter of claim, in the letter of claim.			Pre-action Conduct, para 9.3
For the information to be given by a party who wishes to claim an **additional liability in respect of a funding arrangement** see			Costs PD, para 19
The court will normally order a claimant who **discontinues** his claim to pay the defendant's costs but retains a discretion as to such costs: see *Everton v World Professional Billiards and Snooker Association (Promotions) Ltd* [2001] All ER (D) 172 (Dec) and *Re Walker Windsail Systems Ltd; Walker v Walker* [2005] EWCA Civ 247, [2006] 1 All ER 272.		38.6	

The presumption is that the defendant will be entitled to costs and the burden is on the claimant to rebut that presumption. The claimant would need to show a change of circumstances which was more than a mere re-evaluation and which had something to do with the facts of the claim, not for example running out of money. see *Teasdale v HSBC Bank plc and conjoined claims* [2010] EWHC 612 (QB), 23 March 2010, (2010) NLJ, 18 June, page 87.			
Guidance was given in relation to the liability for costs of claimants following the discontinuance of claims under s 78 of the Consumer Credit Act 1974 in *Teasdale* (see para above).			
It is open for the parties to agree that, notwithstanding the general rule, in consideration of the claimant serving a notice of discontinuance the defendant will not seek costs; a court order could be obtained reciting the agreement and making an order that there be no order as to costs.			
For the availability of a *Bullock* order to a claimant where one of two defendants has discontinued see *Whitney v Monster Worldwide Ltd* [2010] EWHC 1298 (Ch).			
Where neither party is completely successful it does not of itself justify making no order for costs: *Day v Day (Costs)* [2006] EWCA Civ 415, [2006] All ER (D) 184 (Mar) where the importance of who had ultimately to sign the cheque was stressed; see also *Cantor Gaming Ltd v Gameaccount Global Ltd* [2007] EWHC 1914 (Ch), [2007] All ER (D) 02 (Aug), where the successful claimant was awarded costs only until 14 days after the service of witness statements with no order for costs thereafter			

Substantial assistance as to the costs position where each party has claims and maintains a balance is owing to it is provided by Jackson J in the case of *Multiplex Construction (UK) Ltd v Cleveland Bridge (UK) Ltd (No 7)* [2008] EWHC 2280. He concluded *Carver v BAA plc* [2008] EWCA Civ 412 to be of general application and derived eight principles from that decision. The principles and his decision on applying them are full set out and discussed in NLJ 2 and 9 January 2009 at page 31 in an article by the costs team at Kings Chambers, entitled 'Multiplex lessons'.			
The 'Medway Oil' principle as to the costs recoverable on a successful counter claim was revisited and affirmed in *Dyson Technology Ltd v Strutt* [2007] EWHC 1756 (Ch), [2007] All ER (D) 381 (Jul)			
For the relevance and for the effect of this principle to an application for security of the costs of a counterclaim see *Jones v Environcom Ltd* [2009] EWHC 16 (Comm), [2009] All ER (D) 115 (Jan).			
For consideration of the reasonableness of instructing solicitors in Central London in a personal injury claim see *Higgins v Ministry of Defence* [2010] EWHC 654 (QB), 30 March where *Wraith v Sheffield Forgemasters Ltd* [1998] 1 WLR 132 was considered. It was held that the master had been entitled to have regard to the claimant's age and the urgency of the case when deciding it was reasonable to instruct solicitors in Central London.			
For consideration of the court's jurisdiction on an order for agreed costs to give guidance to the costs' judge as to how he should determine certain matters on his assessment of those costs see *Richardson Roofing Co Ltd v The Colman Partnership Ltd* [2009] EWCA Civ 839, 13 February where it was considered 'highly' doubtful that there was jurisdiction for the judge to do so.			

For the circumstances in which the fixed cost regime operates and tables setting out the **fixed costs** recoverable see CPR 45. The figures given include VAT but exclude disbursements. CPR 45.1 and 45.3 give the court a discretion to order more than fixed costs where it considers it appropriate to do so; see *Amber Construction Service Ltd v London Interspace HG Ltd* [2007] EWHC 3042 (TCC), [2008] 09 EG 202 where the defendant filed an acknowledgement admitting the claim and the court exercised its discretion not to limit costs to fixed costs.		45.1 and 45.3	
Where the misconduct of the paying party falls to be taken into account, the trial judge should make it clear in his order whether he has taken it into account in his costs order so that it cannot be further taken into account on assessment: *Ultraframe (UK) Ltd v Fielding* [2006] EWCA Civ 1660, [2006] All ER (D) 81 (Dec).			
In *Drew v Whitbread* [2010] EWCA Civ 53 the judge made no special order as to costs but the costs judge was urged on assessment to assess the costs on a fast track basis although the claim had proceeded on the multi track and the costs order was for costs on a standard basis.			
In *O'Beirne v Hudson* [2010] EWCA Civ 52, where an action had been settled with a costs order on a standard basis, the court was urged to assess the costs as if it were a small claim as on allocation it would have been so allocated.			
In each case the arguments of the paying party succeeded on the first appeal but failed before the Court of Appeal.			
It was held that in the absence of any special order by the trial judge the costs judge is entitled to take into account all the circumstances (see CPR 44.5(1)) and the question of the track that was appropriate is clearly one. That does not mean, however, that the costs can be assessed under a different regime with different rules.			

The Court of Appeal stressed that there is no rule that a paying party who has not raised a matter before the trial judge is precluded from raising it before the costs judge. If it is clear that the costs judge would be assisted on the assessment by some indication about the way in which the trial was conducted, an indication should be sought from the trial judge.			
For detailed consideration of these decisions see article in NLJ (2010) 2 and 9 April, page 491 by King's Chambers costs team entitled 'At the double' and Sol Jo Costs update (2010) 16 March, page 24 by Simon Gibbs.			
Where there has been exaggeration by the claimant who rejects but fails to better a Part 36 offer see *Cunningham v Ast Express Ltd* [2009] EWCA Civ 767 and (2009) Sol Jo, 29 September 'Update: Personal Injury', page 20.			
Section 51 of the Senior Courts Act 1981 provides that the court may disallow or order a legal representative to pay costs where there is an improper, unreasonable or negligent act by that legal representative: a **wasted costs order**. The principles are set out in *Ridehalgh v Horsfield* [1994] 3 All ER 848, CA. see further **CPR 48 GUIDE COG 16.4** and for discussion see Civil Litigation Brief, NLJ 29 January 2008, page 21, by Gordon Exall. It should be noted in particular that the service of a notice to show cause does not reverse the burden of proof and that generally an application for a wasted costs order should be left to the end of the trial. See further below at C Detailed Assessment, paras 11.8–11.10 and 11.13.			
See *Hedrich v Standard Bank Ltd* [2008] EWCA Civ 905, 30 July where the application against solicitors for a wasted costs order failed and the court stressed the summary nature of applications under CPR r 48.7 and deprecated the use of prolix submissions and evidence			

A wasted costs order against solicitors will be waived if the receiving party waives the order for costs against the other party to the proceedings: *D v H* [2008] EWHC 559 (Fam), [2008] All ER (D) 286 (Mar), NLJ, 28 March 2008, page 448.		48.7	
Costs of pre-action mediation are not 'costs of and incidental to the proceedings' within s 51 of the Senior Courts Act 1981: *Lobster Group Ltd v Heidelberg Graphic Equipment Ltd* [2008] EWHC 413 (TCC), [2008] 2 All ER 1173 per Toulson J. Mediation costs incurred after proceedings are recoverable and see *Roundstone Nurseries Ltd v Stephenson Holdings Ltd* [2009] EWHC 1431 (TCC) where costs thrown away by the late cancellation of mediation were held to be recoverable.			
Costs of attending a coroner's inquest are capable of being recoverable as costs incidental to subsequent civil proceedings: *Roach v Home Office, Matthews v Home Office* [2009] EWHC 312 (QB), [2009] 3 All ER 510. A coroner has no power to award costs. See generally on recovery of inquest costs (2009) Sol Jo 29 September, page 20.			
The cost of obtaining a bank guarantee to provide security for costs as required by an order of the court was held to be 'incidental to' proceedings and recoverable within s 51 of the Senior Courts Act 1981: *Ene Kos v Petroleo Brasileiro SA (The 'Kos')* [2009] EWHC 1843 (Comm), [2010] Lloyd's Rep 87.		43.4, 44.3 and 44.7	

For recovery of disbursements by a litigant in person and for recovery of disbursements for pre-action work when solicitors are instructed (the work in the case was investigation by loss adjusters) see *Cuthbert v Gair and Gair (t/a Bowes Manor Equestrian Centre)* [2008] Supreme Court Costs Office, 3 September, (2008) Gazette LR 16 October, page 22. The cases applied included *Agassi v Robinson (Inspector of Taxes) (Bar Council intervening)* [2005] EWCA Civ 1507, [2006] 1 All ER 900, [2008] 1 WLR 2126, see **TAB 16**, section 3, final para.			
For the question of whether entering into an arrangement whereby a solicitor, representing a client on a conditional fee agreement, agrees to indemnify the client if the claim fails is **champerty** see *Morris v Southwark London Borough Council* [2010] AlL ER (D) 103 (Apr); leave to appeal has been granted against the decision that, in the circumstances of this case, it was not.			
For discussion of the **Defamation Costs Management pilot scheme** see LexisNexis Human Rights updater for October 2009. The scheme has been extended to 31 March 2011.			51D
A pilot scheme for the provisional assessment of county court bills with base costs of up to £25,000 on paper from 1 October 2010 to 30 September 2011 will operate at the county courts for Leeds, York and Scarborough. The courts will provisionally assess bills falling within the financial limit within 6 weeks of receipt of the request for detailed assessment and the supporting papers. Either party may request an oral hearing within 21 days of receipt of the provisional assessment. There are costs sanctions where the costs are increased or decreased by 20% or more.			51E

A judge when making an order as to costs following submission by the parties is required to give reasons for preferring one side's argument to the other's: *R (Mendes) v Southwark London Borough Council* (2009) Times, 17 April, CA, a case in which the submissions were written.			
On the filing of a request for detailed assessment by a legally aided or LSC funded party where no other party is ordered to pay the cost the fee payable is £120 in the High Court and £105 in the county court For any other detailed assessment the fees are on a sliding scale presently £300 to £5,000 depending on the amount of costs to be assessed; see **FEE 1.8**, Sch 1, para 5.2 below			

A. COSTS ONLY PROCEEDINGS

	Form No	CPR Rule	PD
1. Preliminary			
1.1 Note **CPR 12A [3]–CPR 12A [4]**, and in particular:		44.12A	
• costs only proceedings cannot continue if the making of an order for costs is **opposed**		44.12A(4)(b)	
• if the order for costs is made, the costs will be quantified by the **detailed assessment** procedure. The costs ordered are not to be summarily assessed			Costs PD, para 17.8(1)
• the court can allow a success fee and an after the event insurance premium as recoverable costs: see			Costs PD, para 17.8(2)
• for recovery of the cost of an insurance premium in publication cases see		44.12B	

	Form No	CPR Rule	PD
• In *Crane v Canons Leisure Centre* [2007] EWCA Civ 1352 the court held by a majority that the fees of external costs draftsmen are profit costs and not disbursements so that solicitors can charge a success fee upon them. There remains the problem of what is the appropriate band of fee earner for a costs draftsman generally and in particular cases.			
1.2 The procedure is available where: (a) the parties to a dispute have reached agreement on all issues (including which party is to pay costs) (b) the agreement is in writing or confirmed in writing (c) they have failed to agree the amount of those costs (d) no proceedings have been started		44.12A(1)	
1.3 The procedure set out in para 2 below is also available in **Road Traffic Accidents** (including those where the proceedings are for the approval of a settlement in favour of an infant) where the costs recoverable are **fixed costs**; that is where		45.7	Costs PD, paras 25A.1–25A.10
(a) the dispute arises from a road traffic accident that occurred on or after 6 October 2003			Costs PD, para 25A.1
(b) the agreed damages include damages in respect of personal injury, damage to property, or both (c) the total value of the agreed damages does not exceed £10,000 and			Costs PD, para 25A.2
(d) if the claim had been issued for the agreed amount the small claims track would not have been its normal track			Costs PD, para 25A.2
The only costs recoverable are (a) fixed recoverable costs calculated in accordance with rule 45.9			

	Form No	CPR Rule	PD
(b) disbursements allowed pursuant to rule 45.10 include the amount of an insurance premium or where a party is funded by a body which indemnifies its members against costs of other parties to the proceedings, a sum not exceeding such sum as would be allowed under s 30 Access to Justice Act 1999 in respect of provision made against the risk of having to meet such liabilities. A medical agency fee is recoverable as a disbursement pursuant to rule 45.10: see *Woollard v Fowler* [2006] May SCCO Ref 050071 provided it is reasonable and proportionate although there are conflicting decisions in *Earle v Centrica* [2005] LTL, 5 October and other similar cases An appeal against the decision in Woollard was filed but withdrawn after mediation between the Association of Medical Reporting Organizations (AMRO) and the insurers which resulted in agreement between those bodies in respect of orthopaedic, accident and emergency and general practitioner reports in those cases where damages do not exceed £15,000. The agreement was to remain in force until 1 April 2009 (c) a success fee allowed in accordance with rule 45.11 of 12.5% of the fixed recoverable costs to be calculated as therein set out (but the claimant cannot claim 12.5% on any additional amount payable if the solicitor practises in the London area)		45.8 and 45.11	

	Form No	CPR Rule	PD
• The entitlement to fixed recoverable costs under 45.9 and a success fee under 45.11 is not dependant on there being a valid conditional fee agreement: *Nizami v Butt; Kamaluden v Butt* [2006] EWHC 159 (QB), [2006] 2 All ER 140			
Unless the court considers there are **exceptional circumstances** which make greater costs than the fixed recoverable costs appropriate		45.12–45.14	
Where the claimant is claiming a sum greater than the amount of the fixed recoverable costs he must include in the claim form details of the exceptional circumstances on which he relies			Costs PD, para 25A.8
For the amount of the fixed costs recoverable and VAT on them see		45.9	Costs PD, para 25A.5
For the 12.5% increase in the fixed recoverable costs where the claimant lives or works in one of the specified areas and instructs a solicitor who practises in one of those areas		45.9(2)	Costs PD, para 25A.6
'Fixed recoverable costs' when considering a claim for 'greater costs' excludes any success fee or disbursements		45.12(1)	
It remains vital on achieving a compromise in such cases to include in the agreement a clause making it clear that predictable costs are to be paid. See article 'A Question of Costs' (2007) NLJ 25 May, page 730			
1.4 Where a dispute arises from a **Road Traffic Accident** which is not a small claim that occurred on or after 6 October 2003 and the claimant has entered into a conditional fee agreement or collective conditional fee agreement which provides for a **success fee** the **percentage increase** allowed is determined by Section III of Part 45		45.15	

	Form No	CPR Rule	PD
The percentage increase allowed in respect of solicitors fees is 100% where the case concludes at trial and 12.5% where the claim concludes before a trial is commenced or the dispute is settled before a claim is issued		45.16	
The hearing of a summons for the assessment of costs (liability, quantum and the liability for costs, but not the amount, having been agreed) is not a trial as it is not a final contested hearing and the percentage increase applicable was accordingly 12.5%: *Thenga v Quinn* [2009] EWCA Civ 151, 28 January 2009.			
The percentage increase in counsel's fees is set out in		45.17	
The only circumstances in which the court can allow a success fee different from that prescribed by r 45.16 in relation to solicitors' costs are those prescribed by r 45.18 below: see *Lamont v Burton* [2007] EWCA Civ 429, (2007) Times, 7 June. In this case the claimant was successful at trial but failed to 'beat' a payment into court, nevertheless the claimant was held to be entitled to the full prescribed success fee			
In *Kilby v Gawith* (2008) Times, 13 June, 152 Sol Jo (no 21) 28 the Court of Appeal decided that the claimant's solicitor can recover the 12.5% success fee allowed under the scheme even if there is before-the-event (BTE) insurance in place. The court agreed with the lower court that the rules allowed no discretion. See Gazette, 22 May 2008, page 3.			
A party may apply for an increased percentage in relation to solicitors' fees or counsel's fees where damages are awarded or agreed in an amount of £500,000 or more ignoring any reduction for contributory negligence		45.18	
The procedure under para 2 below may be used			Costs PD, para 25A.10
The court will determine the alternative percentage in accordance with		49.19	

	Form No	CPR Rule	PD
Note that the alternative percentage increase can only be sought where otherwise the increase would be 12.5% **1.5** Where there is a dispute between **an employer and his employee** arising from a **bodily injury** sustained by the employee in the course of his employment on or after 1 October 2004 and the claimant has entered into a conditional fee agreement or collective conditional fee agreement which provides for a **success fee** the **percentage increase** which is allowed is determined by Section IV of Part 45		45.18(1) 45.20–45.21	
But note that the above provision **does not apply** where the dispute (a) relates to a disease or (b) arises from a road traffic accident as defined in rule 45.7(4) or (c) related to an injury to which Part V of Part 45 (fixed recoverable success fees in employer's liability disease claims) applies or to a claim which: (a) has been allocated to the small claims track or (b) has not been allocated but for which the small claims track is the normal track The **percentage increase** to be allowed for **solicitors fees** is 100% where the case concludes at trial and where the claim is settled before trial or issue the percentage increase is: (a) 27.5% if a membership organisation has undertaken to meet the claimant's liability for legal costs and (b) 25% in any other case The percentage increase which is to be allowed for counsel's fees is 25%		45.20(2) 45.21(a)(i)	
For **alternative percentage increase** see		45.22	

	Form No	CPR Rule	PD
1.6 Where there is dispute between **an employee** (or his estate) **and his employer** (or a person alleged to be liable for the employer's alleged breach of statutory or common law duties of care) relating to a **disease** alleged to have been contracted as a consequence of the employer's alleged breach of duty in the course of the employee's employment and the claimant has entered into a funding agreement under CPR 43.2(1)(k)(i) **the percentage increase** by way of success fee allowed is determined by Section V of Part 45			
But note the provision does not apply where:			
(a) the claimant sent a letter of claim to the defendant containing a summary of the facts and main allegations of fault before 1 October 2005, or			
(b) where the claim has been allocated to the small claims track or would normally be so allocated if not yet allocated		45.23(2)	
The **percentage increase** to be allowed in **solicitors fees** is: (a) 100% if the claim concludes at trial, or (b) if the claim concludes before trial or issue: (i) in Type A claims (see CPR 45.23(3)(c)) 30% if a membership organisation has undertaken to meet the claimants liability for legal costs, and 27.5% in any other case (ii) In type B claims (see CPR 45.23(3)(d) – 100% (iii) In type C claims (see CPR 45.23(3)(e)) 70% if a membership organisation has undertaken to meet the claimant's liability for legal costs and 62.5% in any other cases			
The decision of the Court of Appeal in *Lamont v Burton* [2007] EWCA Civ 429, [2007] 3 All ER 173 (see section 1.4 of this TAB above) applies to employer's liability claims as it does to road traffic claims			

	Form No	CPR Rule	PD
The percentage increase in counsel's fees is 100% if the claim concludes at trial. If the claim concludes before trial or issue see CPR 45.25(2) Where a trial period has been fixed see 45.25(3)		45.25	
For **alternative percentage increase** where the damages are greater than £250,000 see		45.26	
For non-exclusive list of diseases that fall within Class A and within Class B see			Costs PD, Section 25B
2. Procedure for issue			
2.1 Either party to agreement can start the proceedings by issuing **a Part 8 claim form** (reduced fee £30) which has the agreement or confirmation contained in it or with it	N208	44.12A and 44.12A(3)	Costs PD, para 17.4
2.2 The claim form should be issued in the court that would have been appropriate under CPR 47.4 if proceedings had been brought in relation to the substantive claim			Costs PD, para 17.1
2.3 For contents of the claim form, see			Costs PD, para 17.3
2.4 The evidence filed and served with the claim form under CPR 8.5 must include copies of the documents on which the claimant relies to prove the defendant's agreement to pay costs			Costs PD, para 17.4
3. Defendant's acknowledgement of service			
3.1 If the defendant files an acknowledgement of service indicating he intends to contest the proceedings or to seek a different remedy, the court will dismiss the claim		44.12A(4)(b)	Costs PD, para 17.9
3.2 If the defendant has not filed an acknowledgement of service and the time for doing so has expired, the claimant may by letter request an order in the terms of his claim			Costs PD, para 17.6

	Form No	CPR Rule	PD
4. The order			
The order may be made by a costs judge or a district judge whatever the amount of costs in issue	See SCCO Guide, Appendix A5		Costs PD, para 17.5
The court **may** make an order for costs or dismiss the application. If the claim is opposed it **must** be dismissed		44.12A(4)(b)	
See *Brawley v Marczynski* [2002] EWCA Civ 756, [2002] 4 All ER 1060 where matters that can usefully be taken into consideration are set out			
5. Effect of the order			
The order will be treated as an order for costs to be decided by detailed assessment pursuant to CPR Pt 47 and the Practice Directions relating to it. See Section C of this table for detailed assessment			Costs PD, para 17.8(1)
The basis of assessment will be on a standard basis unless cases are claimed on an indemnity basis			Costs PD, para 17.3(5)
The court may, when making the order, additionally give any directions it considers necessary. If the parties are agreed on the directions these require they can usefully be lodged with the defendant's acknowledgement of service with evidence of the claimant's agreement			

B. SUMMARY ASSESSMENT

	Form No	CPR Rule	PD
1. Preliminary			
1.1 Unless costs awarded are fixed costs, the court may either: (a) make a summary assessment of the costs, or (b) order a detailed assessment of the costs			
1.2 See paras **CPR 44.7 [1]–CPR 44.7 [8]** and in particular note that summary assessment cannot take place if the receiving party is LSC funded		44.7	

	Form No	CPR Rule	PD
1.3 Summary assessment means the procedure by which the court, making an order for costs, makes an order for a fixed sum of money instead of fixed costs or detailed assessment		43.3	
1.4 An order for costs will be treated as an order for detailed assessment unless the order provides otherwise			Costs PD, para 12.2
1.5 For considerations of **proportionality** of costs being assessed see *Lownds v Home Office* [2002] EWCA Civ 365, [2002] 4 All ER 775			
Where there has been a failure to serve a costs schedule see *Macdonald v Taree Holdings* (2000) Times, 28 December, per Neuberger J it is not fatal to the costs application but should be taken into account, but the re-action should be proportionate. See also			Costs PD, Section 6
2. When summary assessment is appropriate			
2.1 The general rule is that the court should summarily assess costs:			Costs PD, para 13.2
(a) at the end of a fast track trial (summary assessment of the whole of the costs of the case) (b) at the end of a hearing which lasted not more than one day (the summary assessment will be of the costs of the application or issue but if the hearing disposes of the whole application the order may deal with the costs of the whole claim) (c) of hearings in the Court of Appeal when para 14 of the Practice Direction to CPR Pt 52 (Appeals) applies			

	Form No	CPR Rule	PD
The Court of Appeal in *Coyne v DRC Distribution Ltd* [2008] EWCA Civ 488, [2008] All ER (D) 193 (May) confirmed that a court may exercise its discretion to make a costs order when substantive proceedings have been resolved without a trial but without the parties reaching an agreement as to costs. The court should adopt a summary approach and it is only in exceptional cases where it is impossible to make a summary assessment that the court should direct oral evidence be taken. See also *Business Environment Bowlane Ltd v Deanwater Estates Ltd* [2008] EWHC 2003 (TCC) and articles (2008) NLJ Law Digest, 3 October, page 1376 **2.2** The general rule will not apply "if there is good reason not to do so". The fact a case lasts longer than a day does not raise a rebuttable presumption against summary assessment: *Q v Q (Family Proceedings: Costs Order)* (2002) Times, 16 July			Costs PD, para 13.2 proviso
3. When summary assessment is not appropriate			
Summary assessment is not appropriate when a case involves: (a) mortgagee's costs			Costs PD, para 13.3
(b) the costs of a receiving party who is an assisted person or LSC funded client			Costs PD, para 13.9
(c) the costs of a receiving party who is a child or patient, unless the solicitor acting for the child or patient has waived the right to further costs		Pt 21	Costs PD, para 13.11
(d) an "additional liability" before the conclusion of the proceedings or the part of the proceedings to which the funding arrangement relates. Where this applies the court should summarily assess the base costs unless there is a good reason for not so doing		44.3A	Costs PD, para 13.12

	Form No	CPR Rule	PD
4. The statement of costs			
4.1 It is the duty of the parties and their legal representatives to assist the judge in making a summary assessment of costs			Costs PD, para 13.5(1)
4.2 Each party intending to claim costs must prepare a written statement of costs in schedule form. For the information required, see			Costs PD, para 13.5(2)
The statement should follow as closely as possible **Form N260** and be signed by the party or his legal representative	N260		
4.3 The certificate (as to the indemnity principle) at the end of Form N260 does not have to be signed if the client is legally assisted or LSC funded			Costs PD, para 13.5(3)
4.4 Where the litigant may be entitled to claim or does claim an additional liability, the statement need not reveal the amount of that liability			Costs PD, para 13.5(5)
5. Procedure			
5.1 The statement of costs must be filed at court and copies served on any party against whom an order for payment of those costs is sought It is sensible to amend Form N260 so that the number of letters and telephone calls can be shown separately Filing and service must be effected as soon as possible and in any event not later than 24 hours before the date fixed for the hearing			Costs PD, para 13.5(4)
5.2 Failure without reasonable excuse to comply with the provisions as to filing and service will be taken into account in deciding what order for costs should be made			Costs PD, para 13.6
5.3 The court will make its summary assessment at the conclusion of the hearing after considering the schedule of costs of the party whose costs are to be assessed Normally brief submissions will be made by or on behalf of both parties and reference may be made to the schedule of costs filed by the receiving party			

	Form No	CPR Rule	PD
If the court has summarily assessed the costs of the proceedings it will specify separately: (a) the base costs and, if appropriate, the additional liability allowed as solicitor's costs, counsel's fees, other disbursements and any VAT, and (b) the amount which is awarded under CPR Pt 46 (Fast Track Trial Costs) If the summary assessment cannot be made on the same day as the hearing it will have to be done at a further hearing before the same judge			Costs PD, para 13.7(1) and (2) Costs PD, para 13.8
6. Effect of order for costs that have been summarily assessed			
Unless the court gives an extended time, the costs will be payable within 14 days		44.8	
7. Summary assessment where there is an additional liability			
The existence of a conditional fee agreement or other funding arrangement is not of itself a sufficient reason for not carrying out a summary assessment			Costs PD, para 14.1
Where there is a summary assessment of costs **before the conclusion of the proceedings** and there is a conditional fee agreement or other funding arrangement in existence in respect of the receiving party's costs, reference should be made to			Costs PD, paras 14.1–14.4
Summary assessment before the conclusion of the proceedings will not extend to any additional liability		44.3A(1)	Costs PD, para 14.2
Where there is a summary assessment of costs **at the conclusion of proceedings** and there is a conditional fee agreement or other funding arrangement in existence, in respect of the receiving party's costs, reference should be made to		44.3A(2)	Costs PD, paras 14.5–14.9

					Form No	CPR Rule	PD
8. Annual Guide							
Guidelines on hourly rates from 1 April 2010 have been published after acceptance by the Master of the Rolls of the recommendation of the Advisory Committee on Costs (Bands A-D, London and national):							Costs PD 48 – Guideline Figures for the Summary Assessment of costs, solicitors' hourly rates and counsel's fees
New guideline hourly rates for 2010:							
	A	B	C	D			
London 1	409	296	226	138			
London 2	317	242	196	126			
London 3	229–267	172–229	165	121			
National 1	217	192	161	118			
National 2	201	177	146	111			
The guidelines are reproduced in NLJ 16 April 2010, page 543.							
9. Where an appeal is contemplated							
Consideration should be given as to whether clarification should be sought of the decision of the Costs Judge or District Judge: see per Peter Smith J in his judgment on the costs appeal in *Lloyds TSB Bank plc v Lampert and Lampert* [2003] EWHC 249 (Ch), [2003] 2 Costs LR 286 and see *Hosking v Michaelides* [2003] EWHC 3029 (Ch), [2004] 03 LS Gaz R 32, (2003) Times, 17 December (Ch)							

C. DETAILED ASSESSMENT

	Form No	CPR Rule	PD
1. Preliminary • This Section does not deal with the costs of a funded or assisted person where costs are payable out of the community Legal Service fund.		47.17	Costs PD, para 43
• This Section applies where a costs officer is to make a detailed assessment of: (a) costs which are payable by on party to another; or		47.5	Costs PD, para 43

	Form No	CPR Rule	PD
(b) the sum payable by one party to the prescribed charity pursuant to s 194(3) of the Legal Services Act 2007.			
• Unless the court otherwise orders, the costs of any proceedings or any part of proceedings are not to be assessed by the detailed procedure until the **conclusion of the proceedings**		47.1	Costs PD, para 28.1
• Detailed assessment is not stayed **pending an appeal** unless the court so orders		47.2	Costs PD, para 29.1
• The fee payable on a detailed assessment depends on the amount of the bill. The minimum fee is £300 (in the High Court £600) and increases by steps to a maximum of £5,000			
• The venue for detailed assessment is the "**appropriate court**", generally the district registry or county court which dealt with the case when the judgment or order was made or, in all other cases, the Costs Office. A pilot scheme which originally operated until 5 July 2004 for detailed assessment by the Supreme Court Costs Office (now the Costs Office) of the costs of civil proceedings in the London County Courts has been made permanent. The scheme now also covers the determination of legally aided parties means to pay costs		47.4	Costs PD, para 31, 31A and 47B
• For considerations of **proportionality** of costs subject to assessment see *Lownds v Home Office v* [2002] EWCA Civ 365, [2002] 4 All ER 775			

	Form No	CPR Rule	PD
• With effect from 6 April 2010 a charge for e-mails out was made allowable with a 6 minute unit for routine items, but e-mails received are not normally allowed.			Costs PD, paras 4.8 and 4.16
• For provisions relating to **VAT** see **2. Commencement of detailed assessment proceedings**			Costs PD, Section 5
2.1 Commencement is effected when the receiving party serves on the paying party: (a) notice of commencement duly completed, and (b) a copy of the bill of costs	N252	47.6(1)	Costs PD, para 32.8 Costs PD, para 33.3
2.2 If the detailed assessment is **of costs without any additional liability** the further documents to be served are: (a) fee notes of counsel and any experts (b) written evidence as to any disbursement which is claimed and exceeds £250 (c) a statement giving the name and address for service of any person on whom the receiving party intends to serve notice of commencement			Costs PD, para 32.3
2.3 If the detailed assessment is in respect of an **additional liability only**, the further documents to be served are: (a) the relevant details of the additional liability (b) a statement giving the name and address of any person upon whom the receiving party intends to serve the notice of commencement			Costs PD, para 32.4
• For the relevant details in the case of a conditional fee agreement with a success fee, see (as amended by the Civil Procedure (Amendment No 2) Rules 2009 with effect from 6 April 2010)			Costs PD, para 32.5(1)–(3)

	Form No	CPR Rule	PD
• For the relevant details where the additional liability is an insurance premium, see (as expanded by thee Civil Procedure (Amendment No 2) Rules 2009)			Costs PD, para 32.5(2)
• The bill of costs can be brief; a total figure can be shown for each of the agreed costs and disbursements without a detailed breakdown **2.4** If the detailed assessment is in respect of **base costs and an additional liability** the further documents to be served are those listed in 2.2 and 2.3 above			Costs PD, para 32.7
2.5 There is no compulsory form for a **bill of costs** but there are Precedents A, B and C in the schedule to the Costs Practice Direction			Costs PD, para 3.5
If the model form of bill of costs is not followed an explanation should be given for the departure			Costs PD, para 3.7
• For the form and contents of bills of costs, see			Costs PD, para 4
• For provisions as to VAT, see			Costs PD, para 5
• The court may at any time after the receiving party has filed a request for a detailed assessment hearing issue, amend or cancel an **interim costs certificate** for such sum as it considers appropriate	N244 (for application) N257 (interim certificate)	47.15	Costs PD, para 41
3. Time by which detailed assessment proceedings must be commenced		47.7	
3.1 After a **judgment, direction, order, award or other determination** – must be commenced within 3 months or, if there is a stay pending appeal, 3 months after the date of the order lifting the stay			
3.2 After **discontinuance** – 3 months after the date of service of the notice of discontinuance or 3 months after the date of dismissal of an application to set aside the notice of discontinuance		38.3 38.4	

	Form No	CPR Rule	PD
3.3 After **acceptance of an offer** to settle – 3 months after the right to costs arose			
3.4 *Note:* • The time limits may be varied by the parties by agreement			Costs PD, para 33.1
• The court may extend or shorten time on application			Costs PD, para 33.2
• For sanctions for delay in commencing detailed assessment, see *Less v Benedict* [2005] LSG 102/33, 1 September where three years' delay in bringing the proceedings for detailed assessment did not breach the paying party's ECHR right to a hearing within a reasonable time or merit a sanction under CPR 44.14 and see *Haji-Ioannou v Frangos* [2006] EWCA Civ 1663, [2007] 3 All ER 938 where it was held that the sanction under 47.8 for delay in starting detailed proceedings is that all or part of interest can be disallowed but not any part of the costs unless the non-compliance by the receiving party amounted to misconduct. In this case misconduct was not found to have occurred. See further		47.8 and 44.14	Costs PD, para 34.1
• In *Haji-Ioannou (No 2) Practice Note* [2006] EWCA Civ 1663 the Court of Appeal indicated that the court was loth to depart from the sanction of disallowance because of the danger of satellite litigation that would result from such a departure.			
• Permission to commence assessment proceedings out of time is not required			Costs PD, para 33.4
• For sanction for delay in filing request for a detailed assessment hearing see		47.14	

	Form No	CPR Rule	PD
4. Points of dispute			
4.1 The paying party and any other party to the detailed assessment may dispute any item in the bill by serving **within 21 days** after the date of service of the notice of commencement **points of dispute** on:		47.9(1) and (2)	
(a) the receiving party, and (b) every other party to the detailed assessment **4.2** If points of dispute are served out of time the party in default can only be heard on the assessment if the court gives permission		47.9(3)	
4.3 For **the form of points of dispute** see Precedent G of the Schedule of Costs Precedents annexed to CPR PD 48 and also see			Costs PD, paras 35.2 and 35.3
5. Where points of dispute are not served			
5.1 The receiving party may file a request for a **default costs certificate** if the period for filing points of dispute has expired and they have not been filed	N254	47.9(4)	
But if any party, including the paying party, serves points of dispute before the issue of the default costs certificate the court may not issue the default costs certificate		47.9(5)	
Note: • The time limits may be varied by the parties			Costs PD, para 35.1
• The receiving party can draw up the default costs certificate	N255		Costs PD, para 37.4
• The solicitors fixed costs on issue of the default costs certificate are £80			Costs PD, para 37.8
• For setting aside a default costs certificate, see		47.12	Costs PD, para 38
• Where a receiving party obtains a default certificate in respect of de bono representation proceedings a copy must be sent to the prescribed charity		47.11, 47.12(5)	

	Form No	CPR Rule	PD
6. Where points of dispute are served			
6.1 Where any party to the assessment proceedings serves points of dispute, the receiving party **may** within 21 days of service on him of the points of dispute serve a **reply** on the other parties to the assessment		47.13(1) and (2)	Costs PD, para 39.1(1)
6.2 A reply is: (a) a separate document prepared by the receiving party, or (b) his written comments added to the points of dispute			Costs PD, para 39.1(2)
It must be signed by the party serving it or his **solicitor**			Costs PD, para 39.1(3)
7. Detailed assessment hearing			
7.1 Where points of dispute are served, the receiving party must file a request for a detailed assessment hearing with the necessary accompanying documents. He must do this within 3 months of the expiry of the period for commencing detailed assessment proceedings as specified: (a) in CPR 47.7 (see the last paragraph of para 1 above), or (b) by any direction of the court	N258	47.14(1) 47.14(2)	Costs PD, paras 40.2–40.4
7.2 If the receiving party fails to comply with his obligation to file a request for a hearing, the paying party may apply for an order requiring the receiving party to do so within such time as the court shall specify. The court may specify the disallowance of all or part of the costs if the order is not complied with	N244	47.14(3) 47.14(4)	
Note: • As to the court's power to disallow interest, see		47.14(5)	Costs PD, para 40.7(2)
• As to the availability of an **interim costs certificate**, see	N257	47.15	Costs PD, para 41.1
• As to the parties who can be heard on a detailed assessment hearing, see		47.14(6)	

	Form No	CPR Rule	PD
• Only items specified in the points of dispute may be raised unless the court gives permission		47.14(7)	
• As to the **documents to be filed in support of the bill**, see **7.3** On receipt of the request for a detailed assessment hearing the court will fix an appointment for the hearing or will give directions or fix a date for a preliminary hearing			Costs PD, para 40.12 Costs PD, para 40.5
At least 14 days' notice of the hearing will be given and the court will serve on any party who has served points of dispute a copy of those points of dispute annotated by the receiving party as required by CPR PD 47, para 40.2(d)			Costs PD, para 40.6(1) and (2)
7.4 A useful guide to preparation and conduct of the hearing is to be found in the booklet *Costs Advocacy – A Practical Guide* by DISTRICT JUDGE SEGAL (2001) Butterworths			
7.5 The court will, after hearing arguments, make any reductions it considers appropriate in respect of the items that remain in dispute and make a note on the bill of each reduction or disallowance			Costs PD, para 42.1
8. Costs of the detailed assessment			
8.1 Generally the court will assess the receiving party's costs of the detailed assessment proceedings and add them to the bill of costs			Costs PD, para 45.1
8.2 If the costs of the detailed assessment are awarded to the paying party the court will usually summarily assess them but sometimes will make an order for them to be the subject of detailed assessment			Costs PD, para 45.2
Note: • Parties should not file or serve statements of the costs of the detailed assessment unless ordered to do so			Costs PD, para 45.3

	Form No	CPR Rule	PD
• As to the matters to which the court must have regard when deciding which order for costs of the detailed assessment is appropriate, see			Costs PD, para 45.4
9. Completion of the assessment			
9.1 At the conclusion of the assessment the receiving party or his representatives must remove the papers filed in support of the bill			Costs PD, para 40.16
9.2 The receiving party must complete the bill with the figures agreed or allowed and re-calculate the summary			Costs PD, para 42.2
9.3 The completed bill must be filed no later than **14 days after the hearing** with the necessary accompanying documents. To obtain a final costs certificate all relevant court fees must be paid		47.16(2) 47.16(4)	Costs PD, paras 42.3, 42.4, 42.5
9.4 The court will then issue a **final costs certificate**, including an order to pay the costs and serve it on the parties to the detailed assessment proceedings and, where there was de bono representation, on the prescribed charity		4.16(3), (5) and (6)	
For the form of the final costs certificate, see the Costs Practice Direction and the Schedule of Costs Forms, Form 12	N256(CC) N256(HC)		Costs PD, para 42
10. Settlement			
10.1 For **offers to settle** without prejudice save as to costs, see		47.19	Costs PD, para 46
This Rule will not apply where the receiving party is LSC funded or an assisted person			
Where costs are agreed either the paying or receiving party may apply for a costs certificate (either interim or final)		47.10	
For procedure, see			Costs PD, para 36
11. Funding of Legal Services			
11.1 See **III FUND** in Vol 2			

	Form No	CPR Rule	PD
11.2 The statutory authority for the abrogation of the indemnity principle is s 31 Access to Justice Act 1999 enabling changes to be made to the CPR in respect of compliant CFAs		43.2(3) and (4)	
11.3 A commercial funder who financed the costs of litigation in a manner which facilitated access to justice which was not otherwise objectionable should be potentially liable for the costs of the opposing party to the extent of the funding provided; *Arkin v Borchard Lines Ltd (Nos 2 and 3)* [2005] 1 WLR 3055, CA For discussion of whether liability could extend to the lawyers of the losing party see article by Professor John Peysner entitled 'Arkin again' [2005] NLJ 9 September, p 1326			
The judgment of Wyn Williams J in *R (on the application of Hide) v Staffordshire County Council* [2007] EWHC 2441 (Admin), [2007] All ER (D) 402 (Oct) provides interesting guidance although it was a case concerning a wasted costs order. This was refused as the court found, on the evidence, that it would be highly likely that such an order would result in the solicitor's bankruptcy which would be a disproportionate consequence			
11.4 Where one party is legally funded, an order for costs in favour of the other party could direct that those costs be set off against either damages or costs to which the legally aided person had become, or might in future become, entitled: *Lockley v National Blood Transfusion Service* [1992] 2 All ER 589, [1992] 1 WLR 492; *R (on the application of Burkett) v Hammersmith and Fulham London Borough Council (No 2)* [2004] EWCA Civ 1342			
11.4A Where a legally assisted person's solicitor has ceased to act and (a) no other solicitor has been appointed under the legal aid certificate, and (b) the other party has been so informed,			

	Form No	CPR Rule	PD
the litigant ceases to be legally assisted and becomes liable for costs: *Mohamadi v Shellpoint Trustees Ltd* [2009] EWHC 1098 (Ch), [2009] NLJR 823.			
11.5 The court has no power to direct that a success fee was recoverable under a conditional fee agreement at different rates for different periods of proceedings; *U (a child) v Liverpool City Council* [2005] EWCA Civ 475, [2005] 1 WLR 2657			
11.5A It should be noted when there is a challenge to a staged ATE insurance premium that it cannot be compared with the premium of a policy which made provision for a single payment: *Rogers v Merthyr Tydfil Borough Council* [2006] EWCA Civ 1134, [2007] 1 All ER 354.			
11.6 The Court of Appeal has expressed its grave concern at inflated success fees; *Begum v Klarit* [2005] EWCA Civ 234, (2005) Times, 18 March. See also *Atack v Lee* [2004] EWCA Civ 1712, [2005] 1 WLR 2643 and for discussion of these cases and generally *Burton v Kingsbury* [2005] EWHC 1034 (QB), [2005] All ER (D) 378 (May)			

	Form No	CPR Rule	PD
11.7 Where a person is 'the real party' litigating for his own benefit through a party to proceedings that person may be made the subject of an order under the wide powers vested in the court by s 51 of the Senior Courts Act 1981 for all or part of the costs of the proceedings. See *Hamilton v Al Fayed* [2002] EWCA Civ 665, [2003] QB 1175, [2002] 3 All ER 641; *Dymocks Franchise Systems v Todd* [2004] UKPC 39, [2004] 1 WLR 2807; *CIBC Mellon Trust Co v Stolzenburg* [2005] EWCA Civ 628, [2005] 2 BCLC 618; and *Arkin v Borchard Lines* [2005] EWCA Civ 655, [2005] 3 All ER 613. For a case where such an application failed see *Barndeal Ltd v Richmond-on-Thames London Borough Council* [2005] EWHC 1377 (QB), [2005] All ER (D) 369 (Jun). In *BE Studios v Smith & Williamson Ltd* [2005] EWHC 2730 (Ch), [2006] 2 All ER 811 the court stated that impropriety in the way the claim was prosecuted did not have to be shown before the finding could be made In *Thomson v Berkhamsted Collegiate School* [2009] EWHC 2374 (QB), [2009] NLJR 1440, 2 October the court confirmed the principles set out in the case of *Dymocks* (see above) to be:			
(1) such orders were exceptional; (2) such orders should, in the normal course, be dealt with by the trial judge; (3) pure funders with no personal interest would not normally have the discretion to make a third party costs order exercised against them.			

	Form No	CPR Rule	PD
In *Total Spares and Supplies Ltd v Antares SRL* [2006] EWHC 1537 (Ch), [2006] BPIR 1330, p 1074 Richards J observed 'Causation will often be a vital factor but there may be cases where it is just to make an order for costs against a non-party who cannot be said to have caused the costs in question'. See further as to liability, causation and participation in the dissipation of the paying party's assets to put them beyond the reach of the receiving party *PR Records v Vinyl 2000 Ltd* [2008] EWHC 192 (Ch), [2008] All ER (D) 27 (Jan).			
11.8 The relevant test for causation in an application for a third party costs order under the Senior Courts Act 1981, s 51 is whether the funding provided by the third party caused the applicant to incur costs that he would not otherwise have incurred and whether the funded party was only in court because of the funds that had been made available: *Jackson v Thakrar* [2007] EWHC Civ 626 (TCC), [2007] NLJR 483. There is a presumption that unless there is good reason a s 51 order will not be made against a 'pure funder': see authorities referred to in *Thakrar* starting with *Aiden Shipping Co Ltd v Interbulk Ltd* [1986] AC 965, HL; and see **CPR 48.2 [1]** above			
Excessive citation of the authorities on the principles which should guide a judge as to the making of a third party costs order is unnecessary: *Alan Phillips and Associates v Dowling* [2007] EWCA Civ 64, [2007] BLR 151. In this case the court made a third party costs order because 'given the way the third party had conducted his affairs through the company it would be unjust for him to rely on the separate legal entity of the company to avoid liability for costs			
See also the cases cited at **TAB 19**, para 9 above			

	Form No	CPR Rule	PD
11.9 The determination of who is he real party is not 'all or nothing' and it is for the judge to fix the point of time at which personal motives rather than the interest of the party to the action took over: see *Sims v Hawkins* [2007] EWCA Civ 1175, [2007] All ER (D) 247 (Nov) and article in (2007) Sol Jo, 14 December, page 1593, 'Who's Paying?' by Andrew Davies			
The court can make a third party costs order after the costs have already been assessed: *Nelson v Greening and Sykes (Builders) Ltd* [2007] EWCA Civ 1358, [2008] 08 EG 158. The ability to do so is of importance if the losing party is not able to pay the costs awarded against him.			
11.10 For the distinction in practice in relation to applications for wasted costs orders and for non party costs see *PR Records Ltd v Vinyl 2000 Ltd* [2007] EWHC 1721 (Ch), [2007] All ER (D) 265 (Jul) where it is considered and explained. The tests for adding parties under CPR 19.2 and CPR 48.2(1)(a) are also compared.		19.2 48.2(1)(a)	
Where a claim for costs against a non-party is being seriously considered, making him a party to the original proceedings for the purpose of costs should also be seriously considered. Even if he is not joined as a party notice should be given to him as soon as possible in a 'non-intimidatory' way that this course may be taken: see *Orakhiel v Vickers* [2008] EWCA Civ 748, [2008] All ER (D) 69 (Jul) where it was stated that non-party costs orders are 'exceptional' and that the non-party will normally have a connection with the claim that has given rise to the costs.			

	Form No	CPR Rule	PD
For a case where a firm of solicitors was joined in proceedings as an additional party for the purpose of an application for non-party costs pursuant to CPR 48.2 see *Mohamed Adris v Cartel Client Review Ltd (1) Richard Burley (2) Carl Wright (3) and other conjoined claims* [2010] EWCA Civ 941 (QB), 29 April, where the failure of solicitors to obtain legal costs insurance for unsuccessful claimants alleging breaches of s 78 of the Consumer Credit Act 1974 was held to be a serious breach of the duty owed to them rendering the solicitors liable to a non-party costs order in favour of the defendant when the claims were discontinued.			
The judgment of Andrew Scott J in *Equitas and Additional Underwriting Agencies (No 9) Ltd v Horace Holman & Co Ltd and Powell* [2008] EWHC 2287 (Comm) is very informative and fully discussed in an article 'Time and Tide …' by Jonathan Cohen in (2008) NLJ, 21 November , page 1636			
11.11 As to the question of the liability for costs of insurers when they had funded the defence and the insured was financially worthless see *Plymouth & South-West Co-operative Society Ltd v Architecture, Structure and Management Ltd* [2006] EWHC 3252 (TCC), [2006] All ER (D) 284 (Dec). See also *Palmer v Palmer* [2008] EWCA Civ 46, [2008] Lloyd's Rep IR 535 where the court did uphold an order for costs against the insurance company having stated that the judge was entitled to conclude that the claim was funded, controlled and directed by the insurer solely in its own interest.			
A credit hire company may be liable for a successful defendant's costs when the claimant has failed in his claim for hire charges and subsequently failed to pay the defendant's costs: *Farrell v Direct Accident Management Services* [2009] EWCA Civ 769, [2009] All ER (D) 172 (Jun), 17 June.			

	Form No	CPR Rule	PD
11.12 For procedure when the court disallows any part of a success fee under a Conditional Fee Agreement entered into before 1 November 2005 and the legal representative applies for the disallowed part to the payable by his client, see		44.16	Costs PD, paras 20.1–20.8
12. Variation of costs order			
It was held in *Latimer Management Consultants Ltd v Ellingham Investments Ltd* [2007] EWHC 3682 (Ch), [2007] 3 All ER 485, [2007] 1 WLR 2569 that the court had jurisdiction on an application under CPR 3.1 to vary a costs order so as to make a party to the litigation responsible for paying the costs of another party against whom a costs order had already been made. That party had at the trial been regarded as 'good' in relation to the order for costs but proved to be insolvent. The three conditions that had to be satisfied for the exercise of this jurisdiction must be carefully noted and satisfied			
13. Costs against solicitors			
Under s 51 of the Senior Courts Act 1981 the court has jurisdiction to make a costs order against a party's solicitor and in *Tolstoy-Miloslavsky v Aldington* [1996] 2 All ER 556, [1996] 1 WLR 736, CA Rose LJ found there are only three categories of conduct which can give rise to an order for costs against a solicitor; the third of which is: 'where a solicitor acts outside the role of a solicitor'. In *Myatt v National Coal Board (No 2)* [2007] EWCA Civ 307, [2007] 4 All ER 1094, [2007] 1 WLR 1559 Dyson LJ stated: 'I have no doubt there is jurisdiction to make an order under s 51(3) against a solicitor where the litigation is pursued by the client for the benefit or to a substantial degree for the benefit of the solicitor'			

	Form No	CPR Rule	PD
The solicitors had been joined as parties to the appeal pursuant to CPR 48.2 but the court emphasised the need for parties who think they may apply for costs against solicitors to warn them at an early stage to give them reasonable opportunity to consider whether to continue the proceedings. The solicitors were ordered to pay 50% of the appeal costs taking into account the client's partial interest and the failure to give warning			
Wasted costs orders should only be made against lawyers under 2 52(6) of the Senior Courts Act 1981 'where, and to the extent that, the conduct so characterised has been established as directly causative of wasted costs': *Harrison v Harrison* [2009] EWHC 428 (QB), [2009] 1 FLR 1434. The Court of Appeal when allowing an appeal by solicitors against a wasted costs order made against them found that the solicitors had not acted unreasonably in raising a new point at a late stage in possession proceedings and that their conduct did not amount to a breach of their duty to the court: *Hallam Peel & Co v Southwark London Borough Council* [2008] EWCA Civ 1120, [2008] All ER (D) 200 (Oct).			
For applications against solicitors for a wasted costs order and to make the solicitors third party funders where they were acting under a conditional fee agreement (CFA) but there was after the event insurance see the unreported case of *Poppy Kitts v City of Westminster Council* (4 May 2010, Central London County Court), discussed by Helene Pines Richman in an article entitled 'Avoiding non-party costs' in NLJ (2010) 18 June, page 873; the applications failed.			
14 Interest on costs			
An unpaid order for costs gives rise to a judgment debt on which interest is payable. The statutory provisions are the Judgments Act 1838 (as amended) for High Court judgments and s 74 of the County Courts Act 1984 for county court judgments.			

	Form No	CPR Rule	PD
Interest in the county court is generally not payable on sums of less that £5,000 but this is in respect of the total of the damages and costs. Interest in the county court is suspended on the issue of enforcement proceedings that produce some payment: County Court (Interest on Judgment Debts) Order 1991. Interest in the High Courts and county courts is payable at the rate specified in the Judgments Act 1838, s 7 and is presently 8%.			
For a detailed consideration of this topic, including the discretion that is vested in the court, see NLJ, 11 April 2008, page 514 for an article entitled 'Interest on costs: a definitive guide'.			

TABLE 25A—COSTS CAPPING ORDERS

TAB 25A

	Form No	CPR	PD
1. Nature of costs capping orders			
1.1 Such an order limits the amount of future costs (including disbursements) which a party can recover pursuant to a future order for costs and may be made at any stage in the proceedings. It does not affect the amount that a party can spend but he will not be able to recover costs in excess of the cap.			
The order may be sought by any of the parties against any other party or parties.			
CPR 44.18-CPR 44.20 largely implement the existing case law (see *King v Telegraph Group Ltd (Practice Note)* [2004] EWCA Civ 613, [2005] 1 WLR 2282, [2004] 25 LS Gaz R 27) and clearly the intention is not to encourage cost capping applications in routine cases.			Costs PD, para 23A.1–23A.5
1.2 It may relate to (a) the whole litigation, or (b) any issue ordered to be tried separately			

	Form No	CPR	PD
1.3 It does not apply to protective costs orders (PCOs): see *Eweida (Nadia) v British Airways* [2009] EWCA Civ 1025, 153 Sol Jo (no 40) 37, 15 October.			
1.4 Future costs means costs incurred after the date of the costs capping order but not any additional liability (ie base costs only not any percentage increase under a CFA or an ATE insurance premium).		44.18(1)–(4)	
2. Pre-conditions to be established			
2.1 The court must be satisfied (a) It is in the interests of justice that an order be made (b) There is a substantial risk that without such an order costs will be disproportionately incurred (c) That the risk of disproportionate costs cannot be adequately controlled by (i) case management directions or Part 3 orders (ii) detailed assessment of costs		44.18(5)	
For detailed consideration by the Court of Appeal see *Willis v Nicholson* [2007] EWCA Civ 375, [2007] All ER (D) 205 (Mar)			
3. The exercise of the court's discretion			
The court's power is discretionary and it will consider all the circumstances of the case including: (a) whether there is a substantial financial imbalance between the position of the parties (b) whether the costs of determining the amount of the cap are likely to be proportionate to the overall costs of the litigation (c) the stage the proceedings have reached (d) the amount of the costs incurred to date and the future costs		44.18(6)	Costs PD, para 23A.1

	Form No	CPR	PD
Costly satellite litigation is to be avoided; see for example *Dawson v First Choice Holidays* (unreported, Birmingham DR No 5 BM 15097), Macduff J and note article 'If the cap fits' by Chris Letham (2009) NLJ 27 March, page 469 and article of the same title by Andrew Butler (2009) Sol Jo, 27 October, page 11. Judges can be expected to be astute to prevent cost capping being used to stifle a party's case and will make such an order 'only in exceptional circumstances'.			
For the meaning of 'proportionate' in this context (ie proportionate to what?) see *Barr v Biffa Waste Services Ltd (No 2)* [2009] EWHC 2444 (TCC), [2009] NLJR 1513 per Coulson J and *Eweida v British Airways plc*, above in this TAB at 1.3.			
In *Peacock v MGN Ltd* [2009] EWHC 769 (QB), [2009] AlL ER (D) 88 (Apr) the Judge indicated he was: 'inhibited both by the exceptionality principle and by the fact he was satisfied that the risk of disproportionality could be adequately controlled by a costs judge at the stage of detailed assessment' He refused to make the order but it must be observed that the costs judge would be faced with a fait accompli.			
Where claimants are conducting group litigation and have the benefit of after the event insurance a costs capping order linked to the limit of the ATE insurance is not appropriate and costs management directions and the assessment of costs should control the level of costs: see *Barr v Biffa Waste* above.			
4. The effect of the costs capping order			
4.1 Once the order is made it will limit the costs recoverable by the party against whom the order was made unless a party successfully applies to vary the order			
4.2 A variation will not be made unless:			

	Form No	CPR	PD
(a) there has been a material and substantial change of circumstances, or (b) there is some other compelling reason		44.18(7)	
5. The procedure for obtaining a costs capping order			
5.1 Such an order must be sought by application on notice in accordance with Part 23 and generally not before a CMC; see *Eli Lilly & Co Ltd v James* [2009] EWHC 198 (QB) albeit Coulson J in *Barr v Biffa Waste* (see above) stated it was important that costs capping applications be made 'as soon as possible' and in *Willis v Nicholson* [2007] EWCA Civ 199, [2007] PIQR P318, 151 Sol Jo LB 394 it was stated that the application should be made before or at the first case management conference.	N244		
5.2 The application must specify the matters set out in CPR 44.19(2)(a) and be accompanied by estimates of costs in accordance with CPR 44.19(2)(b)			
5.3 The court may give directions and these may: (a) direct any party to file: (i) a schedule of costs in the form set out in the Practice Direction supplementing this rule (ii) written submission on all or any part of the issue arising (b) fix the date and time estimate for the hearing of the application (c) indicate whether the judge hearing the application will sit with an assessor and (d) include any further directions it thinks fit			Schedule of Costs Precedents annexed to Costs PD – form illustrated in Precedent H

	Form No	CPR	PD
6. The procedure for obtaining a variation of the order An application to vary must be in accordance with Part 23 and can only be varied on a substantial change of circumstances or of there is some other compelling reason An order can be made to vary a cap retrospectively but it ifs likely to be only in a case where the circumstances are exceptional that a judge will be persuaded to make an order for retrospective variation.	N244	44.18 and 44.20	
7. An alternative solution			
In *Barr v Biffa Waste* (above) as a result of observations made by Coulson J the claimants consented to an order that the eventual recovery of future costs would not exceed the amount of their costs estimate. For more detailed discussion see article (2009) NLJ, 13 November, page 1578 by Julia Mowbray.			

TABLE 26—CHANGE OF SOLICITOR

TAB 26

	Form No	CPR	PD
1. Preliminary			
For the importance that the court attaches to the freedom of a litigant to instruct the lawyer of his choice see *British Sky Broadcasting Group plc v Virgin Media Communications Ltd (formerly NTL Communications Ltd)* [2008] EWCA Civ 612, [2008] 4 All ER 1026, [2008] 1 WLR 2854			
See CPR Pt 6 and the Practice Direction to CPR Pt 6 as to the necessity of establishing the address for service of a party who is being represented by a solicitor See also the General Notes to CPR Pt 42 at para **CPR 42 [1]** Where a party has provided the business address of his solicitor as his address for service, that address will remain the address for service until CPR Pt 42 (Change of Solicitor) is complied with			

	Form No	CPR	PD
2. Failure to comply with CPR Pt 42		42.1	42, para 1(1)
The solicitor whose business address has been given will be considered as still acting until compliance			
Rules 6.7 and 6.23 contain provisions about service on the business address of a solicitor			
3. When notice is required			
Notice is required when:		42.2	
(a) there is a change of solicitor (b) where a party appoints a solicitor having previously acted in person (except where the solicitor is only employed as an advocate at a hearing)			42, para 1(3)
(c) where a party who was previously represented by a solicitor intends to act in person			
4. Procedure			
The party or his new solicitor must serve notice of change on every other party and, where appropriate, the former solicitor and then file notice of change		42.2(2)	
The notice filed at the court should be in the prescribed form which includes a statement that notice of the change has been served on all parties and any former solicitor and gives a new address for service	N434	42.2(3) and (4)	
Note: • The former solicitor will still be considered to be acting as the party's solicitor until the notice is filed or the court makes an order – see below			
• The court cannot order a party to appoint new solicitors: *SMC Engineering (Bristol) Ltd v Fraser* (2001) Times, 26 January, CA			

	Form No	CPR	PD
5. Special provisions when a party changing solicitor is an "assisted person", etc			
Where the certificate of a LSC funded litigant or an assisted person is revoked or discharged, the solicitor who acted for that person will cease to be the solicitor acting The solicitor must give notice of the revocation or discharge to the court, the other parties and to counsel		42.2(6)(a)	
If the former funded or assisted person wishes to continue any solicitor appointed must comply with CPR 42.2 or if a solicitor is not appointed the party must give an address for service within the United Kingdom (Rules 6.23 and 6.24 contain provisions about a party's address for service)		42.2(6)(b)	42, para 2.4
6. Order that a solicitor has ceased to act			
A solicitor may apply for an order that he has ceased to be the solicitor acting for a party		42.3	
The application must be served on the party, unless the court otherwise orders and must be supported by evidence	N244, PF 149		
Where the court makes the order it must be served on all parties and a certificate of service filed	PF 150	42.3(3)	
The solicitor will still be considered the party's solicitor until the order is filed and served in accordance with CPR 42.3(3); see note immediately below		42.2(5)	42, para 1.2
Note: • The application for an order must not be served on the other parties, service is only to be effected on the party who was formerly the client			

	Form No	CPR	PD
• It has been held to be appropriate in a simple case for the application to be made in writing by letter: *Miller v Allied Sainif (UK)* (2000) Times, 31 October, NEUBERGER J so that the costs of an attendance at court can be avoided • There are differing views as to whether costs would have to be sought by separate action against the client. In many courts costs are ordered on the pragmatic view that this saves the expense of further proceedings		42.3(3)	70, para 4
Where solicitors are plainly unwilling to continue to act due to a serious breakdown in their relationship with their client they cannot be forced to continue acting and an order will be made removing them form the record: *UCB Bank plc v Hedworth* [2002] All ER (D) 173 (Dec) The Court of Appeal in *Buxton v Mills-Owen* [2010] EWCA Civ 122 considered the circumstances in which a solicitor can 'reasonably' terminate a retainer and the entitlement of the solicitor to recover costs and disbursements up to the date of termination. The case was one where the client required a case to be put forward that the solicitor and counsel regarded as 'bound to fail'. The Court held that the solicitors were officers of the court and as such, and by the Code of Conduct 2007, 'not to put forward any contention not considered to be reasonably arguable'. Therefore the solicitors' termination of the retainer was on reasonable grounds and although the contract between the parties was an 'entire contract', the retainer having been terminated on reasonable grounds they were entitled to be paid for work done and to be reimbursed for disbursements incurred prior to the termination. For a decision based on the terms and limits of a solicitor's retainer see *Tom Hoskins plc v EMW Law (a firm)* [2010] EWHC 479, [2010] All ER (D) 54 (Apr).			

	Form No	CPR	PD
7. Removal of solicitor who has ceased to act on the application of another party			
See **CPR 42.4** and note the court has an inherent power to remove a solicitor where facts exist which give rise to a reasonable lay apprehension of bias: *Re L (minors) (care proceedings: cohabiting solicitors)* [2000] 1 WLR 100			
8. Solicitor ceasing to act by reason of death, etc			
For application for declaratory order see	PF 147		
For declaratory order see	PF 148		
9. Solicitor ceasing to act by reason of conflict etc			
See *Marks & Spencer plc v Freshfields Bruckhaus Deringer (a firm)* [2004] EWHC 1337 (Ch), [2004] 3 All ER 773, [2004] 1 WLR 2331 where it was stressed that the 'double employment rule' which prevented solicitors acting for two clients with conflicting interests is not limited to conflicts in the same transaction. An injunction was granted to the claimants preventing the defendants acting See also as to 'conflict' *Hilton v Barker Booth and Eastwood (a firm)* (2005) Times, 4 February, HL			
10. New address for service			
Where the court makes an order under r 42.3 (that a solicitor has ceased to act) or under r 42.4 (declaration that a solicitor has ceased to be a solicitor for the party) the party for whom the solicitor was acting must give a new address for service to comply with rr 6.23(1) and 6.24.			42, para 5.1

TABLE 27—ORDERS TO OBTAIN INFORMATION FROM JUDGMENT DEBTOR

TAB 27

	Form No	CPR	PD
1. Preliminary			
During the course of any litigation, care should be taken to preserve any information that will be relevant when trying to establish the defendant's financial position; as to transfer between county courts and within the High Court see CPR 30.1–30.5 and as to transfer between Divisions and to and form a specialist list see CPR 30.5 and note *National Amusements (UK) Ltd v White City (Shepherds Bush) LLP* [2009] EWHC 2524 (TCC), [2010] BLR 24.			
If the debtor owns land, official copies can be obtained of any title registered under the Land Registration Act 1925 without quoting the title number or having the permission of the registered proprietor *Note:* CPR Pt 71 and the Practice Direction supplementing it		71	71
The court exercised its inherent jurisdiction under s 34(2) of the Senior Courts Act 1981 to make an order enabling an applicant, other than a registered proprietor, to obtain access to the index of properties at the Land Registry in *Parkinson v Hawthorn* [2008] EWHC 3499 (Ch), [2009] 1 WLR 1665. This was to facilitate enforcement of orders made in separate proceedings.			
S 95 et seq of the **Tribunals, Courts and Enforcement Act 2007** makes amendments but their implementation is being delayed by the Ministry of Justice: see note at **TAB 30**, para 1 below.			
2. Retained CCR provisions – CCR Ord 25			
Of the retained provisions note in particular: • CCR Ord 25 r 1 as to definitions of "judgment debtor" and "judgment creditor"			

	Form No	CPR	PD
• CCR Ord 25 r 6 as to descriptions of parties			
3. Application for an order requiring the debtor to attend court to provide information			
If the judgment debtor is a company or corporation, the application will be to enforce the attendance of one of its officers. The information that it is sought to obtain will be as to the judgment debtor's means and any other information needed for enforcement of the judgment		71.2	
The application may be made at any time the judgment or order became enforceable without notice and must be made to the court which made the judgment or order unless the proceedings have been transferred to another court		71.1 71.2(2)	
The application must be in the form required by the CPR PD 71 fee £50 and contain the information that is required. The application form does not need to be served on the judgment debtor	N316 (individual) N316A (company or corpora-tion)	71.2(3)	71, para 1.1 71, para 1.2(1)–(7)
4. The order			
The application may be dealt with by a court officer and, if it complies with the rule, an order will be made for the judgment debtor to attend court at a place and time there specified to answer questions on oath. He will also be ordered to produce such documents as are specified	N39	71.2(4) 71.2(5) and (6)	
The order will contain a notice that:		71.2(7)	
"You must obey the order, if you do not you may be sent to prison for contempt" The court officer may refer the application to a judge if appropriate and will refer it to a judge if the application is for the judgment debtor to be questioned before a judge			71, para 1.2(5)

	Form No	CPR	PD
It should be noted that the making of the order is a matter for the discretion of the court. In practice the order is invariably made unless the amount is considered to be too small or there has been such delay as to be regarded as prejudicial			
5. Service			
Personal service must be effected not less than 14 days before the hearing. If the judgment creditor is to serve he must inform the court at least 7 days prior to the hearing if he has not done so		71.3	71, para 3
The alternatives to service by or on behalf of the judgment creditor are: (i) service by a High Court enforcement officer; (ii) service by a county court bailiff			
Service by an alternative method can be ordered but the court will be reluctant to commit if the debtor does not appear and service has not been personal		6.8	6, para 9.1
It was held in *Vitol SA v Capri Marine Ltd* [2008] EWHC 378 (Comm), [2008] All ER (D) 437 (Feb) that an order under the CPR against an officer of a corporate judgment debtor requiring him to attend and produce documents was not an order against the judgment debtor and accordingly there is no jurisdiction to give permission for service of an order made under CPR 71.2 and an order permitting service out of the jurisdiction. Both orders were set aside.			
The House of Lords decided in *Masri v Consolidated Contractors International Co SAL* [2009] UKHL 43, [2009] All ER (D) 340 (Jul), (2009) NLJ 7 August, page 1137 that an order under CPR 71 cannot be made against a company officer who is outside the jurisdiction.			

	Form No	CPR	PD
6. Travelling expenses			
A person ordered to attend may, within 7 days of being served request payment of a sum "reasonably sufficient to cover his travelling to and from court" This must be paid by the judgment creditor if requested		71.4	
7. The judgment creditor's affidavit			
The judgment creditor must file an affidavit by the person who served the order (unless it was served by the court):		71.5(1)	
• giving details of service • stating that no request for travelling expenses has been made or that the judgment debtor has been paid the requested sum • stating how much of the judgment debt remains unpaid The affidavit must be filed at least 2 days prior to the hearing or the judgment creditor must produce it at the hearing		71.5(2)	
If it is not possible to deal with all the required matters in one affidavit, additional affidavits may be filed			
8A. The hearing (**other than before a judge**)			
The person attending will be questioned on oath		71.6	
The court officer will ask a standard series of questions as set out in Appendices A and B to the Practice Direction to CPR Pt 71			71, para 4.1
The judgment creditor or his representative may attend and put questions himself or request the court officer to ask additional questions by attaching a list of them to his application notice			71, paras 4.1 and 4.2
The court officer will make a record of the evidence, read the evidence over to the person being questioned and request him to sign the record. If he refuses to sign that fact will be recorded			71, para 4.3

	Form No	CPR	PD
Note: If the proceedings are tape recorded these steps will be unnecessary			
An order to attend court for questioning shall be initially listed for a hearing in private unless the court otherwise orders.		39.2(3)(c)	39, paras 1.5(6) and 1.8
8B. The hearing – before a judge			
If the hearing is before a judge, the questioning will be by the judgment creditor or his representative and standard question forms will not be used. The proceedings will be tape recorded		71.6(3)	71, para 5
The order will provide for questioning before a judge only if the judge considering the request decides there are compelling reasons to make such an order			71, para 2(2)
8C. The hearing – adjournment			
If the hearing is adjourned for any reason the court will give directions as to the service of the new hearing date on the judgment debtor		71.7	
9. Failure by judgment debtor to comply with the order			
9.1 If the person against whom the order is made:		71.8	
(a) fails to attend (b) refuses to take the oath or to answer any questions (c) otherwise fails to comply with the order, the officer or judge must certify in writing the nature of the failure to comply and refer the matter to a High Court judge or a circuit judge		71.8(1)	71, para 6
Provided any travelling expenses requested have been paid and the judgment creditor's affidavit complies with the rules, the judge **may** make a committal order	N79A	71.8(2)	
9.2 If the committal order is made, the judge will direct that the order be suspended provided that person: (a) attends court at a time and place specified in the order, and			

	Form No	CPR	PD
(b) complies with the terms of the original order and of the suspended committal order		71.8(4)	
9.3 The appointment will before a judge if: (a) the original order was to attend before a judge, or (b) the judge making the committal order so directs, but otherwise will be before a court officer. The provisions of CPR 71.3 and para 3 of the CPR PD 71 apply to the service of the order and CPR 71.5(1)(a) and (2) apply as to the affidavit of service			
10. Failure of debtor to comply with the terms of the suspended committal order			
10.1 If the judgment debtor fails to attend and it appears to the judge or court officer that he has been duly served, the judge or court officer will certify in writing the non-attendance			71, para 8.1
Similarly, if the debtor fails to comply with any other term of the suspension it will be so certified in writing			71, para 8.2
10.2 A warrant to bring the judgment debtor before a judge may be issued on the basis of a certificate of non-attendance	N40A		71, para 8.3
The hearing may take place before a Master or district judge			71, para 8.4
10.3 The judge will discharge the committal order unless he is satisfied beyond reasonable doubt that:			
(a) the judgment debtor had failed to comply with– (i) the original order to attend court, and (ii) the terms on which the committal order was suspended, and (b) both orders have been duly served on the judgment debtor *Note*: If the debtor is prepared to submit to the original order to provide information and does answer the questions put the court is likely to discharge the order despite the debtor's breach			71, para 8.5

	Form No	CPR	PD
10.4 If the judge decides the committal order should not be discharged a warrant of committal shall be issued immediately			71, para 8.6
11. Human Rights Act 1988			
When deciding whether the committal order should be enforced by the issue of a warrant, the court will seek to ensure that the defendant's human rights are respected, e g provision of written details of contempt, adequate opportunity to obtain legal advice, opportunity to mitigate			
12. Costs			
For fixed costs as to service, see CPR 45.5, Table 4 (£15) For fixed costs of attendance to question the debtor, see CPR 45.6, Table 5 (£15 for each half hour or part thereof)			

TABLE 28—TRANSFER OF PROCEEDINGS FOR ENFORCEMENT AND OTHER GENERAL ENFORCEMENT RULES

TAB 28

	Form No	CPR	PD
1. Preliminary			
See CPR Pt 70 and the Practice Direction to that Part. As to transfer from county court to High Court, see CCR Ord 25 r 13			
1.1 Prior to enforcement it is sensible to check on the debtor's financial position for there is no point in paying court fees and incurring costs if there is no real prospect of recovery. A search of the Register of Judgments, Orders and Fines (RJOF) maintained by Registry Trust Ltd, 173–175 Cleveland Street, London, W1T 6QR (or DX 137592 Euston 4) may be well worth while Since 6 April 2006 High Court money judgments are registered along with county court judgments etc A 'Request for Search of the Register' form will have to be completed. A fee is payable; the fee for a search against a single name on one of the registers is £8			

	Form No	CPR	PD
A search can be requested online at www.registry-trust.org.uk with payment by credit or debit card			
The telephone number is 010 7380 0133 and the e-mail address is info@registry-trust.org.uk			
These tables do not deal with enforcement by service of a statutory demand but see para **III INS [27]** in Volume 2 and *Collier v P&MJ Wright (Holdings)* [2007] EWCA Civ 1329, [2007] All ER (D) 233 (Dec) and articles by Duncan Adam (2008) Gazette, 15 May, page 30, by Michael Walsh (2009) NLJ, 12 June, page 857 and by Veronica Cocks 'An unreasonable demand' in (2009) Sol Jo, 9 June, page 11.			
2. Enforcement of High Court judgment or order in a county court			
A judgment creditor seeking to enforce a High Court judgment or order in the county court must first apply to the High Court for an order transferring the proceedings to the appropriate county court: County Court Act 1984 s 40(4), (6) and (7)	N244	70.3	
Note: • Section 1(2)(b) and (c) of the Attachment of Earnings Act 1971 and s 1(2) of the Charging Orders Act 1979 • The appropriate court for enforcement is the court where the debtor resides or carried on his business After transfer the judgment, the creditor must file, in addition to his application or request for enforcement: (a) a copy of the judgment or order (b) a certificate verifying the amount due (c) a copy of the relevant enforcement officer's return to any writ of execution issued in the High Court (d) a copy of the order transferring the proceedings to the county court			70, para 3

	Form No	CPR	PD
• 'enforcement officer' means an individual who is authorised to act as an enforcement officer under the Courts Act 2003, and 'relevant enforcement officer' means (a) in relation to a writ of execution which is directed to a single enforcement officer, that officer; (b) in relation to a writ of execution directed to two or more enforcement officers, the officer to whom the writ is allocated **3. Transfer of county court proceedings to another county court for enforcement**			70, para 3.2
Where a judgment creditor is required by Rule or Practice Direction to enforce a judgment or order of one county court in another county court, he must make a written request for transfer. A court officer will then transfer the proceedings and the court will give notice of transfer to the parties			70, para 2
The Production Centre will transfer claims issued in the Northampton County Court to the defendant's home court for oral examination or where enforcement of a judgment (other than by warrant of execution, charging order or third party debt order) is to follow			7C, para 1.3 (f)
4. Transfer of county court proceedings to the High Court			
The judgment creditor may request a certificate of judgment under CCR Ord 22 r 8(1) for enforcing a county court judgment or order in the High Court by execution against goods or where the order to be enforced is an order for possession of land against trespassers The grant of the certificate will have effect as an order to transfer the proceedings to the High Court and the transfer will have effect on the grant of the certificate			

	Form No	CPR	PD
No discretion arises where the enforcement sought is against trespassers but if the enforcement sought is against non-trespassers an application must be made to the court under s 42 of the County Courts Act 1984.		CCR Ord 22 r 8(1) and (1A)	
A combined certificate of judgment and request for a writ of fieri facias may be used		CCR Ord 25 r 13	
Note: • For transfer for enforcement of a possession order against trespassers, see **TAB 22** para 4.7	N239A		
• *The Senior Master's Practice Direction of 31 August 1998* [1998] 4 All ER 63 (see **CCR 25r13 [2]**) and in particular that interest will run from the date of the certificate • The judgment creditor will be notified forthwith • Enforcement in the county court is mandatory where the sum to be enforced is less than £600: see **II HCJ [7]**	N328		
• Judgments of the county court in relation to agreements regulated by Consumer Credit Act 1974 cannot be enforced in the High Court: see **II HCJ [7.3]**			
5. General enforcement provisions			
As to payment of whole or part of judgment debt after the issue of enforcement proceedings, see			70, paras 7.1 and 7.2
As to enforcement of judgment against a non party, see		70.4	
As to enforcement against a partnership see			70, paras 6A.1 and 6A.4
As to creditor's ability to use **any method of enforcement** available **either at the same time or one after another, see**		70.2	

	Form No	CPR	PD
6. Interest			
If a judgment creditor claims interest on a judgment he must include in his application or request to issue enforcement proceedings (a) the amount of interest claimed and the amount on which it is claimed (b) the dates from which and to which interest has accrued and (c) the rate or rates of interest claimed			70 para 6
For the entitlement to interest on county court judgments see the County Courts (Interest of Judgment Debts) Order 1991, SI 1991/1184 and note interest only accrues on a judgment debt of at least £5,000 and an enforcement step that proves to any extent successful stops interest accruing. An application for a charging order does not have this effect. A judgment creditor can enforce in the High Court to avoid the provision that enforcement stops interest accruing.			
7. Limitation			
In *Ridgeway Motors (Isleworth) Ltd v Altis Ltd* [2004] EWHC 1843 (Ch) it was held that s 24(1) of the Limitation Act 1980 which bars rights of action after 6 years applies only to the bringing of a fresh action and does not include proceedings by way of execution of a judgment in the same action			
8. Substitution after judgment			
There is power under CPR 19.2 to substitute a party after judgment as well as before it: see *Prescott v Dunwoody Sports Marketing* [2007] EWCA Civ 461, [2007] 1 WLR 2343, (2007) Times, 25 May, CA		19.2(4)	

TABLE 29—ENFORCEMENT OF DECISIONS OF BODIES OTHER THAN THE HIGH COURT AND COUNTY COURTS AND COMPROMISES ENFORCEABLE BY ENACTMENT

TAB 29

	Form No	CPR	PD
1. Preliminary			
1.1 The rule applies where an enactment provides that: (a) a decision of court, tribunal, body or person other than the High Court or a county court; or (b) a compromise may be enforced as if it were a court order or that any sum of money payable under that decision or compromise may be recoverable as if payable under a court order		70.5(1)	
Save in very limited exceptional circumstances tribunals cannot enforce their awards lacking jurisdiction to do so; but see *Rank Nemo (DMS) Ltd v Coutinho* [2009] EWCA Civ 454, [2009] IRLR 672 and discussion of the decision by Bryden and Seldon in NLJ (2009) 3 July, page 943.			
1.2 There are **excluded** from the provision of CPR 70.5(1). (a) any judgment to which Part 74 (see CPR 74) applies. This provides for registration in the High Court of judgments from other jurisdictions and European Community judgments for enforcement (b) arbitration awards (c) any order to which RSC Ord 115 applies, i e confiscation and forfeiture in connection with criminal proceedings (d) proceedings to which CPR 75 (traffic enforcement) applies		70.5(2)	
1.3 The amendments to Part 70 by the 49th CPR update were to enable enforcement of ACAS compromise agreements by court orders although some agreements are not agreements only for the payment of money.			

	Form No	CPR	PD
2. Procedure where it is necessary to obtain a court order to permit enforcement			
2.1 If an enactment provides that a decision or compromise is enforceable or a sum or money is recoverable if the court so orders an application must be made to the court for the district where the person against whom the order is sought resides or carries on business, unless the court otherwise orders		70.5(3) and (4)	
2.2 The application may be made without notice unless it relates to a compromise which requires the person who is to receive payment to do anything in addition to discontinuing or not starting proceedings (a 'conditional compromise'). In this situation the application must be made on notice.			
2.3 The application must be in the form and contain the information set out in CPR PD 70 and must be accompanied by a copy of the decision or compromise	N322A	70.5, 70.6	70, paras 4.2, 4.3
2.4 An application other than the one relating to a conditional compromise may be dealt with by a court officer without a hearing		70.5(7)	
2.5 Where the application relates to a conditional compromise and accordingly has to be made on notice, if the application notice is served on the respondent by the applicant the applicant must file a certificate of service within 7 days of service of the application notice			70, para 4.4
2.6 If the respondent to an application to a conditional compromise opposes it by filing a response within 14 days see		70.5(7A)	

	Form No	CPR	PD
3. Procedure where it is not necessary to obtain a court order for enforcement			
3.1 Unless CPR 70.5(3) applies, i e because the enactment or compromise states it is enforceable or recoverable if a court so orders, a party may enforce the decision or compromise by applying for a specific method of enforcement under CPR Parts 71 to 73 (obtaining information, third party debt order and charging orders, stop orders and stop notices) or RSC Orders 45 to 47 (execution) or RSC Order 52 (committal) or CCR 25 to 29 (warrant of execution, attachment of earnings, judgment summons and committal)		70.5(2A)	
3.2 The party enforcing must (a) file with the court a copy of the decision or compromise being enforced and (b) provide the court with the information required by the PD	N322B	70.5(2A)	70, para 4.1
3.3 Where the decision to be enforced is: (i) a decision of an employment tribunal; or (ii) the application is for the recovery of a compromise sum under s 19A(3) of the Employment Tribunals Act 1996 and enforcement is to be by issue of a writ of fieri facias the form to be used is form	N471 in situation (i) N471A in situation (ii)		70, para 4.1A
This method of enforcement of tribunal awards was introduced with effect from 6 April 2010 and amended with effect from 1 October 2010.			

TABLE 30—SEIZURE OF GOODS – WRIT OF FI FA AND WARRANT OF EXECUTION

TAB 30

	Form No	CPR	PD
1. Preliminary			
Part 3, ss 62–90 and Schedules 13 and 23 of the **Tribunals, Courts and Enforcement Act 2007** make considerable changes in the enforcement of judgment by the taking of goods. The Ministry of Justice has announced it will delay implementation of Parts 3 and 4 and it is Part 3 which reforms the enforcement rules and introduces a code dealing with the position comprehensively including rights of entry, what goods can be seized and fees payable. See article by Monty Trent in Sol Jo for 21 April 2009, page 16 and Sara Partington's 'Update – commercial' in Sol Jo (2009) 16 June, page 21. In the High Court a writ of fieri facias is issued to the enforcement officer or enforcement officers authorised to enforce writs of execution to seize and sell the judgment debtor's goods to satisfy the money due under the judgment and the costs of execution. In the county court the warrant of execution will be issued to the bailiff In either case the judgment creditor should try to satisfy himself that the judgment debtor has goods that can be seized and should supply as much relevant information as he can to the enforcement officer or the bailiff, as the case may be, to facilitate the execution *Note:* • As to **goods protected against execution**, see the Senior Courts Act 1981 s 138 and the County Courts Act 1984 s 9 • For the dire consequences that can result from the seizure of protected goods see *Brookes v Harris* [1995] 1 WLR 918, QBD			

	Form No	CPR	PD
• The bailiff may not **break open doors** or force his way into the judgment debtor's home to execute a warrant of execution: *Vaughan v McKenzie* [1969] 1 QB 557, [1968] 1 All ER 1154 • See II CCA [87.2] for the nature and effect of a **walking possession** agreement and *McLeod v Butterwick* [1996] 3 All ER 236 with the appeals *Khazanchi v Fairfield* and *McLeod v Butterwick* [1998] 2 All ER 901, CA and **II CCA [87.3]**. A bailiff distraining is not entitled to re-enter a dwelling-house by force except where having entered peaceably he was expelled by force or has been deliberately excluded by the occupier and prevented thereby from re-entering lawfully As to the position when the bailiff has taken walking possession of goods and the debtor becomes bankrupt or being a limited company enters into liquidation, see para CCR 26 r 8[1] • Where judgment is in the name of a firm, permission will be necessary to enforce against **the goods of individual partners** unless they are not limited partners and come within one of the categories set out in paragraph 6A.2(1)–(4) of the Practice Direction to Part 70 For enforcement against a limited partner or a partner who is normally resident outside the jurisdiction see paragraph 6A.3 of the Practice Direction			70, para 6A

	Form No	CPR	PD
• A warrant cannot be issued in a county court where there is an **instalment order** in existence which is not in arrears: County Courts Act 1984 s 86. If the payments are in arrears a warrant can be issued for all or part of the unpaid debt (subject to a minimum of £50 or one month's of 4 weeks' instalments)		CCR Ord 26 r 1(3)	
2. Which court			
2.1 High Court judgment or order			
A judgment or order of the High Court or a judgment, order, decree or award which is or has become enforceable as if it were a High Court judgment can be enforced in the High Court or in any county court for the district in which the levy is to be effected		CCR Ord 26 r 2(1)	
For requirement of transfer of the proceedings to the county court, see **TAB 28** para 2			
2.2 County court judgment or order			
Judgment or orders where the amount sought to be enforced is less than £600 or arising under an agreement regulated by the Consumer Credit Act 1974 can only be enforced in the county court Judgments or orders where the sum sought to be enforced is £5,000 or more can only be enforced in the High Court In any other case judgments or orders of the county court can be enforced in the High Court or county court: High Court and County Courts Jurisdiction Order 1991 in particular Article 8(1) It is clear the amount sought to be enforced, as opposed to the amount of the judgment, is determinative. Where enforcement is sought in the High Court, see **TAB 28** para 4			
3. Permission to issue			
For cases where permission is required in the High Court, see		RSC Ord 46 r 2(1)	

	Form No	CPR	PD
For cases where permission is required in the county court, see		CCR Ord 26 r5(1)	
Note: • The most frequent case where permission must be sought is where 6 years have elapsed since the date of the judgment or order: see *Duer v Fraser* [2001] 1 All ER 249. Permission can be sought by application supported by witness statement or affidavit made initially without notice	N244		
• The one situation where permission is needed in the High Court but not in the county court is where the entitlement to the remedy is subject to any condition which it is alleged has been fulfilled			
4. Procedure			
4.1 High Court		RSC Ord 46 r 6	
A praecipe must be filed signed by or on behalf of the solicitor together with the writ for sealing.	PF 86 No 53–63		
At the time of issue there must be produced: (a) the judgment or order on which the writ is to issue (or the certificate of the county court judgment or order) (b) the order giving permission to issue in those cases where this is necessary There are special provisions where the judgment was obtained in default of appearance against a state			
If the court officer is satisfied that the time allowed for compliance has elapsed he will seal the writ		RSC Ord 46 r 6(4)(b)	
The writ is then served on or sent to: (a) an enforcement officer assigned to the district in which the writ is to be executed, or			

	Form No	CPR	PD
(b) if no enforcement officer has been assigned to the district to the National Information Centre for Enforcement (NICE) at 20–21 Tooks Court (off Chancery Lane), London, EC4A 1LB for allocation, or (c) to an enforcement officer whether or not assigned to that district who has undertaken to execute the writ			
There is a directory of High Court Enforcement Officers which is available at www.dca.gov.uk/enforcement/egeneral.htm			
4.2 County court			
A judgment creditor files a form of request (fee in county court £100 reduced to £70 for bulk issue) and if it is a High Court judgment or order to be enforced he must also file:	N323	CCR Ord 26 r 1	70, para 3
(a) an office copy of the judgment or order (b) a certificate verifying the amount due (c) if a writ of execution has been issued, a copy of the relevant enforcement officer's return (d) a copy of the order for transfer The court officer will issue the warrant, give it a number, give notice to the judgment debtor and forward the warrant to the bailiff On a request for a further attempt at execution of a warrant at a new address following a notice of non-execution a further fee of £25 is payable (except for a further attempt following suspension and bulk order cases).	N326 or N327		
5. Duration of a warrant and renewal			
Renewal is not a formality particularly if it raises questions of **priority**			
5.1 High Court			
A writ of execution is valid in the first instance from 12 months from the date of issue		RSC Ord 46 r 8	

	Form No	CPR	PD
A writ of execution not wholly executed can be extended from time to time for a period of 12 months at any one time. It must be sealed showing the date of the order of extension			
A notice sealed by the court must be served on the High Court enforcement officer informing him of the making of the order and its date			
Application will be without notice supported by a witness statement or affidavit explaining the delay in enforcement			
5.2 County court			
A warrant shall, for the purpose of execution, be valid in the first instance for 12 months from the date of issue. It may be renewed for a period of 12 months at any one time: (a)from the day after its expiry if it is renewed pursuant to an application made before that day, or (b)from that day or such later day (if any) as the court shall allow if not made until after expiry County courts will frequently accept a letter as sufficient application for renewal		CCR Ord 26 r 6	
6. Withdrawal and suspension of warrant at creditor's request			
The warrant may be suspended by the court at the creditor's request normally as a result of an arrangement made with the debtor. If the debtor defaults, the creditor can request the re-issue of the warrant. The warrant when reissued will, however, have lost its priority against warrants issued during the period of suspension		CCR Ord 26 r 10	
7. Stay of execution			
7.1 High Court			
Where the court is satisfied on application by the judgment debtor made to it at the time of the judgment or order or at any time thereafter that:	N244	RSC Ord 47 r 1	

	Form No	CPR	PD
(a) there are special circumstances that make it inexpedient to enforce the judgment or order, or (b) the applicant debtor is unable to pay the money, it may stay enforcement by writ of fieri facias either absolutely or for such period and on such conditions as the court thinks fit			
Note: There is also the power to stay on ground of matters that have occurred since the date of the judgment or order		RSC Ord 45 r 11	
7.2 County court			
The power of the court to suspend or stay a warrant of execution is exercisable by a district judge and in accordance with the rules by a proper officer		CCR Ord 25 r 8	
See notes at **CCR 25r8 [1]–CCR 25r8 [3]**			
The debtor's application is in Form	N245		
The judgment creditor's reply is in Form	N246A		
If the judgment or order is suspended the order is in Form	N41		

TABLE 31—WRIT OR WARRANT OF DELIVERY

TAB 31

	Form No	CPR	PD
1. Preliminary			
See note at **TAB 30**, para 1 above. The form of writ or warrant depends on the nature of the relief given by the court. The warrant can either be one which allows the judgment debtor to **return the goods or pay their value** or one for **specific delivery** which directs the seizure of the goods and their delivery to the claimant The writ of delivery issued by the High Court is directed to the relevant enforcement officer whilst a warrant for delivery issued by the county court is directed to the bailiff			

	Form No	CPR	PD
2. Permission to issue			
Permission is required in the same circumstances as for seizure of goods: see **TAB 30** para 3 and see also below, para 3.1			
3. Procedure			
3.1 High Court			
Where the judgment or order is for the return of goods without the alternative of payment, enforcement will be by writ of specific delivery	No 64	RSC Ord 45 r 4(1)	
Where the judgment or order is for the return of goods but gives the alternative of payment of the assessed value, enforcement may be:	No 65	RSC Ord 45 r 4(2)	
(a) by writ of delivery without permission, or (b) by writ of specific delivery with prior permission of the court A writ of delivery or a writ of specific delivery can include provision for enforcement of any money to be paid pursuant to the judgment being enforced		RCS Ord 45 r 4(3)	
The permission necessary to issue a writ of specific delivery, notwithstanding that the judgment or order gave the alternative of payment of assessed value, should be sought by application supported by evidence. The court has a discretion to grant the permission and the application should be made on notice	N244	RSC Ord 45 r 4(2)	
The judgment creditor seeking **issue** of a writ of delivery or specific delivery must file a praecipe with the form of writ for sealing	PF 90		
He must also produce at the time of issue: (a) the judgment or order on which the writ is to issue, and (b) any necessary order giving permission to issue The writ form number 64 is appropriate for specific delivery. The form number 65 is appropriate for delivery. The writ is then served on the appropriate under-sheriff by the judgment creditor			

	Form No	CPR	PD
The writ of delivery will contain a recital of the judgment or order requiring the defendant to deliver 'the goods'. It must contain a sufficient description of the goods			
3.2 County court			
The judgment creditor files a request for the issue of a warrant for delivery (fee £95)	N324		
If the judgment or order gives the alternative of payment of assessed value, permission of the court will have to be obtained for the issue of a warrant of specific delivery. The application on notice will be supported by evidence	N244		
The appropriate warrant for specific delivery is Form	N46	CCR Ord 26 r 16	
The appropriate warrant for delivery is Form	N48		
The warrant will be directed to the bailiff. If the goods are in the district of another county court the warrant will be endorsed to the district judge of that court for execution	N53		
4. Stay or suspension of execution			
The position in the High Court and the county court is the same as for seizure of goods: see **TAB 30** paras 6 and 7			

TABLE 32—ATTACHMENT OF EARNINGS

TAB 32

	Form No	CPR	PD
1. Tribunals, Courts and Enforcement Act 2007			
By ss 91 and 92 of this Act and Sch 15 substantial amendments are made to the Attachment of Earnings Act 1971. The Ministry of Justice has indicated it will delay implementation of parts of the Act. See note at **TAB 30**, para 1 above. The amendment to attachment of earnings is amongst those whose implementation has been delayed. For text see **CCR 27r1 [1]** to **CCR 27r1 [25]**.			

	Form No	CPR	PD
1A. Preliminary			
See CCR Ord 27 and note: • **"the Act of 1971"** means the Attachment of Earnings Act 1971 • **"the normal deduction rate"** (**NDR**) is the periodic rate at which the court thinks it reasonable for the debtor's earnings to be applied towards the judgment debt or debts – the Act of 1971 s 6(1)(5)(a) • **"the protected earnings rate"** (**PER**) is the rate below which the court thinks it reasonable that the earnings actually paid to the debtor should not be reduced – the Act of 1971 s 6(1)(5)(b) • **"earnings"** are wages or salary or pension payments other than the guaranteed minimum pension under the Social Security Pensions Act 1975. For a full definition, see s 24 of the 1971 Act and note in particular that pay or allowances of a member of HM Forces are not earnings • Payments under a contract for services (self-employment) are not included in contrast to payments under a contract of service (employment) • s 16 of the Act of 1971 enables an application to be made for the court to determine whether particular payments are earnings: CCR Ord 27 r 1(16)			

	Form No	CPR	PD
• **the name and address of the judgment debtor's employer** does not have to be known to the judgment creditor before the issue of the application for attachment of earnings as the court will ask the judgment debtor for this information and for any job number. It is preferable if the judgment debtor can give this information as it enables the court to enquire direct of the employer for wage details if the judgment debtor fails to respond to the enquiry	N338		
2. The enforcement of maintenance payments under the Act of 1971			
Such enforcement is governed by a somewhat different procedure under the Act of 1971 and is not dealt with in this Procedural Table			
3. Jurisdiction of the county court			
The county court can make attachment of earnings orders to secure: (a) payments under a High Court or county court maintenance order (not dealt with in this Procedural Table) (b) the payment of a judgment debt if not less than £50 or for the balance remaining due under a judgment debt for not less than £50 (for definition of "judgment debt", see s 2(c)(1) of the 1971 Act)			
(c) payments under an administration order – s 1(2)(c) of the Act of 1971 *Note*: any one of the creditors scheduled to the administration order may make the application: s 3 of the 1971 Act		CCR Ord 27 r 7(9)	
4. The appropriate county court			
Generally, an application for an attachment of earnings order may be made to the court for the district in which the debtor resides		CCR Ord 27 r 3(1)	

	Form No	CPR	PD
If the debtor resides outside England or Wales or his address is unknown, see		CCR Ord 27 r 3(2)	
If the application is against 2 or more debtors jointly liable, see		CCR Ord 27 r 3(3)	
For transfer to defendant's court when judgment was obtained in another county court see **TAB 28** para 3			70, para 2
5. Issue			
5.1 Prior to issue it is prudent to search the **Index** kept by each county court of the debtors within its district against whom there are attachment of earnings in force. Any person having a judgment or order against a person residing within the district can cause a search to be made	N336		
5.2 The judgment creditor on issue must file his application form (county court fee £100 for each defendant against whom an order is sought), certifying:	N337	CCR Ord 27 r 4(1)	
(a) the amount of money remaining due under the judgment or order, and (b) that the whole or part of any instalment due remains unpaid If the order to be enforced is a High Court judgment or order it will also be necessary to file: (a) a copy of the judgment or order, and (b) if a writ of execution has been issued in the High Court, a copy of the relevant enforcement officer's return			70, para 3
No order for transfer from the High Court would seem necessary: see definition of judgment debt in s 2(c) of the 1971 Act. However, the court on issue may maintain transfer is necessary to comply with CPR 70.3 and para 70.3 of the Practice Direction to CPR Pt 70 A certificate verifying the amount due is incorporated in the application form, which also requires the court where the judgment was obtained to be specified if it was not the court of issue	N337		

	Form No	CPR	PD
5.3 On receipt of the relevant documents and payment of the court fee of £60, a court officer: (a) enters the issue in the court records (b) endorses the copy request with the number and date of the application and sends a copy to the creditor (c) makes out notice of application and form of reply in the appropriate forms with copies for service	N55 and 56	CCR Ord 27 r 5(1)	
6. Service and reply			
Service will be in accordance with CPR 6.20		CCR Ord 27 r 5(1)	
The debtor shall within 8 days of service of the documents on him file a reply in the form provided, but no proceedings for failing to do so shall be taken unless the documents have been served on him personally or the court is satisfied that they came to his knowledge in time for him to do so	N56	CCR Ord 27 r 5(2)	
Note: • A debtor who pays the judgment within the time stated need not reply. The creditor must inform the court of payment • The court will send a copy of any reply to the applicant • The court may at any time send a **notice to any person apparently employing** the debtor to give the court within the time specified a statement of the debtor's earnings or anticipated earnings	N338	CCR Ord 27 r 6	
• If the employer fails to respond, enforcement is by service of any order endorsed with a penal notice requiring production of the earnings statement: s 14(1)(b) of the Act of 1971	N61A		

	Form No	CPR	PD
7. The order			
7.1 On receiving the debtor's reply, provided he has sufficient information, the court officer will make an attachment of earnings order. Unless the order is suspended a copy will be sent to the parties and to the debtor's employer	N60	CCR Ord 27 r 7	
7.2 If the court officer makes a suspended order, the order will not be sent to the employer to make deductions so long as the debtor makes the payments that have been ordered direct to the creditor: s 71(2) of the County Courts Act 1984	N64		
Note: • If there is default the creditor can request the order to be directed to the employer by letter giving details of the default • Whether or not the order is suspended it will fix the PER and the NDR – s6(5) of the Act of 1971			
7.3 Where the court officer does not have sufficient information he will refer the application to the district judge who will decide the application either without a hearing, if he is able to do so, or after a hearing of which the parties must be given at least 8 days' notice		CCR Ord 27 r 7(3) CCR Ord 27 r 7(4) CCR Ord 27 r 7(5)	
8. Reconsideration of the order			
8.1 Where the order is made by a court officer or by a district judge (without a hearing), the judgment creditor or the debtor may, within 14 days of receipt of the order, apply on notice, giving reasons, for the order to be reconsidered. The court will fix an appointment before the district judge and the parties will be given at least 8 days' notice of the hearing		CCR Ord 27 r 7(2) and (6)	
8.2 On the hearing the district judge may confirm the order made or set it aside and make a new order		CCR Ord 27 r 7(7)	
For the position where the creditor does not appear, see		CCR Ord 27 r 7(8)	

	Form No	CPR	PD
9. Failure by the debtor to return reply form or pay debt			
9.1 If the debtor fails to file his reply in the prescribed form or make payment to the judgment creditor, the court officer may, pursuant to s 14 of the Act of 1971, order the **production of a statement of means**		CCR Ord 27 r 7A	
The order will incorporate or be endorsed with a notice warning the debtor of the **consequences of his disobedience** (committal for up to 14 days or fine up to £250) and must be **personally served** on the debtor. The order will also direct that all future payments must be paid into court and not direct to the **judgment creditor**	N61	CCR Ord 27 r 7A(1)	
9.2 If the debtor **fails either to pay or file his statement of means** the court officer will issue a notice for the debtor to show cause **why he should not be imprisoned** and fix a **date for the hearing** before a district judge. This order must be served personally	N63	CCR Ord 27 r 7A(2)	
Note: if the debtor files the statement of means or pays the debt immediately the hearing will be cancelled			
10. Hearing for debtor to show cause			
The judge or district judge has power to **suspend any committal** order made and is likely to do so on terms that the debtor attends court at a specific date and time and completes the statement of means form within 8 days of service	N118		
Note: • The ability of the court to order that the defendant be arrested and brought before the court forthwith or at a particular time and date for the disobedience of an order under s 23(1) of the Act of 1971	N112A		

	Form No	CPR	PD
• The judge or district judge may direct that when a debtor is arrested, pursuant to a committal order made as a result of the debtor's failure to attend a hearing to show cause, that the debtor be brought before him after arrest and before he is imprisoned: s 23(1A) of the Act of 1971			
• The jurisdiction to commit may be exercised by the district judge as well as by the judge: s 23(11) of the Act of 1971 **11. Variation, discharge and lapse of orders**			
Provisions as to these matters are set out in s 9 of the Act of 1971 Where the debtor leaves the employment of the employer to whom the order is directed the order will **lapse** and will have no effect unless and until the court directs it to a person who appears to have the debtor in employment			
12. Consolidated orders			
Where two or more attachment of earnings orders are in force or the court receives an application for such an order and an attachment of earnings order is already in force the court may make a consolidated attachment of earnings orders		CCR Ord 27 r 18	
See further:		CCR Ord 27 rr 19–22	
13. Guide to Employers			
HM Courts Service has published a revised guide to employers explaining how an attachment of earnings order should be operated			

TABLE 33—THIRD PARTY DEBT ORDERS

TAB 33

	Form No	CPR	PD
1. Preliminary			
Third party debt orders were previously called garnishee orders and can be sought by a judgment creditor having an unsatisfied money judgment, payment of which by the judgment debtor (who is within the jurisdiction) is overdue		72.1	
For the priority enjoyed by the holder of an interim third party debt and the effect of that interim order being made final see *FG Hemisphere Associates LLC v Republic of Congo* (2006) Times, 27 February			
Third party debt orders are not subject to limitations as to time. Part 72 makes no reference to the time elapsed from the date of the judgment. A lapse of 6 years was held in *Westacre Investments Inc v Yugoimport SDPR* [2008] EWCA Civ 801 (Comm), [2008] 1 All ER (Comm) 780 to be of no special significance for third party debt orders; it was just one factor to be taken into account in the overall exercise of discretion.			
Note: CPR 70.2, which provides that a judgment creditor (defined in CPR 70.1(2)) may use more than one method of enforcement at the same time or one after another *Note:* CPR 72 and in particular the provision for a "hardship payment order" at CPR 72.7			
Note: Where the third party is a deposit-taking institution it can deduct a prescribed sum, presently £55, towards the costs and expenses of responding to the order; see further CPR 72.4 and Attachment of Debts (Expenses) Order 1996 in CPR 72.4[4] above			
For cases where the LSC has a charge on the debt see *Beechwood Construction Ltd v Afza* [2008] EWHC 2671 (Ch), 31 October			

	Form No	CPR	PD
For consideration of the difficulties and litigation that can arise from the payment of a debt by a third party see *Treasure & Son Ltd v Dawes* [2008] EWHC 2420 (TCC), [2007] All ER (D) 386 (Oct) and article 'Disputed treasure' by Daniels and Milliner in NLJ, 12 December 2008, page 1748			
2. Debts not susceptible to third party debt orders			
These include: (a) money in court under a judgment, but see CPR 72.10 (b) a debt owed to the debtor and another (who is not subject to the judgment) jointly: *Macdonald v Tacquah Gold Mines Co* (1884) 13 QBD 535, CA (c) a joint bank account: *Hirshorn v Evans* [1938] 2 KB 801. See also *Cohen v Cohen* (1982) 12 Fam Law 251 (d) salary accruing but not yet due or a debt that is contingent, see *Kier Regional Ltd v City and General (Holborn) Ltd* [2008] EWHC 2454 (TCC), [2008] All ER (D) 189 (Oct) (e) money payable to the Crown: see s 27 of the Crown Proceedings Act 1947 at **III CRO [19]** (f) unliquidated damages (g) a legacy in the hands of an executor prior to an account stated (h) credit balance governed by Hong Kong law or money held in judgment debtor's Swiss bank account; see *Societe Eram Shipping Co Ltd v Compagnie Internationale de Navigation* [2003] UKHL 30, [2003] 3 All ER 465 and *Kuwait Oil Tanker SAK v Qabezara* [2003] UKHL 31, [2003] 3 All ER 501			72, para 3.2(1) and (2)

	Form No	CPR	PD
But note: A debt that is not payable until a date in the future is nevertheless capable of being the subject of a third party debt order: *Tapp v Jones* (1875) LR 10 QB 591 and see generally CPR 72.2[6]–[7]. However the debt must be actually owed in the name of the judgment debtor: *Continental Transfert Technique Ltd v The Federal Government of Nigeria* [2009] EWHC 2898 (Comm), [2009] All ER (D) 239 (Nov).			
3. Application			
This may be made without notice but must be in the form and contain the information required by the relevant Practice Direction	N349	72.3(1) 72.3(2)	72, para 1.2(1)–(10)
It must be verified by a statement of truth			22, para 1.4(1)
The application must be to the court which made the judgment order or, if the proceedings have been transferred to another court, to that court		72.3(1)(b)	
A user of the Production Centre wishing to enforce a judgment by third party debt order may ask for transfer to the court of his choice for this purpose			
The court will not grant speculative applications for third party debt orders			72, para 1.3
The application will not be served on the judgment creditor			
On the application of a judgment debtor who wishes to oppose the application, the court must transfer to the court where the debtor resides or carries on business, or to another court			72, para 4
The court fee on issue is £100 and is payable in respect of every party against whom the order is requested			

	Form No	CPR	PD
4. Interim third party debt order			
The application will be dealt with without a hearing and, if he is satisfied that there is sufficient evidence that the third party is within the jurisdiction and owes money to the judgment creditor, the judge **may** make an interim order which will:		72.4 72.4(2)	
(a) fix a hearing to consider whether a final order should be made		72.4(2) and (3)	
(b) direct that the third party must not make any payment which would reduce the sum owed to the judgment debtor below the sum specified in the order (c) specify the amount of money which the third party must retain, being the total of the judgment debt remaining due and the creditor's fixed costs			72, para 2
For consideration of the cogency of the evidence that is likely to be required for the grant of an interim debt order see *Alawiye v Mahmood* [2005] EWHC 277 (Ch), [2006] 3 All ER 668 where Lindsay J explained that the whole point of the interim stage, where a bank or building society is the proposed third party, is to establish that there is evidence to substantiate the belief that the judgment debtor has an account with the bank or building society in question but not that it is presently in credit The reason why it is believed the third party is indebted to the defendant and the source of the information that forms the basis of the belief must be given. For a case where the court was prepared to pierce the corporate veil when it found it to be a sham see *Kensington International Ltd v Republic of Congo* [2005] EWHC 2684 (Comm), [2005] All ER (D) 370 (Nov) and article by Friedman and Wilcox [2006] 156 NLJ 27 January, p 148			72, para 1.3

	Form No	CPR	PD
The interim order will bind the third party from the time it is served on him but only freezes the required sum not the whole of the third party's debt.		72.4(4)	
For the priority of a judgment creditor who has obtained an interim third party debt order see *FG Hemisphere Associates LLC v Republic of Congo* (2006) Times, 27 February			
The hearing date must be no less than 28 days after the interim order		72.4(5)	
5. Service			
Service of the interim order, with the application notice and any documents filed in support, must be effected:		72.5	
(a) on the third party not less than 21 days before the hearing date (b) on the judgment debtor not less than 7 days after service on the third party and not less than 7 days before the hearing date Where the judgment creditor serves, he must either file a certificate of service not less than 2 days before the hearing or produce the certificate at the hearing			
For the attachment of debts owed by partnership for provisions as to service see			72, para 3A.2
6. Third party's obligations after being served			
After the service of the interim order, the third party must within 7 days: (a) **if a bank or building society**, inform the court and the creditor –		72.6 72.6(1)–(3)	72, para 3.1 and 3.2
(i) whether, or not, the judgment debtor has an account which can be identified and, if so, the account number (ii) whether there is sufficient credit to cover the amount specified in the order or, if not, the amount of the credit balance at the date of service			

	Form No	CPR	PD
(iii) whether the bank or building society asserts any right to the money in the account			
(b) **if not a bank or building society**, inform the court and the creditor if he claims not to owe any money to the judgment debtor or that he owes less than the amount specified in the order		72.6(4)	
7. Hardship payment orders			
7.1 A judgment debtor who is an individual who is suffering hardship in meeting ordinary living expenses, by reason of a third party debt order, preventing him withdrawing money from a bank or building society, can make an application for a hardship payment order		72.7 72.7(1)	
7.2 The application for a hardship payment order will be dealt with by the court to which it is made (in the county court to any county court) and must provide detailed evidence of the debtor's needs and be verified by a statement of truth		72.7(4)	72, paras 5.1–5.3 and 5.6 22 para 1.4(1)
The applicant should attach relevant documents to show the truth of his statements of fact			
The application must be served on the judgment creditor at least 2 days before the hearing but if there is exceptional urgency see the Practice Direction to CPR Pt 72 para 5.4		72.7(5)	72, paras 5.4 and 5.5
7.3 If the hardship order is made it can permit the third party to make one or more payments of specified amounts out of the account to specified persons		72.7(6)	
8. Hearing of the application for a final third party debt order			
If the judgment debtor or the third party objects to the court making the order or knows, or believes that some person other than the judgment debtor has a claim to the money, he must file and serve written evidence of his objection or knowledge		72.8(1) and (2)	

	Form No	CPR	PD
If the judgment creditor disputes the third party's case he must file and serve written evidence setting out his grounds		72.8(3)	
All evidence must be filed as soon as possible and in any event not less than 3 days before the hearing		72.8(4)	
A person, other than the judgment debtor, who the court is informed has a claim to the money specified in the interim order, will be served with notice of the application and the hearing		72.8(5)	
For the appropriate response to submissions by other creditors, at the final hearing, that the interim order should be discharged, see *FG Hemisphere Associates Ltd v Republic of Congo* (2006) Times, 27 February, CA			
9. The order			
At the hearing the court **may**: (a) discharge the interim debt order and dismiss the application (b) decide any issues in dispute		72.8(6)	
(c) direct a trial of an issue and give necessary directions (d) make a final third party debt order requiring the third party to pay to the judgment creditor –		72.2(1)	
(i) so much of the debt due from him as is sufficient to satisfy the balance outstanding of the judgment debt and the costs of the application, or (ii) where the amount owing to the judgment debtor is not sufficient to satisfy the amounts specified in (i) above, the whole of the debt owed by the third party to the judgment creditor A final third party debtor order will not require a payment which leaves less than £1 in the debtor's account with a building society or credit union			72, para 6

	Form No	CPR	PD
10. Costs			
Any costs of the application awarded to the judgment creditor shall be retained by him from the moneys recovered and the moneys recovered should be treated as having first been used for this purpose		72.11	
The court fee payable on issue is £100 in respect of each person against whom an order is sought			
The fixed costs are: • if the amount recovered is less than £150, one half of the amount recovered • otherwise, £98.50		45.6, Table 4	
11. Enforcement			
A third party debt order is enforceable as an order to pay money Any moneys paid in compliance with the order or as a result of its enforcement shall be treated as reducing or extinguishing the amount due by the third party to the judgment debtor For enforcement of third party debt orders against an unincorporated association see *Huntingdon Life Sciences Group plc v Stop Huntingdon Animal Cruelty* [2005] EWHC 2233, (2005) Times, 2 November			
12. Money in court			
An application for a third party debt order cannot be made against such moneys but the judgment creditor can apply for an order for the payment out to him of such part of the moneys as will satisfy his debt	N244	72.10	
The moneys in court cannot be paid out until the application is disposed of			

TABLE 34—CHARGING ORDERS

TAB 34

	Form No	CPR	PD
1. Preliminary			
1.1 See CPR Pt 73 and the Practice Direction supplementing it, and note in particular:			

	Form No	CPR	PD
• "the 1979 Act", meaning the **Charging Orders Act 1979** • "the 1992 Regulations", meaning the **Council Tax (Administration & Enforcement) Regulations 1992** Before making the application, an attempt should be made to calculate whether **the equity** in the property justifies the application. Information should be sought from office copies of the Register if the land is registered and, in appropriate cases, by oral examination			
1.2 The court has a **discretion** to make a charging order and s 11(5) of the 1979 Act requires the court to consider all the circumstances of the case and in particular any evidence before it as to: (a) the personal circumstances of the debtor, and (b) whether any other creditor would be likely to be unduly prejudiced by the making of the order			
1.3 As to the discretion and its exercise, the following should be noted: • the burden of showing cause why an order nisi should not be made absolute is on the debtor: *Rosseel NV v Oriental Commercial and Shipping (UK) Ltd* [1990] 3 All ER 545 • prejudice to other creditors does not preclude the making of a charging order although it may be considered as one of the circumstances of the case. Generally the law recognises the rights of the diligent, see per Denning LJ in *Pritchard v Westminster Bank Ltd* [1969] 1 All ER 999, CA. The rights of another creditor actually objecting to the making of the charging order are of more significance than the rights of other creditors generally which are raised by the debtor.			

	Form No	CPR	PD
• a charging order may be made and an order for sale can be made to enforce it even if it is only for a small amount compared to the value of the property: see *Packman Lucas Ltd v Mentmore Towers Ltd* [2010] EWHC 1037 (TCC). • the court has no power to make a charging order unless the debtor is in default under the court order or judgment: *Mercantile Credit Co Ltd v Ellis* (1987) Times, 1 April but if the interim charging order precedes the instalment order the interim charging order may be made final: *Ropaigealach v Allied Irish Bank* [2001] EWCA Civ 1790, [2002] 03 EG 130 • judgment interest accruing in the future will be secured by the charging order although not specifically mentioned: *Ezekiel v Orakpo* [1997] 1 WLR 340, CA (the rate of such interest is presently 8%) • a charging order can be expressed in a foreign currency, being the currency in which the parties had chosen to deal; *Carnegie v Giessen* [2005] EWCA Civ 191, [2005] 1 WLR 2510 • a debtor cannot sit back and await enforcement before making an application to set aside judgment; *Nolan v Devonport (decd)* [2006] EWHC 2025 (QB) where such an application was held to be an abuse of process and an attempt to frustrate enforcement			
Sections 93 and 94 of the **Tribunals, Courts and Enforcement Act 2007** makes amendments to the 1979 Act and insert s 3A which will deal with the power to set financial thresholds. See note at **TAB 30**, para 1 above as to the delay in implementation. For text see **CPR 73 [12]** to **CPR 73 [16]**.			

	Form No	CPR	PD
2. The property that may be charged			
2.1 The beneficial interest of the debtor in the following property may be charged to enforce a judgment or order of the High Court or county court to pay money to another person: (a) land (b) government stock (c) stock of any body (other than a building society) incorporated within England and Wales (d) stock registered in a register kept within England and Wales even though the body is incorporated outside England and Wales (e) unit trusts (f) funds in court (g) any interest under a trust (s 2(2) of the 1979 Act) (h) any property, within the jurisdiction, belonging to a judgment debtor that is a partnership (see para 4A of PD 73)			
2.2 Section 23 of the Partnership Act 1890 provides that (i) execution shall not issue against partnership property except on a judgment against a firm; (ii) on an application by summons of any judgment creditor of a partner the court may make an order charging that partners' interests in the partnership property and profits with payment of the judgment debt.			
See **III PAR [43]** in Volume 2.			
The application must be made in accordance with CPR 23. For procedure see		73.22	73, para 6
3. Jurisdiction – appropriate court			
See s 1(2) 1979 Act			73, para 2
(a) Where the property to be charged is a **fund in court**, that court is the appropriate court: s 1(2)(a)			

	Form No	CPR	PD
(b) Where (a) does not apply and the order to be enforced is a **maintenance order of the High Court**, the application can be appropriately made to the High Court or a county court: s 1(2)(b) (c) Where neither (a) or (b) apply and the judgment to be enforced is a **High Court judgment or order** or one that has been **transferred to the High Court** and which **exceeds £5,000** (the county court limit), the application can be made to a High Court or a county court: s 1(2)(c) (d) **In all other cases** a county court is the appropriate court: s 1(2)(d) (e) A user of the Production Centre wishing to enforce a judgment by charging order may ask for transfer to the court of his choice for this purpose			
4. The application			
4.1 The application may be made without notice. Where the application is made to a county court it must be issued in the court where the judgment or order was made unless the proceedings have been transferred to another court (fee payable £100)		73.3(1) and (2)	
4.2 A judgment debtor who wishes to oppose an application for a charging order may apply for transfer to the court where he resides or carries on business			73, para 3
4.3 Note that if the application is made under the 1992 Regulations it must be issued in the county court for the district in which the property is situated but the claimant can seek a transfer to another county court for enforcement		73.3(2)(b)	
5. The form of the application			
The application notice must contain:	N379 (land) N380 (securities)		

	Form No	CPR	PD
(a) the name and address of the judgment debtor (b) details of the judgment or order sought to be enforced (c) the amount of money remaining due under the judgment or order (d) if the judgment debt is payable by instalments, the amount of any instalments which have fallen due and remain unpaid (e) if the judgment creditor knows of the existence of any other creditors of the judgment debtor, their names and (if known) their addresses (f) identification of the asset or assets which it is intended to charge (g) details of the judgment debtor's interest in the asset, and (h) the names and addresses of the persons on whom an interim charging order must be served under CPR 73.5(1)			73, para 1.2
The application must be verified by a statement of truth		73.3(4)(b)	
Note: • The application is not served on the respondent/debtor • A judgment creditor may make a single application in respect of one or more judgments or orders against the same debtor • A judgment creditor may make a single application to charge more than one asset, although separate orders have to be drawn in respect of each asset charged		73.3(3)	73, para 1.3
• If the asset is registered land, an official copy of the Register provides the best evidence of the asset and the judgment debtor's interest in it			

	Form No	CPR	PD
6. The interim charging order			
The application will be dealt with by a judge without a hearing and if he is satisfied there is sufficient evidence of the judgment debtor's ownership of or interest in the property and that the procedure has been complied with, he **may** make an **interim charging order** and fix a **hearing date** when consideration will be given to making a final charging order		73.4	
Where the asset is land or an interest in it, the charging order should be protected by registration of a notice (where the legal estate is charged) or restriction in Form K (where a beneficial interest only is charged) under **the Land Registration Act 2002** (for registered land) or the registration of a land charge under **the Land Charges Act 1972** (for unregistered land) to fix a prospective purchaser with notice: s 3(2) of the 1979 Act Where the interest of a joint owner of registered land is the subject of a charging order the right or claim in relation to the registered estate can be protected by a restriction; see Rouff and Roper, para 42.023.04 Great care must be taken when registering under the Land Charges Act 1972 to ensure the full and correct name of the judgment debtor is given			
For the effect of an interim order on securities held by the judgment debtor, see		73.6	
Where an interim charging order is protected by a notice on the register a further application should be made to protect a subsequent absolute order			
For the effect of an interim order in respect of funds in court, see		73.7	
The appropriate Land Registry form to be lodged to register a restriction is RX1			

	Form No	CPR	PD
7. Service			
Copies of the interim charging order, the application notice, and any documents filed in support of it, must be served not less than 21 days before the hearing and must be served on: (a) the judgment debtor		73.5(1)(a)	
(b) such other creditors as the court directs		73.5(1)(b)	
(c) if the order relates to an interest under a trust, on such of the trustees as the court directs		73.5(1)(c)	
Note: • If land is held in joint names a trust of land is created and if the beneficial interest charged is that of one of the beneficial owners the court will order service on the other joint owner as a trustee			
(d) If the interest charged is in funds in court, the order will direct service on the Accountant General at the Court Funds Office		73.5(1)(e)	
(e) If the interest charged is in securities, see		73.5(1)(d)	
(f) If the property to be charged is the property of a partnership			73, para 4A.2
Note: If the judgment creditor serves, he must file a **certificate of service** not less than 2 days before the hearing or produce the certificate at the hearing		73.5(2)	
8. Adjournment of the hearing for the final charging order			
If there is to be an adjournment it is important to ensure the court order provides that **the charging order nisi will remain effective** until the adjourned hearing date.			

	Form No	CPR	PD
9. The hearing to decide whether a final charging order should be made			
Any person who objects to the making of the order must do so not less than 7 days prior to the hearing file and serve **written evidence of the ground of his objection**		73.8(1)	
At the hearing the court may:		73.8(2)	
(a) make a final charging order confirming that the charge imposed by the interim charging order shall continue, with or without modification (b) discharge the interim charging order and dismiss the application (c) decide any issues in dispute between the parties, or between any of the parties and any other person who objects to the court making a final charge order, or (d) direct a trial of any such issues, and if necessary give directions *Note:* • If the court discharges the interim charging order and dismisses the application, the defendant should request the court to include in its order a requirement for the claimant to cause any entries protecting the interim order under the Land Registration Acts or Land Charges Act 1979 to be cancelled. The order should specify which of the parties is to make the application, within what time and at whose expense. • For the position where the debtor becomes the subject of a bankruptcy order between the interim charging and the hearing to make that order final see *Togo Investments SA v Official Receiver* [2009] All ER (D) 63 (Jan) and note that the discretion of the court to make the order final is only to be exercised in an exceptional case.			

	Form No	CPR	PD
Where a bankruptcy petition is presented against the debtor between the interim order and the final charging order the judgment creditor is not to be deprived of his security by reason of the petition resulting in a bankruptcy order made after the final order: *Wright v Nationwide Building Society* [2009] EWCA Civ 811, [2009] All ER (D) 305 (Jul). The charging order is however susceptible to discharge under the Charging Orders Act 1979, s 3(5): *Berry Ltd v Armstrong and Noakes decd* [2007] EWHC 2010 (QB), [2007] BPIR 1199. For the position where an interim Individual Voluntary Arrangement is in force when the application is made to make the Interim Charging Order final see *Clarke v Coutts & Co* [2002] EWCA Civ 943, [2002] BPIR 916, [2002] 26 LS Gaz R 40 and s 252(2) of the Insolvency Act 1986. • If the court makes a final charging order charging securities other than securities in court it must include a stop order unless the court otherwise directs			
For stop orders, see		73.11	
• The court will also make an order for costs (normally fixed costs of £110) and the judgment creditor should have a **list of disbursements** incurred, with a copy for the judgment debtor so that a request can be made for an order that these be paid. The position as to costs in Table 5 to CPR 45.6 refers to 'reasonable disbursements' in respect of search fees and the registration of the order. The court fee on issue is £50 for every party against whom the charging order is sought.		45.6, Table 4	

	Form No	CPR	PD
• The position under the **Land Registration Act 2002** or the **Land Charges Act 1972**, as the case may be, should be considered again to ensure that the final order is duly protected or whether a further registration is required. For registered land see Land Registry Practice Guide 19 which is obtainable free of charge from any Land Registry Office			
10. Discharge or variation of the final charging order			
Section 3(5) of the 1979 Act and reg 51(4) of the 1992 Regulations provide that the court, on application, may make an order discharging or varying the charging order	N244		
The application must be made to the court which made the charging order		73.9(1)	
The court may direct that any interested person be joined or served with the application		73.9(2)	
Any order discharging or varying the charging order must be served on all the persons on whom the charging order was required to be served		73.9(3)	
The court should be asked to make clear in the order who is responsible for making any application necessary, because of the discharge or the variation, under the Land Registration Act 2002 or the Land Charges Act 1972			
11. Enforcement of charging order by sale			
A county court has jurisdiction to deal with an application to enforce if the amount owing under the charge does not exceed the county court limit (£30,000 pursuant to s 23 of the County Courts Act 1984 and the County Courts Jurisdiction Order 1981)			

	Form No	CPR	PD
An application to enforce a charging order by way of sale made to the High Court may be transferred by that court to the county court although the proceedings would otherwise fall outside the jurisdiction of the county court (for the extent of that jurisdiction see the immediately preceding sub-para): *National Westminster Bank plc v King* [2008] EWHC 208 (Ch), (2008) Times, 14 April. The court transferred down under CCA 1984, s 40(2) having decided that the county court was the appropriate tier in the court system.			
Enforcement of a charging order by sale is not an action on a judgment but a fresh action taken by the judgment creditor and is accordingly not subject to a 6 year limitation period for the recovery of interest under s 24 of the Limitation Act 1980: *Ezekiel v Orakpo* [1997] 1 WLR 340, CA and see *Yorkshire Bank Finance Ltd v Mulhall and Mulhall* [2008] EWCA Civ 1156, [2008] All ER (D) 241 (Oct) where the Court of Appeal further held that a charging order is not extinguished after the 12 year limitation period in the Limitation Act 1980, s 20(1). See further **III LIM [25]** in Volume 2.		73.10(2)	55, para 7.2
The Court of Appeal held that a charging order is not a judgment and accordingly Limitation Act 1980 s 24(1) which limits actions n a judgment to 6 years does not apply and further s 24(2) which limits interest to 6 years also does not apply. The charging order is an equitable charge which has no associated right to possession of the property charged and therefore could be distinguished from *National Westminster Bank v Ashe* [2008] EWCA Civ 55; see **TAB 22**, part 3, para 3.8 above.			
For the date of accrual of the chargee's right to receive money within s 20(1) Limitation Act 1980 see *Doodes v Gotham* (2006) Times, 14 August, CA			

	Form No	CPR	PD
A claim to enforce in the High Court must be started in Chancery Chambers at the Royal Courts of Justice or a Chancery district registry			73, para 4.2
The court **may** order the sale of property to enforce a charging order to which it is subject, see cases at para **CPR 73.10 [5]** above			
Note: • This method of enforcement where the property is jointly owned but **the charging order is sought against the interests of some, but not all, of the joint owners** can be made by application under CPR 73.10, with the Court applying the provisions of s 14 of the Trusts of Land and Appointment of Trustees Act 1996 or (more usually) by application under that Act (see the final paragraph of this **TAB**). In either case the co-owner of the property should be made a party (to the application or to the claim as the case may be). An application under s 14 of the Trusts of Land and Appointment of Trustees Act 1996 can be made. Careful consideration should be given to the statutory guidelines for the court contained in s 15 of the Trusts of Land and Appointment of Trustees Act 1996 before commencing proceedings. An application under ss 13 and 14 of this Act can be made to the county court by virtue of s 2(1)(p) of the High Court and County Courts Jurisdiction Order 1991 (SI 1991/724) whatever the value			

	Form No	CPR	PD
• Even if application is made under CPR 73.10 the judgment creditor should establish whether there is any equity in the property that will be realised by the sale if ordered. The court is unlikely to order sale, particularly of a family home, lightly (see, however, *Pickering v Wells* [2002] 2 FLR 798, (2002) Times, 4 June, Ch D – sale ordered despite interests of children). Note however *Packman Lucas Ltd v Mentmore Towers Ltd* at para 1.3 above of this TAB and the judgment of Coulson J which sets out the principles to be applied. • If the court that made the order has jurisdiction to determine an application for an order for sale the application should be made there • If the application is made in the High Court it must be made in the Chancery Division • When using the **Part 8 procedure** a copy of the charging order must be filed with the claim form. A hearing date will be given on issue		73.10(4)	
• The **claimant's written evidence** must: (i) identify the charging order and the property sought to be sold (ii) state the amount in respect of which the charge was imposed and the amount due at the date of issue of the claim (iii) verify, so far as known, the debtor's title to the property charged (iv) state, so far as he is able to identify – • the names and addresses of any other creditors who have a prior charge or other security over the property, and • the amount owed to each such creditor, and			

	Form No	CPR	PD
(v) give an estimate of the price which would be obtained on sale of the property (vi) if the claim relates to land give details of every person to the best of the claimant's knowledge is in possession, and (vii) if the claim relates to residential property – (a) state whether – (i) a land charge of Class F; or (ii) a notice under s 31(10) of the Family Law Act 1996, or under any provision of any Act that preceded that section has been registered, and (b) if so state – (i) on whose behalf the land charge or notice has been registered and (ii) that the claimant will serve notice of the claim on that person			
The claimant must take all reasonable steps to obtain the names and addresses of any creditors who may have a prior charge or security over the property and the amount owing in each case			73, para 4.4
The claim form (and any particulars of claim) must be verified by a statement of truth		22.1(1)	
For precedents of claims and the evidence to support them where the debtor is the sole owner and where the debtor is a joint owner, see **BCCP H[33]-BCCP H[36]**			
A sample order for sale, for use when the property is solely owned by the judgment debtor, is set out in Appendix A to the Practice Direction to CPR Pt 73 Note the grant of a term of 3,000 years to the judgment creditor is a conveyancing device to enable him to effect a sale. A prospective purchaser may need considerable explanation			

	Form No	CPR	PD
Where the order for sale is sought to enforce a charging order over the interest of one or some (but not all) co-owners. The application may be made under CPR 73.10 or under s 14 of the Trusts of Land and Appointment of Trustees Act 1996; see above in this section. If the application is made under CPR 73.10 the court will apply the provisions of the 1996 Act and to enable it to do so the co-owner must be made a party to the proceedings. A specimen order for such a sale, if an application under s 14 is successfully made, is also set out in Appendix A to PD 73			73, para 4.5

TABLE 35—WRITS AND WARRANTS OF POSSESSION OF LAND AND THEIR SUSPENSION

TAB 35

	Form No	CPR	PD
1. Preliminary			
• See RSC Ord 45 (but note rr 1(1), 1(2), 1(3), 9, 10, 13 and 14 have been revoked) and CCR Ord 26	N244		
• For transfer of proceedings for enforcement see **TAB 28** • A writ or warrant of possession is enforceable against all persons on the premises whether or not named in the writ or warrant: *R v Wandsworth County Court, ex p London Borough of Wandsworth* [1975] 3 All ER 390, [1975] 1 WLR 1314, CA			

	Form No	CPR	PD
• Occupiers who are not parties may apply to be made parties: CPR 19.2 and 19.4. The court is only likely to make them parties if they have rights against the party seeking to enforce the judgment as opposed to rights against the person against whom the judgment was made or is sought but see **TAB 22**, para 3.6A and this **TAB**, para 3.2 below and the Mortgage Repossessions (Protection of Tenants etc) Act 2010. • Helpful information for a person facing eviction is provided by Community Legal Advice leaflet 'Losing your home' No C6 which additionally provides information about possible sources of assistance in paying the deposit on rented accommodation: CLA telephone number 0845 345 4 345; web address www.communitylegaladvice.org.uk.			
2. Where permission is required for issue			
2.1 In the **High Court** the permission of the court is required to enforce a judgment or order for the giving of possession except: (a) where the order was made in mortgage proceedings as defined in		RSC Ord 45 r 3 RSC Ord 45 r 3(2)	
(b) where the possession order is against trespassers. See further **RSC 45r3 [1]** In the High Court permission will also be necessary where possession was given subject to the fulfilment of a condition, which it is alleged has been fulfilled	N244	55.6 RSC Ord 113 r 7 RSC Ord 46 r 2(1)(d)	

	Form No	CPR	PD
An application on notice supported by evidence is required. There is accordingly an important difference between enforcement of suspended possession orders in the High Court and the county court The application for permission to enforce a judgment must be supported by evidence.	N244	RSC Ord 45 r 3(3) RSC Ord 46 r 4	
Where permission is sought in respect of a house in multi occupancy see **QBG 11.2.3**			
2.2 In the **High Court and the county court** permission will be required where: (a) 6 years have elapsed since the judgment		RSC Ord 46 r 2(1)(a) and (b)	
(b) there has been a change of parties Where permission is not required execution can be issued as soon as the time for delivery up of possession has passed		CCR Ord 26 r 5(1)(a) and (b)	
3. Procedure on issue			
3.1 High Court			
High Court judgments for possession on county court judgments transferred to the High Court for enforcement (see **TAB 25** para 4.7) are enforced by the relevant enforcement officer and not the court bailiff	No 66	RSC Ord 46 r 6(1)	
Issue of a **writ of possession** takes place on its being sealed and a **praecipe** for its issue signed by or on behalf of the solicitors must be filed	PF 88 or 89	RSC Ord 46 r 6(2) and (3)	
At the time of issue there must be produced:		RSC Ord 46 r 6(4)	
(a) the judgment or order on which the writ is to be issued (b) any order giving permission where that is necessary There are special requirements where judgment has been entered against a state in default of appearance		RSC Ord 46 r 6(4)(iii)	

	Form No	CPR	PD
The court, if satisfied that any time given for the delivery of possession has expired: (a) seals a copy of the writ (b) returns it to the solicitors who will send it to the High Court enforcement officer for the district or if one has not been appointed to the National Information Centre for Enforcement (see **TAB 30**, para 4.1)			
3.2 County court			
The judgment creditor files in the court office a request incorporating a certificate of the balance outstanding of any money claim and a certificate that the land which is the subject of the judgment or order has not been vacated	N325	CCR Ord 26 r 17	
Additionally, by reason of an amendment to CPR Ord 26, r 7 made in July 2010, lenders applying for a warrant of possession must certify that they have given 14 days' notice of the execution of a possession order to all tenants or occupiers by first class or registered post or recorded delivery, or by leaving the notice at the property as required by the Execution of Possession Orders (Prescribed Particulars and Notices) (England and Wales) Regulations 2010. The notice has to be given in a prescribed form set out in the schedule to the regulations. Form N325 has been amended accordingly.			
If the judgment or order to be enforced is a High Court judgment or order see **TAB 28** para 2 for further documents that must accompany the request to issue			70, para 3
The court office: (a) allocates next warrant number (b) prepares and seals warrants of possession (c) endorses the warrant with the time of filing (d) adds the appropriate fixed costs	N49		

	Form No	CPR	PD
(e) endorses the request with the date of issue, number of warrant and the receipt for the fee and sends it to the creditor (f) forwards the warrant to the bailiff in whose area the warrant is to be executed *Note:* • Where a warrant for possession is issued, the judgment creditor shall be entitled by the same or a separate warrant to execution against the debtor's goods for any money payable under the judgment		CCR Ord 26 r 17(3)	
• Where an order for possession was suspended on instalment payments, the judgment creditor must certify that the whole or part of any instalment due remains unpaid		CCR Ord 26 r 17(3A)	
4. Duration of a writ or warrant of possession and renewal			
4.1 High Court			
A writ of possession is valid in the first instance from 12 months from the date of issue		RSC Ord 46 r 8	
A writ not wholly executed can be extended from time to time for a period of 12 months at any one time. The writ must be sealed showing the date of the order of extension A notice sealed by the court must be served on the High Court enforcement officer informing him of the making of the order and its date. Application will be without notice supported by a witness statement explaining the delay in enforcement	No 71		
4.2 County court			
A warrant shall, for the purpose of execution, be valid in the first instance for 12 months from the date of issue. It may be renewed for a period of 12 months at any one time: (a) from the date after its expiry if it is renewed pursuant to any application made before that day, or			

	Form No	CPR	PD
(b) from that day or such later day (if any) as the court shall allow if not made until after expiry		CCR Ord 26.17(6) CCR Ord 26.6	
County courts will normally accept a letter as a request for renewal			
5. Suspension of a warrant			
5.1 Secure or assured tenancies			
In the county court the landlord is not required to seek permission to issue the warrant; nor is there any requirements that notice is to be given to the defendant: *Leicester City Council v Aldwinkle* (1991) 24 HLR 40, CA			
It is necessary to establish whether the ground for possession was mandatory or discretionary (all orders should state on their face the ground on which made and whether it was mandatory or discretionary).			
Mandatory orders include: (a) local authority introductory tenancies (b) demoted tenancies (c) assured tenancies (d) persons housed by a local authority discharging its duty to homeless persons			
Where the ground was **mandatory** the normal order for suspension is 14 days; in cases of exceptional hardship the maximum period of suspension is 42 days form the date of the original order: Housing Act 1980, s 89.			
The restrictions imposed by s 89(1) on the court's power to postpone the giving of possession does not prevent an appellate court which has either: (a) granted permission to appeal; or (b) was considering granting such permission, from staying the order for possession until the appeal or application for permission is determined; see *Admiral Taverns (Cygnet) Ltd v Daniel* [2008] EWCA Civ 1501, [2009] 4 All ER 71, [2009] 1 WLR 2192.			

	Form No	CPR	PD
Where orders are made on a **discretionary** ground (even if not suspended) or in a mortgage claim there is a general discretion to suspend.			
The court may stay or suspend execution of the warrant or postpone the date for possession for such period or periods as the court thinks fit: Housing Act 1985 s 85(2) and Housing Act 1988 s 9(2). However an application to suspend cannot be made once possession has been given up: *Dunn v Bradford Metropolitan District Council; Marston v Leeds City Council* [2002] EWCA Civ 1137, [2002] All ER (D) 479 (Jul) If the tenant disputes the landlord's calculation of the arrears of rent, the up to date position has to be accurately established before hearing the tenant's application to suspend: *Haringey London Borough Council v Powell* [1996] 28 HLR 798, CA For application to suspend use:	N244		
The fee payable on the making of an application to suspend a warrant for possession is £35: Civil Proceedings Fees Order 2008, SI 2008/1053.			
The warrant cannot be suspended or set aside after eviction unless: (a) the warrant is defective (b) the warrant was obtained by fraud, or (c) there has been an abuse of process or oppression in the application See *Hammersmith and Fulham Borough Council v Hill* (1995) 27 HLR 368, CA As to "oppressive" see, for example, *Hammersmith and Fulham London Borough Council v Lemeh* (2000) 33 HLR 231, CA and *Jephson Housing v Moisejevs* [2001] 2 All ER 901, CA			

	Form No	CPR	PD
See *Circle 33 Housing Trust v Desmond Ellis* [2005] LTL 17 August (unreported elsewhere) where it was held that, in the circumstances, the execution of a warrant of possession against a tenant who was in receipt of housing benefit was oppressive as it amounted to an unjust exercise of the power granted by the warrant. Prior to evicting the tenant the landlord should have contacted the housing benefit department to find out why the benefit had ceased and whether the rent arrears were likely to be made up *Note:* consideration should be given as to whether the judgment or order on which the warrant is based can be set aside			
5.2 Mortgages			
As to stay or suspension of execution or postponement of date for delivery of possession **by the borrower**, see paras **CPR 55.10 [5]** and **III REA [22]** Note the Protocol for Possession Claims based on Mortgage or House Purchase Plan Arrears in respect of Residential Property (see para **CPR 55 PRO 2**). Note in particular that the powers of the court under the Administration of Justice Acts 1970 and 1973 are available on an application to suspend a warrant to the same extent as they are when hearing an application for a possession order For the **judgment creditor** seeking to oppose an application to suspend, a chronology showing the history of the mortgage account is essential A **judgment debtor** should deal with the reasons for breaches in the past and the effect of having to deliver up possession. In addition, a financial statement showing that his proposals for paying the current instalments and monthly payments of the arrears are realistic is essential. A vital point to make, if it is available, is that there is a sufficient equity in the property that the lender's money is not "at risk"			

	Form No	CPR	PD
If the basis of the application to stay or suspend is that the mortgage debt will be repaid from the proceeds of sale of the property it will be necessary to satisfy the court that the sale can be effected in a reasonable time; see *National and Provincial Building society v Lloyd* [1996] 1 All ER 630 and *Bristol and West Building Society v Ellis* (1996) 73 P & CR 158, CA and note that in *Cheltenham & Gloucester Building Society v Grant* (1994) 26 HLR 703, CA the Court of Appeal declined to lay down rigid rules on how district judges should satisfy themselves about the requirements of s 36 of the Administration of Justice Act 1990			
5.2A As to stay or postponement of the execution of a possession order on application by **an unprotected tenant of the borrower** see **TAB 22**, para 3.6, and this **TAB**, para 3.2 above as to the Mortgage Repossessions (Protection of Tenants) Act 2010 and the Execution of Possession Orders (Prescribed Particulars and Notices) (England and Wales) Regulations 2010 respectively.			
5.3 Former tenants and service occupiers			
Section 89 of the Housing Act 1980 gives the Court making possession orders power to suspend or stay for 14 days and for 6 weeks in cases of exceptional hardship. The restriction under this section does not apply to those actions specified in s 89(2): see **III L&T [98]** in Volume 2. The power given by s 89 is exercisable by the High Court or a county court: *Admiral Taverns (Cygnet) Ltd v Daniel* [2008] EWCA Civ 1501, [2009] 4 All ER 71, [2009] 1 WLR 2192			

	Form No	CPR	PD
5A. Stay of warrant for possession pending an appeal			
The provision in s 89 of the Housing Act 1980 is that an order for possession must take effect not later than 14 days after the hearing of the order and 6 weeks from the order in cases of exceptional hardship but those restrictions do not apply where an appellate court had either granted permission to appeal or was still considering the grant of permission. In these circumstances a stay could be granted pending determination of the appeal or the application for permission to appeal: *Admiral Taverns (Cygnet) Ltd v Daniel* [2008] EWHC 1688 (QB), [2008] 37 EG 153, [2008] All ER (D) 274 (Jul)		3.1(2)(f)	
6. Execution of the warrant			
It is not necessary on the execution of a county court warrant for possession for a bailiff to remove any goods from the premises: s 111 of the County Courts Act 1984 For the position of persons in the premises and not named in the warrant, see para 1 of this Procedural Table The judgment creditor will be required to attend upon the appointment fixed to execute the warrant to change the locks A person may be guilty of contempt of court if he fails to give up possession as required by the order or obstructs a bailiff seeking to execute a lawful warrant of possession: *Robert Arnold Tuohy v Gary Bell* [2002] EWCA Civ 423, [2002] 3 All ER 975			
The court stated it was prepared to take a hard line against those who persistently flaunt final orders when committing the defendant for contempt for his failures to comply with a court order to give up possession in *Canty (a bankrupt) (Trustee of the estate of) v Canty* [2007] EWCA Civ 241, [2007] All ER (D) 63 (Mar)			

	Form No	CPR	PD
7. Restitution			
In the county court a warrant of restitution may be issued with the **permission of the court** where there has been wrongful re-entry by the person evicted	N50	CCR Ord 26 r 17(4)	
The application for permission may be made without notice	N244	CCR Ord 26 r 17(5)	
In the High Court a similar procedure is provided by:		RSC Ord 46 r 3	
See also **QBG 11.2** *Note:* • Form 68 is the form of writ of restitution • Where there have been proceedings for the possession of land against trespassers and the re-entry is by others or includes others, a writ of restitution may be available if there is a sufficient connection between the original defendants and those who have re-entered: *Wiltshire County Council v Fraser* [1986] 1 All ER 65		Part 55	

TABLE 36—COMMITTAL FOR BREACH OF ORDER OR UNDERTAKING (COUNTY COURT)

TAB 36

	Form No	CPR	PD
1. Preliminary			
See paras **CCR 29.1 [0]–CCR 29.1 [33]** and the PD on Committal Applications and note in particular:			
(a) a committal order cannot be made against the Crown		66.6	
(b) an injunction or order against a corporation may be enforced by committal against any officer of the corporation: *Biba Ltd v Stratford Investments* [1973] Ch 281		CCR Ord 29 r 1(1)	
(c) where the alleged contempt is based upon – (i) disobedience of a county court order		CCR Ord 29 r 1	

	Form No	CPR	PD
(ii) breach of an undertaking given to a county court, or		CCR Ord 29 r 1A	
(iii) an act done in the course of proceedings in a county court; or where in any other way the alleged contempt is one the county court has power to punish,			CCR PD 29, para 1.2 and paras 12–14
the committal application may be made to the county court in question			
In any other case the application has to be made to the High Court. For an example of the exercise by the High Court of its power of committal for contempt see *Walton v Kirk* [2009] EWHC 703 (QB), [2009] All ER (D) 70 (Apr) where orders were made for the payment of the defendant's costs from the payment into court and for payment of a fine for contempt where there had been 'exaggeration of symptoms to a considerable and unconscionable degree'. See articles in by Jonathan Scriven NLJ (2009) 29 May, page 786 and by Pedley and Thackeray Sol Jo (2009) 23 June, page 16. In particular note that the standard of proof required is the criminal standard, the importance of properly pleading all allegations and the consideration of the jurisdiction issue by Coulson J.			CCR PD 29, para 1.3
The immense financial consequences of solicitors' failures to perform fully undertakings given by then to discharge a mortgage or charge against a property they are conveying for a client can be seen from the cases of *Thames Valley Housing Association Ltd v Elegant Homes (Guernsey) Ltd* [2009] EWHC 2647 (Ch), [2010] 1 P & CR D39 (£1.35 million liability) and *Clark v Lucas Solicitors LLP* [2009] EWHC 1953 (Ch), [2009] 46 EG 144, [2009] 32 EG 69 (CS).			

	Form No	CPR	PD
There are special provisions where the breach is of an order made pursuant to the Attachment of Earnings Act 1971 (see **TAB 32**) or an order made for obtaining information from a judgment debtor (see **TAB 27**). There are special provisions for Anti-Social Behaviour Injunctions (ASBI) under the Housing Act 1996 (see **CPR 65.5**)			
1A. Committal is a 'last resort'			
It was stressed in *R v Huggins* [2007] EWCA Crim 732, [2007] 2 Cr App Rep 107, [2007] Crim LR 798, criminal division, that committal to prison summarily is a last resort and that the judge hearing the contempt proceedings had to consider whether the object necessary could be achieved by any other step			
1B. Breach of undertaking			
The breach of an undertaking given to the court as part of a consent settlement is actionable by the other party to the settlement as a breach of contract: *Independiente v Music Trading On-line (HK) Ltd* [2007] EWCA Civ 111, [2007] 4 All ER 736, [2008] 1 WLR 608			
In *Zipher v Markem Systems Ltd* [2009] EWCA Civ 44, (200() Times, 27 February the basic issue was whether a binding undertaking had been given or offered to the High Court when it had not been committed in writing. The judgment of Lord Neuberger requires careful consideration, in particular paras 19 to 25. An undertaking to the court does not have to be recorded in writing. Whether an undertaking has been given is a question of fact in every case.			
2. Requirements for issue			
2.1 Committal may be sought where: (a) a person who is required by a judgment or order **to do an act refuses or neglects to do so** within the time fixed by that or any subsequent order, or			

	Form No	CPR	PD
(b) a person disobeys a judgment or order requiring him to **abstain from doing an act**		CCR Ord 29 r 1	
This provision is subject to the Debtors Acts 1869 and 1878, which limit the power to commit for non-payment of a debt to: (a) arrears under a maintenance order, and (b) recovery of income tax and certain other taxes			
2.2 A judgment or order shall not be enforced by committal unless: (a) a copy of the order has been personally served (in the case of a corporation, on a director or other officer)		CCR Ord 29 r 1(2)(a)	
(b) if the order is one requiring an act to be done, the order and any further order made before its service were served before the expiry of the time within which the defendant was required to do the act, and		CCR Ord 29 r 1(2)(b)	
(c) a **penal notice**, i e a notice warning of the consequences of disobedience, was incorporated in or endorsed on the order served		CCR Ord 29 r 1(3)	
The endorsement of a penal notice on an order which the court has made is a mandatory act and a ministerial act as to which there is no discretion. It is an act that can be performed by a court officer.			
The endorsement of a penal notice is not necessary to enable a court to deal with public bodies by contempt or sequestration for failing to deal with the court's orders: see *MSA v Croydon London Borough Council* [2009] EWHC 2474.			
Note:			

	Form No	CPR	PD
• A judgment or order requiring a person to abstain from doing an act may be enforced by committal, notwithstanding he has not been served with a copy of it, if the judge is satisfied the defendant has notice because he was present when the judgment or order was made or he has been notified of its terms whether by "telephone, fax, e-mail or otherwise"		CCR Ord 29 r 1(6)	
• The court may **dispense with service** of a copy of the judgment or order or the claim form or application for committal if the court "thinks it just to do so"		CCR Ord 29 r 1(7)	
• Where service of the claim form or application to commit is dispensed with, the judge may fix a date and time for the defendant to be brought before him or the court		CCR Ord 29 r 1(8)	
• Where an ex parte order was made freezing the absent party's assets it was held he should have been heard before a finding of contempt was made: *Raja v van Hoogstraten* [2004] EWCA Civ 968, (2004) Times, 27 July			
3. Procedure for commencement of committal proceedings			
3.1 If there are existing proceedings, the committal application must be made within these proceedings and an application to commit for breach of an undertaking or order must be made in the proceedings in which the undertaking was given or order made	N244		CCR PD 29, para 2.2
In all other cases it must be started by the issue of a Part 8 claim form	N208		CCR PD 29, para 2.1
3.2 The claim form or application (as the case may be) shall		CCR Ord 29 r 1(4A)	

	Form No	CPR	PD
(a) identify the provisions of the injunction or undertaking which it is alleged have been disobeyed or broken (b) list the ways in which it is alleged that the injunction has been disobeyed or the undertaking broken (c) be supported by filing an **affidavit** stating grounds on which the application is made		CCR Ord 29 r 1(4A)(c)	CCR PD 29, paras 2.5 and 2.6
If the proceedings are by application notice in existing proceedings the notice must quote the title and reference number of those proceedings			CCR PD 29, para 2.2(3)
A copy of the affidavit shall be served with the application form unless service is dispensed with			
A precedent for an application for a committal order is at **BCCP H[44]**			
The old form N78 should not be used without considerable adaptation necessary to make it Human Rights Act 1998 compliant			
A judge has jurisdiction to institute committal proceedings himself without any application being made but if he does so another judge should hear the committal application: *Re H (Minors)* (1998) Times, 31 December, CA			
4. Service			
4.1 If the application is made by the issue of a claim form, Part 8 applies and the claim form together with copies of all written evidence must, unless the court otherwise directs, be **personally served** on the respondent and must contain a **prominent notice of the possible consequences** of the court making a committal order and of the respondent's failure to attend			CCR PD 29, para 2.5(v)

	Form No	CPR	PD
4.2 If the committal application is commenced by application notice, CPR Pt 23 will apply but the provisions as to personal service and a prominent notice as set out in 4.1 above apply and the application cannot be dealt with without a hearing			CCR PD 29, para 4.1
4.3 The court may dispense with service of the claim form or application seeking committal if it thinks it just to do so and fix a date for the defendant to be brought before the court. The evidence in support of such an application must make it clear why it is appropriate for the court to depart from the normal rule requiring service: *Hickling v Baker* [2007] EWCA Civ 287, [2007] All ER (D) 51 (Apr) and see para 6(c) below in this TAB		CCR Ord 29 r 1(7) and (8)	
It will be only in exceptional circumstances that service will be dispensed with: see the cases cited at **CCR 29r1 [17]** A form of warning notice is annexed to the Practice Direction			CCR PD 29, Annex
4.4 As to enforcement before service against as person who was (a) present when the judgment or order was made or (b) has been notified of its terms by telephone, fax, e-mail or otherwise, see:		CCR Ord 29 r 1(5A) and 1(6)	
4A. Human Rights			
Committal proceedings are criminal proceedings for the purpose of ECHR Art 6 because they affect the liberty of the subject. The respondent is entitled to a fair and public hearing before an independent tribunal established by law. By virtue of Art 6.3 the respondent will have the following minimum rights:			
• to be informed promptly, in a language which he understands and in detail, of the nature and cause of the accusation against him; • to have adequate time and facilities for the preparation of his defence;			

	Form No	CPR	PD
• to defend himself in person or through legal assistance of his own choosing or, if he has not sufficient means to pay for legal assistance, to be given it free when the interests of justice so require; • to examine or have examined witnesses against him and to obtain the attendance and examination of witnesses on his behalf under the same conditions as witnesses against him; and • to have the free assistance of an interpreter if he cannot understand or speak the language used in court			
See further Gazette (2007) 6 December, page 28, article 'Proceeding with care' by Margaret Langley and NLJ (2010) 10 February, page 201 'Extreme Sanctions' by David Burrows.			
For the discretion of the court to hear a contemnor whose contempt is not complying with a court order see *Blue Sky One Ltd v Mahan Air* [2010] EWHC 128 (Comm), [2010] All ER (D) 25 (Feb), (2010) NLJ, 12 February, page 219.			
5. Evidence and the hearing			
5.1 The evidence in support of the application will have been served with the application and filed Written evidence in opposition must be given by affidavit and filed unless the court otherwise directs			CCR PD 29, para 3.2
Even if the respondent has not filed or served written evidence he may give oral evidence at the hearing if he wishes. If he does he may be cross-examined			CCR PD 29, para 3.3
The respondent may, with the permission of the court, call a witness to give oral evidence notwithstanding the witness has not filed an affidavit			CCR PD 29, para 3.4
5.2 An **amendment** to the claim form or application can only be made if the court gives permission			CCR PD 29, paras 2.5 and 2.6

	Form No	CPR	PD
5.3 The **hearing date** of the committal application shall be not less than 14 days after service. The hearing date must be specified in the claim form or application notice or in a separate notice served at the same time. The court may also give **case management directions** or may convene a directions hearing			CCR PD 29, paras 4.2 and 4.3
5.4 If the matter is **adjourned** the notice giving the date of the adjourned hearing must be personally served unless the respondent was present to hear the new date or was remanded in custody			
5.5 On an application to commit, the court will not exercise its **powers to cure procedure defects** that effect the essential rights of the defendant			CCR PD 29, para 10
5.6 If at the hearing the **defendant is unrepresented** he should be asked by the judge if he wishes to be legally represented and, in appropriate cases, informed of the availability of assistance from the Community Legal Service and how to contact that Service; see further **CCR 29r1 [21]** and **CCR 29r1 [31]** and *Berry Trade Ltd v Moussavi* [2002] 1 WLR 1910, CA as to a request for an adjournment to exercise the right given by the Human Rights Act 1998			CCR PD 29, para 4.6
5.7 The **burden of proof,** in view of the fact that the defendant may be sent to prison, is "beyond reasonable doubt": s 1 of the Human Rights Act 1998 and see **CCR 29r1 [22]**			CCR PD 29, para 1.4
5.8 A committal hearing will normally be **in public** but if it is in private and the respondent is found guilty of contempt the judge must make an announcement in open court containing the particulars set out in			CCR PD 29, para 9
5.9 A committal application cannot be **discontinued** without the permission of the court but there are provisions to **strike out** a committal application			CCR PD 29, paras 8 and 5

	Form No	CPR	PD
5.10 Except where under an enactment a Master or district judge has power to make a committal order, a committal order may only be made by a **circuit judge** or a person authorised to so act or capable by virtue of his office of so acting			CCR PD 29, para 11
5.11 Committal is a remedy of the last resort and the court will expect the claimant to have exhausted any other available remedy: *Danchevsky v Danchevsky* [1974] Fam 17, CA			
6. The order			
If a committal order is made, the order will be for the issue of a **warrant of committal** and unless the judge otherwise orders:	N79	CCR Ord 29 r 1(5)	
(a) a copy of the order will be served on the person to be committed before or at the time of execution of the warrant, or		RSC Ord 52 r 7A	
(b) where the order has been signed by the judge, the order for issue of the warrant may be served on the person to be committed any time within 36 hours after the execution of the warrant (c) if the order was made in the absence of the defendant it should make provision for the person committed to be brought before the court at an early opportunity: *Hickling v Baker*, a bankruptcy case, see para 4.3 above *Note:* • For "imprisonment is not an automatic result of a breach", see **CCR 29r1 [6]** • For further guidance as to the order, see **CCR 29r1 [23]** • For **suspension of the order**, see **CCR 29 r1 [24]**			

	Form No	CPR	PD
• The standard of proof to be applied by the court in deciding whether there has been a breach of the terms of an order suspending an order for committal to prison is the civil standard: *Alfa Laval Tumba AB v Separator Spares International Ltd (in liquidation)* [2010] EWHC 674 (Ch), 30 March. For provision that a warrant of arrest or of committal shall not be enforced more than 2 years after the date it was issued see Either party can appeal a committal order; the right of appeal is not limited to the contemptor: *Wood v Collins* (2006) Times, 26 June, CA		CCR Ord 29 r 1(5A)	
7. Committal of a party for breach of his undertaking			
7.1 An undertaking given by a party cannot be enforced by committal unless a copy of the document recording the undertaking was delivered by the court officer to the party giving it:	N117		
(a) by handing a copy to him before he left the court building (b) where his place of residence is known, by posting a copy to him at his place of residence, or		CCR Ord 29 r 1A(2)	
(c) through a solicitor Where delivery cannot be effected in this way, the court officer must deliver a copy of the document to the party having the benefit of the undertaking to cause it to be personally served as soon as possible		CCR Ord 29 r 1A(2)	
7.2 As to enforcement of an undertaking as if it were an order see *Gandolpho v Gandolpho (Standard Chartered Bank Garnishee)* [1981] QB 359. For the position where there is a breach of a consent order see para 1B of this TAB above			

	Form No	CPR	PD
Where a judge considers an undertaking given by a party in earlier proceedings was inappropriate the appropriate course is not for him to re-consider it at first instance but to give leave to appeal; *Mid-Suffolk District Council v Clarke* [2006] EWCA Civ 71, (2006) Times, 10 March, CA			
8. Committal of a solicitor for breach of an undertaking			
An undertaking given by a solicitor in relation to any proceedings in a county court may be enforced, by order of the judge, by committal. This may be:		CCR Ord 29 r 2	
(a) by a judge of his own initiative where it appears to him a solicitor has failed to carry out any such undertaking, or (b) on the application by a party to the proceedings supported by an affidavit setting out the facts Notice will be served on the solicitor calling him to show cause why he should not be committed to prison In *Udall v Capri Lighting Ltd* [1988] QB 907, Balcombe LJ stated that there are three ways to enforce a solicitor's undertaking (other than as set out above): (a) by action (b) by an application to the High Court to exercise its inherent jurisdiction over solicitors (the first order will normally order the solicitor to do '**now**' the act he has undertaken to do even if the payment required '**now**' may be greater than if the undertaking had been complied with earlier (c) an application to the Law Society			

	Form No	CPR	PD
For recent cases on solicitors' undertakings see *Austin v London Borough of Southwark* [2009] EWCA Civ 66, [2009] All ER (D) 145 (Feb) and *Clark v Lucas Solicitors LLP* [2009] EWHC 1952 (Ch), [2009] AlL ER (D) 11 (Aug) (where impossibility of performance was considered and the court issued the warning to solicitors that by their code of conduct an undertaking to make a payment out of the proceeds of sale is binding even if the fund turns out to be insufficient). For the position of a solicitor who finds a change of circumstances has affected his ability to comply with his undertaking, see *Hole & Pugsley (a firm) v Sumption* (2002) Times, 29 January			
9. Committal for contempt in the face of the court			
Reference should be made to:			CCR PD 29 Part II
10. Discharge from prison			
A person wishing to apply for his discharge from prison can apply in writing attested by the governor or other officer not below the rank of principal officer		CCR Ord 29 r 3	
The notice must show he has purged his contempt or wishes to purge his contempt. For form of notice see **CCR 29r3 [4]** The notice must be served, not less than 1 day before the hearing, on any party at whose instance the warrant or order was issued If the committal order – (a) does not direct that any application shall be made to a judge, or (b) was made by the district judge under s 118 of the County Courts Act 1984 (wilfully insults the judge, wilfully interrupts proceedings, etc) any application for discharge can be made to the district judge The form of order for discharge is	N83		

TABLE 37—APPEALS TO A CIRCUIT JUDGE FROM A DISTRICT JUDGE IN A COUNTY COURT OR AN APPEAL TO A HIGH COURT JUDGE FROM THE COUNTY COURT OR FROM A MASTER/DISTRICT JUDGE IN THE HIGH COURT

TAB 37

	Form No	CPR Rule	PD
Preliminary			
In *Office of Communications v Floe Telecom Ltd* [2009] EWCA Civ 47, [2009] Bus LR 116, (2009) Times, 23 February, Mummery LJ referred to the 'well established general principle that appeals should be against orders rather than reasons or findings'. In *Brissett v Brissett* [2009] EWCA Civ 679, [2009] 2 FLR 1451, [2009] Fam Law 793 the circuit judge was held to have been wrong to communicate with the district judge, whose decision was the subject of the appeal, about the substance of the appeal he was to hear. In these circumstances the circuit judge has to build a Chinese Wall between himself and the district judge. The Court of Appeal allowed an appeal against the circuit judge's decision because of his communication.			
For guidance on appeal documentation see also **BCCP F[15]-BCCP F[17]**, **BCCP F[52]** and **BCCP F[201]**			
1. Routes of appeal			
Subject to obtaining any necessary permission, appeal from the decision (a) of a district judge of a county court is to a circuit judge (b) from a master or district judge of the High Court is to a High Court Judge			52, para 2A.1 (and Table 1 within this sub-paragraph)
Note: where the appeal is of a final decision in a Part 7 claim allocated to the multi track or in certain specialist proceedings appeal (subject to obtaining permission) is to the Court of Appeal. See further **CPR 52 [5]** above.			52, para 2A.2
There are flow charts at **CPR FC 52** in Volume 1 of the Civil Court Practice			

	Form No	CPR Rule	PD
There is an interactive guide to the different routes of appeal on the website of the Court of Appeal's Civil Division: www.civilappeals.gov.uk			
The Designated Civil Judge in consultation with the Presiding Judge has responsibility for allocating appeals from decisions of district judges to circuit judges			52, para 8A.1
For the venue for an appeal to a High Court Judge from the decision of a county court or district judge of the High Court see			52, paras 8.1–8.9
Note: for final decision see			52, paras 2A.2–2A.4
2. Permission to Appeal sought at hearing			
2.1 The district judge or master should be asked to give permission to appeal (if that course is seriously contemplated) immediately after delivery of judgment. If this is not done or permission is refused permission must be sought from the court to which the appeal is to be made in the appeal notice. A note should be carefully taken of the reasons given whether or not permission is given.		52.3(2)	52, para 4.6
See 'Appeals Action Checklist' at **BCCP F[200]** It is vital that the steps are followed.			
2.2 Permission is not required to appeal against a committal order		52.3(1)	
2.3 Form N460 should be completed by the lower court whether permission is given or refused	N460		
2.4 Permission to appeal may only be given where the court considers that the appeal would have a real prospect of success or that there is some other compelling reason why the appeal should be heard		52.3(6)	
2.5 As to 'new grounds' see **CPR 52.3[4]**			

	Form No	CPR Rule	PD
2.6 If the Court dismisses an application for permission to appeal as totally without merit it should at the same time consider whether it is appropriate to make a civil restraint order		3.3(7), 23.12	3C
2.7 Where a party applies for permission to appeal against a judgment or order at the hearing at which it was made the judgment or order shall state: (a) whether or not the judgment is final (b) whether an appeal lies and if so to which court (c) whether permission to appeal has been granted and (d) if not, the appropriate appeal court that can grant permission		40.2(3) and (4)	
For precedents see **BCCP F[191]** and **BCCP F[192]**			
2.8 If the court makes an order granting permission to appeal but not mentioning costs, it will be deemed to include an order for applicants' costs in the case		44.13(1A)	
For **Appeals Action Checklist** that should be followed at the hearing before leaving court see BCCP [200] – every advocate should be aware of its contents. Note in particular the request for a stay of execution pending the appeal and to extend time for filing the appellant's note on the appeal court			
If leave is granted and that grant is to be challenged it will be too late to do this at the hearing of the appeal when considerable work will have been done: *Tradigrain SA v Intertek Testing Services (ITS) Canada Ltd* [2007] EWCA Civ 154, (2007) Times, 20 March			

	Form No	CPR Rule	PD
3. Application for permission to Appeal sought from the Appeal court			
3.1 Within such period as directed by the lower court (which may be more or less than the time allowed if no period is specified but which should not normally exceed 35 days) or where no such direction is given the appellant must file the appellant's notice at the appeal court within 21 days after the decision being appealed. If the parties wish to vary the time limit they cannot do so by agreement but must seek an order form the appeal court.	N161 or N164 for a small claim	52.6	52, para 5.19
The time for permission to appeal (no application having been made at the hearing) was extended, pursuant to the discretion to do so, in *Jackson v Marima Homes Ltd* [2007] EWCA Civ 1404, 13 November, Civil Procedure News, February 2008. Where an unsuccessful defendant does not appeal a new party may apply for permission to appeal: *R (George Wimpey UK Ltd) v Tewkesbury Borough Council* [2008] EWCA Civ 12, [2008] 3 All ER 859.			
Guidance notes on completing form N161 – Appellant's Notice (all appeals except small claims track appeals) are to be found in	N161A		
Where the appellant seeks permission to appeal from the appeal court it must be sought in the appellant's appeal notice.		52.4	
The court may dispense with the requirement for service of the notice on a respondent. Any application to dispense with service should set out the reasons relied on and be verified by a statement of truth.		6.28	52, para 5.23
3.2 Where the appellant is applying for permission to appeal in his appellant's notice he must serve it on the respondent with a skeleton argument but not the appeal bundle unless the appeal court otherwise directs		52.4(1)	52, para 5.24

	Form No	CPR Rule	PD
3.3 Unless the court otherwise orders an appeal notice must be served on each respondent as soon as practicable and in any event not later than 7 days after it was filed		52.42	
3.4 For the role of the Respondent at the permission to appeal stage, see **CPR PD 52 PARA 5 [5]** and *Jolly v Jay* [2002] EWCA Civ 277, (2002) Times, 3 April mentioned there.			
4. Refusal of permission by Appeal Court without a hearing			
4.1 Where the appeal court without a hearing refuses permission to appeal the party wishing to appeal may request the decision to be reconsidered at a hearing		52.3(4)	
4.2 Such a request must be filed within 7 days after service of the notice that permission has been refused		52.3(5)	
4.3 The appellant's advocate must, at least 4 days before the hearing in a brief written statement (a) inform the court and the respondent of the points which he proposes to raise at the hearing (b) set out the reasons why permission should be granted notwithstanding the reasons given for the refusal of permission and (c) confirm where applicable that the requirements of CPR PD 52 para 4.17 (see 4.6 below) have been complied with			52, para 4.14A(2)
4.4 Unless the court otherwise directs a respondent need not take any action when served with the appellant's notice unless notice is given to him that permission to appeal has been given. The Court of Appeal in *Jolly v Jay* [2002] EWCA Civ 277 indicated that where a respondent believes the appeal notice is defective he may file submissions limited to failure to meet the relevant threshold test or a material inaccuracy in the notice.			52, para 4.15

	Form No	CPR Rule	PD
4.5 If the High Court Judge or circuit judge refuses permission to appeal at the oral hearing there is no further appeal – Access to Justice Act 1999, s 54(4)			
4.6 A publicly funded appellant must send a copy of the reasons for refusing permission to the Legal Services Commission as soon as they are received form the court		52.3(3) and (4)	52, para 4.17
4.7 If the application for permission to appeal is dismissed as being totally without merit see para 2.6 of this TAB above		3.3(7), 23.12	3C
4.8 For extension of time for filing the appellant's notice see			52, paras 5.2–5.4
4.9 For applications to the appeal court for a remedy incidental to the appeal see			52, para 5.5
5. Documents to be filed with Appellant's Notice of Appeal			
5.1 In every case, except where the appeal relates to a small claim and is being heard in a county court or the High Court, the appellant must file the following documents with his appellant's notice: (a) two additional copies of the appellant's notice for the appeal court and (b) one copy of the appellant's notice for each of the respondents (c) one copy of his skeleton argument for each copy of the appellant's notice that is filed (d) a sealed copy of the order being appealed (e) a copy of any order giving or refusing permission to appeal together with a copy of the judge's reasons for allowing or refusing permission (f) any witness statements or affidavits in support of any application, such as a stay of execution, included in the applicant's notice (g) a copy of the order allocating a case to track, if any			52, para 5.6

	Form No	CPR Rule	PD
5.2 The appellant's appeal bundle must be filed with the appeal notice and include the following documents:			
(a) a sealed copy of the appellant's notice (b) a sealed copy of the order being appealed (c) a copy of any order giving or refusing permission to appeal together with a copy of the judge's reasons (d) any affidavit or witness statement filed in support of any application included in the appellant's notice (e) a copy of his skeleton argument (f) a transcript or note of judgment and in cases where permission to appeal was given by the lower court or is not required those parts of any transcript of evidence which are directly relevant to any question at issue on the appeal (g) the claim form and statement of case (when relevant to the subject of the appeal) (h) any application notice (or case management documentation) relevant to the subject of the appeal ((i), (j) and (k) are not relevant to appeals form district judges or masters) (l) any other documents which the appellant reasonably considers necessary to enable the court to reach its decision (m) such other documents as the court may direct			52, para 5.6A
Note • Where the appellant is represented the appeal bundle must contain a certificate signed by his solicitor that he has read and understood the direction and that material extraneous to the issues to be considered must be excluded			52, para 5.6A(3)
• for skeleton arguments see			52, para 5.9–5.10
• for chronologies etc see			52, para 5.11

	Form No	CPR Rule	PD
• for suitable record of the judgment see			52, paras 5.12–5.14
• for transcripts or notes of evidence see			52, paras 5.15–5.16
• for transcripts at public expense see			52, paras 5.17–5.20
• for requirement of certificate of service see			52, para 5.21(2)
• where it is not possible to file all the required documents see			52, para 5.9(2)
5.3 For fee payable on filing an appeal see Civil Proceedings Fees Order 2004, paras 2.4 and 2.5 at **FEE 1.8**			
The fee in county court for filing an appellant's notice or a respondent's notice is £100 in the small claims track and £120 for all other claims. The fee in the High Court is £200.			
6. Small claims			
Where the appeal relates to a claim allocated to the small claims track and the appeal is being heard in a county court or the High Court, the appellant must file the following documents with the appellant's notice: (a) a sealed copy of the order being appealed and (b) any order giving or refusing permission to appeal together with a copy of the reasons for the decision	N460		52, para 5.8(2)
The appellant may file any other document relevant to the appeal listed in the document to be filed with the appellant's notice or in the appeal bundle (see paras 5.1 and 5.2 above)			52, para 5.8(3)
The court may order a suitable record of the reasons for the judgment of the lower court (see CPR PD 52, para 5.12) to be filed: (a) to enable it to decide if permission should be granted or (b) to decide the appeal			52, para 5.8(5)

	Form No	CPR Rule	PD
The appellant's notice must be accompanied by a skeleton argument or it may be included in the appellant's notice but: (i) if this cannot be done it must be filed and served within 14 days of filing of the appellant's notice (ii) an appellant who is not represented need not file a skeleton argument but is encouraged to do so			52, paras 5.9–5.11
7. Procedure after permission is obtained			
7.1 Where permission is given by the appeal court or the appellant's notice is filed in the appeal court and permission has been given in the lower court or is not necessary the following procedure must be observed			52, para 6.1
7.2 If the appeal court gives permission to appeal the appeal bundle must be served on each respondent within 7 days of receiving the order giving permission to appeal			
7.3 The appeal court will send the parties: (a) notification of the date of the hearing or the listing window (b) where permission has been granted by the appeal court a copy of the order giving permission to appeal and (c) any other direction given by the court			
7.4 Where the appeal court gives permission to appeal the appellant must add the following documents to the appeal bundle: (a) the Respondent's notice and skeleton argument (if any) (b) those parts of the transcript of evidence which are directly relevant to any question at issue on the appeal (c) the order giving permission to appeal and if given at an oral hearing the transcript or note of any judgment which was given and			

	Form No	CPR Rule	PD
(d) any document that the parties have agreed to add upon the respondent's request pursuant to CPR PD 52, para 7.11		52.5	52, para 6.3A
(e) As to the respondent's notice see			52, para 7
If the respondent does not file a respondent's notice he is not entitled, except with the permission of the court, to rely on any reason not relied on in the lower court			52, para 7.3(2)
• As to the requirement that the respondent file a skeleton argument where he wishes to address the court (unless the appeal relates to a small claim or the respondent is not represented) see			52, para 7.6, 7.7A and 7.7B
7.5 As to the filing of the respondent's notices and skeleton arguments see			52, para 7.10–7.13
7.6 As to the content of the respondent's skeleton argument see			52, para 7.8
It should identify the copy of the diagram, plan or map which shows the location of all the relevant features in the appeal to assist pre-reading: *Hunte v E Bottomley & Sons Ltd* [2007] EWCA Civ 1168, (2007) Times, 21 November.			
8 Hearing			
The court notifies the parties of the hearing date. The appeal is generally by way of review and not rehearing		52.11(1)	
8.1 The venues for High Court appeals are listed by Circuit in PD 52, paras 8.1–8.8 and the relevant general provisions are set out in paras 8.9–8.14			52, paras 8.1–8.14
8.2 The Designated Civil Judge, in consultation with the Presiding Judges, deals with the allocation of appeals from district judges to circuit judges			52, para 8A.1
8.3 For disposal of applications or appeals by consent see			52, paras 12 and 13
8.4 For hearings at which costs are likely to be assessed see			52, para 14

	Form No	CPR Rule	PD
8.5 If either party wishes to appeal against the circuit judge's decision on an application for permission it must be made to the Court of Appeal. The circuit judge has no jurisdiction to either grant or refuse permission: Administration of Justice Act 1999, s 55		52.13	
8.6 It is too late to challenge the grant of leave to appeal at the hearing of the appeal itself when considerable work will have been done: *Tradigrain v Intertek Testing Services* [2007] EWCA Civ 154, (2007) Times, 20 March			
9. For admission of fresh evidence on appeal see CPR 52.11(2) at **TAB 38**, para 13. This provision applies to all appeals			

TABLE 38—COURT OF APPEAL

TAB 38

	Form No	CPR Rule	PD
1. Preliminary			
1.1 Relevant documents must be filed in the Civil Appeals Office Registry, Room E 307, Royal Courts of Justice, Strand London WC2A 2LL			52, para 15.1(1)
1.1A An appellant's notice, a respondent's notice and an application notice may be filed by e-mail using the e-mail account specified in the 'Guidelines for Filing by E-mail' where those guidelines permit it. For website details see 1.1B below			52, para 15A(1)
1.1B Provision is made for certain notices to be filed electronically at the Court of Appeal, Civil Division using the online forms service on the Court of Appeal, Civil Division website at www.civilappeals.gov.uk			52, para 15.1B

	Form No	CPR Rule	PD
1.1C There is not separate Practice Direction for the Court of Appeal. The same time limit applies for filing an appellant's notice (21 days including Saturdays, Sundays, Bank Holidays, etc) after the date of the decision appealed unless a longer or shorter period is directed by the lower court. For applications for an extension of time for filing an appellant's notice see			52, para 5.2
1.2 All documents required to be served must be served by the parties			52, para 15.1(2)
1.3 A court officer assigned to the Civil Appeals Office who is a barrister or solicitor may with the consent of the Master of Rolls (and subject to review on the request of a party) deal with - (a) any matter incidental to any proceedings in the Court of Appeal (b) other matters where there is no substantial dispute (c) dismissal of an appeal or application for failure to comply with any order, rule or practice direction		52.16(2)	52, para 15.5
A Court officer may not decide an application for: (a) permission to appeal (b) bail pending an appeal (c) an injunction a stay (save in limited (d) circumstances)		52.16(3)	
1.4 At the request of a party filed within 7 days after service of notice of the decision, a hearing will be held to reconsider a decision of a court officer or a single judge without a hearing		52.16(5), (6) and (6A)	
1.5 Substantial changes in civil appeal procedure came into effect in 30 June 2004 and on 29 June 2004 the Court of Appeal handed down a Practice Note to explain and give notice of the substantial changes to PD 52; *Scribes West Ltd v Relsa Anstalt* [2004] EWCA Civ 835, (2004) Times, 8 July per Brookes LJ, V-P			

	Form No	CPR Rule	PD
1.6 In *Jeyapragash v Secretary of State for the Home Department* [2004] EWCA Civ 1260, (2004) Times, 12 October the necessity for everyone who practised and appeared before the Court of Appeal to understand the new regime and comply with it were stated. The costs and consequences of failure to do so were stressed			
2. Permission to Appeal			
2.1 Permission to appeal is required from a decision of a judge in the county court or of the High Court except where the appeal is against (a) a committal order (b) a refusal to grant habeas corpus (c) a secure accommodation order made under s25 of the Children Act 1989		52.3(1)	
2.2 Application can be made (a) to the lower court at the hearing of decision sought to be appealed or (b) to the appeal court in an appeal notice		52.3(2)	
For time limit for an appellant's notice see **TAB 36** para 3.1 and also see		52.4(2)	
For time limits for a respondent's notice see		52.5(4) and (5)	
Where a decision has been made to appeal or that an appeal is likely application should be made to the lower court. If the application to appeal is refused by the lower court a further application for permission may be made to the appeal court in an appellant's notice		52.3(3)	
2.3 Permission is required from the Court of Appeal for all appeals to that court from a decision of a county court or the High Court which was itself made on appeal		52.13(1)	52, paras 4.8 and 4.9
2.4 If permission is to be sought to appeal because of the failure of the judge to give reasons for his decision it would be prudent first to consider the practice set out in *English v Emery Reimold and Strick Ltd* [2002] EWCA Civ 605, [2002] 3 All ER 385			

	Form No	CPR Rule	PD
2.5 Applications for leave to appeal are not to be listed to suit the convenience of counsel even if the appeal was to follow if permission was granted: *Bracknell Forest Borough Council v N* (2006) Times, 6 November, CA			
2.6 It is only in exceptional circumstances that permission would be given for a second appeal; *Uphill v BRB (Residuary) Ltd* [2005] EWCA Civ 60, [2005] 3 All ER 264. See Dyson LJ's guidance as to rule 52.13(2)(a) and (b)		52.13(2)(a) and (b)	
Unless (a) the appeal court or the lower court otherwise orders; or (b) the appeal is from the Asylum and Immigration Tribunal, an appeal does not operate as a stay of any order or decision of the lower court.			
For the principles to be applied when an application is made to the Court of Appeal for stay of enforcement proceedings pending an appeal to the Court of Appeal against an order of the trial judge see *Gater Assets Ltd v Nak Naftogaz Ukrainy* [2008] EWCA Civ 1051, 8 August (Mummery LJ)		52.7	
For the jurisdiction to suspend an order which falls within s 89(1) of the Housing Act 1980 see *Admiral Taverns (Cygnet) Ltd v Daniel* [2008] EWCA Civ 1501 discussed at **CPR 52.7 [1]** above.			
3. Filing of Appellant's Notice and documents to accompany			
3.1 The appellant must complete and file the appellant's notice	N161		
An application to the appeal court incidental to the appeal (including for a stay of execution) may be included in the appeal or a separate Part 23 application notice. The provisions of Part 23 apply to such an application			52, paras 5.5 and 7.9
3.2 It must be filed with the documents specified in **CPR PD 52**, para 5.6(2) (see **TAB 37** para 5.1) including an appeal bundle.			52, para 5.6(2)

	Form No	CPR Rule	PD
For the contents of the appeal bundle see **CPR PD 52**, para 5.6A(1) (see **TAB 37** para 5.2) and note documents: (i) in cases where the decision appealed was itself an appeal (e.g. an appeal from a district judge) the first order, the reasons given and the appellant's notice used to appeal from that order (j) in the case of judicial review or statutory appeal the original decision which was the subject of the application to the lower court (k) in cases where the appeal is from a Tribunal, a copy of the Tribunal's reasons for the decision which was the subject of the application to the lower court			52, para 5.6A(1)
Whilst these are not relevant on appeals from District Judges or Masters to a circuit judge or to a High Court judge they will be relevant to appeals in the Court of Appeal			
A skeleton argument filed in the Court of Appeal, Civil Division on behalf of the appellant should contain in paragraph 1 the advocate's time estimate for the hearing of the appeal			52, para 5.10(7)
The court fee will be payable on filing the appellant's notice		SCFO fee 9.1	
4. Procedure where permission is being sought from the Court of Appeal			
4.1 Where the appellant is applying for permission in the appellant's notice he must serve on the respondents his appellant's notice and skeleton argument but not the appeal bundle (if permission to appeal has been given by the lower court or is not necessary) the appeal bundle must be served on the respondents with the appeal notice			52, para 5.24(1)

	Form No	CPR Rule	PD
4.2 Within 7 days after service of the notice that permission has been refused without a hearing, the appellant files a request for the decision to be reconsidered at an oral hearing at the appeal court with the statement required by CPR PD 52, para 4.14A and serves a copy of the request and the statement on the respondent at the same time. The hearing may be before the same judge who refused leave on paper; *Sengupta v Holmes* [2002] EWCA Civ 1104			52, para 4.14, 4.14A
Where the Court of Appeal refuses permission without a hearing it may, if it considers the application is totally without merit, make an order that its refusal cannot be reconsidered at a hearing. This does not apply to family proceedings **4.3** When permission is granted, the Civil Appeals Office sends: (a) notification of listing window or of hearing (b) notification of hear by date (c) a copy of the order granting permission (d) the court's directions (e) appeal questionnaire			52, para 4A 52, paras 6.3 and 6.4
5. Procedure when permission obtained or is not necessary			
5.1 If the appeal court gives permission the appeal bundle must be served on each of the respondents within 7 days of receiving the order giving permission			52, para 6.2
For the documents to be added to the appeal bundle see TAB 37 para 7.4			52, para 6.3A
5.2 If permission is not necessary, or has been given by the lower court or has been given by the appeal court the appeal court will send to the parties (a) notification of the hearing date or listing window during which the appeal is likely to be heard (b) the date by which the appeal will be heard (the hear- by date) (c) any other directions (d) an appeal questionnaire			52, paras 6.3 and 6.4

	Form No	CPR Rule	PD
5.3 Within 14 days of the date of the letter of notification the appellant must complete and file the Appeal Questionnaire which must contain: (a) if the appellant is represented the advocate's time estimate (b) where a transcript of evidence is relevant to the appeal, confirmation as to what parts of a transcript have been ordered where this is not already in the bundle (c) confirmation that copies of the appeal bundle are being prepared, that they will be held ready and an undertaking that they will be supplied to the court on request. The transcripts included in the appeal bundle may be photostats (d) confirmation that copies of the Appeal Questionnaire and the appeal bundle have been served and the date of that service			
Note: the time estimate specified in the Appeal Questionnaire must be that of the advocate who will argue the appeal. If the respondent disagrees with the time estimate he must so inform the court within 7 days of its receipt or he will be deemed to have accepted the time proposed by the appellant			52, para 6.5 and 6.6
5.4 For the requirement that a respondent must notify within 21 days to inform the Civil Appeals Office in writing whether he intends to file a respondent's notice see			52, para 15.6
If a respondent proposes to address arguments to the court he must file a respondent's notice and skeleton argument			52, para 7.6
5.5 Where the appeal bundle comprises more than 500 pages the appellant's solicitors after consultation with the respondent's solicitors must file in addition to the appeal bundle the requisite number of copies of a **core bundle**			

	Form No	CPR Rule	PD
This must be done within 28 days of receipt of the order giving permission to appeal or where permission was given by the lower court or is not required within 28 days of service of the appellant's notice on the respondent The core bundle must contain the documents that are central to the appeal and not exceed 150 pages			52, paras 15.2 and 15.3
6. Preparation of Bundles			
The importance of precise compliance with the requirements of the Practice Direction cannot be overstated. Failure to do so is likely to result in costs sanctions and consideration of dismissal for non compliance The Practice Direction deals in detail with: (1) Rejection of bundles			52, para 15.4(1)
(2) Avoidance of duplication			52, para 15.4(2)
(3) Pagination			52, para 15.4(3)
(4) Format and Presentation			52, para 15.4(4)
(5) Binding			52, para 15.4(5)
(6) Indices and Labels			52, para 15.4(6)
(7) Identification			52, para 15.4(7)
(8) Staples			52, para 15.4(8)
(9) Statements of case			52, para 15.4(9)
(10) New documents			52, para 15.4(10)
(11) Inter-solicitor correspondence			52, para 15.4(11)
(12) Sanctions for non-compliance			52, para 15.4(12)
7. Listing and hear by dates			
7.1 Management of the list will be dealt with by the listing officer under the direction of the master. The Civil Appeals list of the Court of Appeal is divided into: • the applications list • the appeals list • the expedited list; see for the current practice of the Court of Appeal *Unilever plc v Chefaro Proprietories Ltd (Practice Note)* [1995] 1 WLR 243 • the stand out list			

	Form No	CPR Rule	PD
• the special fixtures list (for special provisions for this list see CPR 52, para 15.9A) • the second fixtures list • the short warned list (for special provisions for this list see CPR 52, para 5.9) **7.2** Requests for directions (whether as to listing or other matters) should be made to the Civil Appeals Office **7.3** Once the parties have been notified of the hearing date the appellant's advocate after consultation with his opponent shall file a **bundle of photocopies of the authorities** relied on. Unless the period of notice is less than 7 days the bundle must be filed at least 7 days prior to the hearing date and the requirements of CPR PD 52, para 15.11 must be complied with			
7.4 A **supplementary skeleton argument** on which the appellant wishes to rely must be filed at least 14 days before the hearing. A supplementary bundle from the respondent must be filed at least 7 days before the hearing. The requirement of CPR PD 52, para 15(11)(a) must be complied with and the sanctions in sub-paragraph (4) should be noted			52, para 15(11)(A)
The appellant cannot present the Court of Appeal with a totally new argument not stated in the grounds of appeal when the point had not been taken below; *Gover v Propertycare Ltd* [2006] EWCA Civ 286, [2006] 4 All ER 69			
All documents that are needed for the appeal hearing must be filed at least 7 days prior to the hearing			52, para 15(11)(b)
8. The fact that **a Part 36 offer** (or a per-April 2007 payment into court) has been made must not be disclosed to any judge of the appeal court who is to hear or determine: (a) an application for permission to appeal, or (b) an appeal until all questions (other than costs) have been determined		52.12(1)	

	Form No	CPR Rule	PD
CPR 52.12(1) above does not: (a) apply if the Part 36 offer or payment into court is relevant to the substance of the appeal;		52.12(2)	
(b) prevent disclosure of any application in the appeal proceedings if disclosure of the fact that a Part 36 offer or payment into court has been made is properly relevant to the matter to be decided		52.12(3)	
Note rule 36.3 has the effect that a Part 36 offer made in proceedings at first instance will not have consequences in any appeal proceedings. Therefore, a fresh Part 36 offer needs to be made in appeal proceedings. However, rule 52.12 applies to a Part 36 offer whether made in the original proceedings or in the appeal			
9. Video-link facility at the Court of Appeal			
Where counsel are to present short appointments, particularly where considerable travelling time will be involved, they should consider whether the use of the video-link facility would be appropriate: see *Babbings v Kirklees Metropolitan Council* [2004] EWCA Civ 1431, (2004) Times, 4 November			
10. Court of Appeal – general civil restraint order			
The Court of Appeal has power when making a general civil restraint order to prevent proceedings being brought in the county court as well as in the High Court and the Court of Appeal: *R (Mahajan) v Central London County Court* [2004] EWCA Civ 946, (2004) Times, 13 July			
10A. Declaratory Relief			
The jurisdiction of the Court of Appeal to grant declaratory relief is fully examined in the case of *Rolls Royce plc v Unite* [2009] EWCA Civ 387, [2010] 1 WLR 318, [2010] ICR 1 and in particular by Wall LJ in paras 14 to 28 of his judgment.			

	Form No	CPR Rule	PD
11. Checklists			
11.1 For a checklist for filing papers in the Court of Appeal, see **BCCP F[201.1]**			
11.2 For guidance on appeal documentation, see **BCCP F[15]**, **BCCP F[17]**, **BCCP F[52]**, **BCCP F[201]** and for judicial guidance in complex appeals see *Leofelis SA v Lonsdale Sports Ltd* [2008] EWCA Civ 640, [2008] NLJR 1041, [2008] All ER (D) 87 (Jul).			
12. New Evidence			
CPR 52.11(2) provides that an appeal court subject to the CPR will not (a) fresh oral evidence (b) evidence which was not before the lower court unless the court otherwise orders			
Note the three part test for deciding whether leave should be granted set out in *Ladd v Marshall* [1954] 3 All ER 745 and post-CPR see *Lifely v Lifely* [2008] EWC Civ 904, [2008] All ER (D) 396 (Jul), *Marchmont Investment Ltd v BFO SA (formerly Banque de l'Orient)* [2007] EWCA Civ 677, [2007] All ER (D) 104 (Jun) and *Khetami v Kanbi* [2006] EWCA Civ 1621			
For detailed discussion and consideration of the Commercial Court Working Party's recommendation on witness statements see article by Kagon and Barton 'Mind the gaps' in (2008) NLJ, 3 October, page 208			
13. Reserved Judgments			
The practice direction supplementing Part 40 (Reserved Judgments) contains provisions relating to reserved judgments			52, para 15.12
14. Costs			
When the court makes an order for costs the general rule is that the unsuccessful party will be ordered to pay the costs of the successful party but the court may make a different order.			

	Form No	CPR Rule	PD
In *Phillips v Phillips* [2009] EWCA Civ 185, 25 February the court considered the application of the general rule when a party decided not to pursue the appeal which was thereupon dismissed.		44.3(2)	

INDEX

[all references are to table number]

References in *italic* are to page numbers.

References in *italic* are to page numbers.